MILLENNIAL JEWISH STARS

Millennial Jewish Stars

Navigating Racial Antisemitism, Masculinity, and White Supremacy

Jonathan Branfman

NEW YORK UNIVERSITY PRESS

New York

NEW YORK UNIVERSITY PRESS
New York
www.nyupress.org

Library of Congress Cataloging-in-Publication Data
Names: Branfman, Jonathan, author.
Title: Millennial Jewish stars : navigating racial antisemitism, masculinity,
and white supremacy / Jonathan Branfman.
Description: [New York]: New York University Press, [2024] |
Includes bibliographical references and index.
Identifiers: LCCN 2023038894 (print) | LCCN 2023038895 (ebook) |
ISBN 9781479820764 (hardback) | ISBN 9781479820795 (paperback) |
ISBN 9781479820818 (ebook) | ISBN 9781479820849 (ebook other)
Subjects: LCSH: Jewish actors—United States—Biography. | Jewish entertainers—
United States—Biography. | Generation Y—United States—Biography. | Stereotypes
(Social psychology) in mass media. | Drake, 1986– | Lil Dicky, 1988– | Jacobson, Abbi. |
Glazer, Ilana. | Rogen, Seth, 1982– | Efron, Zac.
Classification: LCC PN3035 .B69 2024 (print) | LCC PN3035 (ebook) | DDC
791.4302/8092273 [B]—dc23/eng/20231031
LC record available at https://lccn.loc.gov/2023038894
LC ebook record available at https://lccn.loc.gov/2023038895

This book is printed on acid-free paper, and its binding materials are chosen for strength
and durability. We strive to use environmentally responsible suppliers and materials to the
greatest extent possible in publishing our books.

Manufactured in the United States of America

10 9 8 7 6 5 4 3 2 1

Also available as an ebook

CONTENTS

LIST OF FIGURES

Introduction

Getting Racy

Beware the comments on YouTube, for they often distill viewers' crudest biases. For instance, misinformed comments about Jews of color lurk below many clips of the biracial Jewish rap superstar Drake—comments like "OMFG, I found the first Black Jew!"[1] More polite but equally sharp surprise sweeps my college classes on media, race, gender, and Jewish culture whenever I mention Drake's Black Jewish identity. Yet these same classes are just as startled to hear that the blue-eyed, sandy-haired, brawny film star Zac Efron is also Jewish: I routinely hear twin gasps that "Drake is *Jewish?!*" and "Zac Efron is *Jewish?!*" Upon reflection, students consistently trace their surprise to a perception that Drake looks too Black, Efron too white, and both too muscular and handsome to "look Jewish." But even while voicing preconceptions about Jewish skin, hair, faces, and muscles, many students state that they do not consider Jewishness a bodily trait, but a religious identity. Indeed, for many students, it is as novel to notice their own racial perceptions about Jewish bodies as to find those perceptions shattered by Drake and Efron. And these surprised reactions only grow as we begin tracing how such stereotypes descend from at least eight centuries of religious, artistic, and racial stigmas on Jewish bodies. By examining millennial Jewish stars, many students thus newly recognize their own conflicting definitions of Jewishness, their own preset images of Jewish bodies, and the antisemitic history that shapes both.

My students' classroom epiphanies reflect pervasive racial contradictions around Jewishness in twenty-first-century America. On one hand, many Americans assume that all Jews look white, erasing Jews of color like Drake. Yet if Drake's Blackness "looks un-Jewish" to many people, so does Efron's whiteness, both men's muscularity, and both men's handsomeness. These contradictions emerge partly because US media circulate racial antisemitism: historically traceable stigmas that depict Jews as bodily different from and inferior to white gentiles (non-Jews). Even for Americans who do not consciously deem Jews a "race," these stigmas fuel racial stereotypes about Jewish bodies and prompt questions about how to racially define Jews. Such questions grabbed headlines in 2019, after reports that Donald Trump might legally reclassify Jewishness from a religion to a "race or nationality."[2] This controversy only dramatized racial contradictions that many Jews navigate daily. For instance, I grew up Jewish in the 1990s hearing peers ask, "Are Jews a religion or a race?" without knowing why the answer seemed hazy. Jewish racial discrepancies also went unexplained at home: although my family checked "white" on school forms, we tracked monthly reports about white supremacists who committed racial violence against Jews because they deemed us "nonwhite."

While far-right violence can target Jews of all colors, this violence especially illustrates how Euro-American Jews navigate contradictory relationships to white supremacy and white supremacists. White supremacy describes how racism systematically awards greater rights, opportunities, and safety to people labeled white, including many Jews. The Jewish comedic rapper Lil Dicky details these advantages in his 2013 rap "White Dude," observing that "I ain't gotta worry where the cops at," since "they ain't suspicious of Jews," so "it's a damn good day to be a white dude."[3] Yet even as white supremacy advantages Euro-American Jews over people of color (including Jews of color), self-declared white supremacists revile all Jews as nonwhite "race enemies." The former KKK grand wizard David Duke captured this hostility in 2016 when tweeting, "JEWS ARE NOT WHITE!"[4] White supremacists like Duke specifically accuse Jews of puppeteering the Black, feminist, and gay civil rights movements, plus Muslim and Latinx immigration, to eradicate white Christian Americans.[5] This conspiracy theory, called "white genocide" or "the great replacement," is what motivated the 2017 Charlottesville white supremacist rally to chant "Jews will not replace us!"[6] In 2018, this myth motivated a white gentile gunman to massacre eleven congregants at Pittsburgh's Tree of Life Synagogue. Before attacking, the gunman ranted online against a Jewish American refugee-resettlement nonprofit, which he claimed was "bring[ing] invaders in that kill our people."[7] In response to this imagined threat, the gunman stormed Tree of Life while shouting, "All Jews must die!"[8] This Pittsburgh attack, like the Charlottesville rally before it, illustrates that antisemitism remains central to white supremacists' ecosystem of hate, intimately bound to anti-Blackness, Islamophobia, xenophobia, homophobia, and sexism.

These contradictions make racial antisemitism vital to challenge but tricky to visualize in America today. If few Americans consciously label Jews a "race," how can they racially stereotype Jewish bodies? How can this racial antisemitism impact Jews of color like Drake, who "don't look Jewish?" Why do Euro-American Jews experience safety from racist police violence, but not from racist alt-right violence? How can Euro-American Jews acknowledge their white privilege and fight color-based racism without downplaying antisemitism, and vice versa? Unwinding these paradoxes is essential to combat antisemitism and to fully grasp how race operates in America. It is also essential for American Jews who wish to decode their own unpredictable racial statuses and to dismantle racism inside and outside Jewish communities. Until such questions about Jewishness and race receive clarity, they will keep fueling harmful miseducation, imprecise scholarship, and misinformed activism.

To clarify how America racially envisions Jews, this book spotlights the screens where many people already gaze at Jewish bodies. Like classroom dialogues on Drake and Zac Efron, this book dissects the way millennial Jewish stars market their bodies and the way audiences consume those bodies. In turn, this analysis reveals how racial antisemitism permeates twenty-first-century American racial "common sense." Millennial Jewish stars make such helpful exemplars for this study because they tend to spotlight Jewish identity and antisemitic stigma in unusually provocative ways, as we will see.

As the examples of Drake and Efron suggest, this book specifically aims to demystify how US media racially envision North American-born Jews of Ashkenazi (Central and Eastern European) descent with black or white skin. Future scholarship must also explore how US media racially envision Jews of Middle Eastern, North African, or Sephardic (Iberian) descent, like the pop star Paula Abdul; Jews who are Latinx, Indigenous, or Asian American, like the Venezuelan-American Jewish comedian Joanna Hausmann; and Jews descended from sub-Saharan Jewish communities, like the Jewish Eritrean-American comedian Tiffany Haddish.[9] While this book may contribute tools for deciphering how US media racially envision all Jews, its focus is Ashkenazi North American-born Jews with black or white skin.

To analyze these Jewish bodies onscreen, this book extends forty years of Jewish feminist scholarship that has urged deeper analysis of Jewishness and antisemitism within feminist studies, queer studies, critical race studies, media studies, and Jewish studies; within activist communities; and within Jewish communities.[10] Across these contexts, many people invisibilize antisemitism by oversimplifying race into a color-based dichotomy, which the feminist scholar Susan Stanford Friedman calls "the white/people of color binary."[11] To nuance this binary, Jewish feminists sometimes note how racial antisemitism manifests through stigmas of queer (strange) gender and sexuality rather than skin color. "Queer" here does not simply mean "gay," but more broadly "nonnormative." Jewish gender and sexuality carry this queer (odd) connotation because Christian cultures have long accused Jews of strange gender and sexuality to help "prove" that Jewish bodies differ from gentile bodies. We will soon see how these stigmas historically depict Jewish men as emasculated, Jewish women as masculinized, and both as sexually perverse— for instance, by alleging that Jewish men menstruate.[12] Scholars such as Marla Brettschneider and Sarah Imhoff note that this history still leads many Americans to envision Jews' gender and sexuality as visibly different from gentiles', as in stereotypes of emasculated "nice Jewish boys."[13] Similarly, when analyzing white-skinned Ashkenazi Jews in US film, David Reznik writes that antisemitic racial stigma remains most visible "in cinema today [in] the portrayal of American Jewish male characters as effeminate, emasculated, [or] passive."[14]

Although I agree that stigmas of queer (odd) masculinity symbolize Jewish racial difference in US media today, these masculine stigmas actually reach beyond Euro-American Jews, Jewish men, and conventional cinema. And these masculine stigmas convey different racial statuses when intersecting with different skin tones. Also important, Jewish performers are not passive canvases for antisemitic masculine tropes. Instead, Jewish stars often counterintuitively *harness* these stigmas to market themselves. Therefore, to clarify how US media racially envision Jews, this book stakes five scaffolded claims about race, masculinity, and millennial Jewish stardom:

1. Queer (strange) masculinity often symbolizes Jewish racial difference in twenty-first-century US media for Jews who are both women and men, black- and white-skinned, across diverse platforms from cinema to YouTube. Alongside images of beaked noses, swarthy skin, and dark curly hair, historical stigmas of queer masculinity remain primary tools by which US media racially distinguish Jews from gentiles.

2. Recognizing how queer masculinity symbolizes Jewish racial difference is one key to visualizing how racial antisemitism intersects with America's white/people of color (white/POC) binary: how US media depict antisemitism interacting with white privilege and color-based racism. Stigmas of queer Jewish masculinity position Jewishness as a racial difference that is *distinct from* but *intersects with* skin color.

3. To pinpoint how stigmas of queer Jewish masculinity intersect with white privilege and color-based racism onscreen, millennial Jewish stars make ideal exemplars. Before these millennials, earlier mainstream Jewish stars were nearly all Euro-American and often obeyed industry pressures to keep Jewish identity tacit. By contrast, new social activism and digital media have aided millennial Jewish stars of diverse colors and genders to win mass appeal without sacrificing creative control. Many millennial stars use this newfound freedom to sensationally flaunt Jewish identity, antisemitic racial stigmas, and Jewish racial contradictions in once-taboo ways.

4. Jewish masculinity's racial symbolism appears most sharply when millennial Jewish stars *instrumentalize* stigmas of queer Jewish masculinity to perform *ideological labor.* "Ideological labor," per the media scholar Janice Peck, is a process that helps audiences to perceive social conflicts in soothing ways that uphold the status quo.[15] However, the stars examined in this book perform more contradictory ideological labor: they sculpt antisemitic stigmas into public personae that ambivalently *challenge and/or renormalize white, straight, Christian male supremacy.* For instance, these personae shape the way that each star depicts sexual violence, class mobility, childrearing, cultural

appropriation, sex work, queer identity, and male bonding. These social commentaries fuel each star's appeal by helping viewers to fantasize about challenging oppression, sustaining their own privilege, or both at once. But whether disrupting and/or naturalizing inequality, each star's persona utilizes (and thereby exposes) America's commonplace racial assumption that Jews look, speak, move, and lust differently from gentiles. Thus, even stars who harmfully normalize inequality against others simultaneously illustrate the antisemitic racial stigmas that expose Jews to mockery, discrimination, and violence.

5. When these millennial Jewish stars achieve mass appeal by enlisting popular assumptions about Jewish bodies, they demonstrate that racial antisemitism is not limited to America's past or to its far-right extremists. Instead, racial antisemitism widely shapes American racial "common sense."

To realize these arguments, this book offers case studies on six of America's best-known millennial stars who self-identify as Jewish: the biracial rap superstar Drake, comedic rapper Lil Dicky, TV comedy duo Abbi Jacobson and Ilana Glazer, "man-baby" film star Seth Rogen, and chiseled film star Zac Efron. Although Drake and Rogen are Canadian, they are two of the most prominent explicitly Jewish stars in US media, and we will see that both vividly riff on racial tropes of Jewish emasculation. All six case studies inspect many facets of the performer's "star text,"[16] a term coined by Richard Dyer to name the countless materials by and about a star that build their public image, from films to memes, interviews, YouTube clips, Instagram posts, and congressional hearings.

Because the six stars in this book present diverse genders, skin tones, Jewish upbringings, and media genres, they offer a cross-section of Ashkenazi North American-born millennial Jewish stardom. Yet despite their differences, all six weave racial stereotypes about Jewish masculinity into racially caricatured public personae, using a technique that I define below as *subliminal postmodern minstrelsy*. By making this minstrelsy their hallmark, these stars differ from peers who riff on Jewish stereotypes without racially caricaturing themselves so sharply or consistently—peers like Rachel Bloom, Amy Schumer, Andy Samberg,

Ben Platt, Gal Gadot, Joseph Gordon-Levitt, and Natasha Lyonne. For this book's six stars, each minstrel persona enables their ideological labor: the way they thrill audiences by challenging and/or renaturalizing straight white Christian male supremacy. And this ideological effect grants all six stars an unconventional allure that I define below as *queer glamor*. These commonalities make all six stars cohere as foils who mirror-yet-invert each other. For instance, Drake and Efron's "opposite" skin tones and similar musculature compel both men to craft minstrel personae that reconcile Jewish identity with "un-Jewish-looking" bodies. Likewise, individually and side by side, all six stars spotlight how queer masculinity racially distinguishes Jews from gentiles in today's US media, and thus how racial antisemitism permeates American thought. Examining these stars particularly opens new directions for scholarship about Jewish masculinities, which has mainly investigated how antisemitic tropes emasculate European and Euro-American Jewish men.[17] Broadening this scope, I analyze how antisemitic racial stigmas about masculinity can shape the self-representation of Black Jewish men, Euro-American Jewish women, and Euro-American Jewish men in America today, including some men who are famous for performing hypermasculinity rather than emasculation.

In turn, this multifaceted analysis draws feminist, queer, critical race, media, and Jewish studies into new dialogues about Jewishness and antisemitism, inviting all these fields to better map how race itself operates in twenty-first-century America.

Queer Glamor and Subliminal Postmodern Minstrelsy

This book's stars exemplify how stigmas of queer (strange) masculinity racially distinguish Jews from gentiles in US media, because each star sculpts these stigmas into different *racial minstrel* personae. Racial minstrelsy is a genre of racial caricature in which Jews historically serve as both white-privileged performers *and* racially stigmatized targets. This genre prominently includes blackface minstrelsy, which originated in the United States in the late 1820s,[18] when white performers began rubbing burnt cork on their faces to caricature Black dance, speech, and song. On stages and then screens, such performances spread widely alongside Jewface, redface

(Native American), yellowface (Asian), and brownface (Latinx, Arab, or South Asian) impersonations.[19] Jewface minstrelsy also extended the longer legacy of Christians caricaturing Jews onstage, a practice that stretches back to medieval Passion plays.[20]

As Jewface, blackface, brownface, yellowface, and redface minstrelsy all proliferated in the late nineteenth and early twentieth centuries, they became key arenas for contesting Euro-American Jews' racial status. On one hand, Jewface used fake noses, dark beards, dark wigs, and dark greasy makeup to racially distinguish Jews from white gentiles.[21] On the other hand, scholars have argued that performing blackface helped early twentieth-century Jewish performers like Al Jolson and Eddie Cantor establish their own whiteness.[22] For instance, by performing blackface, these stars participated in white racism. Meanwhile, the Jewish star Sophie Tucker ended minstrel routines by revealing her light skin and blond hair, thus urging audiences to perceive her as "really" white.[23]

Today, this book's millennial Jewish stars update Jews' ambivalent role as performers and targets of racial minstrelsy. For instance, we will see that Lil Dicky performs Jewface by caricaturing himself as (in his words) a "nappy-headed, greasy Jew" with "frail, Jewish shoulders" and a "little dicky."[24] As Lil Dicky's stage name suggests, his Jewface persona forefronts racial stigmas of Jewish emasculation. Conversely, Zac Efron sometimes *contrasts* himself against emasculated Jewish foils to exaggerate his own "un-Jewish" (blue-eyed, button-nosed, brawny) beauty. This juxtaposition helps Efron to perform what I call "goyface," which racially caricatures straight white gentile masculinity. Like Dicky and Efron, this book's other millennial Jewish stars each weave racial stigmas of queer Jewish masculinity into different styles of racial minstrelsy, including Jewface, goyface, blackface, brownface, a blackface variant called "blackfishing,"[25] and a rarer style that I term "Jewessface."

Yet even as this minstrelsy defines each star's allure, neither the stars nor their audiences seem aware of it. This paradox arises because all six stars perform *subliminal postmodern minstrelsy*: racial caricatures that stars and audiences rarely recognize as synthetic caricatures at all, and which ambivalently challenge/renormalize inequality. Subliminal postmodern minstrelsy escapes conscious attention because many people narrowly define minstrelsy as deliberate, blatant, cosmetic facial distortion to caricature a different racial group from one's own (such as Al Jolson's blackface). Instead, subliminal postmodern minstrelsy is frequently *inadvertent*; it often subtly caricatures the star's *own* identity or appearance; it uses *minimal or no cosmetics* but instead uses choreography, fashion, accents, camera angles, and verbal self-descriptions to racially caricature a performer; and it therefore extends *beyond the face*, and sometimes even *beyond the body*. Further, these self-caricaturing techniques may not converge simultaneously. More subtly, these techniques may appear piecemeal throughout a star's oeuvre, accumulating into a tacit but cohesive minstrel persona. This visual elusiveness helps subliminal postmodern minstrelsy to stay ideologically elusive, neither blatantly oppressive nor liberatory. Indeed, subliminal postmodern minstrelsy proves marketable precisely *because* it is so visually and ideologically nebulous: this ambiguity aids the audience to guiltlessly consume minstrelsy and its oppressive messages without noticing either, or while plausibly denying both. This book dissects that elusive minstrelsy into concrete gestures, fabrics, lighting tactics, camera angles, hairstyles, jokes—and concrete ideological effects.

This definition of subliminal postmodern minstrelsy extends insights from the dance scholar Hannah Schwadron and the media scholar Simon Weaver. Schwadron notes that minstrelsy often "extends beyond the use of makeup [and] . . . manipulations of the face" to include "props, costumes, and humorous narrative devices."[26] I add that minstrelsy which minimizes cosmetics and/or does not manipulate the face easily stays subliminal: it escapes conscious notice even while mesmerizing audiences. Such subliminal caricatures put a more elusive twist on Simon Weaver's concept of "postmodern minstrelsy." Weaver defines postmodern minstrelsy as racial caricatures that may stay cosmetically subtle;[27] may fuse multiple contradictory racist and/or antiracist meanings;[28] and may camouflage or even *lack* political intentions, despite conveying political meanings.[29] These subtleties and contradictions allow postmodern minstrelsy to produce "slippery" (not plainly derogatory) ideological meanings,[30] and especially to produce *liquid racism*: racism that is difficult to concretely recognize or confront.[31] However, Weaver applies this analysis only to minstrelsy that I call *semi-subliminal*: racial caricatures that are *often* recognized as artificial, cartoonish, and separate from the performer's own identity, but *rarely* recognized as minstrelsy because they eschew face paint.

Weaver's prime example of (semi-subliminal) postmodern minstrelsy is the Gen-X British Jewish comedian Sacha Baron Cohen, who helpfully contrasts against this book's millennial Jewish stars. Cohen specializes in buffoonish racial alter egos constructed from costumes, facial hair, accents, and gestures, but never face paint. Weaver spotlights Cohen's character Ali G, most popular from 1998 to 2007: Ali G is a goateed British working-class man who ambiguously seems white or South Asian, but who mimics stereotypical Black American "ghetto" speech and dress.[32] Cohen and millions of viewers explicitly recognize Ali G as an artificial, clownish caricature who sharply differs from Cohen's real self, but because Cohen eschews face paint, neither he nor most viewers recognize his Ali G performances as minstrelsy.[33] Further, this character stays subtle enough to pass as nonsynthetic: when playing Ali G, Cohen often interviews passerby or politicians who misperceive this fabricated caricature as an actual (albeit odd) person. Alongside this visual ambiguity, Cohen fostered political ambiguity throughout the 2000s by saying little about his political aims for Ali G.[34] Weaver finds that Cohen's political ambiguity and cosmetic subtlety let viewers interpret Ali G in many contradictory ways: as a white man who commits *anti-Black racism* by caricaturing Black men, a white man who commits *anti-Asian racism* by caricaturing South Asian men who imitate Blackness, or a white man who only caricatures *his fellow whites* who appropriate Black culture.[35] In turn, Weaver finds that this whirl of anti-Black, anti-Asian, and intra-white mockery creates liquid racism that makes Ali G ideologically marketable. For instance, this ambiguity may help viewers to believe that they enjoy only Ali G's mockery of white people—and thus to guiltlessly enjoy his anti-Black and anti-Asian meanings as well.[36]

This book's millennial Jewish stars perform racial caricatures even more visually and ideologically elusive than Cohen's, producing *subliminal* postmodern minstrelsy. As mentioned above, neither these stars nor their viewers tend to recognize that the stars are performing synthetic racial caricatures at all. On one hand, all six stars do deliberately spotlight stereotypes about Jewish appearance and masculinity, such as when Lil Dicky mocks his "frail, Jewish shoulders."[37] However, none seems to plan or recognize how this pattern caricatures them into racial minstrels, nor how this minstrelsy thrills viewers with ambivalent messages about inequality. Instead, in their minstrelsy, these stars are akin to the comedian who tries a new joke that unleashes riotous laughter and therefore repeats similar jokes, without quite knowing why this shtick electrifies audiences. Similarly, this book's stars have achieved greatest success when their hair, subtle makeup, costumes, choreography, speech, and sexual antics converge toward subliminal postmodern minstrelsy, which fuels their appeal but seems to escape their own notice.

Just as these millennial Jewish stars perform minstrelsy more subliminal than Sacha Baron Cohen's, so does their minstrelsy produce more postmodern (ambivalent and nebulous) political meanings, by often seeming *apolitical*. Cohen's comedy is explicitly political even if his meanings are open-ended. For instance, Cohen often uses his minstrel personae to interview high-profile politicians, such as former US vice president Dick Cheney,[38] about topics like race, war, and gun violence. Conversely, excepting the self-identified feminists Abbi Jacobson and Ilana Glazer, this book's stars rarely seem to intend *any* political commentaries in their performances. Further, their performances often seem intuitively apolitical. For example, critics dismissed Zac Efron's 2017 slapstick comedy *Baywatch* as a "mindless summer diversion."[39] However, we will see that *Baywatch* actually wields subliminal postmodern goyface to convey ambivalent messages about racism, misogyny, and class mobility—political messages that are palatable *because* the film seems like fluff. Likewise, many of this book's stars can thrill viewers with elusive, contradictory, deniable meanings precisely because the stars and audiences misperceive their performances as apolitical.

Further, each star's elusive ideological effects flow beyond Weaver's concept of liquid racism. We will see that through subliminal postmodern minstrelsy, these millennial Jewish stars not only blend many contradictory streams of racism and antiracism, but also blend misogyny with feminism, blend homophobia with homoeroticism or queer pride, and blend antisemitism with Jewish pride. These swirling contradictions often produce racist, misogynist, homophobic, and antisemitic meanings that are exceptionally difficult to notice, articulate, or confront. Further, both the stars and their audiences may enjoy these contradictions for reasons broader (but no less problematic) than Weaver envisions. Weaver emphasizes that liquid racism may help some audiences to enjoy-but-disavow racist jokes.[40] I argue more expansively that subliminal postmodern minstrelsy *helps audiences to pleasurably reconcile contradictory fantasies about challenging/upholding straight white Christian male supremacy.* This fusion can range from "getting away with" bigoted laughter to earnestly misbelieving that one has grown into a perfect antiracist.

Additionally, this book's stars illustrate how the "slippery" appearances and meanings of postmodern minstrelsy *can flow from a performer's own unstable racial status.* Weaver overlooks this point despite using Sacha Baron Cohen, an explicitly Jewish star, to exemplify postmodern minstrelsy. Conversely, when analyzing how millennial Jewish stars perform subliminal postmodern minstrelsy, I emphasize how this minstrelsy harnesses (and thus demonstrates) the contradictory racial perceptions that many viewers already hold about Jewish bodies.

If subliminal postmodern minstrelsy helps these millennial Jewish stars to reconcile liberatory and oppressive fantasies, then this effect has grown ever more electrifying across the Obama, Trump, and Biden eras, as US debates about inequality have grown more explicit. Before these presidencies, during the 1990s and early 2000s, many Americans embraced the myth that America was a post-racial and post-feminist meritocracy, cured of systemic inequality. Conversely, from Barack Obama's second term onward, American politics have increasingly centered around dueling narratives about the extent, cause, and solution of inequality. In this clash, the fact-based perspective recognizes that the US was founded on violent inequality, including Black chattel slavery, Indigenous genocide, racist and antisemitic immigration bans, women's disenfranchisement, and prohibitions against queer gender and sexuality. Emerging from this history, the US systematically limits and harms all who are not white, straight, Christian, and male. This harm will continue until the US proactively ends discriminatory systems, such as by reinventing policing to prevent anti-Black brutality. This fact-based perspective has especially gained visibility via the emergence of #BlackLivesMatter and #MeToo, and the rise of new dialogues about cultural appropriation and racial minstrelsy.

Against these progressive insights has risen a myth-based backlash that denies the existence of white, straight, Christian male supremacy even while defending that system as a necessary good. This backlash variously denies that violent inequality ever existed in America; justifies this inequality as a biological or divine hierarchy; or duplicitously claims that such inequality has ended. This backlash misrepresents social justice movements as deceitful propaganda by nasty women, perverse queers, criminal people of color, and/or greedy Jews who are allegedly pursuing two ends: either to seize "special rights" or to destroy white, straight, Christian, and/or male communities altogether. Although this myth-based backlash has deep roots in American politics, it found raw new expression in Donald Trump; in Trump supporters who idealize America's "great" racist, sexist, homophobic yesteryear; in the alt-right militias whom Trump has called "very fine people"; and in far-right disinformation stars like Tucker Carlson.

Because these clashing narratives about social inequality are so salient in twenty-first-century American life, the ability to reconcile them (as this book's stars do) can prove especially thrilling. Further, some millennial Jewish stars have taken on new valences as America's political landscape has shifted. For instance, we will see how Seth Rogen's early hit *Knocked Up* (2007) presaged far-right misogyny of the 2010s.

By wielding their Jewish bodies to produce subliminal postmodern minstrelsy that ideologically thrills audiences, this book's millennial Jewish stars become gilded with *queer glamor*. I define queer glamor as *an unexpected allure rooted in racial stigmas of queer (odd) Jewish masculinity*, which flips "normative" Hollywood glamor. Normative glamor requires what the philosopher Mikhail Bakhtin calls "classical bodies":[41] svelte, poised, often white gentile bodies like Daniel Craig's. Conversely, racial antisemitism casts Jews as what Bakhtin calls "grotesque bodies"[42] (lumpy, leaky, vulgar) that spark scorn and revulsion. Further, Hollywood has historically pressured Jewish stars to mute their Jewishness, as we will see. Even today, some openly Jewish millennial stars like Scarlett Johansson and Jake Gyllenhaal achieve normative glamor by playing gentile characters and by rarely referencing antisemitic bodily stigmas. Conversely, against industry norms, this book's stars have found success by *spotlighting* racial stigmas of queer Jewish masculinity to create subliminal minstrel personae that seem inherently pathetic and unappealing, but which instead *magnetize* audiences with their tacit ideological meanings. This unexpected appeal is queer glamor. And by deciphering how each star recruits antisemitic tropes into minstrelsy that produces queer glamor, this book clarifies how stigmas of queer masculinity racially distinguish Jews from gentiles onscreen.

Missed Connections and Conditional Whiteness

Spotting racial antisemitism onscreen is essential because scholars, students, activists, and Jewish communities often lack tools to analyze antisemitism at all. For instance, because US culture lacks language for Jewish racial status, even students who racially perceive Zac Efron as "too white to look Jewish" struggle to analyze racial antisemitism when discussing the 2017 Charlottesville rally. Perplexed by white supremacists chanting "Jews will not replace us!," students often ask, "Aren't Jews white? Isn't Judaism a religion?" Beyond the classroom, oversimplifying Jewish racial status this way can derail progressive social activism. For example, in 2018 the Women's March splintered over accusations that its leaders had trivialized antisemitism because they deemed Jews white.[43]

This tendency for progressive thought communities to overlook antisemitism and oversimplify Jewish racial status sparked much larger nationwide tensions in October 2023, in response to renewed violence in Israel-and-Palestine. On October 7, an infiltration team from the Palestinian Islamist militant group Hamas swept through Israeli towns to shoot, stab, beat, and burn to death more than 1,200 Israeli adults and children, often gang-raping and genitally mutilating their victims.[44] Across America, many progressives interpreted these atrocities through a simplified racial narrative which inaccurately imagines all Jews everywhere as white; which therefore envisions the Israeli-Palestinian conflict as a simple struggle between Indigenous people of color (Palestinians) and white colonizers (Israelis); and which can therefore imply that Israelis deserve any and all violence in the name of decolonization.[45] This narrative led many activist and student groups to publicly minimize, justify, or even celebrate Hamas's massacre as admirable anticolonial resistance—for instance, publicly declaring that "I was exhilarated" by Hamas's attack.[46] By endorsing the mass torture and murder of Jews abroad as a supposed moral good, these American progressive thought communities illustrated how ill-equipped they are to analyze antisemitism in any context, including within themselves. Extensively covered in national news, these reactions sparked soul-searching among many progressive Jews, broader Jewish communities, broader left-leaning communities, and university leaders. As of this writing, such onlookers are questioning how progressive groups that claim to advance critical thought and human dignity have fallen into hyper-simplified narratives that invisibilize antisemitism and normalize grisly murder.[47] Likewise, many progressive American Jews who participate in causes like LGBTQ+ advocacy are now questioning their place within left-leaning movements that so vividly excuse (and even glorify) Jewish death.[48] More broadly, these events have shone a new national spotlight on the way American progressive thought communities constantly and harmfully misapprehend antisemitism and Jewish racial status, both when discussing international and US affairs.

When progressive activists and students misconceive Jewish experience, they reflect gaps in feminist, queer, and critical race scholarship. Although these fields respectively examine gender, sexuality, and race, they overlap by emphasizing how multiple oppressions intersect—for instance, how racism and sexism jointly harm Black women differently from white women or Black men.[49] This intersectional approach, pioneered by the feminist scholar Kimberlé Crenshaw, leads all three fields to examine many facets of identity, especially race, class, gender, sexuality, and disability. Jewishness and antisemitism seem natural concerns for this intersectional analysis. Nevertheless, antisemitism often goes unnamed in feminist, queer, and critical race theory: these fields often conflate Jews with white gentiles or mention Jews only as oppressive colonizers in Israel-and-Palestine. Although Jewish feminists have critiqued this silence since 1982,[50] it remains common today. America's feminist scholarly organization, the National Women's Studies Association (NWSA), illustrated this gap after the 2017 Charlottesville white supremacist rally. When condemning that rally, NWSA detailed how "white supremacy and fascism have always been intricately connected with misogyny, patriarchy, transphobia, homophobia, ableism, and settler-colonial logics."[51] This expansive list omitted how white supremacy integrates antisemitism, even though the Charlottesville marchers had chanted "Jews will not replace us!" on national television.[52] Although later corrected, this omission exemplified how even blatant antisemitism routinely goes unnoticed in feminist, queer, and critical race scholarship.

In turn, these fields often dismiss efforts to challenge antisemitism. Such efforts often get rebuked as ploys to evade white guilt, distract from "real" injustices, or rationalize Israeli violence against Palestinians. When feminist, queer, and critical race theory do recognize antisemitism, they often narrowly deem it religious stigma, neatly detached from racial status. This perspective dismisses "white Jews" purely as privileged whites who might occasionally face religious discrimination. Likewise, when these fields (rarely) mention Jews of color, they usually discount how such Jews face antisemitism, instead solely discussing how Jews of color face racism from lighter Jews.[53] Although media studies and Jewish studies have stronger histories of analyzing Jewish racial status, both still tend to overlook Jews of color and to oversimplify how race operates for twenty-first-century Euro-American Jews. However, by analyzing millennial Jewish stardom, this book draws Jewish, feminist, queer, critical race, and media studies toward a fuller understanding of American racial ideologies in general and racial antisemitism in particular.

By investigating how racial antisemitism shapes millennial Jewish stardom, this book especially expands star studies, a strand within media studies. Built on scholarship by Chris Holmlund, Richard Dyer, Diane Negra, Linda Mizejewski, Priscilla Peña Ovalle, and Russell Meeuf, star studies examines how stars perform ideological labor for their audiences.[54] And this field observes that even when minoritized stars break barriers in representation, their performances may not challenge inequality. Instead, many minoritized stars build appeal by subtly *normalizing* inequality, no matter whether they intend or notice this effect. For instance, in *Rebellious Bodies* (2017), Russell Meeuf analyzes six twenty-first-century American stars with stigmatized identities, including the fat Black actress Gabourey Sidibe, elderly white actress Betty White, and the "world's sexiest dwarf," Peter Dinklage.[55] Meeuf argues that these stars build appeal by endorsing a soothing but oppressive myth: that marginalized people can conquer adversity just by expressing self-confidence and performing "proper" middle-class gender. For example, Gabourey Sidibe charms audiences by implying that fat, poor Black women can transcend racism, sexism, and classism just by presenting a bubbly personality and consuming high-end fashion.[56] In turn, some audiences may love Sidibe, White, and Dinklage precisely for the opportunity to feel progressive while actually ignoring legal, economic, and social discrimination.

I note that *Rebellious Bodies* insightfully analyzes gentile stars, but no Jewish ones. Indeed, Jewishness and antisemitism have received little attention in star studies, excepting Linda Mizejewski's work on Fanny Brice and Sarah Silverman.[57] Noticing Jewishness opens new insights about how stars can wield gender to market their stigmatized bodies. For comparison, when analyzing gentile stars in *Rebellious Bodies*, Russell Meeuf concludes that twenty-first-century stars with stigmatized "race or ethnicity, body shape, age, or ability" must counterbalance this stigma by emphasizing "traditional gender roles."[58] Gabourey Sidibe's image as a bubbly and fashion-loving (conventionally feminine) fat Black woman exemplifies this pattern. But if traditional gender styles are vital for making stigmatized bodies palatable, why would some millennial Jewish stars *exaggerate* stigmas of queer Jewish masculinity? And why would this strategy prove marketable? The reason is that—unlike Sidibe's Blackness and fatness, Betty White's old age, or Peter Dinklage's short stature—Jewish racial stigma often *primarily* appears onscreen through queer masculinity. Therefore, performing normative masculinity would invisibilize (not just downplay) Jewish stigma. Yet this book's millennial Jewish stars need to keep that stigma visible, so that they can *enlist* their "nonnormative" bodies to channel national fantasies about inequality. Therefore, to fuel their queer glamor, this book's stars must spectacularize (not mute) stigmas of queer Jewish masculinity. But like Meeuf's gentile stars, this book's Jewish stars often use their stigmatized bodies to subtly or strongly normalize inequality, regardless of intention.

When inviting readers to better recognize racial antisemitism, it may seem counterproductive to examine Jewish stars whose ideological labor normalizes inequality. This focus might encourage readers to keep perceiving Jews (especially Euro-American Jews) simply as privileged oppressors, and therefore to keep trivializing antisemitism. However, when examining how Gabourey Sidibe, Peter Dinklage, and Betty White tacitly assist inequality, no reader would conclude that racism, misogyny, fatphobia, ableism, or ageism have vanished. Instead, these stigmas are precisely what make minoritized stars into potent symbols who can cloak white, straight, Christian male supremacy in a marketable veneer of meritocracy. Likewise, when this book's Jewish stars ambivalently challenge and reaffirm inequality, this ideological labor always enlists Americans' ongoing racial assumption that Jews bodily differ from gentiles. And although this racial stigma may help individual stars to market themselves, it can expose these same stars (and countless other Jews) to stigma and violence. For instance, soon after the Pittsburgh synagogue shooting in 2018, Ilana Glazer had to cancel a speech at a Brooklyn synagogue because the building was graffitied with "Die Jew Rats."[59]

Oversimplifying Jewish racial status prevents many scholars (both Jewish and gentile) from recognizing that such antisemitism remains a threat. The same oversights also discourage some Euro-American Jews from addressing their white privilege. *Time* magazine exemplified this problem with a 2014 op-ed, "Why I'll Never Apologize for My White Male Privilege," by Jewish Princeton student Tal Fortgang.[60] Fortgang asserts that because his grandparents reached America as penniless Holocaust survivors, neither they nor he benefit from any white privilege. Fortgang's narrative overlooks how white skin helped Ashkenazi Holocaust refugees to obtain legal entry, citizenship, or employment in America, and how America rebuffs darker refugees today. Fortgang also overlooks how Euro-American Jews receive better acceptance within American Jewish communities than Jews of color. For instance, he has probably never been mistaken for "the help" at Jewish events, as the Black Jewish comedian Tiffany Haddish has: Haddish relates that "I've been to like over five hundred bar mitzvahs, and I'm getting tired of people telling me to go to the kitchen. No motherfucker, I'm supposed to be here!"[61]

It is tempting but inadequate to dismiss Fortgang's defensiveness as willful ignorance. When refusing to notice white privilege, Fortgang actually mirrors the NWSA statement that disregarded neo-Nazi antisemitism at Charlottesville: both gaps result from trying to ignore Jews of color and to label Euro-American Jews as stably racially privileged or oppressed. Further, both miss how Jews can encounter racial antisemitism simultaneously with white privilege or color-based oppression.

For instance, both Fortgang's and the NWSA's statements overlook how twenty-first-century Euro-American Jews experience *a gap between legal and social race*. On legal documents, these Jews are stably white. Yet in social interactions, they experience racial instability that legal scholar David Schraub calls *conditional whiteness*.[62] I specify that such Jews are conditionally white *with unpredictable conditions*. Even people who deem these Jews white often assume they can spot Jews by noses or hair, assumptions rooted in racial antisemitism. Ultra-Orthodox Jews with distinct clothing may seem "less white" than secular Jews. Sephardi,

Mizrahi, and/or Latinx Jews, no matter how fair-skinned, may find their white status more precarious than that of Ashkenazi North American–born Jews.[63] And even secular Ashkenazi, non-Latinx, Euro-American Jews who get initially read as white cannot predict if this advantageous white status will falter once a name or nose reveals their Jewishness. Likewise, conditionally white Jews cannot foretell what consequence may follow losing whiteness, from mockery to murder.

Feminist, queer, and critical race studies often worry that acknowledging antisemitism and conditional whiteness may aid Jewish communities to deny their white privilege as Fortgang does, to employ evasions like "I'm not white, I'm Jewish."[64] However, *erasing* racial antisemitism actually promotes this evasion. Unlike Fortgang, many conditionally white Jews do wish to challenge white privilege. But when hearing anyone deny their Jewish stigma and danger, such Jews can jointly experience a rightful urge to acknowledge antisemitism *and* a wrongful urge to avoid white guilt. Together, these reactions encourage some conditionally white Jews (like Fortgang) to reject antiracist insights altogether. Instead, accurately naming how antisemitism intersects with white privilege and color-based racism sets the stage for Jews and gentiles of all colors to ally in dismantling white supremacy.

To support this precision, this book helps readers to articulate how US media depict Jewish racial status onscreen. Although Jewish racial contradictions can seem abstract, they are really as familiar to many Americans as their favorite sitcom or star.

Racial Trajectories of Jewishness and Gentility

Abbi Jacobson and Ilana Glazer forefront these racial contradictions in their hit sitcom, *Broad City* (2014–2019): both stars call themselves white but emphasize bodily stereotypes that historically *distance* Jews from whiteness. For instance, Glazer quips that she irons her hair because "I look like a true Jew if I don't straighten" it.[65] By implying that Jews have identifiably curly dark hair, this wisecrack invokes centuries-old antisemitic stigmas that intersect with anti-Blackness. The notion that "red or black curly hair" physically marks Jews descends from the Middle Ages.[66] This trope later informed nineteenth-century racial pseudoscience, which sometimes stigmatized Jews as "Africanized" people who allegedly possessed dark coiled hair, swarthy skin, and large noses and lips.[67] The Polish nobleman Adam Gurowski illustrated this fusion of antisemitism with anti-Blackness when visiting America in the 1850s: Gurowski journaled about mistaking "every light-skinned mulatto for a Jew."[68] Over a century and a half later, Glazer's joke exemplifies how deep-rooted racial beliefs about Jewish hair still shape American racial assumptions.

By flaunting Jewish racial stigmas and contradictions, stars like Glazer disrupt tidy narratives about Jews' *racial trajectory*. I repurpose the term "racial trajectory" from the critical race scholars Michael Omi and Howard Winant, who analyze how racial categories emerge and fluctuate over time.[69] Though often misperceived as a biological fact, race is actually a cultural *myth* about biology:[70] it shoehorns human diversity into artificial boxes like "Black," "white," and "Jew," while asserting that different "races" merit unequal treatment. But like national borders, racial categories can unpredictably appear, shift, and vanish as social consensus changes, producing new beliefs about how many races exist and who fits in each. Omi and Winant name this process "racial formation."[71] They likewise coin "racial trajectory" to describe a given society's historical path across different styles of racial politics, such as eras of blatant or subtler racism.[72] Restyling this term, I use "racial trajectory" to name a given group's historical path *across racial categories*: how that group gets racially defined and redefined over time by the wider flux of racial formation.

American Jews' racial trajectory flows from roots older than the idea of race itself. Some scholars argue that Europeans first conceived race in the seventeenth to eighteenth centuries in order to justify colonizing, enslaving, and exterminating darker peoples.[73] For instance, colonial Virginian documents show how racial thinking gradually crystallized there, as European colonists first called themselves "white" in the 1680s and first wrote this term into law in 1691.[74] Other scholars trace racism's roots back further to the late fifteenth century, when the Spanish Inquisition began defining Jewish and Muslim identity as heritable blood taints rather than religions.[75] Indeed, the word "race" descends from the medieval Spanish *raza*, which stigmatized Jews and Muslims as physically, unchangeably inferior to Christians.[76] Meanwhile, the literary scholar Geraldine Heng has argued that Europeans first articulated racial thinking—including about Jews—by the thirteenth century.[77]

Like Heng, this book embraces the view that racial antisemitism descends from medieval bodily stigmas that predate widespread statements about blood, race, or biology. Of course, anti-Jewish bodily stigmas stretch back even farther than the medieval era. For example, by the second century CE, Christian theologians were already depicting Jews as "sexually deviant, lascivious, emasculated, bestial, and contagious."[78] Although such early accusations may inform today's racial stereotypes about Jewish bodies, a particularly traceable lineage anchors today's racial antisemitism in twelfth-century European Christian art. The art historian Sara Lipton explains that this era saw Christian art newly begin distorting Jewish bodies.[79] Christian art had long used shaggy beards and beaked noses as "visual indicators of bestiality, brutality, irrationality, and evil,"[80] but now attached these traits to Jews.[81] Visual stereotypes of Jewish male faces with a "bony hooked nose and a pointed beard" first emerged in the mid-thirteenth century, as did textual assertions that Jews have darker hair and skin.[82] These associations even prompted one thirteenth-century Jewish scholar to pen instructions for fellow Jews on how to retort if asked why "gentiles are . . . white and attractive while the majority of Jews are black and ugly."[83] Since medieval imagery linked Jewish bodily deviance to sin rather than heredity, Lipton distinguishes such depictions from modern racism.[84] Yet this early anti-Jewishness constituted what some scholars term "proto-racism" or "race before race,"[85] by *initiating* patterns that later shaped secular racial antisemitism. For instance, thirteenth-century sources accused Jews of a *foetor Judaicus* ("Jewish stench") in religious terms, claiming that Jews' disbelief in Jesus caused them to reek unless baptized,[86] and this religious accusation grew more racial over time. For example, in 1646, the English author Thomas Browne noted the common opinion that baptism could not cure Jews' stench, but rather that "Jews stink naturally" because "in their race and nation there is an evil savour."[87] Nearly three centuries later, Nazi pseudoscientists embraced such claims to allege that Jews emit a cloying "'faint-sweet' racial odor."[88]

Most scholarship on race disregards how this eight-century lineage of bodily stigmas still steers American Jews' racial trajectory in contradictory ways. On one hand, critical race studies, American studies, and Jewish studies do accurately note that Ashkenazi Jews were racially stigmatized across the eighteenth to early twentieth centuries. That era's pseudoscience often labeled Jews an inferior "Oriental," "Semitic," "Asiatic," or "Hebrew" race.[89] However, scholars tend to erroneously flatline Ashkenazi Jews' racial trajectory by asserting that American society firmly relabeled these Jews white by the 1950s or 1960s. This "stably white by midcentury" narrative, proposed by scholars such as David Roediger, Matthew Frye Jacobson, Karen Brodkin, and Michael Rogin, asserts that Ashkenazi Jews paralleled the racial trajectories of gentile Irish, Italian, Greek, and Slavic immigrants. In the mid-nineteenth to early twentieth centuries, American society commonly deemed all these groups distinct "races" that were ambivalently viewed as nonwhite, as lesser varieties of white, or as in-between, though always privileged above people of color. However, across the 1920s to 1960s, American racial ideologies "whitened" these European groups by largely reimagining them as "ethnicities" within a single white race.[90] Matthew Frye Jacobson observes that this "whitening" partly responded to the Nazi Holocaust.[91] While racism had long exposed people of color to genocide, the Holocaust had turned this genocidal racism against other Europeans.[92] In response to these intra-European atrocities, it became gauche for Americans to label any Europeans "separate races," thus prompting the turn toward "ethnicity." The 1947 novel and film *Gentleman's Agreement* exemplified this shift by adamantly informing viewers that, contrary to earlier scientific claims, "there's no such thing as a Jewish race."[93]

However, when scholars assume that Jewishness fully and stably equals whiteness after midcentury, they erase Jews of color, oversimply how Euro-American Jews experience conditional whiteness, and discount how both still encounter deep-rooted antisemitic racial stigmas. To better map Jewish racial status, Jewish scholars such as Melanie Kaye/Kantrowitz, Marla Brettschneider, Rachel Silverman, Sander Gilman, Helene Meyers, Laura Levitt, Jonathan Freedman, David Reznik, Nathan Abrams, Jon Stratton, Jonathan Boyarin, Carol Siegel, and Hannah Schwadron have all striven to articulate how Euro-American Jews waver inside/outside whiteness. Likewise, Katya Gibel Mevorach, Melanie Kaye/Kantrowitz, and Marla Brettschneider have drawn scholarly attention to Jews of color, while Jews of color including Mevorach, Rebecca Walker, Tiffany Haddish, Gen Slosberg, and Siona Benjamin have theorized their own experiences in scholarship, memoir, poetry, comedy, film, and art.[94]

To clarify Jews' racial trajectory, some Jewish feminists have also emphasized how today's secular racial categories interact with older religious stigmas that tie whiteness to Christianity. As mentioned above, secular "scientific" racism of the seventeenth to twentieth centuries developed from earlier religious stigmas. Marla Brettschneider and Rachel Silverman emphasize how this history continues to link present-day American white supremacy with Christian supremacy.[95] While Christian supremacy includes violence and discrimination such as the 2017 Muslim travel ban, it also includes subtler "Christonormativity."[96] Christonormativity assumes that Christian identity, custom, and appearance form the neutral default, against which all other religions (and the bodies who perform them) appear "strange."

Because Christonormativity co-shapes racism, presenting as fully white in America still depends on hailing from Christian roots, even if one is unreligious—that is, being *gentile*. The etymology of "gentile" clarifies how this identity shapes racial status: literary scholar Marjorie Garber traces "gentile" to its shared root with "gentle," which "initially meant well-behaved because 'well-born.'"[97] Shakespeare's *The Merchant of Venice* (approximately 1596) exemplifies this racialized presumption that white gentile ancestry creates better-behaved bodies: it famously presents the phrase "gentle Jew" as an oxymoron.[98] Over four centuries later, gentility remains central but underexamined in US racial ideologies. Like the specific racial stigmas concerning Jews, this wider link between gentility and whiteness explains why Euro-American Jews have remained conditionally white rather than following gentile Irish, Slavic, Greek, and Italian Americans into stable whiteness.

Linear narratives about Jewish whitening preclude asking how racial antisemitism and Christonormativity still impact American Jews of all colors. Yet this book's millennial Jewish stars vividly illustrate how racial antisemitism, white privilege, and color-based racism continue to swirl unstably together.

Glamorous Provocations: Goodbye to "Double-Coding"

When this book's millennial Jewish stars spotlight Jewish racial contradictions, they not only destabilize scholarly narratives about race; they also breach historical Hollywood taboos. Two early American blockbusters did scrutinize Jewish racial status: Al Jolson's *The Jazz Singer* (1927) and Eddie Cantor's *Whoopee!* (1930) use the racist tool of blackface to question how their Jewish leading men fit between Blackness and whiteness.[99] However, as American antisemitism escalated in the 1930s, Hollywood films began repressing Jewishness to avoid backlash from Christian audiences. Hollywood executives (including Jewish ones) discouraged explicitly Jewish characters and intensified the pressure on Jewish actors to closet their Jewishness.[100] This censorship began loosening in the 1970s with films by Woody Allen, Barbra Streisand, and Richard Benjamin, but unapologetically Jewish stars and characters remained rare until the 1990s.[101] Even when the comedians Fran Drescher and Jerry Seinfeld broke this barrier by starring as Jewish leads in their own sitcoms, NBC's president critiqued Seinfeld's series as "too Jewish" and Drescher's sponsors pressured her to restyle her leading lady as Italian.[102] Although Drescher refused, the words "Jew" and "Jewish" rarely appear in her series *The Nanny* (1993–1999) or Seinfeld's series *Seinfeld* (1989–1998).[103] Instead, like most twentieth-century American media, both employ a subtler strategy that theater scholar Henry Bial calls *double-coding*: they use stereotypical accents or mannerisms to hint at Jewishness, but often keep these hints subtle enough not to tip off gentile viewers who might reject an "overly Jewish" show.[104]

Shattering such restraints, this book's millennial Jewish stars flaunt Jewishness and its racial contradictions to once-unthinkable degrees— for instance, when Seth Rogen quips that "my face is circumcised" (self-evidently Jewish) in the trailer for *Funny People* (2009).[105] This new freedom to publicly explore Jewish racial status has overlapped with new diversity in mainstream Jewish stardom. Since the late 2000s, Jewish men of color like Drake, Jewish women of color like Tiffany Haddish, and conditionally white Jewish women like Abbi Jacobson and Ilana Glazer have gained new space to assert their perspectives onscreen while attracting wide audiences. This leeway for diverse Jewish stars to openly explore Jewish racial contradictions builds on Seinfeld's and Drescher's breakthroughs of the 1990s, and on wider feminist, antiracist, and LGBTQ+ advances.

This leeway also frequently mobilizes digital media that originated in the 2000s, like Facebook, Twitter, and YouTube. Media scholar A.J. Christian writes that these platforms have enabled *open TV*: they aid independent artists to create and widely circulate homemade media, thereby proving their marketability before approaching industry gatekeepers.[106] This pathway grants greater freedom for minoritized artists to assert their identities and perspectives, rather than censoring themselves to please more privileged executives. However, when analyzing how open TV has uncensored Black, women, and/or queer mediamakers, Christian omits how this medium has enabled millennial Jewish stars to uncensor their Jewishness. This silence is especially striking when Christian discusses *Broad City*, Abbi Jacobson and Ilana Glazer's webseries turned network comedy, in which they provocatively self-identify as "Jewesses."[107] This outdated and flamboyantly Jewish label illustrates how Jacobson and Glazer flaunt Jewishness far more sensationally than predecessors like Fran Drescher or Jerry Seinfeld. Similarly, Lil Dicky rocketed to YouTube stardom by mocking himself as a "nappy-headed, greasy Jew,"[108] and then he parlayed this YouTube success into a network sitcom. Dicky, Jacobson, and Glazer all thus exemplify how open TV has newly enabled millennial Jewish stars to spectacularize Jewishness and its racial stigmas.

Little Dicks: Historicizing "Racially Queer" Jewish Masculinity

And Lil Dicky's self-emasculating stage name signals how he specifically flaunts racial stigmas about Jewish *masculinity*. Likewise, all this book's stars particularly harness the long-running notion that Jewish men are emasculated, Jewish women are masculinized, and both are sexually perverse. These masculine stigmas constitute key threads in the eight-century lineage of antisemitic bodily stigmas that shape present-day American stereotypes.

In other words, Europeans and Americans have commonly envisioned Jews as *racially queer*. "Racial queerness," coined by the literary scholar Steven Kruger,[109] describes *stereotypes of strange gender and sexuality that are projected onto racially stigmatized communities*. As many queer theorists have observed, these racially queer stereotypes reflect the commonplace assumption that different races possess different types of gender and sexuality.[110] For instance, saying "all-American football player" conjures a heroic white gentile masculinity very different from stereotypes of menacing "Black rapists" or feeble "nice Jewish boys." Likewise, stereotypes of negligent Black "welfare queens," authoritarian Asian "tiger moms," or emasculating "Jewish mothers" cast women who are not white and gentile as aberrant mothers. As the phrase "all-American" suggests, racist ideologies often stereotype white gentiles with wholesome gender and sexuality, and so as good citizens. Conversely, these ideologies stereotype each racial outgroup with specific types of racially queer (deviant, dirty, excessive, or deficient) gender and sexuality, and so as bad citizens. In turn, these racially queer stereotypes *amplify the stigma* on racial outgroups.

While "racial queerness" aptly names stigmas on many communities, Steven Kruger initially used this term to analyze thirteenth-century antisemitism.[111] He thus illuminated the early roots of today's antisemitic masculine stigmas, which millennial Jewish stars now harness. Kruger writes that medieval Christians commonly deemed Jews "unnatural" for denying that Jesus was messiah.[112] In turn, this Jewish intellectual "deviance" allegedly caused "unnatural" gender and sexuality. For instance, medieval Christians often alleged that Jewish men were effeminate, spread the sin of sodomy, and even menstruated as punishment for crucifying Jesus.[113]

The thirteenth century also planted the seeds of racially queer masculine stereotypes about Jewish *women*, centering around a stock figure called the "beautiful Jewess." This figure was first recorded circa 1292 in Iberian tales of a Christian king who becomes sexually entranced by a Jewish woman, possibly ensnared by "spells and love magic that she knew."[114] Subsequently, the "beautiful Jewess" trope spread and reached peak popularity in the eighteenth to early twentieth centuries across American, British, and European popular culture.[115] This trope depicted Jewish women as racially exotic temptresses who might conceal dangerous masculinity behind their seductive façades.[116] This image drew inspiration from, and was retroactively projected onto, Near Eastern biblical characters like Judith: Judith (whose name means "Jewess") seduces the enemy general Holofernes only to behead him, thus revealing "masculinized" aggression, deceit, and swordsmanship.[117] Likewise, although some nineteenth-century Jewess characters were passive victims awaiting rescue by white Christian heroes, others were dark femmes fatales whose "masculine" sexual deceit and assertiveness lured Christian men to ruin. This pattern has led the performance studies scholar Ann Pellegrini to observe that the "hyperbolic femininity of the *belle juive* [beautiful Jewess] conceals her perverse masculinity."[118]

These images of deceptively masculinized Jewish women and perversely emasculated Jewish men formed early links in a chain that threads through US media today. As pseudoscientific racism emerged over the seventeenth to twentieth centuries, it incorporated queer stereotypes about Jewish masculinity to help racially differentiate Jews from white gentiles. The antisemitic industrialist Henry Ford captured this link between racial, gendered, and sexual antisemitism when he alleged in 1921 that Jewish male filmmakers were sexually corrupting America with "Oriental," lascivious art.[119] This accusation cast Jews as racially dark "Orientals" (Near Easterners) and equated their racial difference with sexual deviance. The French Nazi-sympathizer Louis-Ferdinand Céline even more bluntly illustrated the links between racial, gendered, and sexual antisemitism: in a single sentence, he smeared Jews as "unbridled fornicators" and "Afro-Asiatic hybrids, quadroons, half-negroes, and Near-Easterners."[120] This lineage of antisemitic beliefs about Jewish appearance, masculinity, and sexuality still fuels the conviction among white supremacists like David Duke that no Jew is white. It also explains why many Americans who would never speak like Duke still find Jewish racial status confusing, and still assume that Jews look, speak, move, and lust differently from white gentiles. Thus, although US science, policy, and media no longer officially label Jews a race, historical antisemitism still shapes today's commonsense notion that Jews are racially queer.

In turn, this racial queerness *tints Jewish bodies with unacknowledged racial subtext*. Although American pop culture often depicts Jewish masculinity as self-evidently strange, it rarely recognizes this assumption as a racial perception rooted in traceable racist histories. These poorly understood perceptions cast many conditionally white Jews into a socially recognized identity ("Jew") with an implicitly incoherent racial status: racially white by color but racially Jewish by masculinity. In contrast, stereotypes of racially queer Jewish masculinity impose more explicit racial incoherence on Jews of color, on conditionally white Jews who look "too white," and on all Jews whose masculinity seems "too normal." Such performers appear onscreen as socially unthinkable identities for which audiences demand explanation, such as when students perceive Zac Efron and Drake as "impossibly" white, Black, or muscular Jews.

Yet even when Jewish masculinity's racial symbolism is strongly felt onscreen, this racial meaning often goes unacknowledged, because articulating it requires noticing that:

1. Different parts of one body (like skin tone and penis shape) can simultaneously connote different racial statuses.
2. Racial symbolism can attach not only to concrete body parts like noses, but also to intangible bodily effects called *ephemera* (like voices).
3. Present-day images reproduce well-documented antisemitic bodily stigmas from earlier periods that explicitly labeled Jews an inferior race.

These insights, detailed below, not only clarify how queer masculinity racially stigmatizes Jewish bodies onscreen; they also clarify how millennial Jewish stars creatively *enlist* that stigma to market themselves.

Disidentifying and Counteridentifying with the "Mythical Jew"

Antisemitic stigmas make such effective marketing tools because they are not simply insults, but *tropes* that link Jews into wider narratives about dominance, deviance, and decency. "Tropes" are stock characters, images, or storylines that each convey a cluster of cultural beliefs, like the fairytale princess whose journey teaches children that good women must be white, gentile, thin, passive, and straight. Similarly, the emasculated Jewish man and seductive-but-masculinized Jewess are two prominent tropes in European and Euro-American cultures, conveying preset narratives. Of course, tropes of racially queer Jewish masculinity have evolved from medieval European manuscripts to American vaudeville plays to YouTube raps. But across eras, regions, and genres, these tropes provide familiar building blocks for storytelling: they constantly enable artists to reshuffle audiences' preset antisemitic expectations into new storylines, jokes, or characters.

Antisemitic tropes have always positioned Jews as symbols for wider narratives about social difference and hierarchy. For instance, when analyzing medieval anti-Jewish imagery, the art historian Sara Lipton writes that medieval Christians circulated images of Jews *not* to understand Jews' actual appearance or customs, but to symbolize philosophical issues like "knowledge, vision, and representation."[121] For example, these images played on the Christian belief that Jews were "blind" to the Bible's true meaning because they did not recognize Jesus's divinity. Thus, for as long as European and Euro-American cultures have circulated antisemitic images, these images have performed ideological labor about topics far beyond Jews' own lives.

However, only more recently have real live Jews like Drake gained some say in their own representation and ideological labor. Historically, Christians in regions with no Jews often produced artistic, literary, and theatrical images of Jews, positioning Jews as passive objects of Christian imaginations. The "mythical Jew"[122] is one term for such imagery, which Christian societies spun from their own biases for their own ends.[123] Two well-known "mythical Jews" are the spiteful merchant Shylock and his lovely daughter Jessica in Shakespeare's *The Merchant of Venice*, written three centuries after England expelled its Jews. Shylock and Jessica were imagined, performed, and consumed by white Christians to assert Christian superiority, which Jessica affirms by converting to wed a Christian.[124] Shylock and Jessica were also among the first Jewish characters consumed by Euro-American audiences when *Merchant of Venice* became the first professional play staged in Britain's North American colonies in 1752.[125] These characters thus form two links in the chain of mythical Jews presaging today's millennial Jewish stars and their ideological labor.

But as authors of their own image, today's millennial Jewish stars embody a recent shift: American Jewish media representation now reflects input from Jewish executives, writers, directors, and actors. The theater scholar Harley Erdman traces this shift to American theater of the 1870s.[126] For instance, the Jewish playwright Milton Nobles described his 1876 play *The Phoenix* as "the first to place on the stage a modern young American Jew, a jolly, up-to-date man about town, and not a villain."[127] Forty years after *The Phoenix*, real live Jews gained exceptional new opportunities for self-representation when Hollywood emerged in the 1910s. Jewish immigrants like Carl Laemmle (co-founder of Universal Studios) and Jack Warner (co-founder of Warner Brothers) founded Hollywood, becoming filmmakers partly because more established industries would not hire Jews.[128] These Jewish executives gained wealth, prestige, and cultural impact unimaginable for almost any Jew in history—but also endured antisemitic backlash, like Henry Ford's tirade against "Oriental" Jewish filmmakers. As noted earlier, studio executives forestalled backlash by erasing Jewish characters. Another method to placate gentile audiences was to confirm their biases by stereotyping Jewish characters as foreign, emasculated comic relief.[129] As early as 1928, the *Jewish Forum* periodical critiqued Jewish Hollywood executives for promoting "the comic movie Jew," an "easily grasped version of the Jew" who is short, greasy, and vulgar[130]—a cinematic twist on older "mythical Jews." As this critique illustrates, Jews seeking employment or representation in US media have always negotiated with preexisting tropes about Jewish gender, sexuality, and race.

Yet Jewish stars have not passively mirrored these antisemitic stereotypes. In Harley Erdman's words, Jewish stars have instead "resisted, assimilated, or reordered images that a dominant culture constructed for them" to assert their own perspectives.[131] In other words, many Jewish performers *counteridentify* and *disidentify* with antisemitic racial tropes. The terms "counteridentify" and "disidentify," coined by linguist Michel Pêcheux, have gained prominence in queer theory through José Muñoz's book *Disidentifications*. For minoritized people, "counteridentifying" means rejecting the dominant culture's images of oneself by crafting an opposite image; for instance, rebuffing stereotypes of weak Jewish men by bodybuilding in the gym.[132] Yet Pêcheux and Muñoz caution that counteridentification can feed the stigmatizing images that it flees: it throws these images into sharper relief and displaces them onto other members of the same minoritized community, an effect called *counterdetermination*.[133] For instance, we will see that Drake and Zac Efron sometimes use their skin tones and muscles to actively rebuff racial stigmas of Jewish emasculation onto more stereotypically Jewish-looking peers like Seth Rogen. This counterdetermination validates and sharpens antisemitic stigma, while elevating Drake and Efron as sexy exceptions.

Unlike counteridentifying, to *disidentify* is neither to strictly accept nor reject dominant images of oneself, but to *creatively reinhabit* them.[134] Muñoz specifically uses "disidentification" to name how (gentile) queer people of color reinvent racist and queerphobic images for liberatory ends.[135] For instance, he analyzes how the lesbian Cuban American performer Marga Gomez refashions a homophobic caricature of lesbian truck drivers that she saw on television as a child: in her one-woman show, Gomez restages these stigmatized TV lesbians as beloved role models who assure younger lesbian viewers that they are not alone.[136] Similarly, I will show that Seth Rogen, Lil Dicky, Ilana Glazer, and Abbi Jacobson disidentify with antisemitic tropes like the emasculated Jew or the seductive-yet-masculinized Jewess: they refashion these tropes to express their own views and fuel their own stardom.

By analyzing how millennial Jewish stars disidentify and counteridentify with racial antisemitism, this book promotes dialogue between scholarship on Jews (of all colors) and on (both Jewish and gentile) people of color. Indeed, this analysis reveals that gentile scholars of color and conditionally white Jewish scholars already investigate similar questions, frequently without realizing it. For instance, when Harley Erdman writes that Jewish performers have "resisted, assimilated, or reordered images that a dominant culture constructed for them,"[137] his words mirror Muñoz's work on disidentification and counteridentification. Further, although Muñoz focuses on gentile queer performers of color in *Disidentifications*, he uses one Jewish example to illustrate disidentification: the comic book superhero Superman, created by Ashkenazi Jewish American artists in the 1930s.[138] That decade's racial ideologies exalted German gentile men as "Übermensches" (supermen)[139] and Jewish men in British Palestine as strong "muscle Jews,"[140] explicitly defining both against "emasculated" diasporic Jewish men. Disidentifying with these stigmas, Jewish American comic artists invented a diasporic alien refugee with the Hebrew-sounding name "Kal El" ("El" means "God"), who acculturates to Midwestern America and becomes the nation's heroic "superman." This tale reshuffled antisemitic racial stigmas into an affirming model for diasporic Jewish masculinity. And by citing this example, Muñoz established that his model of disidentification can encompass how Jews of any color remold antisemitic tropes.

While prior scholarship has asked how Jewish stars "resist, assimilate, or reorder" antisemitic tropes to assert their own self-image, this book also asks why this disidentification and counteridentification prove so *marketable*. This analysis crystallizes antisemitic racial stigmas that often stay nebulous.

Something Funny: Spotting Racialized Ephemera and Hauntings

Indeed, this book's stars sometimes dramatize just how vivid-but-nebulous racial antisemitism can be. Seth Rogen spotlights this ambiguity in his 2015 comedy *The Night Before*,[141] when father-to-be

Isaac Greenberg (Rogen) hosts a Christmas party with his white Christian wife. When their icily white, thin, blond Christian twin nieces learn Isaac is Jewish, one niece asks, "Is that why you look different?" Isaac stammers for her to clarify, but her twin just squints in distaste while musing, "You just look . . . funny." The girls seem baffled because they cannot pin Isaac's Otherness to concrete traits like color—he inexplicably "looks different" in a "funny" (strange and amusing) way. Rogen's wider star text specifically links this ethereal funniness to Jewish masculinity: many of Rogen's comedies, including *The Night Before*, package him as a Jewish man-baby struggling into fatherhood.

The nebulous "funniness" of Rogen's Jewish body illustrates how tropes of racially queer Jewish masculinity can reside not only in concrete physical traits like Lil Dicky's penis, but also in *ephemera*. In my usage, ephemera are fleeting bodily effects such as speech, gesture, posture, eye contact, or facial expression, which can bear racial stigma, becoming *racialized ephemera*. This notion of racialized ephemera builds on José Muñoz's *Cruising Utopia*, which draws in turn from the Jewish philosophers Ernst Bloch and Jacques Derrida.[142] Muñoz explains that American society often visualizes queer identity in ephemera like fleeting gestures, tones, and traces,[143] as captured by the homophobic jeer "limp wrist." Therefore, even when queerness makes a powerful impression, it is less a concrete object than an ethereal sensation, at once present and absent.[144] The same fleeting yet powerful sensation often defines racial tropes about Jewish masculinity. This evanescence often makes racial antisemitism slippery to analyze, but Muñoz's paradigm offers language for crystallizing how antisemitic racial tropes attach to ephemera. In US media today, ephemera like voices and body language weightily symbolize Jewish racial difference. Indeed, this ephemerality is one reason why Jewish stars can channel antisemitic racial stigmas into *subliminal* postmodern minstrelsy.

Whether stigmas of racially queer Jewish masculinity attach to ephemera or to concrete body parts, they often go unrecognized even when strongly *felt*. This disconnect between sensing and comprehending such stigmas poses another obstacle to noticing racial antisemitism. The Black Jewish rap superstar Drake illustrated this disconnect in 2014, when performing Jewish racialized ephemera on *Saturday Night Live*.[145] While restaging his own bar mitzvah (Jewish manhood ceremony),

Drake briefly adopts a nasal "Jew voice" to complain about a Jewish deli's pickles. The studio audience chuckles at his quip: they "get" that Drake is vocally caricaturing himself as a neurotic, fussy, emasculated Jewish man. But Drake and his audiences likely do not recall the antisemitic racial beliefs that first produced this emasculating "Jew voice" stereotype: nineteenth-century racial pseudoscience accused Jews of possessing distinct facial muscles that supposedly produced deviant voices (and in men's case, feminine voices).[146] The German language even had a verb for "speaking like a Jew," *Mauscheln.*[147] Germans thus commonly depicted Jews as people with racially distinct bodies that produced feminized and foreign speech. Drake's nasal quip in 2014 fleetingly conveyed these centuries of antisemitic racial stigma to American viewers who may not know that Jews were ever labeled a "race"—but an audience still primed by this history to assume that Jewish men physically differ from gentile men.

Drake's *SNL* "Jew voice" exemplifies how antisemitic racial beliefs tint our view of Jewish bodies in potent yet ghostly ways. Indeed, Marjorie Garber writes that racial antisemitism has a visibility that is "spectral— the visibility of a ghost."[148] A useful lens to reveal this ghostly influence is José Muñoz's notion of queer "hauntology."[149] Building on Jewish philosopher Jacques Derrida, Muñoz explains in *Cruising Utopia* how queerness can appear not only in fleeting impressions (ephemera), but also as a ghostly haunting sensation. For instance, Muñoz describes New York City's many spaces where gay men sexually cruised before the HIV crisis shut them down: piers, movie theaters, and bathhouses all closed, scrubbed, and gentrified.[150] For men who once cruised these spaces, New York's sanitized new face conveys a haunting history—the traces of an exuberant gay subculture that social panic, gentrification, and janitorial labor could never fully erase.

Likewise, racial antisemitism haunts Jews and all who watch Jewish bodies onscreen today. Just as New York's makeover has never fully erased queer subcultures, America's post-1950 racial formation has never fully erased the popular impression that Jews bodily differ from gentiles. It especially has not erased tropes of racially queer Jewish masculinity. This book's millennial Jewish stars—like all Jews in the US—remain haunted by those racial stigmas, stigmas always waiting to solidify into view through the lilt of a voice or flick of a wrist. And noticing how present-day performances invoke this racial haunting is vital for recognizing how queer masculinity connotes Jewish racial difference onscreen.

Invisible Intersections: Layering the White/POC Binary

In turn, recognizing Jewish masculinity's racial symbolism makes visible how racial antisemitism intersects with both white privilege and color-based oppression on Jewish bodies. As mentioned above, this nuance often goes unrecognized because American conversations on race frequently presume a white/people of color (white/POC) binary that fully equates race with skin color. On one hand, this binary is informative because skin tone centrally shapes American racial definitions, discrimination, and violence. As Frederick Douglass and W. E. B. Dubois each wrote near the turn of the twentieth century, America enforces a "color line" dividing people deemed visually white from brown or black.[151] This division still holds deadly importance today, such as when police officers' implicit biases endanger Black lives.

However, while the white/POC binary illuminates this division, it also raises the question: how do we recognize racial stigma that is not primarily attached to skin color? For instance, how can a conditionally white Jew like Lil Dicky, who benefits from the system of white supremacy, simultaneously experience racial harassment or violence? Even when feminist, queer, and critical race scholarship look beyond color to analyze how hair textures, facial features, gender styles, and sexual behaviors also symbolize race, they often assume that these non-melanin-based stigmas *reinforce* white/POC color assignments. This approach valuably clarifies how racially queer stereotypes vilify people primarily marked by color. For instance, when politicians stereotype Latino men as violent "bad hombres," they project non-melanin-based stigma (criminal masculinity) onto people who are primarily visualized as "brown." However, presuming that all facets of racial stigma cohere into one color status precludes asking how racial stigmas attached to hair, noses, or masculinity may *contradict* one's color status. For instance, presuming such harmony forestalls asking how Drake may face discordant racial tropes of Black hypermasculinity and Jewish emasculation.

For scholars, students, and activists who have not faced antisemitism, the white/POC binary makes racial antisemitism hard to spot or even imagine. For Jews who have experienced antisemitism, this binary compels a false choice: either conflate antisemitism with color-based racism or deny their own experiences of Jewish stigma, fear, and violence. And for conditionally white Jews, conflating antisemitism with color-based racism often entails denying their own white privilege while erasing Jews of color, precisely the problems in Tal Fortgang's op-ed above.

To visualize how Jewish stars simultaneously embody racial antisemitism *and* white privilege or color-based racism, this book *layers the lens of masculinity-as-race alongside the white/POC binary*. Recognizing Jewish masculinity's racial symbolism moves beyond the false choice between ignoring racial antisemitism or conflating it with color-based racism. Instead, acknowledging how queer masculinity symbolizes Jewish racial difference onscreen makes visible how racial antisemitism intersects with both white and POC color statuses in US media.

Linking Queer of Color Critique with Jewish Cultural Studies

Visualizing how racially queer Jewish masculinity intersects with the white/POC binary reveals unexplored directions for many fields, but especially for *Jewish cultural studies* and *queer of color critique*. Although these fields have separately trailblazed scholarship about racial queerness, they have never yet acknowledged each other. And although both fields emphasize how gender and sexuality structure race, each has examined just one side of the white/POC binary, leading both to oversimplify Jewish racial status. Jewish cultural studies emerged in the 1990s as a thread within Jewish studies that examines Jewish experiences of race, gender, and sexuality, especially analyzing how European and North American nations have labeled Jews racially queer.[152] For example, John Efron notes that during the late eighteenth and nineteenth centuries, European gentiles debated whether Jewish men were masculine enough to join gentile men in military service, and thus to merit legal equality with gentile men.[153] Queer of color critique emerged from queer theory and women of color feminism in the early 2000s to analyze how stigmas of racial queerness fuel large-scale violence.[154] For example, Jasbir Puar and Amit Rai have analyzed how US media depict Arab men as "monster terrorist fags": viciously perverse brown misogynists who allegedly deserve white American violence.[155] Both Jewish cultural studies and queer of color critique draw from earlier work by gentile Black, Latina, and Asian American feminists like Gloria Anzaldúa about the intersection of race with gender.[156]

Jewish cultural studies and queer of color critique share near-identical claims about how race, gender, and sexuality co-define each other. From Jewish cultural studies, for instance, Ann Pellegrini writes that "gender, race, [and] sexuality . . . are not mutually exclusive but interimplicating and interstructured."[157] This claim mirrors that of Roderick Ferguson, a founder of queer of color critique, who writes that "the decisive intervention of queer of color analysis is that racist practice articulates itself generally as gender and sexual regulation, and that gender and sexual differences variegate racial formations."[158] That is, gender and sexual stigmas often define the supposed difference between racial groups, and these stigmas "justify" racist discrimination. Jewish cultural studies and queer of color critique also overlap when describing how these racial-gendered-sexual stigmas impact diasporic identities like Jewishness. Daniel Boyarin, a founder of Jewish cultural studies, writes that "diaspora is essentially queer."[159] Similarly, Roderick Ferguson describes "diaspora as a gendered and eroticized process."[160] That is, the stigma on diasporic identities—the sense that certain groups really belong elsewhere, thus blurring national boundaries—often appears through racially queer gender and sexual stereotypes like the emasculated Jew. Likewise, this stigma often appears through efforts to regulate, punish, or fix diasporic people's "deviant" gender and sexuality.

Partly because they speak past each other, Jewish cultural studies and queer of color critique each overlook a side of the white/POC binary that logically invites their attention. For instance, Jewish cultural studies has only asked how racially queer stigmas impact Jews with white skin like Seth Rogen, not Jews of color like Drake. This absence is striking because Jewish cultural studies often traces how racial antisemitism co-developed with anti-Black racism, anti-Indigenous racism, and Orientalism (racist stereotypes about the Near East). For instance, the field discusses how antisemitism and Orientalism merged in the darkly exotic "beautiful Jewess" stereotype.[161] It is time to ask not only how antisemitism co-shapes other stigmas, but also how these stigmas jointly harm Jews of color today. Meanwhile, some Jewish cultural studies scholars like Karen Brodkin and Matthew Frye Jacobson have described

Euro-American Jews as stably (not conditionally) white after midcentury,[162] thereby erasing how racial antisemitism continues to circulate.

Queer of color critique inverts Jewish cultural studies' silences: it analyzes how race, gender, and sexuality co-construct each other for gentile people of color, but never addresses how Jews of any color encounter racial antisemitism. The field mentions Jewishness almost exclusively when discussing Israel-and-Palestine, the sole region where Jewishness is a dominant and non-diasporic identity. This narrow geography normalizes the field's silence about Jewishness and antisemitism. And this silence sticks out because racial antisemitism is historically central to many topics that queer of color critique investigates: how race, gender, and sexuality jointly shape nationalism, citizenship, migration, diaspora, and genocide.

This silence is also intriguing because queer of color critique's founding texts rely on Jewish perspectives in central but unexamined ways. One such text, mentioned above, is José Muñoz's *Disidentifications*, which cites Superman's Jewish roots to help define disidentification.[163] Muñoz's later book *Cruising Utopia* also draws heavily from two Jewish philosophers to analyze both queerness and utopia: Ernst Bloch, who penned his work after fleeing the Nazis, and Jacques Derrida, whose philosophies reflect his youth as a Jewish outsider in French Algeria.[164] Although Jewish perspectives underpin Muñoz's concepts of disidentification and queer utopia, neither Jewishness nor antisemitism arises in the extensive queer of color scholarship that Muñoz has inspired.

A key book that builds on Muñoz is Roderick Ferguson's *Aberrations in Black*, which first named the field of queer of color critique and which vividly erases Jewishness. Ferguson defines queer of color critique in relation to Karl Marx's 1844 essay "On the Jewish Question," which tackles the (then controversial) question of whether Jews were fit to receive legal and social equality with Christians in European nations.[165] Marx's text serves Ferguson as a negative example: Marx acknowledges only how the state distinguishes citizens based on their class, education, religion, and occupation, while queer of color critique reveals how people also differently experience citizenship based on race, gender, and sexuality. Yet Jews disappear from Ferguson's analysis. First, his long quotation from "On the Jewish Question" cites no lines about Jews. Second, Ferguson never mentions that antisemitic racial, gender, and sexual stigmas often foreclosed citizenship to European Jews. For instance, as mentioned above, European gentiles long debated whether Jewish men were masculine enough for military service, and thus for legal equality with gentiles.[166] In other words, European Jews exemplified the racial, gendered, and sexual exclusions that Ferguson intends for queer of color critique to scrutinize, and Ferguson springboards off Marx's essay (about whether Jews could gain citizenship) to theorize those exclusions—but he mentions neither Jewishness nor antisemitism. This silence continues in the many queer of color works inspired by *Aberrations in Black*. This erasure illustrates how "Jewish questions" hide in plain sight at queer of color critique's core, just as unasked questions about Jews of color await Jewish cultural studies.

To begin answering these questions, this book invites Jewish cultural studies and queer of color critique to recognize their common interests in racial queerness and in disidentification. It also invites these fields to visualize how both Jews of color and conditionally white Jews embody racial queerness onscreen.

Double Meanings: Jewishness as a Threat/Resource to White Supremacy

Understanding how Jews embody race onscreen also requires understanding how some white gentile Americans paradoxically stigmatize *and* identify with Jewishness—especially with Jewish victimhood. While this ambivalence is clearest among self-declared white supremacists like David Duke, it also permeates the broader system of straight, white, Christian, male supremacy shaping daily American life and media. This ambivalence underpins the way this book's millennial Jewish stars harness racial stigmas on Jewish masculinity to critique and/or normalize inequality, thereby thrilling audiences.

White supremacists like the KKK often invoke Jewishness as both a *threat* to white Christian survival and *a resource that white supremacists can embrace to justify their violence*. This paradox underpins far-right conspiracy theories that invert the Holocaust by accusing Jews of orchestrating "white genocide." While depicting Jews as aggressors, these accusations cast white, straight, Christian men as metaphorical Jews. For instance, the far-right Christian talk show "TruNews," which the

Trump White House granted press accreditation, reported that the 2019 impeachment proceedings against Trump comprised a "Jew coup" and warned that, "when Jews take over the country," they will "kill millions of Christians."[167] White supremacists sometimes even more explicitly "borrow" Jewish vulnerability to label themselves victims of liberal plots, the same plots they pin on Jews. The conspiracy theorist Paul Craig Roberts—who served as Ronald Reagan's assistant secretary of the Treasury for economic policy—exemplified this pattern in a 2018 blog post, writing that liberal "Identity Politics" place "white people" in "the same position as Jews in Nazi Germany."[168] This claim captures a wider white supremacist zeitgeist that imagines white, straight, Christian, and/ or male Americans as "the Jews" (imperiled outcasts) of twenty-first-century America. Appropriating Jewish victimhood in this way serves to "justify" white supremacist violence as self-defense, including violence against Jews. The 2018 Pittsburgh synagogue shooter epitomized this contradiction: he justified his massacre by claiming that Jews were "committing genocide to his people."[169] In twenty-first-century America, then, the same extremist communities that explicitly promote racial antisemitism also think themselves the victims of a Jewish conspiracy. In turn, they appropriate Jewish suffering to articulate their own victimhood and legitimize "defensive" violence.

While hate groups like the KKK position Jewishness as both threat and resource, Jewishness also holds this dual symbolism for America's broader system of white, straight, Christian and/or male supremacist beliefs. Likewise, the fringe conspiracy theory about a Jewish-led "white genocide" is only the most extreme version of mainstream backlash narratives which claim that white, straight, Christian men are today's "true victims," dispossessed by aggressive women, queers, Jews, and/or people of color.[170] The literary theorist Sally Robinson calls this mindset an "identity politics of the dominant," since it twists ideas from the Black, Native American, feminist, and gay civil rights movements to cast straight, white, Christian men as disenfranchised underdogs.[171]

Jewish identity's double meaning as a threat/resource to white supremacy is precisely why some millennial Jewish stars can gain marketability by sculpting Jewish racial stigmas into subliminal postmodern (ideologically ambiguous) minstrel personae. In turn, this double meaning is why each star's ideological labor can range from fairly liberatory to grossly oppressive. As we will see, Lil Dicky falls on the most deplorable end of this spectrum by using his Jewface to closely mirror alt-right racism, misogyny, and sadism. Conversely, Abbi Jacobson and Ilana Glazer fall on the liberatory end by striving (but not always succeeding) to challenge misogyny, queerphobia, and racism. Meanwhile, Drake, Seth Rogen, and Zac Efron fall in the middle, by subtly but consistently normalizing mainstream (rather than far-right) prejudices and resentments.

Mapping This Book

Chapter 1, "Drake's Jewish Pickle: Chameleonic Minstrelsy, Detachable Judaism, and Black Violability," argues that Drake's success depends on a chameleonic form of subliminal postmodern minstrelsy: rather than producing one fixed persona, Drake produces *endless variations of subtle blackface, brownface, whiteface, and Jewface, all with racially distinct masculinities.* But across all these personae (even explicitly Jewish ones), Drake's minstrelsy strives to *delink* his body from racial stigmas of Jewish emasculation. Rebuffing these Jewish stigmas vitally aids Drake to balance and glide between the most appealing tropes of gentile whiter, Blacker, Afro-Latino, and Afro-Caribbean masculinities. On one hand, this chameleonic minstrelsy elevates Drake as an icon of multicultural harmony, whose biracial Jewish body reconciles many different identities. However, Drake's utopic multicultural image actually depends on an oppressive *respectability politics*: Drake's chameleonic minstrelsy often glamorizes him by contrast against other minoritized men whose masculinity appears "too" (and too permanently) Jewish, dark, urban, or foreign. Thus, Drake's chameleonic minstrelsy often normalizes racism, antisemitism, and xenophobia against others while celebrating Drake as a debonair exception.

Whereas Drake rebuffs racial stigmas of Jewish emasculation, the conditionally white Jewish rapper Lil Dicky embraces them to craft subliminal postmodern Jewface. Chapter 2, "'Redpill Me on Lil Dicky': Vicarious Jewface and 'Soft' Deplorable Satire," analyzes this strategy. Although Dicky's self-emasculating Jewface seems only to mock himself, it actually validates the resentment of white-privileged men (both Jewish and gentile) who misperceive themselves as the emasculated victims of feminism and multiculturalism. In fact, Dicky specifically mirrors alt-right racist and misogynist doctrine. This knack for marketing white male rage deceptively as "harmless" self-satire has fueled Dicky's rise from fringe YouTube stardom to network television and musical collaborations with A-list stars like Katy Perry.

Like Lil Dicky, the comedy duo Abbi Jacobson and Ilana Glazer have used racial tropes of Jewish masculinity to rise from YouTube comedy to network television. Unlike Dicky, they wield these tropes to promote feminist, queer, and antiracist liberation—but often fall into subtle racist missteps. These patterns receive analysis in chapter 3, "Ecstatic Jewessface: Blending Feminist, Queer, and Racist/Antiracist Fantasies with Abbi Jacobson and Ilana Glazer." This chapter argues that Jacobson and Glazer's allure depends on "Jewessfacing" themselves by resurrecting historical tropes of exotic, seductive-yet-masculinized Jewesses. Through subliminal postmodern Jewessface, Jacobson and Glazer offer two fantasies that (like the "beautiful Jewess" trope itself) are both exhilarating and paradoxical: (1) the liberatory dream of reconciling "masculine," "filthy," or "perverse" freedoms with glamorous femininity, but also (2) the oppressive dream of reconciling white privilege and racist microaggressions with guilt-free antiracist identity. These Jewesses thus (1) channel the liberatory desire of progressive straight women, queer women, and queer men to break free from misogyny and heteronormativity without being labeled disgusting, but also (2) channel the oppressive desire of *white-privileged* progressive straight women, queer women, and queer men to shed white guilt without shedding white privilege or racist pleasures. This dual ideological labor fuels their appeal.

The film actor Seth Rogen, who has guest-starred on Jacobson and Glazer's sitcom, is one of Hollywood's highest-grossing comedic stars. Chapter 4, "Boys Just Want to Have Fun? Seth Rogen's Beta Male Patriarchy, Post-Meninist Violence, and Fun Fatherhood," analyzes his ideological labor. Despite invoking the same dirty, emasculated Jewish tropes as Lil Dicky, Rogen crafts these tropes into an adorable, babyish, innocent Jewface persona that I call "the gently messy Jewish man-baby." Although this subliminal postmodern Jewface seems gentle and thus progressive, it actually packages straight white-privileged male supremacy in cuddly form. For instance, Rogen's bumbling, emasculated, babyish Jewface protagonists often model "blameless"-looking white male violence against women and/or people of color. Rogen thus reassures straight, white-privileged male viewers (both Jewish and gentile) that they can sustain dominance while still deeming themselves sweet guys who just want to have fun.

Rogen's babyish Jewface persona makes him an ideal foil for the brawny, blue-eyed, button-nosed, sandy-haired film star Zac Efron. Indeed, their film roles as comedic opposites provide key material for chapter 5, "From Blue-Eyed Demon to Nice Jew-ish Goy: Zac Efron's 'Goyface' as Sexy Abject Hegemony." This chapter shows that Efron sometimes contrasts his gentile appearance against more "Jewish-looking" stars like Rogen to achieve subliminal postmodern goyface: a racial caricature of sexy but self-destructive straight white gentile masculinity. Efron deploys this caricature within *redemptive goyface comedies*—films that seem to deride and punish straight white gentile male privilege, but actually renew it in lovelier form. And this renewal often requires Efron's goyface characters to absorb the most likable *invisible* stereotypes of Jewish emasculation (like wit and kindness) while displacing the most repulsive *physical* stereotypes of Jewish emasculation onto his Jewish foils. These narratives offer straight white gentile men the dream of earning validation as good enlightened citizens while still sustaining accustomed privileges in gentler guise.

Lastly, the conclusion unites these threads to reemphasize how queer masculinity racially distinguishes Jewish from gentile bodies in US media. This insight illuminates how viewers can better notice and challenge antisemitism without discounting the white, male, or straight privilege that some Jews experience. In turn, the conclusion illustrates why Jewishness and antisemitism are vital lenses for all the fields that aim to comprehend and challenge straight white gentile male supremacy.

1

Drake's Jewish Pickle

Chameleonic Minstrelsy, Detachable Judaism,
and Black Violability

The 2021 Billboard Music Awards bestowed Artist of the Decade upon Drake, a biracial Jewish Canadian rap superstar.[1] Drake was born Aubrey Drake Graham in 1986 to a Black gentile American father and conditionally white Jewish Canadian mother.[2] After a 1991 divorce, Drake's mother raised him in Toronto, eventually settling in the affluent Forest Hill neighborhood, although Drake emphasizes that their own household was at times "very poor" and at most middle-class.[3] In Forest Hill, his upbringing included Jewish day school and a bar mitzvah (Jewish manhood ceremony).[4] In 2001, Drake made his media debut by playing a sweet and artistic middle-class student on the Canadian soap opera *Degrassi* (on which he appeared until 2008), before breaking into America's rap scene in 2006–2010. Drake quickly gained fame for pushing rap's boundaries to integrate more singing and more vulnerable lyrics. For instance, his 2011 hit "Take Care" tenderly reflects on how "I've loved and I've lost."[5] Further expanding rap's borders, Drake soon became known as a "musical chameleon"[6] for blending hip hop with other genres such as R&B, pop, house, trap, Jamaican dancehall, and reggae.

On one hand, becoming Artist of the Decade reflects Drake's stellar success: his music has garnered a record-breaking thirty-nine Billboard Music Awards[7] and a reported $260 million net worth.[8] He has also become a sexual icon since revealing a newly muscular body in 2015.[9] Yet Drake's enduring appeal coexists with enduring bafflement and disdain about his identity, masculinity, and rap authenticity. For instance, countless online "Drake memes" deride him as "not really Black," "not a real man," and "not a real rapper."[10] Just one exemplar depicts Drake proclaiming that "I'm a massive fa**ot."[11]

Both Drake's stigma and success illuminate how racial antisemitism can intersect with anti-Blackness onscreen, placing unique constraints on Black Jewish performers. In turn, these constraints illustrate how tropes of queer (strange) masculinity racially distinguish both black- and white-skinned Jewish bodies from gentile peers in US media. These racial boundaries become visible as Drake labors to reconcile all the mismatched stereotypes of race and masculinity that his various identities carry, like opposite stigmas of Black hypermasculinity and Jewish emasculation.

One performance offers an especially sharp snapshot of these stereotypes, of how Drake strives to tame them, and how he thereby shapes American racial beliefs in return. This performance is his 2014 role as guest star on the American sketch-comedy show *Saturday Night Live*.

SNL Bar Mitzvah: Becoming a (Marketable) Man

Drake's very first sketch on *SNL* restaged his bar mitzvah, with *SNL* comedians playing his family (figure 1.1).[12] Despite depicting a Black Jewish manhood ceremony, this sketch presents Jewishness and Blackness as incompatible because they connote differently queer (non-normative) masculinities. To evoke this clash, *SNL* sandwiches Drake between two racially caricatured uncles whose rhyming names (Barry/ Larry) link them as mirror opposites. The Black gentile "Uncle Larry" performs stereotypes of hypersexual, coarse, loud Black masculinity: he nearly shouts in African American Vernacular English (AAVE) while revealing that he has brought his mistress instead of his wife to the party. This dialogue firmly ties Larry's hypersexual masculinity to his Black "ethnolinguistic repertoire," a term coined by the linguist Sarah Bunin Benor to name the vocal tones, grammar, and pronunciation associated with a particular racial or ethnic community.[13] Inverting this Black hypermasculinity, the conditionally white Jewish "Uncle Barry" exemplifies stereotypes of neurotic Jewish emasculation: Barry uses a nasal faux-Yiddish accent to quaver about Jewish tradition, while performing timid and twitchy (emasculated) gesticulations. Like Larry's AAVE, Barry's speech links his "strange" masculinity with racial difference: while spoofing real Jewish ethnolinguistic repertoires, Barry also evokes nineteenth-century antisemitic racial pseudoscience. As we have seen,

Figure 1.1. Drake's *SNL* bar mitzvah sketch (2014) sandwiches him between stereotypes of Black hypermasculinity and Jewish emasculation.
Screenshot from *Saturday Night Live*, season 39, episode 11, aired January 18, 2014, on NBC. Pulled from YouTube.

this pseudoscience accused Jews of possessing distinct facial muscles, which supposedly made Jewish men speak in "feminized" singsong tones and breaking voices,[14] as Barry does.

These vocal stigmas composed one thread in the eight-century lineage of racial antisemitism that historically depicts Jewish men like Drake as emasculated, Jewish women as too masculinized, and both as sexually perverse.[15] We have seen how these gendered accusations long served alongside stereotypes of swarthy skin, black curly hair, and beaked noses to "prove" that Jews racially differ from gentiles. Even today, when few Americans explicitly categorize Jews as a race, this racial history still fuels the expectation that Jews will look, move, and speak differently from gentiles. Although *SNL*'s cast and audience may not know the racial history behind these stereotypes, that history underpins Uncle Barry's emasculated and trembly dialogue. These racial meanings help the sketch to equate Jewishness with emasculation, allegedly incompatible with Blackness.

If Drake's uncles represent "incompatible" Black hypermasculinity and Jewish emasculation, then Drake glamorously reconciles both extremes—at the expense of stigmatizing his uncles. To this end, he balances and glides between his uncles' masculinities, while blending both with the suave connotations of white gentile middle-class masculinity. This smooth balance and motion depend on juxtaposing Drake against his clownish uncles. This contrast emerges from Drake's central position between his uncles; from his light brown skin, which lands halfway between his uncles' complexions; and from his even mix of Black and white formalwear, which contrasts against his uncles' more monochrome suits. These visual signals cumulatively imply that Drake (unlike his uncles) can balance between Black gentile, white gentile, and Jewish masculinities.

Drake's speech, gestures, and emotions all amplify the sense that he can reconcile his uncles' "extreme" Black and Jewish masculinities with white gentile sophistication. Both uncles appear déclassé because their "improper" masculinities include uncontrolled bodies, voices, and emotions. For instance, both uncles use racially stigmatized ethnolinguistic repertoires that are allegedly unrefined (respectively "too loud" or "too shrill"), and both uncles pair their grating speech with jerky gesticulations. Conversely, Drake pairs smooth white gentile middle-class English with elegant but firm gestures, such as when he gracefully spreads his hands in welcome. This linguistic and gestural smoothness aligns him with white gentile middle-class masculinity. Further, Drake emotes polite puzzlement and amusement whenever his uncles violate white gentile middle-class decorum. These reactions convey Drake's mastery of white gentile middle-class masculine norms, while inviting viewers to laugh at his clueless uncles. Indeed, the *SNL* audience joins Drake in chuckling at his uncles' faux pas.

Yet balancing between Black hypermasculinity, Jewish emasculation, and "classy" white gentile masculinity is only half the picture. To further imply that Drake can reconcile his different identities, and to further normalize him at his uncles' expense, the sketch also uses a second tactic: it shows Drake *briefly don and doff* his uncles' racially stigmatized masculinities, before rebounding to his dapper (more white gentile) midpoint. To glide between "whiter," "Blacker," and "more Jewish" masculinities, Drake builds on earlier cues like his light brown skin, black-and-white costume, and physical midpoint onscreen. Specifically, he combines these cues with a rap that invokes many different ethnolinguistic repertoires and racially symbolic topics. This rap first uses white gentile English with slight AAVE inflections to proclaim, "Please don't forget I'm Black / Please don't forget I'm Jewish / I play ball like LeBron and I know what a W-2 is."[16] These lyrics pivot Drake between stereotypes of athletic Black men and effete, brainy Jewish men. However, his ethnolinguistic repertoire excludes any "weak" Jewish quaver, instead embellishing "classy" white gentile English with hints of "harder" AAVE. Only after establishing this balance does Drake dip sharply into AAVE to rap about "my bitches," thus briefly but clearly evoking Black hypermasculinity. Later, his rap dips much more subtly into Jewish emasculation. For a split second, Drake lightly echoes his Uncle Barry's neurotic, nasal Jewish vernacular to warn the audience, "Do *not* go to Feingold's [deli] . . . the pickles are *rubber!*" This line about a Jewish deli, delivered in a stereotypically Jewish vernacular, subtly caricatures Drake as a fussy (feminized) Jewish man like Uncle Barry. Drake then reclaims a deeper tone and his balance of AAVE with white gentile English to conclude that you get "the best of both worlds when you're Jewish with Black in ya!" Although these lyrics reemphasize Drake's Black and Jewish identities, his ethnolinguistic repertoire re-distances him from Jewish emasculation. This conclusion restores his persona as a rapper who can balance Black and Jewish identities with each other and with dapper white gentile masculinity.

By framing Drake between a hypersexual Black gentile uncle and an emasculated, conditionally white Jewish uncle; by showing Drake balance and pivot between these extremes while blending both with white gentile masculinity; and by thus glamorizing Drake at his uncles' expense, this *SNL* bar mitzvah crystallizes the core challenges and solutions of Drake's stardom. *Every facet of Drake's identity, appearance, and career connotes mismatched masculinities*: not only his Blackness and Jewishness, but also his light skin, Canadian middle-class upbringing, soap star origins, and vulnerable lyrics. For example, while Blackness connotes dangerous hypermasculinity and Jewishness connotes neurotic emasculation, Drake's light brown skin can contradict both stereotypes. Colorism equates lighter skin with beauty and refinement while conflating darker skin with ugliness and primitivism, including violent masculinities.[17] These associations can romanticize "lightskin" men like Drake as classy and sweet, but can also stigmatize him as "softer" than dark peers like his rap mentor Lil Wayne.[18]

Indeed, the myriad masculine stereotypes on Drake's body not only contradict each other, but also contradict conventions of rap marketability. The hip hop industry typically equates authenticity with narrow notions of "gangsta" Black American hypermasculinity, which the African American studies scholar Imani Perry calls *double-voiced*.[19] Even as this gangsta image may titillate white suburban audiences with racist fantasies of Black men as hypersexual criminals,[20] the same trope offers "fantasies of masculine power" to impoverished Black men "who feel powerless" in a racist society.[21] This effect transmutes racist imagery into a vehicle for Black dignity and self-expression.[22] But whether conveying racism or Black pride, this gangsta stereotype ill fits Drake's image as a light-skinned, biracial Jewish soap star turned rapper with middle-class roots and sentimental lyrics. His Canadian identity amplifies this mismatch, as the media scholar Alexandra Boutros observes: because rap originated in the US, the genre often predicates "authentic" gangsta masculinity on a connection to US Black communities like those of "the Bronx, Brooklyn, [and] Compton."[23] Drake's distance from gangsta masculinity explains why so many "Drake memes" harshly ridicule his Blackness, masculinity, and rap authenticity.

More gently, the journalist Katie Couric has illustrated how tropes of Jewish emasculation undercut Drake's rap marketability: when interviewing him in 2010, Couric immediately asked, *"what's a nice Jewish boy doing in a career like this?"* (my emphasis).[24] This question saddles Drake with the popular "nice Jewish boy" trope, born in mid-twentieth-century America. Descending from the longer lineage of antisemitic masculine stigmas, this trope casts Jewish men like Drake as sweet but emasculated, neurotic, and twitchy, supposedly because they are smothered by overbearing Jewish mothers.[25] Couric's question exemplifies how this "nice Jewish boy" image contradicts stereotypes of Black hypermasculinity, thereby making Drake seem unfit to rap.

Because popular stereotypes burden Drake's body with mismatched and stigmatized masculinities, his success requires constantly sculpting that fragmented image into a glamorous whole. And Drake's *SNL* bar mitzvah exemplifies his core technique for that labor: *chameleonic minstrelsy*.

Drake's Chameleonic Minstrelsy, Cool Pose, and Queer Glamor

Drake's chameleonic minstrelsy is subtler than conventional (blatant) minstrelsy, which he has performed just once. His single instance of blatant minstrelsy was a 2007 blackface photo (figure 1.2). Drake has since stated that this blatant blackface aimed to critique, not reinforce, anti-Black stereotypes.[26] Regardless, when this initially obscure photo went viral in 2018, he endured scathing criticism.[27]

Whereas this blatant blackface drew condemnation, Drake's chameleonic minstrelsy often goes unrecognized because it is a form of *subliminal postmodern minstrelsy*. As we have seen, subliminal postmodern minstrelsy describes racial caricatures that stars and audiences rarely recognize as synthetic caricatures at all, and which ambivalently challenge/renormalize inequality. Drake's subliminal postmodern minstrelsy is *chameleonic* because it produces *endless variations of subtle blackface,*

Figure 1.2. Drake's single instance of conventional (blatant) blackface minstrelsy, in a 2007 photograph.
Photograph by David Leyes, 2007. Image pulled from *Business Insider,* "Drake Finally Explains Why He Wore Blackface in an Old Photo Uncovered by a Rival Rapper," by Jacob Shamsian, May 31, 2018.

brownface, whiteface, and Jewface, all with racially distinct masculinities, rather than one fixed persona. This chameleonic minstrelsy emerges as Drake pairs his light-skinned biracial Jewish body with different settings, co-stars, ethnolinguistic repertoires, and styles of hair, clothing, music, dance, and gesture. Together, these tools produce myriad minstrel personae who are often versions of Drake's self, but occasionally other characters, and that embody varied tropes of Jewish emasculation or gentile white, Black, Afro-Latino, and Afro-Caribbean masculinities. For instance, Drake's *SNL* bar mitzvah shows him flow chameleonically across "whiter," "Blacker," and "more Jewish" versions of his own masculinity,[28] each constituting different subliminal minstrel personae. The same episode later swathes Drake in a subliminal brownface persona that caricatures Latino and Caribbean masculinities: he plays the Dominican American baseball star Alex Rodriguez (A-Rod), infamously suspended in 2014 for using steroids. For this brownface persona, Drake pairs his light-brown skin with a straight-haired wig while mimicking a Dominican American ethnolinguistic repertoire to deny the steroid allegations. While ostensibly satirizing one ill-behaved athlete, Drake-as-A-Rod evokes broader stereotypes of belligerent, unintelligent, over-passionate Latino masculinity. For instance, Drake combines his faux-Latino accent with cartoonishly angry facial expressions and dramatically flared lips (figure 1.3). If a white man in brown makeup caricatured A-Rod this way, he would clearly be committing racist brownface. However, Drake's racial proximity to A-Rod keeps this minstrelsy visually subtler and supposedly guiltless. Indeed, this racist caricature can even seem a *rightful* critique of dishonest athletes. This A-Rod caricature thus exemplifies how Drake's minstrelsy is chameleonic (encompassing myriad racial personae), subliminal (visually subtle), and postmodern (ideologically ambiguous).

At first glance, only Drake's Afro-Latino and Afro-Caribbean personae may seem to constitute minstrelsy, while his performances of Jewish, Black, or white masculinities might simply seem self-representations. Yet self-caricature is a hallmark of subliminal postmodern minstrelsy, which helps this minstrelsy to stay visually subtle and ideologically ambiguous. Further, we will see that *all* of Drake's racialized masculine personae can be *unpredictably interpreted as offensive caricatures, failed imitations, or authentic self-representations,* regardless

Figure 1.3. Drake plays the Dominican American baseball star Alex Rodriguez on *SNL* (2014). This role constitutes subliminal postmodern brownface that caricatures Latino masculinities.
Screenshot from *Saturday Night Live*, season 39, episode 11, aired January 18, 2014, on NBC. Pulled from YouTube.

of his intentions. This ambivalence emerges from his multifaceted identity and racially ambiguous appearance. This ambivalent authenticity/caricature further positions Drake's chameleonic style as subliminal postmodern minstrelsy.

Although Drake's chameleonic minstrelsy generates countless personae, these personae all help him to pursue just three broader constellations of race and masculinity: *detachable Judaism, racialized masculine balance,* and *racialized masculine mobility.* In "detachable Judaism," Drake's minstrelsy strives to delink his body from racial stigmas of Jewish emasculation, even when his minstrel personae are explicitly Jewish. For contrast, the Jewish comedic rapper Lil Dicky amplifies antisemitic bodily stigmas to craft a Jewface persona that is (in his words) a "nappy-headed, greasy Jew" with "frail, Jewish shoulders."[29] Instead, Drake's detachable Judaism is a technique for "counteridentifying with"[30] (rebuffing and inverting) such stigmas. This detachable Judaism is aided but not assured by Drake's Blackness and his muscles. For example, Katie Couric's "nice Jewish boy" question demonstrates how—despite the myth that Blackness is incompatible with Jewishness—viewers may still project neurotic Jewish emasculation onto Drake's Black Jewish body. To rebuff such stigmas, his minstrelsy harnesses the split between *performing Judaism* and *acting Jewish*, articulated by theater scholar Henry Bial.[31] "Performing Judaism" means depicting Jewish religious symbols or rituals, like Drake's kippah in his *SNL* bar mitzvah.[32] Conversely, "acting Jewish" means depicting stereotypically Jewish speech and body language, such as when Drake's "Uncle Barry" nasally whines on *SNL*. As this sketch illustrates, US media tropes of "acting Jewish" often reflect racial stigmas of Jewish emasculation. To detach these antisemitic stigmas from Drake's body, his chameleonic minstrelsy includes only "performing Judaism," not "acting Jewish." Thus, Drake's minstrelsy *nearly always restricts his Jewish identity to a disembodied religious faith, marked only by religious rituals like a bar mitzvah and removable religious items like a kippah.*

Drake's *SNL* bar mitzvah boy persona exemplifies this detachable Judaism: although he "performs Judaism" by wearing a kippah, he avoids bodily "acting Jewish" like his twitchy and quavery Uncle Barry. Only for one fleeting and subtle moment does Drake mimic Barry's nasal Jewish speech, thereby donning a brief and subtle Jewface persona. However, this ephemeral mimicry marks the single split-second of Drake's career when his minstrel personae have embodied Jewish emasculation. Further, he uses this brief exception only to illustrate how easily he (unlike Barry) can shed Jewish emasculation. This fleeting mimicry highlights that Drake could always choose to perform racially emasculated Jewish minstrel personae as Lil Dicky does. Of course, embracing antisemitic stigmas is not inherently more liberatory than evading them. Regardless, Drake's detachable Judaism requires active, consistent choices across all his minstrel personae to deflect Jewish emasculation.

By counteridentifying with (repelling) antisemitic masculine stigmas, detachable Judaism frees Drake to *disidentify with*[33] (creatively reinhabit) the rap industry's stigmas on his other traits, like his light skin and Canadian middle-class upbringing. Drake's minstrelsy revalorizes these traits from markers of "soft" emasculation to "suave" masculinity. In turn, he has often used this revalorization to unify his "mismatched" racial image into *racialized masculine balance*. That is, his minstrel personae have often blended the most alluring tropes of gentile Black and white masculinities, thus synthesizing gentile black-face and whiteface. Drake's *SNL* bar mitzvah exemplifies this balance by packaging him as a suave, light-brown gentleman between a darker, hypersexual Black gentile uncle and a paler, emasculated, conditionally white Jewish uncle.

Alongside detachable Judaism and racialized masculine balance, Drake's chameleonic minstrelsy has also pursued a third effect: *racialized masculine mobility*. That is, Drake wears-and-discards minstrel personae that embody myriad gentile Afro-Latino, Afro-Caribbean, and Black North American masculinities, but almost never Jewish emasculation. This mobility (like Drake's racialized masculine balance) nearly always depends on shedding Jewish emasculation, and it often entails revalorizing his other "soft" traits. Drake exemplified this mobility on *SNL* by impersonating the Latino athlete A-Rod and by flowing across "whiter," "Blacker," and (very briefly) "more Jewish" personae within his bar mitzvah sketch.

However, from his 2006 rap debut until the early 2020s, Drake's appeal depended on presenting his racialized masculine balance as more "real" than his racialized masculine mobility. That is, Drake often presented his most "balanced" (most white gentile and middle-class) personae as his most candid self. For instance, after dipping into other masculine personae, he typically rebounded to genteel midpoint personae, such as when concluding his *SNL* bar mitzvah. Conversely, we will see how Drake has pursued new forms of racialized masculine mobility in the early 2020s. These new techniques strive (with mixed success) to present "Blacker" and tougher masculine personae as his most candid self.

By identifying how Drake's chameleonic minstrelsy produces detachable Judaism, racialized masculine balance, and racialized masculine mobility, this book inverts earlier claims from Jewish rap studies. Musicologist Uri Dorchin has described Drake's gentler image as "a classic example of self-feminization of the Jewish male."[34] Instead, I find that Drake must *rebuff* stigmas of Jewish emasculation (must perform detachable Judaism) while spotlighting other forms of softness like light skin, which prove more compatible with suave masculinity. Several scholars also argue that Drake downplays Jewish identity to fit the rap industry's Black hypermasculine norms.[35] However, downplaying Jewish bodily stigmas actually helps him to appear not just "Blacker," but more racially "balanced" and "mobile."

By producing chameleonic personae that cumulatively present detachable Judaism, racialized masculine balance, and/or racialized masculine mobility, Drake fuses a racist performance tradition (minstrelsy) with an antiracist performance tradition: *the cool pose.* Defined by Richard Majors and Janet Mancini Billson, the cool pose describes Black male strategies for achieving survival and dignity against daily racism. This cool pose depends on "carefully created performances" that project "pride, strength, and control."[36] To achieve this self-mastery while facing racist coworkers, teachers, police, salespeople, and passerby, many Black men must become "chameleon-like": must modulate clothing, "speech, intonation, gesture[s], and facial expressions" to produce varied "masks, acts, and façades" that each "meet the expectations of a particular situation or audience."[37] Drake's chameleonic personae exemplify this cool pose: against racist stereotypes that both demand and vilify narrow models of Black masculinity, Drake's fluid personae assert his dignity and complexity. Yet Drake's cool pose fully overlaps with minstrelsy: his fluid personae grant him self-mastery at the expense of caricaturing other minoritized people, often to entertain majoritarian viewers—like *SNL*'s largely white[38] audience.

If Drake's chameleonic minstrelsy fuses key elements of racist minstrelsy and the antiracist cool pose, this fusion produces several marketable effects. First, this chameleonic minstrelsy strives to reframe Drake as a nimble master (not an incoherent jumble) of many racialized masculinities. Second, this minstrelsy often invites audiences to feel progressive while actually indulging oppressive biases, as we will see shortly. These paradoxical feelings highlight how Drake's chameleonic minstrelsy (like all subliminal postmodern minstrelsy) reconciles contradictory fantasies about challenging/sustaining straight white gentile male supremacy. In turn, this ambivalence always produces a glamor that is queer in many ways at once: Drake's queer glamor requires him to fluidly embrace-and-rebuff many racially queer masculine minstrel personae, while teetering between suave masculinity and soft emasculation, and while ambivalently disrupting/validating commonplace prejudices.

Drake's Ideological Labor, Respectability Politics, and Nebulous Intentions

On one hand, Drake's chameleonic minstrelsy elevates him into a multicultural icon who can embody a more diverse, egalitarian, and harmonious future. For instance, because American society often erases Jews of color, Drake's Black Jewish bar mitzvah boy persona on *SNL* truly broke boundaries for multicultural representation and vividly illustrated that many "incompatible" identities can coexist. Drake's multicultural image can also appeal by inviting many different demographics to identify with him, as the media scholar Amara Pope notes.[39] For example, Drake's *SNL* bar mitzvah boy persona may jointly affirm Black, Jewish, biracial, and Canadian viewers. Further, consuming Drake's multicultural image may help *any* viewer to pleasurably burnish their own progressive credentials, since celebrating Drake can feel equivalent to celebrating a more diverse future—for instance, a future full of joyful Black Jewish Canadian bar mitzvah boys.

However, Drake's utopic multicultural image actually depends on an oppressive *respectability politics*, a term coined by Evelyn Brooks Higginbotham. "Respectability politics" describes the way some minoritized people package themselves as "good" minorities who embrace dominant norms, while displacing stigma onto "bad" minoritized peers who can't or won't conform.[40] Similarly, when Drake's chameleonic minstrelsy produces detachable Judaism, racialized masculine balance, and racialized masculine mobility, these effects often serve to *elevate Drake above other men who appear "too" Jewish, dark, urban, or foreign*. For instance, although Drake's *SNL* bar mitzvah seems to celebrate his Black and Jewish identities, it actually celebrates his ability to *tame* both identities in accordance with straight white gentile norms. In turn, the sketch relishes his ability (as a "good," well-assimilated minority) to validate stigma against less assimilated peers like Uncle Barry and Uncle Larry. Throughout Drake's oeuvre, this type of comparison has often normalized racism, antisemitism, and xenophobia against others while idealizing Drake as an urbane outlier. Conversely, straight white gentile male characters never serve as derided foils to his minstrel personae. Because Drake's chameleonic minstrelsy seems to celebrate his minoritized identities but tacitly stigmatizes those identities, this minstrelsy can aid audiences to feel guiltlessly progressive while actually normalizing stigma and inequality.

Drake's version of respectability politics particularly harnesses the dichotomy between *classical/grotesque bodies*, a dichotomy identified by the philosopher Mikhail Bakhtin. "Classical bodies" appear elegantly self-contained, while "grotesque bodies" overflow with uncontrolled emotions, appetites, voices, odors, and/or excreta.[41] In Drake's chameleonic minstrel performances, other minoritized men often appear more grotesque than Drake because they get no chance to shed their stigmatized masculinities nor to approximate white gentile middle-class sophistication. Against these grotesque foils, Drake's body appears especially classical because his chameleonic minstrel personae constantly perform detachable Judaism, racialized masculine balance, and/or racialized masculine mobility. For instance, in Drake's *SNL* bar mitzvah, his uncles both appear grotesque because they fail to smoothly compose their bodies: Uncle Larry's stereotypical Black hypermasculinity is loud and hypersexual, while Uncle Barry's stereotypical Jewish emasculation is neurotic and twitchy. Between these uncomposed (grotesque) uncles, Drake's racially "balanced" persona looks particularly dapper (classical). Throughout Drake's career, particularly until the early 2020s, he has similarly displaced stigma onto minoritized foils in order to achieve a classical body and suave masculinity rooted in ideals of whiteness, gentility, and high social class.

While Drake's respectability politics tacitly validates antisemitism, it particularly endangers Black lives—including both Black Jews and gentiles, and including Black people of North American, Afro-Caribbean, Afro-Latino, and African origin. By contrasting his lighter body against darker Black men like Uncle Larry, Drake's respectability politics tacitly normalize the life-and-death inequalities of colorism. Sociologist Margaret Hunter observes that colorism shapes more than personal biases: it fuels structural discrimination that "privileges light-skinned people of color over dark" in "income, education, [and] housing."[42] In addition to naturalizing colorism, Drake's performances have often fed the racist myth that Black men (except Drake) are out-of-control, hypermasculine criminals. We will see below how this tacit message mirrors rhetoric from white conservative pundits like Bill O'Reilly; such pundits often misuse gangsta rap stars like Lil Wayne as evidence that Black men are innately hypermasculine criminals, that Black people's own misbehavior is to blame for racial inequality, and that Black people must be harshly policed to protect (white) society.[43]

By casting Black people as criminals who always deserve violent restraint, these myths expose Black lives to a constant vulnerability that the feminist scholar Treva Lindsey terms *Black violability*.[44] Black violability encompasses both interpersonal and state violence, like wrongful arrest, mass incarceration, and murder by police.[45] For instance, during the #BlackLivesMatter movement, conservative pundits have routinely invoked myths of Black criminality to justify violence against unarmed protesters and against unarmed Black people murdered by police. Indeed, when officer Darren Wilson killed teenager Michael Brown in Ferguson, Missouri, in 2014, Arkansas's ex-governor Mike Huckabee claimed that Brown "could have avoided that if he'd have behaved like something other than a thug."[46] Yet as mentioned above, rap's hypermasculine Black stereotypes are "double-voiced":[47] the same images that help white audiences to "prove" Black deviance also help some Black viewers to channel resistance, self-respect, and creativity.[48] However, rather than asserting Black dignity, Drake's chameleonic minstrelsy has often implied that darker, poorer, and more visibly foreign Black men *really are* hypermasculine criminals.

Importantly, Drake's marketable contrast against "bad" gentile Black, Afro-Latino, and Afro-Caribbean masculinities always depends on using "detachable Judaism" to shed tropes of racially queer Jewish emasculation. If darker gentile masculinities are the "bad" foils that make Drake's balanced masculinity look so appealing, then Jewish emasculation is the embarrassing specter that threatens to undermine it. Thus, Drake's chameleonic minstrelsy illustrates how antisemitic racial tropes structure millennial Jewish stardom *even* for stars who reject such stigmas. The same dynamic characterizes Zac Efron, as we will see. Drake and Efron may seem unrelated to peers like Lil Dicky who parlay Jewish emasculation into comedic stardom. Yet embracing or evading antisemitic racial tropes are two sides of one coin: like Dicky, Drake selectively navigates racial assumptions about how Jewish men look, speak, gesticulate, dance, and lust.

In turn, counteridentifying with stigmas of racially queer Jewish masculinity *counterdetermines* them—throws them into sharper relief. This counterdetermination can be vivid, when Drake displaces antisemitic racial stigmas onto Jewish characters like Uncle Barry on *SNL*.[49] Alternatively, this counterdetermination can delineate antisemitic racial tropes as a *present absence*: a stigma always hovering just out of sight, outlined in reverse by Drake's choices about how *not* to move, speak, or style his body. For instance, emasculated Jewish minstrel personae constitute a conspicuous absence in his palette of racialized masculine personae. This absence is so striking because Drake has commonly performed personae unrelated to his own identities (like the Latino star A-Rod) while avoiding personae related to his own Jewishness. This conspicuous absence establishes a *silent respectability politics* toward other Jewish men, in which Jewish foils rarely appear onscreen and the topic of Jewish emasculation seems effortlessly absent. Drake's *SNL* bar mitzvah clarifies that this silence is always a pregnant one, full of stylistic choices that steer him away from tropes of Jewish emasculation. Likewise, this present absence always implicitly markets Drake through contrast against stereotypically emasculated Jewish men who bear antisemitic stigmas in his place.

When deciphering how Drake's chameleonic minstrelsy produces respectability politics, his *SNL* performances make apt starting points because their artistic origins and intentions are so *untraceable*. These intentions are unknowable because *SNL* famously requires the cast and guest stars like Drake to collaboratively pitch, write, and improvise all sketches.[50] Similarly, nearly all performances by any star reflect team efforts that make intentionality hard to trace. Further, Drake has never declared any intention to perform minstrelsy, detach Judaism from his body, stigmatize other men, nor accomplish any other technique detailed here. Yet regardless of intention, these chameleonic minstrel techniques fuel Drake's appeal on *SNL* and far beyond.

This step from nebulous intent to vivid effect is vital for comprehending Drake's ideological appeal without demonizing him or invalidating his multifaceted identity. As previously mentioned, many postmodern minstrels camouflage or even *lack* political intentions.[51] These blurry intentions enhance the minstrels' appeal, by helping them thrill audiences with elusive, deniable meanings. Drake exemplifies this effect: his minstrel techniques are so potent-yet-palatable partly because he rarely seems to intend them. Rather than premeditating his minstrelsy, Drake has moved toward it while striving to unify, dignify, and market his image in a society that constantly judges his biracial Canadian Jewish body as inconceivable, inauthentic, and pathetic. Describing his performances of Black, brown, and Jewish identity as "minstrelsy" may seem to reinforce such judgments, but that is not my intention. Regardless of Drake's private identities, his public stardom relies on subtle but quantifiable minstrel techniques. Without mislabeling Drake a deliberate bigot, I aim to clarify how his chameleonic minstrelsy glamorizes him by displacing stigma onto other Black, brown, and Jewish targets.

New Connections, Impossible Bodies, and (Ir)redeemable Softness

These insights about chameleonic minstrelsy open new dialogues on race, Jewishness, masculinity, rap, and stardom. Although feminist, queer, and critical race theory often study how race intersects with masculinity in popular media, we have seen that these fields commonly erase Jews of color and disregard antisemitism. And although Jewish studies has written extensively on Jewish racialization and Jewish masculinity, it too has rarely examined Black Jews. As a Black Ashkenazi Jew, Drake especially disrupts the presumption that "Jews of color" and "Ashkenazi Jews" are distinct categories. And for all these fields, Drake's stardom illustrates how antisemitic racial stigmas can intersect with black skin as well as white.

Drake's queer glamor also calls for new connections between hip hop feminism and Jewish hip hop studies. When analyzing how Drake displays or downplays Jewishness, Jewish hip hop studies has not yet asked how these performances channel wider racial debates. Hip hop feminism—feminist theory by Black women of the hip hop generation, often inspired by hip hop's musical and linguistic innovations—enables such analysis.[52] The field emphasizes how Black people can deploy hip hop for self-expression even as white audiences twist hip hop to justify Black violability. This insight clarifies Drake's ideological labor. In turn, this analysis highlights antisemitism and Jewish masculinity as topics already present but unexplored within hip hop feminism.

Drake's allure also requires star studies to rethink the relationships between racial *ambiguity*, Jewishness, gender, and stardom. Drake's racialized masculine balance, mobility, and respectability politics nuance insights from Priscilla Peña Ovalle about "racially in-between" stardom. Ovalle has coined "racial in-betweenness" to analyze how gentile Euro-Latina stars like Jennifer Lopez dance between stereotypes of Black and white femininity.[53] This Latina in-betweenness often thrills white American audiences by evoking the exciting connotations of Blackness (like exotic sensuality) without its threatening connotations (like violence, crime, or sharply visible difference).[54] Drake partly matches Ovalle's paradigm: Ovalle finds that Latina stars must often validate racial stereotypes about Blackness and whiteness to secure their alluring place in the middle,[55] as does Drake.

However, Drake illustrates that racial in-betweenness can prove both more precarious and more malleable than Ovalle envisions. Ovalle analyzes how gentile, monoracial, nearly white-looking Latina women like Jennifer Lopez embody alluring in-betweenness. Instead, Drake bridges *two* racial binaries: an explicitly racial Black/white binary *and* a Jewish/gentile binary that is loaded with racial history but rarely recognized as racial in America today. Further, while colorism often leads the rap industry to eroticize light-skinned women of color,[56] we have seen how colorism often emasculates light-skinned men. Thus, the same American audiences who find Euro-Latinas alluringly "in-between" often find Drake's body *racially incoherent* and *pathetic*, as illustrated by the endless derogatory "Drake memes." But by sculpting his racial "incoherence" into racialized masculine balance and mobility, Drake achieves more agency than Ovalle envisions for racially ambiguous men. Ovalle writes that gentile Euro-Latina women often harness their racial in-betweenness to perform "vertical" racial mobility between gentile Blackness or whiteness depending on speech, body language, costumes, hairstyles, and narrative cues like romance with white men.[57] Conversely, Ovalle finds that Latino men are often cast "horizontally" as ethnically ambiguous characters or other "in-between" ethnicities like Native Americans.[58] Drake illustrates that some racially ambiguous men can take greater control of their racial mobility, as his minstrel personae maneuver "vertically" between Blackness or whiteness *and* "horizontally" toward other in-between racial statuses like Afro-Latinidad.

By wrestling many racially queer masculinities into one marketable package, Drake also expands star studies' paradigm of "impossible bodies." "Impossible bodies" often describes extreme but admired physiques, like Arnold Schwarzenegger's exceptional muscles.[59] Less flatteringly, this phrase can also describe bodies whose stardom seems implausible, like Melissa's McCarthy's unexpected success as a fat film heroine.[60] Past scholarship on Drake often evokes the second meaning without citing star studies' concept of impossible bodies. For instance, in an article on "the impossibility of being Drake,"[61] Alexandra Boutros observes that many audiences find Drake's version of Black rapper masculinity "unimaginable."[62] I clarify how Drake's "unimaginable" stardom reflects a wider pattern of impossible star bodies. Yet I add that he presents *a third type* of impossible body that star studies has not previously considered: viewers not only find Drake's physique exceptional and not only find him an unlikely star, but also commonly assume that Drake's body *cannot hold all his identities*. For instance, Drake has recalled how schoolmates often "didn't understand how I could be Black and Jewish,"[63] and my American students today often echo this startlement. In turn, because Drake's Jewishness joins his light skin, Canadian middle-class upbringing, soap star origins, and vulnerable lyrics to supposedly contradict gangsta Black masculinity, it casts Drake as (to paraphrase Boutros) *impossibly Black*, and thus an *impossible rapper*.

When examining how Drake's identities complicate his marketability, scholars often forefront either his Jewishness *or* his other "soft" traits like light skin. I clarify that these different emasculating traits prove *differently redeemable or irredeemable*. Drake's Jewishness connotes an especially *grotesque* form of emasculation: racial antisemitism historically envisions Jewish emasculation as unequivocally pathetic (weak, neurotic, twitchy, like *SNL*'s "Uncle Barry") and disgusting (greasy, perverse, and foul, like Lil Dicky's rap persona). These stigmas are incompatible with the classical bodies and suave masculinities that Drake seeks to compose across his many minstrel personae. This incompatibility is why his minstrel personae must restrict his Jewish identity to a disembodied, detachable religious faith. By connoting grotesquery, Drake's Jewishness resonates with one other facet of his image that cannot fit his classical, masculinized personae. This other element is Drake's first media role, on the Canadian soap *Degrassi*, in which he played a wheelchair-bound student (Jimmy Brooks) whose paralysis causes erectile dysfunction. While erectile dysfunction can emasculate any character, ableism especially stigmatizes disabled bodies like Jimmy's as grotesque (broken, uncomposed, pathetic).[64] However, Drake's muscular transformation in 2015 has helped him mitigate this ableist stigma. For instance, in "When Exactly Did Drake Get So Swoll?" (2015), *New York Magazine* breathlessly reported that three years of gym training had transformed "wheelchair Jimmy," the "little kid from Toronto," into a "Hulk-style, capital-*M* Man."[65] This phrasing simultaneously stigmatizes "little" "wheelchair Jimmy" and distances him from Drake's new "Hulk"-like body. While bodybuilding has physically masculinized and "classicized" Drake's body, performing detachable Judaism encourages audiences to *interpret* Drake's body in more masculine and classical ways.

Unlike Drake's Jewishness and his past role in a wheelchair, his other "soft" traits prove more redeemable because they are compatible with debonair (classical) masculinity. This difference emerges because Drake's other "soft" traits, like his light skin and Canadian middle-class upbringing, evoke *white gentile masculinity*. As mentioned above, the same colorism that stigmatizes "lightskin" men like Drake as "soft" and "inauthentic" rappers can also romanticize those men as classier (closer to white gentile masculinity) than dark peers like Uncle Larry. Similarly, because Americans often conflate Canada with wholesome gentile whiteness,[66] Drake's Canadian middle-class upbringing jointly feminizes and idealizes him with a more courtly (classical) masculinity. Drake illustrated this genteel effect when first introducing himself to the *SNL* audience in 2014, quipping that he hails from Toronto, "where the rappers are polite."[67] Likewise, although Drake's vulnerable lyrics and melodious singing can emasculate him, they also romanticize him and sell marvelously, assisting his rise into 2021's Artist of the Decade.

To see how Drake harnesses these "redeemable" forms of softness, a deeper look at his racialized masculine balance is illuminating.

Prince Charming: Racialized Masculine Balance

Across many different minstrel personae, Drake has striven to balance the most alluring tropes of "classy" white gentile masculinity and "hard" Black gentile hypermasculinity into one classical body. As mentioned above, Drake especially pursued this balance from 2006 to the early 2020s. For instance, in his 2014 *SNL* bar mitzvah, he achieves this balance by playing the suave host to his racially caricatured uncles.

Meanwhile, in Nicki Minaj's 2011 music video, "Moment 4 Life,"[68] Drake achieves this balance by blending the tropes of the Black gentile rapper and white gentile Prince Charming. Set in a fairytale palace, the video restages Cinderella's ball with Nicki and Drake as the leading lovers. The video elegantly costumes Drake in a black, high-collared blazer and a single gold chain, fusing the fashions of European and rap royalty. He also strolls through the palace with a subtle swagger that blends tropes of Black hypermasculinity and white gentile princely grace. And like a fairytale prince, Drake offers Nicki chocolate and strawberries before wedding her at midnight.

This Prince Charming persona exemplifies how Drake's racialized masculine balance labors to depict him as edgy yet sophisticated, sensual but not sexually menacing, and thoughtful but not overemotional. Regarding class, Drake's racialized masculine balance fuses elite white styles with subtle markers of Black urban counterculture. In this balance, class relates to wealth but is distinct from it; while marking wealth is a common theme in hip hop masculinities, Drake has often used clothing, language and hairstyle to present his wealth in ways that white middle-class norms deem "tasteful." This effect signals to white viewers that he is well-assimilated, palatable, and "safe," unlike the darker or less assimilated men of color whom white middle-class judgments deem grotesque.

This balance requires more than just rebranding some of Drake's "soft" traits, like Canadian identity. It also requires downplaying some of his well-known behaviors that are objectively unethical and fit stereotypes of "bad" Black hypermasculinity—for instance, brawling in clubs against rival rappers.[69] More ominously, Drake has cultivated friendships with then teenaged stars Millie Bobbie Brown and Billie Eilish, prompting bloggers to speculate from 2018 onward that he might be grooming these (white) girls for romantic relationships.[70] Such grooming would constitute an egregious sexual predation strategy, a strategy now better recognized thanks to the #MeToo movement.[71] And although Eilish and Brown have denied sexual overtones in their connections with Drake,[72] it seems inherently suspicious for any man in his thirties to pursue friendships with teenaged girls. Drake's behavior thus simultaneously evokes real patterns of pernicious sexual abuse *and* racist tropes of Black men preying upon white women. For both reasons, Drake's troubling closeness to teenaged girls clashes against his genteel image of racialized masculine balance. This clash highlights that Drake's balanced persona never automatically results from his identity, appearance, or actions. Instead, this balance depends on how Drake actively *sculpts* the potential meanings of his light-skinned biracial Jewish Canadian body, using chameleonic minstrel techniques like his Prince Charming costume in "Moment 4 Life."

Like in Drake's *SNL* bar mitzvah, this sculpting always depends on his detachable Judaism and how it contrasts him (openly or tacitly) against other Jewish men. This step from detachable Judaism to racialized masculine balance is especially visible in the music video "HYFR" (2012),[73] which also reenacts Drake's bar mitzvah. This video initially swathes Drake's bar mitzvah boy persona in external symbols of Jewish identity: he appears in a kippah and *tallis* (prayer shawl), which signal pious masculinity by the Jewish community's internal norms, while reading from a Torah (Hebrew Bible scroll) on a synagogue's *bima* (stage), framed by *menurot* (ritual candelabras). Yet Drake swiftly sheds these Jewish symbols: an ensuing shot shows him blocking the *bima* from view as he raps about sexual conquests alongside the Black gentile rapper Birdman and Muslim Palestinian-American rapper DJ Khaled, without any Jewish symbols. This transition *sheds Drake's bar mitzvah boy persona* even as he dances at his own bar mitzvah, substituting a more generic rapper persona who embodies racialized masculine balance. For instance, Drake often glides through the video in elegant black-and-white formalwear that looks equally suited for rap videos (connoting gentile Black hypermasculinity) or James Bond films (connoting classy but forceful elite white gentile masculinity).

"HYFR" also illustrates just how harshly Drake's performances can stigmatize other minoritized men in order to secure his racialized masculine balance. In Drake's light-hearted *SNL* bar mitzvah, his caricatured Black and Jewish uncles appear grotesque only in silly (not repulsive) ways.[74] Conversely, to help Drake achieve detachable Judaism and racialized masculine balance, "HYFR" pins a deeply unpleasant version of Jewish emasculation to a conditionally white Jewish foil. This foil is an older man, introduced in behind-the-scenes footage as a friend of Drake's (Jewish) mother.[75] This Jewish foil disrupts the party with wildly flailing dance moves, then falls to his knees, mouth gaping, as a younger woman grabs him by the tie. This Jewish man then scrunches his wrinkly face to pull in the woman for an unseemly kiss that sends his kippah swinging off his hair. Although *kippot* can represent pious Jewish masculinity, "HYFR" uses the kippah-in-motion to link this man's sweatiness, twitchiness, lewdness, and weakness with Jewishness—to align him with racial tropes of grotesque Jewish emasculation. The camera further links his pathetic and perverse behavior with Jewishness by cutting to a buffet of Jewish foods, like bagels. Against this grotesque Jewish foil, Drake's masculinity appears even more balanced, suave, and sexy.

To bolster Drake's racialized masculine balance, "HYFR" also harshly stigmatizes a grotesque Black gentile foil in ways that normalize colorism and Black violability. This hypermasculine Black gentile foil is Drake's rap mentor, the self-described gangster[76] Lil Wayne. Of "HYFR's" many Black guests and rappers, Wayne is the darkest and the only dreadlocked one. While Lil Wayne often uses his Black gangsta image to assert strength and dignity, "HYFR" instead validates racist fantasies by casting Wayne's dark, ghettoized Black hypermasculinity as violently disruptive. Wayne first appears slumped at a party table, sporting a black-and-white panda mask that looks wildly misplaced in a grand synagogue full of chic guests. Jerking awake, Wayne raps lewdly about rape: he describes getting "aggressive" with a woman who was too "sober," and giving her "a pill" that made her start "undressing." Wayne then becomes the video's most disruptive character by feverishly smashing a flower arrangement, while Drake laughs from the edge of the screen in his debonair white dress shirt and black slacks. This juxtaposition exemplifies how Drake's racialized masculine balance often idealizes him through respectability politics that stigmatize darker Black men as inherently dangerous or wild, thereby normalizing colorism and Black violability.

While Lil Wayne is American, *Caribbean* dark-skinned men also commonly serve as stigmatized foils who enhance Drake's racialized masculine balance. The hit music video "Work" (2016),[77] a collaboration with the Bajan American star Rihanna, exemplifies this pattern. The video depicts a raging dance party in a Caribbean restaurant, mostly featuring dark-skinned Black men and women. The camera casts these dark revelers as grotesque (messily unbounded) bodies by scrutinizing their dripping sweat, lustful facial expressions, revealing clothes, and greasy food. In contrast, Drake presents a classical (gracefully composed) body:

both he and Rihanna appear very light, Drake is fully covered by his clothing, he dances and sweats little, and eats nothing. His lyrics accentuate this "classier" masculinity, such as assuring Rihanna that even "if you had a twin, I would still choose you." By implying that Drake's love transcends simple carnality, these lyrics romanticize his light body above the dark and allegedly hypersexual Caribbean men who gyrate around him. This effect packages Drake's light-skinned North American Black masculinity as "balanced" (classy and suave) rather than weak.

While common styles of speech, clothing, hair, gesture, and emotion link Drake's many "balanced" minstrel personae, he varies his look much more widely when performing racialized masculine mobility. But like his racialized masculine balance, Drake's mobility strives to imply that he can smoothly control his "mismatched" traits, and it often glamorizes him at the expense of stigmatizing other minoritized men.

Racialized Masculine Mobility, Part 1: Caricature vs. (Failed) Earnestness

Drake sometimes achieves racialized masculine mobility through openly artificial and/or exaggerated (but still cosmetically subtle) minstrel personae, like his Latino A-Rod impersonation on *SNL*. Through these caricatures, Drake *plays at being grotesque*: he briefly exaggerates the unseemliness associated with darker, poorer, more foreign, or more stereotypically Jewish men before reclaiming his suave masculine midpoint. This playful grotesquery idealizes Drake by contrast against the very men he plays. It implies that other minoritized men unselfconsciously and inescapably embody "deviant" masculinities, but that Drake possesses enough self-awareness to notice, satirize, and then shed other men's deviance. This distinction not only bolsters his racialized masculine mobility, but also his racialized masculine balance, by illustrating his greater mastery of white gentile middle-class norms.

When Drake caricatures and sheds other minoritized masculinities this way, he resonates with early twentieth-century Jewish stars like Al Jolson and Sophie Tucker. As we have seen, performing blackface sometimes aided these stars to establish their whiteness.[78] For instance, I have mentioned that Tucker ended blackface routines by revealing her light skin and hair, thus stressing her distance from Blackness.[79] On a more subliminal level, Drake's quick motion in and out of "Blacker," "more Jewish," Afro-Latino, and Afro-Caribbean personae often "lightens" and "gentilizes" him: each time he sheds these personae, his "balanced" masculinity appears closer to North American white gentile middle-class norms of sophistication and respectability by comparison.

Drake's racialized masculine mobility also sometimes caricatures his own identities to idealize him above darker or poorer Black men. For instance, when returning to *SNL* in 2016, he performed a skit called "Drake's Beef,"[80] which parodies his well-known feuds with fellow rappers like Chris Brown.[81] In this sketch, Drake initially uses white middle-class gentile vernacular to chat with the *SNL* cast—but when each comedian accidentally offends him, his internal monologue raps furiously against them in African American Vernacular English and fantasizes about shooting them. These different ethnolinguistic repertoires cast Drake as a racially mobile Jekyll-and-Hyde who seesaws between "classy" white masculinity and "violent" Black gentile hypermasculinity. Importantly, Drake is in on the joke: although the skit riffs on his real-world feuds, it does not stigmatize him with gangsta Black masculinity. Instead, he briefly wears that masculinity to mock it for *SNL*'s (majority white)[82] audience, before flowing into other personae throughout the episode. Authorizing white progressive audiences to voice racial disdain that they might usually deny could easily become a critical joke on white viewers themselves, laying bare their racism. Instead, "Drake's Beef" aligns Drake with the white audience to help them mock Black men as irrationally violent.

However, Drake's racialized masculine mobility sometimes inverts these comedic caricatures to pursue a more earnest tack: he sometimes sincerely strives to package himself in hypermasculine Black gangsta personae, to market himself as a more conventional rapper. One such attempt was Drake's 2013 music video "Worst Behavior,"[83] set in his father's hometown of Memphis. The video stages Drake in a ghettoized Black neighborhood, wearing fashion that fits the rap industry's norms of gangsta masculinity: a loose black shirt, multiple gold chains, and a backward baseball cap. Further conforming to tropes of aggressive Black masculinity, he uses AAVE to rap forcefully into the camera, vehemently addressing the viewer as "muh-fuckuh" (motherfucker) while flipping the middle finger. To emphasize that Drake authentically fits this setting, fashion, and speech, the video stresses his ties to Black Memphis: he appears alongside prominent Black gentile Memphis musicians, including his own father as well as MJG, Juicy J, and Project Pat.[84] On one hand, many YouTube commenters under "Worst Behavior" praise it as an authentic expression of Black masculinity, such as a commenter who deems it "one of Drake's hardest tracks." Yet performances like "Worst Behavior" contradict Drake's well-known upbringing and *Degrassi* role, which established that his most candid speech, fashion, and body language actually match white Canadian middle-class norms. Therefore, Drake's racialized masculine mobility never fully lets him control his own image. Instead, his occasional gangsta personae remain open to dismissal as inauthentic, and even as minstrelsy. The Black gentile rapper Pusha T implied this accusation in a 2018 diss track titled "Story of Adidon." This track calls Drake "confused, always thought you weren't Black enough"[85]—and to emphasize this diss, the cover features Drake's aforementioned blatant blackface photo from 2007. By pairing this accusation and image, Pusha T suggests that all Drake's performances of Black masculinity, no matter how earnest, constitute minstrelsy.

Drake's struggle to control his image through racialized masculine mobility has taken new directions in the early 2020s, producing further ambivalence between authenticity and minstrelsy. Historically, only specific performances like "Worst Behavior" have earnestly packaged Drake as a hypermasculine Black rapper. Outside these performances, we have seen how he historically rebounds to racialized masculine balance (for instance, by presenting tightly trimmed hair and white gentile middle-class English), thereby implying that this balanced persona constitutes his true self. However, in the early 2020s, Drake has sought to imply that he candidly embodies Black hypermasculinity in daily life. For instance, in March 2022, he revealed his hair in cornrows for the first time, a hairstyle that evokes ghettoized Black masculinities. Rather than accepting this hairstyle as authentic, fans perceived it as strange and artificial. Exemplifying this perception, the hip hop magazine *XXL* compiled Twitter reactions under the headline, "Drake Gets His Hair Braided and *People Are Confused*" (my emphasis).[86] One illustrative tweet describes Drake's new look as "a new character or personality" invented to market a new album. This phrasing casts his

"Blacker" new image as an artificial persona created to entertain viewers and enrich Drake himself—in other words, a minstrel persona.

However, Drake's vacillation between authenticity and minstrelsy can *help* him as well as hurt him in achieving racialized masculine mobility. On one hand, his hypermasculine Black personae often ring inauthentic despite his Black identity. On the other, his Afro-Latino and Afro-Caribbean personae elicit surprising *validation* despite his penchant for caricaturing these identities and despite his well-known North American roots. The Latinx YouTube comedy channel *Flama* exemplified this validation in a 2016 mini-mockumentary titled "Flama Conspiracies: Drake is Dominican."[87] Analyzed below, this clip satirically claims that Drake actually *is* Dominican. Rather than revealing his true identity, this clip reveals another dimension of Drake's chameleonic minstrelsy: this minstrelsy pursues racialized masculine mobility not only through caricatured personae like A-Rod, but also through subtler *male brownfishing* personae, which produce exoticized but plausibly authentic-seeming versions of Drake's self.

Racialized Masculine Mobility, Part 2: Male Blackfishing and Brownfishing

"Blackfishing," sometimes interchangeably called "brownfishing," describes a recent form of minstrelsy associated with *white women* performers. This term, popularized by media scholar Lauren Michele Jackson in 2018, names how some white women self-exoticize onscreen to appear plausibly Black, Latina, or Arab.[88] These women (called "blackfish") may darken their skin with makeup and tanning; plump their lips with lip-filler; darken, curl, or braid their hair; or don (in Jackson's words) "hood fashions" like gold hoop earrings. Thus, blackfishing is *subtler* than conventional minstrelsy (like blatant blackface), but *more deliberate and noticeable* than subliminal postmodern minstrelsy. Blackfish may enhance their self-exoticization by pairing cosmetics with *preexisting* elements of their image that connote racial in-betweenness. For instance, the Italian American pop star Ariana Grande pairs her Spanish-sounding surname with tanners and lip fillers to invite viewers into misreading her as Latina.[89] By self-exoticizing, blackfish doubly enhance their marketability. First, like the actual Euro-Latina stars analyzed by Priscilla Peña Ovalle,[90] blackfish offer white audiences the "exotic" connotations of racial darkness on less "threatening" (lighter) bodies. Second, blackfish tempt viewers of color into misrecognizing them as "fellow" community members. Blackfish thus appropriate the most pleasurable and profitable elements of racial ambiguity, without facing the racism that confronts actual women of color.

Since 2018, public and scholarly debates over blackfishing have lambasted white women stars like Ariana Grande—but have overlooked Drake's subtle, unusual, and highly marketable version of blackfishing. Unlike typical blackfish, Drake is not a white woman wielding cosmetics and fashion to darken herself. Instead, he is a biracial Jewish man who uses language, music, dance, fashion, and minimal cosmetics to produce plausibly "real-looking" Afro-Latino and Afro-Caribbean versions of himself. And although these personae embody greater exoticism than Drake's own identity, they are not necessarily darker. Indeed, Afro-Latino personae may come across as *lighter* than Drake's Black North American identity because American culture envisions Latinidad as racially in-between Blackness and whiteness.[91] To capture how Drake self-exoticizes into other racial identities without necessarily darkening ("blackening") himself, I describe his techniques specifically as "*brown*fishing." Drake's brownfishing constitutes one key mechanism within his chameleonic minstrelsy, helping him to achieve racialized masculine mobility.

Drake produces especially convincing brownfish personae, which may convey charming authenticity *even* to Latino and Caribbean audiences who recognize these personae as synthetic. His brownfishing personae can seem so authentic because he mirrors but outstrips Ariana Grande's blackfishing techniques. As mentioned above, Grande pairs cosmetics with her racially ambiguous surname to evoke Latina exoticism. Drake pairs his *more robust* racial ambiguity (his biracial identity and appearance) with *visually subtler* self-exoticization techniques. For instance, we will see how he can wield musical chameleonism (without any cosmetics) to produce Afro-Latino and Afro-Caribbean personae. Drake thus *blends the subtlest techniques of brownfishing and of subliminal postmodern minstrelsy.* This fusion generates brownfish personae that look and feel uncommonly "legitimate."

Drake's brownfish personae prove marketable for two reasons. First, these personae invert the effect of his more caricatured Afro-Latino and Afro-Caribbean characters. For contrast, his caricatured personae like A-Rod displace the most grotesque stigmas about Afro-Latino and Afro-Caribbean masculinities onto other men. Instead, Drake's subtler brownfish personae imbue him with the *sexiest* connotations of Afro-Caribbean and Afro-Latino exoticism, granting him a sensually classical body. Second, these brownfish personae enhance Drake's image as a multicultural icon who offers affirming representation to multiple minoritized identities.

Drake's most enduring brownfish persona is *Dominican Drake*: bloggers' term for a public version of Drake who plausibly seems Dominican. "Dominican Drake" cumulatively emerges from dozens of briefer Dominican or generically Latino brownfish personae throughout Drake's career. Two texts that trace this accumulation are the 2015 listicle "The Evolution of Dominican Drake,"[92] from the Latinx blog *Remezcla*, and the aforementioned comedy clip "*Flama* Conspiracies: Drake Is Dominican."[93] Both note the widespread impression that Drake's biracial appearance *naturally* matches visual stereotypes of Dominican men. For instance, both cite a popular 2015 meme of Drake shirtless in a pool with the caption, "Drake looks like a Dominican uncle." However, *Remezcla* and *Flama* also document how, long before 2015, Drake began accentuating this preexisting fit to *encourage* viewers to misread his body as Dominican—in other words, how Drake has brownfished. For example, both *Remezcla* and *Flama* mention his longtime Instagram handle, "@champagnepapi," which I clarify constitutes *rhetorical brownfishing*: the Spanish term *papi* ("daddy," often addressed to male lovers) encourages viewers to misread Drake as Latino, and it rhetorically swathes him in tropes of exotic Latino masculinity. Both *Remezcla* and *Flama* also note how Drake has signaled Dominican identity by waving a Dominican flag in his 2013 music video "Started from the Bottom," which (*Remezcla* observes) is partly set in Casa de Campo, DR. Both also emphasize how he sometimes mimics Dominican men's fashions, like by "smoking a cigar and rocking gold-tinted shades" in the music video "Headlines" (2011) and sporting "all-white, linen yachtwear" in "Pop That" (2012).[94] Likewise, *Remezcla* and *Flama* mention Drake's collaboration with Romeo Santos (an American singer of Dominican and Puerto Rican descent) on the bilingual track "Odio" (2014).[95] This song, which features Drake singing in Spanish, was nominated for the

Billboard Latin Music Award for Tropical Song of the Year.[96] All these performances constitute brownfishing: each pairs Drake's racially ambiguous body with racially symbolic fashions, props, locations, music, language, and/or co-stars to produce a "tropicalized" version of himself, which may tempt Latino audiences into misreading him as a peer.

And like *Flama*'s satirical claim that "Drake is Dominican," *Remezcla*'s "Evolution of Dominican Drake" captures just how *authentic and affirming* his brownfish personae can feel to Latinx viewers. The listicle, by Dominican American author Isabelia Herrera, declares that Drake's white linen yachtwear "rivals some of my dad's own outfits."[97] This familial comparison captures the warmth and pride permeating Herrera's listicle: the sense that "Dominican Drake" pleasurably affirms Dominicanidad rather than mocking or exploiting it. However, unlike Herrera's father, Drake can always shed Latinidad—both its pleasurable and stigmatized connotations. Likewise, he can always invoke the more "wholesome" white gentile connotations of his Canadian identity to produce racialized masculine balance. Further, as Drake's past A-Rod impersonation illustrates, he can also always displace racist stigma onto Latino men to elevate himself as more normative.

Alongside his "Dominican Drake" brownfish persona, Drake also cultivates a "Jamaican Drake" persona. Alexandra Boutros notes that "Drake has adopted Jamaican sounds, accents and language in his work and his public utterances."[98] This pattern is especially salient in his 2015 megahit "Hotline Bling,"[99] which boasts nearly two billion YouTube views. As the Caribbean music blog *LargeUp* observes, "Hotline Bling" incorporates Jamaican dancehall beats and features Drake performing dancehall choreography alongside the Jamaican Canadian choreographer Tanisha Scott.[100] Although many commentators critique Drake's Jamaican speech, music, and dance as appropriation,[101] others assert that these performances authentically reflect his upbringing as a Black Canadian in Toronto, a city with large Caribbean diaspora communities.[102] Yet whether critiquing or validating Drake's use of Jamaican culture, no commenters have recognized how these performances constitute *brownfishing* techniques: these tactics swathe Drake's racially ambiguous body in a Jamaicanized alter ego. Further, those who defend "Jamaican Drake's" authenticity overlook how easily he sheds this brownfish persona in exchange for racialized masculine balance, and how he sometimes stigmatizes Afro-Caribbean men in the process. For instance, less than a year after Jamaicanizing himself in "Hotline Bling," Drake idealized himself above Afro-Caribbean men in Rihanna's hit music video "Work" (2016).[103] As analyzed above, "Work" romanticizes Drake and Rihanna's light bodies while stigmatizing darker Afro-Caribbean characters as grotesque.

Whether eliciting validation or critique, Drake's brownfish personae always depend on more than just performing Latino or Caribbean masculine stereotypes. They (like nearly all his minstrel personae) also depend on *avoiding* antisemitic racial stigmas by performing detachable Judaism. Needless to say, "Dominican Drake" cannot quaver or twitch like the Jewish "Uncle Barry" from *SNL*. And to sustain this detachable Judaism across all his chameleonic minstrel personae, Drake must carefully package one particularly potent symbol: *his Jewish mother*, Sandi Graham.

"Momma Is a Saint": Erasing, Christianizing, and Feminizing the Jewish Mother

Drake's chameleonic minstrelsy often requires linking or distancing his body from *other racially symbolic bodies*. Like his varied costumes, hairstyles, and ethnolinguistic repertoires, these other bodies serve as props that assist Drake's various racialized masculine personae. For instance, we have seen how Drake's "Uncle Barry" and "Uncle Larry" serve as props in his *SNL* bar mitzvah: by variously juxtaposing himself against and linking himself with each uncle's body, Drake achieves his own whiter, Blacker, and more- or less-Jewish masculine personae.

But of all the bodies that sometimes appear around Drake's, his mother's has special power to undercut his detachable Judaism. In turn, her body can undercut the racialized masculine balance, mobility, and respectability politics that require Drake's Judaism to stay detachable. In other words, *Drake's mother can undercut all the effects that make his chameleonic minstrelsy so ideologically marketable.* Drake's mother holds this power thanks to two interwoven stereotypes: the emasculated nice Jewish boy and his castrating Jewish mother.[104] Popularized by works like Philip Roth's 1969 *Portnoy's Complaint*,[105] these tropes depict Jewish mothers as all-consuming harpies who strangle their sons with too much love, controlling them so intrusively that hapless Jewish boys cannot develop proper masculine boundaries, identities, or sexualities. This Jewish mother/son dyad is now so well-established in US pop culture that each trope invokes the other. Therefore, *referencing Drake's Jewish mother always risks tying him to racially queer Jewish emasculation, grotesquery, perversion, and neurosis.*

Drake's *SNL* bar mitzvah exemplifies this threat by initially showing his Jewish mother (played by Jewish comedian Vanessa Bayer) emasculate him. Although Sandi Graham is Canadian, *SNL* depicts her with a brash New York Jewish vernacular that masculinizes her, and which she uses to unman Drake. First, she infantilizes Drake by introducing him as "our little Aubrey."[106] Next, when he tries to assert masculine independence by declaring that "as a man . . . I will now be called *Drake*," his mother sternly forces him to embrace the more Jewish-sounding "Drakeob" (like "Jacob"). These gags position Drake as the weak Jewish son of a domineering Jewish mother. Only after his mother *exits* and gets *replaced* by his uncles does Drake manage to detach this Jewish emasculation, achieve racialized masculine balance, and achieve racialized masculine mobility.

Like on *SNL*, Drake's chameleonic minstrelsy often pursues detachable Judaism by carefully managing when and how his mother appears around him. Analyzing this technique does not question Drake's feelings for his mother, but deciphers how he *presents* his mother and their relationship onscreen. On one hand, Drake is a self-declared "momma's boy" who calls his mother "the most important person in my life" and praises her for raising him solo.[107] Yet even when literally embracing Sandi onscreen, Drake narrowly circumscribes her *and her Jewishness* in ways that assist his detachable Judaism, racialized masculine balance, and racialized masculine mobility. Sometimes, like on *SNL*, this detachment requires literally removing Sandi from a performance.

In other cases, this detachment requires *Christianizing* and thereby *feminizing* Sandi's image. This tactic distances Drake from neurotic "nice Jewish boy" imagery, and thus enhances his various minstrel personae that embody gentile whiter, Blacker, Afro-Latino, and Afro-Caribbean masculinities. Drake exemplified this Christianizing and feminizing effect in 2016: posting from his @champagnepapi Instagram handle, he shared a clip of his mother blowing out her birthday candle. His caption reads, "I do this all for you. Happy birthday, *my angel*" (my emphasis).[108] Although many Black rappers record odes to their mothers (like Snoop Dogg's 1999 track "I Love My Momma"),[109] Drake's phrasing sounds oddly Christianized for a Jewish man addressing his Jewish mother. Even though Jewish theology does include angels, addressing loved ones as "angel" has a Christian ring in North America today. Further, the angels in Euro-American culture often carry Christian religious connotations and white gentile appearances like brilliantly fair skin, hair, and eyes.[110] Regarding gender, American media's angelic women (like Cinderella) usually embody the daintiest traits of stereotypical white gentile femininity, like soft pink skin, gentle voices, and sweet temperaments—the very opposite of stereotypically loud, brash, overbearing Jewish mothers. By invoking these "angelic" white gentile connotations, Drake's Instagram caption Christianizes and feminizes his mother. It thereby helps Drake to present his own masculinity as charmingly genteel rather than shamefully emasculated. Erasing his mother's Jewishness also assists Drake's Instagram brownfish persona "@champagnepapi" by downplaying any perceived clash between stereotypical Jewish emasculation and stereotypical Latino hypermasculinity.

A more extensive performance that Christianizes and feminizes Drake's Jewish mother is the music video "Child's Play" (2016).[111] "Child's Play" especially illustrates how these techniques aid Drake's racialized masculine balance, aid him to displace stigma onto other Black men *and* Black women, and thus aid him to normalize Black violability. Set in a chic restaurant, "Child's Play" converts a lover's quarrel into a confrontation over how Black bodies should occupy public spaces: Drake nervously hushes his girlfriend, played by Black supermodel Tyra Banks, as her speech mounts louder and switches into AAVE. When shaming his girlfriend, Drake invokes a Christianized version of his Jewish mother to depict his respectability politics as admirable rather than inauthentic, and to depict his masculinity as genteel rather than weak.

"Child's Play" initially seems to critique Drake's racial respectability politics and challenge the racist norms that normalize Black violability. This critique begins when Drake's girlfriend confronts him about texting another woman. Rather than apologizing, he focuses on how Banks's rising tone and AAVE may embarrass him before their mostly white fellow diners. Nearly whispering in white gentile vernacular, Drake urges his girlfriend to lower her voice and take the argument outside, even demanding, "Do you wanna get us in trouble?" This question tacitly references Black violability: Black people of all genders face extreme violation on small pretexts like a raised voice. Just one example was the 2015 assault on a Black high school student in South Carolina for refusing to stow her cell phone: in response, a school police officer trapped her in a chokehold, flipped her, dragged her across the room, and handcuffed and arrested her.[112] Such violence is the threat behind white diners' stares as Drake and his girlfriend argue in "Child's Play."

"Child's Play" initially delegitimizes the racist norms that expose Black people to violation: the video portrays Drake as out of line when he treats his girlfriend's rising voice (rather than his own infidelity) as transgressive. Rejecting Drake's authority to hush her, his girlfriend demands, "Why are you lookin' and actin' like I'm crazy?" and adds that "I don't care where we are!" because his infidelity so pains her. She literally claps back against his tone-policing, rhythmically clapping in his face while chanting, "I, am, tired, of, you, Au-brey!" These techniques resonate with the tactic that hip hop feminist scholar Gwendolyn Pough calls "bringing wreck": the way Black women in hip hop wield spectacle to demand recognition as full people and to claim space in public life.[113] This clapback climaxes when Drake's girlfriend smashes her cheesecake into his face and storms off, leaving his face with a racially symbolic smear of white frosting.

Although "Child's Play" initially assigns the moral high ground to Drake's girlfriend, it ultimately rejects her criticisms to reassert that Drake's genteel masculinity makes him both a more deserving citizen and more desirable lover than other Black people. And his (Jewish) mother plays a key role in this reversal. Once his girlfriend exits, Drake raps to the camera as if to her: "You . . . say *I'm actin lightskin*, I can't take you nowhere / This is a place for families that drive / Camrys . . . You wildin', you super childish." He adds, "*Momma is a saint*, yeah she raised me real good / All because of her, I don't do you like I should." Then, sternly wagging a finger into the camera, Drake threatens "*Don't make me give you back to the hood*" (my emphasis). These lyrics imply that he takes pride in "actin lightskin," as the alternative would be to act "wildin'" and "childish" like his girlfriend from "the hood." "Child's Play" thus aligns Tyra Banks's character with Lil Wayne's in "HYFR":[114]

both "prove" that "hood" Black people are inherently wild and disruptive. And by threatening to "give" his girlfriend "back to the hood," Drake conveys that his own allure includes his *distance* from the ghetto, a distance allegedly instilled by the "saintly" mother who "raised me real good." Rather than challenging the racist norms that perceive Black people as innately disruptive, these lyrics cast Drake as better than other Black people at mastering white norms, better at composing a classical body, and therefore more entitled to full citizenship (full inclusion and safety). Further, he credits his (Jewish) mother not just with his "light-skin" appearance, but also *comportment*. While images of a castrating Jewish mother would feminize Drake, the Christian term "saint" Christianizes and feminizes his *mother*. This saintly imagery elevates Drake's classical body with tropes of enlightened Christian self-restraint, rather than weighting him with grotesque Jewish weakness.

By crediting Drake's (Jewish) mother for his respectable Black masculinity, "Child's Play" echoes racist narratives about Black parenting. The racist discourses that blame Black people for their own oppression often claim that racial inequality and police violence reflect Black people's "bad parenting," which allegedly causes Black people's own "bad behavior," including gangsta masculinity. Such accusations stretch back at least to the Moynihan Report, a 1965 study that stereotyped Black households as a "tangle of pathology," and which partly blamed unwed Black mothers for Black poverty.[115] This victim-blaming narrative still commonly dismisses anti-Black discrimination and violence. In June 2020, for instance, during the uprisings that followed George Floyd's murder by Minneapolis police, Fox Nation contributor Tomi Lahren tweeted that "we don't have a policing problem, we have a parenting problem."[116] This tweet implies that unarmed Black people murdered by police are not victims of racist policing, but poorly parented delinquents whose own misbehavior leads them to sticky ends. When "Child's Play" credits a saintly (Christianized) version of Drake's mother for his "better" Black masculinity, it not only validates stigma against Black people who can't or won't obey white middle-class norms, but also feeds the broader accusation that all Black suffering is a self-inflicted "parenting problem." This ability to validate racist stigmas is always part of the ideological labor that makes Drake's racialized masculine balance and mobility marketable.

To extend this anti-Black ideological labor, "Child's Play" also invokes its Christianized version of Drake's Jewish mother to valorize him as a more chivalrous (not more emasculated) boyfriend than fellow Black men. Before he raps about his mother, Drake's efforts to quietly appease his girlfriend can seem ambivalently genteel or weak. However, he valorizes this pacifism in gentlemanly terms by rapping that because his (Jewish) "momma" "raised me real good . . . I don't do you like I should." This lyric may imply that Drake does not physically punish his girlfriend like "real men" are often expected to do. By implying that his "saintly" (Jewish) mother raised him too well to hit women, "Child's Play" contrasts Drake not just against his "wildin'" girlfriend, but also against his fellow light-skinned Black male music star, Chris Brown. Drake's restraint, which allegedly reflects "proper parenting," contrasts against Brown's real-world violence when confronted by an angry girlfriend. In March 2009, Chris Brown was dating Rihanna, whom Drake has also since dated. When Rihanna challenged Brown about texts from another woman, Brown brutally beat her.[117] The ensuing scandal transformed Chris Brown's image from that of a "squeaky-clean," "well-assimilated Black man" to a déclassé, aggressive Black man, as noted by communications scholars Suzanne Marie Enck and Blake McDaniel.[118] Conversely, in "Child's Play," Drake presents himself as a Black man raised too well to hit his girlfriend after she publicly humiliates him. Although "Child's Play" is fictional, it blurs the line with reality: Tyra Banks calls Drake "Aubrey," implying that both are playing themselves. This realism invites viewers to compare Drake's fictional self-discipline with Chris Brown's actual violence. "Child's Play" thus recruits the topic of domestic violence to imbue Drake's image with principled self-restraint, thereby enhancing his racialized masculine balance. And to package Drake's nonviolence as gallant rather than emasculated, "Child's Play" deploys a Christianized image of his Jewish mother.

Conclusion

By Christianizing his mother's image to masculinize his own, Drake once again spotlights his personal Jewish pickle. The tropes of queer (strange) masculinity that racially distinguish Jews from gentiles in US media place Drake in a bind. On one hand, these antisemitic stigmas combine with his light complexion, Canadian identity, white middle-class speech and deportment, and soap opera origins to disqualify him from hip hop's manufactured standard of "authentic" Black hypermasculinity. And while Drake's chameleonic minstrelsy can reframe his other "soft" traits into "suave" personae with classical bodies, none of these classical bodies can incorporate racial tropes of grotesque Jewish emasculation. Therefore, all Drake's minstrel personae strive to detach Jewish identity from his body, restricting antisemitic masculine stigmas to a present absence, while implicitly or explicitly contrasting him against more emasculated Jewish men. In turn, this minstrelsy helps Drake present himself as a "better" (more tasteful and charming) Black man, while displacing stigma onto other men who appear darker, poorer, or more foreign. This effect invites audiences to indulge oppressive biases yet still feel pleasurably progressive for embracing a multicultural icon.

The next chapter turns to Drake's foil, the comedic rapper Lil Dicky, who has found success by exaggerating the most grotesque racial stigmas of Jewish emasculation.

2

"Redpill Me on Lil Dicky"

Vicarious Jewface and "Soft" Deplorable Satire

Newsweek has dubbed Lil Dicky "the Jerry Seinfeld of Rap" for his "curly-haired," "neurotic," "scrawny" Jewish image.[1] Lil Dicky (aka David Burd, b. 1988) has similarly invoked America's lineage of self-deprecating Jewish comedians by calling himself a "white, Jewish, suburban loser"[2] specializing in "stand-up rap" or "satirical rap."[3] Jewish self-mockery launched Dicky's career in 2013, when his first homemade YouTube rap video, "Ex-Boyfriend," broke one million views overnight.[4] Flipping rap conventions about hard Black gentile men who magnetize women, "Ex-Boyfriend" mocks Dicky's failure to get laid and inaugurates the self-emasculating stage name "Lil Dicky."[5] Dicky later explained this moniker as a small-penis pun on "Lil Wayne,"[6] an icon of gangsta Black rapper masculinity. And Dicky routinely links this emasculating "Ex-Boyfriend" debut to Jewishness by stating that he funded the video with "bar mitzvah money,"[7] cash gifts saved from his Jewish manhood ceremony.

Although the rap industry typically markets Black gentile hyper-masculinity, Lil Dicky's emasculated Jewish rapper persona has proven queerly (oddly) alluring. Since his first viral hit, Dicky has attracted fervent fans called "Dickheads" and drawn collaborations with A-list musicians like Katy Perry and Snoop Dogg. In 2015, Snoop helped hoist Dicky from YouTube personality to legitimate rapper by co-starring in Dicky's music video "Professional Rapper."[8] In 2016, hip hop magazine *XXL* further legitimized Dicky by featuring him in its "freshman class" of rising rappers.[9] Dicky has also parlayed this success into an FX television series, *Dave* (2020–2023), starring Dicky as himself. Dicky's incongruous Jewish rap stardom fuels *Dave's* humor about a "suburban neurotic man in his late twenties who has convinced himself that he's destined to be one of the best rappers of all time."[10]

Lil Dicky thus exemplifies "open TV"[11] stardom: the way independent artists can harness social media to prove their marketability before approaching network gatekeepers, and thereby assert minoritized identities that Hollywood has historically muted. Dicky's vividly Jewish and emasculated persona flouts past restrictions on Jewish comedians and Jewish rappers. He consistently degrades (not merely deprecates) his body more luridly than stand-up forebears like Jerry Seinfeld, and he links this degradation more overtly to Jewishness. We have seen that Seinfeld's sitcom (1989–1998) extended Hollywood's tradition of "double-coding,"[12] using clichéd mannerisms to hint that some characters are Jewish without alienating gentile viewers. This choice partly reflected the studio's anxieties: NBC's president Brandon Tartikoff nearly nixed *Seinfeld* as "too Jewish" for wide appeal.[13] Therefore, even as *Seinfeld* broke barriers with openly Jewish characters, it rarely spoke the words "Jew" or "Jewish."[14] And although *Seinfeld* tacitly evokes antisemitic tropes to cast Jewish men as neurotic and unimposing, it never presents Jews as viscerally vile or acknowledges antisemitic racial slurs like "kike." Conversely, Lil Dicky has harnessed YouTube's democratizing power to sidestep gatekeepers like Tartikoff and trumpet his Jewishness in the most degrading terms. Dicky flaunts the word "Jew," which (unlike "Jewish") becomes a slur when paired with antisemitic stereotypes.[15] For instance, in the YouTube rap "$ave Dat Money" (2015), with 187 million views, he brags of being a cheap "Jew biz major."[16] While this slur activates tropes of Jewish greed, Dicky usually invokes racial stigmas that cast Jewish men as emasculated, perverse, and filthy. For example, he racially emasculates himself as a "kike" with a "little dicky" in "All K" (2013) and mocks his "frail, Jewish shoulders" in "Really Scared" (2014).[17] Similarly, when rap-battling Hitler in "Jewish Flow" (2013), Dicky echoes Nazi racial propaganda by calling himself a "nappy-headed, greasy Jew."[18]

While YouTube lets Lil Dicky mock his Jewishness more provocatively than Seinfeld, this self-degradation also separates him from his fellow millennial Jewish rapper, Drake. As we have seen, Drake's appeal depends on "counteridentifying with"[19] (rebuffing) antisemitic tropes of racially queer Jewish masculinity. Shedding these Jewish stigmas, Drake crafts a "classical body"[20] (a cleanly self-contained body) that can balance and glide between tropes of Black gentile hypermasculinity, white gentile sophistication, and Latino or Caribbean gentile exoticism. This tactic has often marketed Drake as a suave superior to darker and more "gangsta" Black men like his mentor, Lil Wayne. Conversely, Lil Dicky "disidentifies"[21] with racially queer Jewish masculinity: he actively paints himself as an emasculated and "grotesque"[22] (messily unbounded) body, marking himself as Lil Wayne's pathetic opposite, yet Dicky turns this humiliation to advantageous ends. Racial tropes of feeble, neurotic, perverse, greasy Jewish men have historically "justified" excluding and slaughtering Jews. Instead, Dicky alchemizes these stigmas into a marketable persona that has helped him build an $8 million net worth.[23]

Spinning extreme Jewish self-degradation into mainstream rap stardom also distinguishes Dicky from other conditionally white Jewish rappers. Although the all-Jewish group the Beastie Boys helped introduce rap to white middle-class audiences with their 1986 album, *Licensed to Ill*, their lyrics did not reference Jewishness until 2004.[24] Rappers who do forefront Jewishness mainly pursue niche Jewish audiences. Such rappers have focused on critiquing antisemitism (like the rap duo Blood of Abraham, who condemn Christian proselytizers in their 1993 single "Stabbed by the Steeple");[25] on promoting Jewish education (like the Chasidic group the Radical Rappin' Rebbes);[26] or on lightly self-deprecating Jewishness (like the comedic rap duo 2 Live Jews, in their 1990 single "Oy, It's So Humid!").[27] Unlike these predecessors, Lil Dicky crafts an exceptionally repulsive, emasculated Jewish image that counterintuitively attracts mainstream audiences.

Vicarious Jewface, White Male Grievance, and Deplorable Disidentification

Lil Dicky's queer (emasculated and counterintuitive) glamor depends on a comedic sleight-of-hand: *disguising white male rage as harmless Jewish self-mockery*. He nearly pinpoints this effect in the 2014 rap video "Really Scared," which proclaims, "Lil Dicky is the voice of the voiceless. In an era where rap is dominated by racial, social, and economic minorities, LD decided to put the upper-middle class on his frail, Jewish shoulders."[28] This caption ridicules Dicky's "frail" body and links this frailty with Jewishness. And this Jewish self-mockery helps Dicky to cast all white-privileged, upper-middle-class men like himself as "voiceless" outsiders in rap, allegedly "dominated by racial, social, and economic minorities." Yet the caption also hints that it might be *satirizing* this white male angst with its overdramatic lament about "the voiceless." As in "Really Scared," Lil Dicky's queer glamor always depends on channeling white male resentment while plausibly claiming to mock that resentment, or just to mock Dicky's own Jewish emasculation.

To this end, Lil Dicky's comedy always mirrors wider myths that cast white men today as dispossessed underdogs, "dominated" by racial, gender, and sexual minorities. Such narratives fuel what sociologist Michael Kimmel calls *aggrieved entitlement*: rage against those who "steal" white men's "rightful" power, respect, and opportunities.[29] Philosopher Kate Manne notes that aggrieved entitlement also accuses women of withholding sexual and emotional labor that men "deserve."[30] These white male victim narratives decry modest gains by minoritized people as "proof" that white men are now persecuted victims. For instance, in 2017 the *New York Times* analyzed a survey of 1,302 American adults about social inequality, in which one interviewee lamented, "The white man is a low person on the totem pole. Everybody else is above the white man."[31] Such narratives have circulated at least since the Black civil rights and women's liberation movements of the 1960s and 1970s,[32] but have intensified since the 2010s in response to Barack Obama's election, the #MeToo movement, and the #BlackLivesMatter movement, with further incitement from Donald Trump, the alt-right, and right-wing disinformation networks like Fox News and OANN. However, while many white male victim narratives accuse Jews of puppeteering white gentile men's downfall, "Really Scared" does the opposite: it invites all white-privileged men (both Jewish and gentile) to embrace Dicky's "frail, Jewish" body as a symbol for their own imagined victimhood, authorizing him to "voice" their misplaced grievances.

In other words, Lil Dicky's queer glamor depends on *Jewfacing himself,* then *vicariously offering that Jewface to all white-privileged men.* Leonard Stein has defined Jewface rappers as those who "exploit their [Jewish] heritage . . . for humor and popularity," such as when 2 Live Jews spoof stereotypical Jewish fussiness in "Oy, It's So Humid!"[33] I define Jewface rappers more narrowly and literally as those who extend the history of theatrical Jewface: "the tradition of codified stage makeup techniques to accentuate stereotypical Jewish features" to depict villainous or clownish

Jews in late nineteenth- to early twentieth-century theater.[34] Theatrical Jewface used cosmetics to caricature racially symbolic body parts like noses and to heighten racialized ephemera like effeminacy and lecherousness. For instance, alongside a "false nose," "heavy black beard," "black Jew wig," and "dark shade of grease paint," male Jewface actors often sported flashy jewelry while shadowing their eyes and rouging their lips for a "thick, sensual look."[35] This cosmetic Jewface conveyed the racial belief that Jewishness generates a "grotesque and garish vulgarity immediately evident to the eye."[36]

Lil Dicky updates this tradition to produce *subliminal postmodern Jewface*, which neither he nor his audience seems to recognize as a synthetic racial caricature at all. This subliminal postmodern Jewface pairs subtle cosmetics (hairstyles, facial grooming, and subtle makeup) with animation and cinematography (lighting and camera angles) to racially caricature Dicky as a filthy, perverse, emasculated Jew. Regarding cosmetic Jewface, Dicky has styled his brown hair into larger, curlier, and greasier mops over the years. Further, his skin and facial scruff always bear a putrid oily sheen, even in network television episodes whose makeup artists would not let such oiliness occur accidentally. Regarding cinematographic Jewface, Dicky's lighting and camera angles accentuate his racially symbolic Jewish traits. For example, his rap battle against Hitler in "Jewish Flow" (2013)[37] opens with a profile shot outlining Dicky's arched nose and curly hair in white light (figure 2.1). Meanwhile, Dicky performs cartoon Jewface in his 2015 animated music video "Professional Rapper," co-starring Black gentile rap superstar Snoop Dogg.[38] The video casts Snoop as CEO of "Rap Game, Inc.," a fictional corporation symbolizing the rap industry, where Dicky seeks employment. Like "Ex-Boyfriend's" plot about sexual failure, "Professional Rapper" comedically contrasts Dicky's emasculated Jewish image against the rap industry's hypermasculine Black gentile norms. The video heightens this mismatch with cartoon Jewface, which exaggerates Dicky's hooked nose, frail and hunched frame, puffy brown curls, and scummy brown facial scruff. While this Jewface initially caricatures Dicky in minor ways, it soon turns monstrously grotesque: a flashback to Dicky's bar mitzvah presents him as a waist-high gremlin whose massive nose overwhelms his goat-like face as he waves envelopes of cash that evoke tropes of Jewish wealth (figure 2.2). Monstrous yet pathetic,

Figure 2.1. Lil Dicky's cinematographic Jewface in "Jewish Flow" (2013).
Screenshot from the music video "Jewish Flow" by Lil Dicky, released August 14, 2013, on YouTube. Pulled from YouTube.

Figure 2.2. Lil Dicky's cartoon Jewface in "Professional Rapper" (2015).
Screenshot from the music video "Professional Rapper" by Lil Dicky, released July 31, 2015, on YouTube. Pulled from YouTube.

this gremlin-bar-mitzvah-boy echoes centuries of European art that painted Jews as animalized demons, translating religious stigmas into proto-racial imagery.[39]

Lil Dicky amplifies his cosmetic, cinematographic, and animated Jewface through a technique I call *rhetorical Jewface*: he verbally coaches audiences to conflate his Jewishness with visibly grotesque emasculation. For instance, Dicky's lyrics variously instruct audiences to view him as a "greasy," "nappy-headed" "kike" with a "little dicky" and "frail, Jewish shoulders." This rhetorical Jewface builds as viewers consume his performances, cumulatively encrusting Dicky like greasy residue.

By Jewfacing himself, Lil Dicky can offer his audiences *vicarious Jewface: Dicky invites all white-privileged men (both Jewish and gentile) to identify with his emasculated Jewface character as a symbol for their alleged disenfranchisement as white men in twenty-first-century America.* When using antisemitic racial tropes to claim victimhood, Dicky's vicarious Jewface never asks audiences to challenge present-day American antisemitism. Instead, this vicarious Jewface only offers Jewishness as a tool to help white-privileged men claim victimhood *as white men.* Likewise, it invites all white-privileged men to embrace Dicky as their Jewfaced avatar of aggrieved victimhood. And this invitation works: although no statistics document Dicky's online viewers, onlookers at his concerts emphasize that most attendees are young middle-class white men.[40] For instance, "Behind the Dick," a 2016 behind-the-scenes series about his concerts, shows mostly white crowds. One Asian man even tells the camera, "I think I'm the only Asian guy here, it's kinda weird."[41] These concert demographics capture elevated engagement with Dicky's work in white male circles. And footage from his first live concerts in 2014 shows just how exuberant this engagement can be, as Dicky receives ecstatic hugs from conventionally masculine, muscular, "bro-y" white young Dickheads.[42]

As these images suggest, many fans in Dicky's concert footage embody white, *straight, gentile* masculinity. His 2018 music video "Freaky Friday"[43] acknowledges this niche appeal by casting the brawny white gentile actor Jimmy Tatro as Dicky's fan. Standing in for the Dickheads, Tatro brings his muscular physique, deep voice, and penchant for masculine white gentile roles. For instance, two months after "Freaky Friday," Tatro appeared in *Camp Manna* as a dreamboat bible camp counselor, described as "the epitome of Christian cool."[44] Likewise, as a Dickhead in "Freaky Friday," Tatro embodies effortless white gentile masculinity that accentuates Lil Dicky's cinematographic Jewface: Tatro's broad shoulders, straight nose, and straight, sun-bleached hair contrast against Dicky's slight build, beaked nose, and greasy brown curls. Yet this macho white gentile fan loves Dicky precisely for his emasculation. Spotting Dicky in a Chinese restaurant, Tatro extols him as a "funny rapper who raps about how small his dick is and how he's a funny-lookin' little white guy." This backhanded compliment highlights Dicky's counterintuitive glamor: the racial queerness that marks Jewish "white guys" like Dicky as "funnier" (more ridiculous, emasculated, and strange) than gentile white guys like Tatro also queerly (oddly) appeals to gentile white guys. And it does so by vicariously validating their misplaced self-image as abused underdogs.

Rap makes an ideal genre to build this vicarious Jewface bond, thanks to the myth that Black men monolithically control the rap industry. Lil Dicky can thus present his "struggle" as a puny, sexually unsuccessful, conditionally white Jewish rapper as an allegory for the "struggle" of all white-privileged men in America today. In reality, although Black New Yorkers originated rap in the 1970s, white-privileged executives (including Jewish ones) have prominently shaped and profited from mainstream rap, often in ways that caricature Black people.[45] Likewise, white-privileged rap executives commonly hold gatekeeping power. For instance, since 2016, Dicky's manager has been the conditionally white Jewish executive Scooter Braun, who has also managed Kanye West (before West's infamous antisemitic tirades).[46] Dicky's work erases these white-privileged gatekeepers, such as when "Professional Rapper" casts Snoop Dogg rather than Braun as "the rap game's" intimidating CEO.[47] This erasure helps to package Dicky as a marginalized outsider in rap, who thereby symbolizes white-privileged men's nationwide "marginalization."

By inviting all white-privileged men to pity themselves as "the Jews" (oppressed victims) of present-day America, Lil Dicky's vicarious Jewface disidentifies with (mirrors-yet-revises) white nationalist rhetoric. Both vicarious Jewface and white nationalist media falsely suggest that social justice efforts have placed "white people . . . [in] the same position as Jews in Nazi Germany."[48] But even while claiming Jewish victimhood, white nationalist media accuse Jews of orchestrating white male oppression or even "white genocide." For instance, the far-right Christian talk show "TruNews" warned that Trump's 2019 impeachment constituted a "Jew coup," and that "when Jews take over the country," they will "kill millions of Christians."[49] Lil Dicky sidesteps these white male victim narratives that blame Jews. Instead, his vicarious Jewface helps him symbolize white-privileged men's victimhood at the hands of (in order of alleged culpability) straight gentile Black men, white women, and Black women. By weaving antisemitic racial stigmas into a persona that benefits Dicky but harms others, his vicarious Jewface comprises a kind of *deplorable disidentification.* José Muñoz theorizes disidentification as a liberating tactic, whereby marginalized people sculpt their own stigmas into alluring identities.[50] Dicky's grotesquely emasculated Jewface persona does just this—but fuels its appeal by channeling white-privileged men's bigotry and rage toward other victims.

Comedic Abject Hegemony

Embodying straight white-privileged men's "victimhood" enables the second key to Lil Dicky's queer glamor: vicariously *voicing white men's serious resentment, fear, disdain, and desire for the groups that "dethrone" them, under the guise of harmless comedy.* After all, Dicky's lyrics are "just jokes," these self-degrading jokes seem to primarily demean their teller, and these emasculating jokes combine with Dicky's frail Jewface image to paint him as a weakling whose animosity poses no danger. Racial tropes of Jewish emasculation also help Dicky pretend his comedy "punches up" at overprivileged people (like Black men who allegedly sideline him in rap), when his comedy really "punches down" at more oppressed people. Thus, as in "Really Scared," his vicarious Jewface always fuels his queer glamor by *(1) validating white-privileged men's baseless sense of grievance; (2) voicing white-privileged men's resentment, fear, disdain, and desire toward the groups who have "wronged" them; and (3) helping audiences claim or even believe that this virulent resentment is harmless humor.*

To further disguise white male backlash as harmless humor, Lil Dicky's Jewface comedy also teases the possibility that he might be satirically *deflating* (not endorsing) the white male victim narratives that he stages. This wavering between sincerity and satire is especially clear in Dicky's 2013 music video "All K."[51] "All K" opens with the kind of corny inspirational music that an uplifting documentary might use to signal virtuous concern about some grievous injustice, like child poverty. Alongside this tune, a solemn black screen presents text in a minimalist white font that gravely declares, "The N word is the most commonly uttered noun in hip hop. But he cannot say it. In a rap landscape littered with hardened criminals, hypermasculinity, and irrational swagger, a mild-mannered Jewish boy can struggle for acceptance." By exaggerating ad ridiculum the cues that convey sincerity in documentaries, this prelude teeters between sincerity and self-satire. Is "All K" earnestly upholding anti-Black stereotypes, earnestly claiming that rap discriminates against white-privileged men, and earnestly asserting that white-privileged men suffer oppression because they cannot (publicly) say the N-word? Is it satirically puncturing these misguided ideas? Is it just ridiculing Dicky as a meek "Jewish boy?" The answer is all three: *Dicky always employs satirical tones and Jewish self-mockery as comedic misdirection, to more freely voice earnest white male bigotry and resentment.* This alluring ambivalence makes Dicky an exemplar of subliminal postmodern minstrelsy more broadly. Such minstrelsy is ideologically slippery because it blends contradictory fantasies about disrupting/sustaining straight white gentile male supremacy. In turn, we have seen that this type of minstrelsy is so marketable precisely because its ideological messages are so elusive, contradictory, and thus deniable.

By helping straight white-privileged men disguise their backlash behind pathetic weakness and self-mockery, Dicky's vicarious Jewface reveals how antisemitic racial tropes can assist *abject hegemony.* "Abject hegemony," coined by communications scholar Claire Sisco King, *describes how dominant groups can feign weakness to stealthily reassert power, by embracing traits they usually despise, expel, and project onto marginalized groups.*[52] King's insight builds on theories by the philosopher Julia Kristeva. Kristeva defines "the abject" as that which *threatens* the boundary between self and other; which individuals must therefore *reject* to delineate their coherent self; and which therefore provokes mingled *disdain, fear, and revulsion.*[53] While the abject includes excreta like feces that blur the body's anatomical boundaries, it also includes traits which blur *social* boundaries between dominant and marginalized groups. For example, historically, many straight white gentile men have delineated their identities and claimed superiority by sharply distinguishing themselves from women, LGBTQ+ people, people of color, and/or Jews. Such men may therefore anxiously deny any "taint" of femininity, homoeroticism, or racial impurity in themselves, since these abject traits threaten to unravel their identities and claims to power. In turn, this fear of social contamination often fuses with fears of physical filth, as analyzed by anthropologist Mary Douglas,[54] philosopher Mikhail Bakhtin,[55] and feminist theorist Kathleen Rowe.[56] Due to this conflation of social and physical impurity, subordinated groups often become stigmatized as what Bakhtin calls "grotesque bodies":[57] bodies that allegedly overflow with nauseating juices, odors, crusts, lusts, and diseases which threaten to infect dominant groups with both abject excreta and abject social traits. The epithet "stinking Jew!" exemplifies this fusion of social and excretal abjection.

While Kristeva stresses how dominant groups shun the abject, King exposes the opposite. Dominant groups sometimes strategically *embrace* abject traits and excreta to *enhance* their privilege by camouflaging it, producing "abject hegemony." King's prime example is the 1999 hit *Fight Club*.[58] To misrepresent straight white gentile men as dispossessed victims, the film casts their bodies as ugly, leaky, penetrable, and vulnerable—stigmas usually displaced onto women, Jews, people of color, and queer people. To this end, *Fight Club* wallows in images of brutalized and bloodied straight white gentile male bodies. By releasing excreta (like blood and scar tissue) that convey wretched vulnerability, this self-inflicted violence cloaks the men's social privilege in physical weakness.

Unlike *Fight Club*'s white gentile leading men (Brad Pitt and Edward Norton), Lil Dicky needn't self-mutilate to perform abject hegemony. Instead, Dicky harnesses the preexisting stigmas on his Jewish body: his Jewface flaunts a historically abject identity (Jewishness) that connotes many abject characteristics (feminization, racial impurity, sexual perversion) and many abject physical excreta (greasiness, odor, disease). King's work on abject hegemony overlooks these links between Jewishness and abjection, but Dicky illustrates how abject hegemony can harness these antisemitic racial stigmas. His putrid, reeking, feminized, homoerotic, weak, racially caricatured Jewface incarnates nearly all the abject social traits and physical excreta that usually disrupt straight white-privileged masculinity. Many straight white-privileged men therefore strive to excise such traits from themselves—but Dicky's Jewface invites them to *relish* such traits instead. By vicariously offering his own abjection to straight white-privileged men, he helps them to disavow their own privilege, validate their misplaced resentment, and guiltlessly unleash their sadistic revenge fantasies. This invitation to abject hegemony is what makes Dicky's *aesthetically repulsive* Jewface so *ideologically alluring*.

And to amplify his Jewish abjection, Lil Dicky wields *self-mockery* rather than the self-brutalization seen in *Fight Club*. He thus spotlights a previously unnoticed *racial dichotomy in American media depictions of abject hegemony*. White gentile performers like *Fight Club*'s stars typically construct abject hegemony by suffering physical violence onscreen. Instead, conditionally white Jewish performers like Lil Dicky typically construct abject hegemony through comedic self-degradation that invokes antisemitic racial tropes. The feminist theorist Kathleen Rowe has hinted at this Jewish brand of abject hegemony when analyzing self-deprecating men's comedy, but Rowe underestimates how deeply such comedy depends on antisemitic racial tropes. In 1995, Rowe coined the term *melodramatized man* to describe any emasculated male comic who weaponizes his aggrieved victimhood to both deny and reassert male privilege[59]—a comedic version of what Claire Sisco King later dubbed "abject hegemony." Significantly, Rowe identified Jewish comedian Woody Allen as America's foremost melodramatized man.[60] Presaging Lil Dicky's paradoxical stardom, Rowe writes that "[i]f certain elements of Allen's persona (he is intellectual, introspective, Jewish, East Coast, urban), have limited . . . his popularity," his "neuroses . . . merely exaggerate more commonly held fears about the impact on men of the changes in the status of women."[61] For instance, Allen's rom-com *Annie Hall* (1977), which debuted during the women's liberation movement, follows a neurotic Jewish New Yorker who resents his white gentile ex for dumping him. However, by listing Jewishness as just one of Allen's defining traits, Rowe overlooks how antisemitic tropes actually drive Allen's whole "melodramatized" image, and thus his comedic version of abject hegemony. All the traits in Rowe's list are common media codes for Jewishness, and these codes are precisely the tools by which Allen emasculates himself, to embody many men's "neuroses" about feminism.

Additionally, the literary theorist Eli Bromberg argues that the border-line whiteness of Euro-American Jews helps to vicariously market Allen's victimized Jewish image to all white-privileged men, letting them feel "unfairly prosecuted even when they're guilty" of racially or sexually abusing others.[62]

Lil Dicky's Jewfaced stardom illustrates even more explicitly how antisemitic racial stigmas can help a Jewish male comedian to vicariously channel many white-privileged men's feelings of "dispossession" and fantasies of reasserting power.

Selling Difference as Sameness: The Mechanics of Blackface and Vicarious Jewface

To perform abject hegemony this way, Dicky must *sell difference as sameness*: he must Jewface himself to embody victimhood, but must also invite all white-privileged men to identify with this racially specific victimhood. For this tightrope act, Dicky's Jewface narratives ambivalently racialize him as white/Jewish; they cherry-pick only antisemitic stigmas that envision Jews as weak, not over-powerful; they avoid pitting Dicky against white gentile men; and they often juxtapose Jewface against blackface techniques.

To balance inside/outside whiteness, Dicky presents his Jewface persona as racially *protean*, an effect that mirrors-yet-inverts Drake's "racial chameleonism." As we have seen, Drake performs chameleonic minstrelsy by cycling through many different and racially specific personae, like an exotic Afro-Latino lover or tough Black gangster. Instead, per the media scholar Simon Weaver, "racially protean" describes how a *single* minstrel persona can appear racially liquid, multiple, and elusive.[63] To achieve this protean effect, Lil Dicky keeps his self-presentation stable but his self-descriptions fluid: he always crafts a grotesquely emasculated Jewface persona, but erratically labels this persona a (nonwhite) greasy kike, a (conditionally white) neurotic Jewish boy, or a generic white boy. The 2013 rap "White Dude" exemplifies this slipperiness by calling Dicky a "kike boy" and "white boy" in back-to-back lyrics.[64] Such racial uncertainty aids Dicky to offer his grotesque Jewish emasculation as a symbol for all white male disenfranchisement.

To better offer his Jewish emasculation to all white-privileged men, Dicky also avoids villainizing Jewish *women*. This absence is striking because self-deprecating Jewish male comics customarily blame their emasculation on Jewish wives or mothers.[65] However, because Dicky symbolizes all white-privileged men, painting himself as a victim of Jewish women would risk marking Jews as threats to white gentile masculinity—thus marking Dicky as an antagonist to (rather than mouthpiece for) many white men. Therefore, Dicky's comedy rarely presents any Jewish women: of all his raps, only his 2018 music video "Freaky Friday" briefly invokes "overbearing Jewish mother" tropes by mentioning that his mother calls too often.[66] Instead, Dicky's vicarious Jewface depends on targeting "common threats" to all straight white-privileged men, whom he depicts as straight gentile Black men, white women, and Black women.

To further avoid suggesting that his Jewishness might threaten white gentile masculinity, Lil Dicky cherry-picks antisemitic tropes to cast himself as *weak*, never *powerful*. While embracing far-right antisemitic racial stigmas and slurs (like "kike") to embody pitiful victimhood, Dicky sidesteps conspiracy theories that accuse Jews of dominating and contaminating white gentile men. His sole rap to break this rule depicts a distant setting, Nazi Germany. This 2013 video, "Jewish Flow,"[67] edits WWII-era footage to stage a rap battle between Dicky and Hitler. Within this battle, Dicky brags of being precisely what Nazi propaganda feared: a "nappy-headed, greasy Jew" who racially pollutes German bloodlines by seducing blond "German bitches." While ogling a beautiful blond actress in cartoonish German garb, Dicky even gloats to Hitler about putting his "seed" in "yo girl." By casting Dicky as a dirty Jew who goads white gentile men by defiling "their" women, "Jewish Flow" presages alt-right anxieties that surfaced at the 2017 Charlottesville "Unite the Right" rally. One alt-right spokesman, Chris Cantwell, railed against then president Donald Trump for "giv[ing] his daughter to a Jew," adding that "I don't think you can feel about race the way I do and watch that Kushner bastard walk around with that beautiful girl."[68] Echoing WWII-era Nazism, Cantwell labels Ivanka Trump a racially white woman who belongs to her white gentile father despite her religious conversion to Judaism. Ivanka's marriage to "that Kushner bastard" specifically threatens Cantwell's "feelings about race," his desire for white gentile racial "purity." Although today's American far-right promotes the same Nazi bigotry that Lil Dicky mocks in "Jewish Flow," Dicky has never presented himself as a racial or sexual threat to American white gentile male supremacists like Cantwell. Indeed, since "Jewish Flow," Dicky has presented no plotlines that depict him dominating, deriding, or contaminating white gentile men. He thus avoids implying that Jews might undermine present-day straight white gentile male dominance.

To emasculate himself as a Jew yet offer this image to all white-privileged men, Lil Dicky also *reroutes* his own resentments away from white gentile men toward Black gentile men. His 2013 viral debut, "Ex-Boyfriend,"[69] exemplifies this redirection. In the video, Dicky's sexual frustration mounts as his beautiful white gentile girlfriend (Katie) delays sex with him and gets distracted by her gorgeous, muscular, massively endowed white ex-boyfriend. The video starkly contrasts Dicky's grotesque Jewfaced body (greasy, frail, curly-haired, and hook-nosed), against his competitor's rosy, chiseled, straighter-haired, button-nosed beauty (figure 2.3). Dicky even compares his nemesis to the pinnacle of classical white male bodies—Greek statues—by calling him "the closest thing I've seen to a Grecian god." Yet Dicky unexpectedly links this adversary's masculine appeal with *Blackness*: Dicky raps that "he's so damn attractive / so damn tan, he gotta have a little Black in him." This lyric implies that Dicky's white gentile "Grecian god" rival is really Black, or at least that Black ancestry makes him "so damn attractive."

This implication reframes "Ex-Boyfriend's" racialized masculine conflict from Jew/gentile to white/Black. It thus channels the racist myths that cast Black men as hypermasculine savages who rape or seduce white women.[70] In turn, "Ex-Boyfriend" invokes the fear, envy, and disdain that white-privileged American men have historically felt toward Black men's alleged hypermasculinity. These mixed emotions grow sharper when the video links Dicky's rival with the myth of the gigantic Black penis:[71] peeping his competitor's penis in a bar bathroom, Dicky discovers that "it's the biggest cock that I've seen in my whole life," making Dicky's penis look "like a raisin" by comparison.

By nearly thrusting Lil Dicky into sexual competition against a white gentile man but then recasting this rival as Black, "Ex-Boyfriend" also adds racial dimensions to Dicky's resentment against his girlfriend, Katie. Katie's frigidity (denying Dicky sex) and promiscuity (flirting with

Figure 2.3. "Ex-Boyfriend" (2013) stresses Lil Dicky's Jewfaced emasculation by contrast against his chiseled rival.
Screenshot from the music video "Ex-Boyfriend" by Lil Dicky, released April 25, 2013, on YouTube. Pulled from YouTube.

her ex) feed white men's historical anxiety that "their" women may emasculate them by preferring Black men. This anxiety includes fearing that white women's sexual "treason" will racially pollute white bloodlines.[72] However, sociologist Abby Ferber notes that white nationalists accuse Jews of promoting "race mixing" as an "organized mutiny of biologically inferior people."[73] Instead, "Ex-Boyfriend" offers Dicky's Jewfaced image as the voice rather than enemy of aggrieved white manhood: he vicariously channels white-privileged men's resentment, anxiety, and lust toward both white gentile femininity and Black gentile hypermasculinity.

If Dicky must wield his specifically Jewfaced persona to symbolize all white-privileged men's "victimhood," then another technique in this balance is to *juxtapose Jewface against blackface minstrelsy*. We have seen that blackface minstrelsy originated in the United States in the late 1820s,[74] when white performers began rubbing burnt cork on their faces to caricature Black dance, speech, and song for white audiences. Scholars including Eric Lott, Jayna Brown, and Krin Gabbard note how these performances aimed to possess the thrilling stereotypes that white people project onto Blackness, but that also naturalize racism—stereotypes like animalistic hypermasculinity.[75] Blackface minstrels conveyed a toxic cocktail of fetishization, envy, and desire (for Black people's allegedly primal bodies, dance, and music) blended with disgust, disdain, and fear (for Black people's allegedly primitive violence, vulgarity, and stupidity).[76] This genre achieved massive popularity over the nineteenth century, remaining prominent on stage and screen through the 1950s.[77] This popularity spawned a wider legacy in which white-privileged people mimic (white fantasies about) Black dance, speech, song, and emotion—with or without painting their faces.[78] As past scholarship observes, many white performers from Elvis to Eminem to Christina Aguilera have built profitable careers by "trying on" Blackness to amplify their perceived sensuality, soulfulness, or toughness.[79] The media scholar Krin Gabbard writes that no matter whether these stars or their audiences realize it, such performances directly descend from blackface minstrel shows.[80]

When Lil Dicky raps and mimics African American Vernacular English (AAVE), he extends this lineage of cosmetic-free blackface minstrelsy. He specifically extends the lineage of Euro-American Jews who have channeled Blackness by "blacking up" (like Sophie Tucker and Al Jolson) or simply mimicking Black performance traditions (like the Beastie Boys).[81] However, while blackface historically conveys disdain, fear, envy, and desire for Black *bodies*, Dicky's juxtaposition of Jewface against blackface also adds new envy for Black people's alleged *social power*: power to withhold the cool masculinity, sex life, and rap career that Dicky covets.

Therefore, rather than embodying Black men's alleged coolness, Dicky uses Jewface to stress his comedic *failure* at Black masculinity. For instance, spotting his (supposedly) Black rival's "long," "thick," "smooth" penis in "Ex-Boyfriend" prompts Dicky to rhetorically Jewface his own penis as a shriveled "raisin." Dicky's Jewfaced failure to appropriate Black traits always implies that Black gentile men are unjustly *monopolizing* opportunities at white-privileged men's expense, such as when Dicky fears that his rival in "Ex-Boyfriend" will steal his girlfriend. Juxtaposing Jewface against blackface thus helps Dicky channel white-privileged men's sense that they are America's mentally superior but physically, sexually, and politically marginalized underdogs.

Blackface's contradictory fear, disdain, and lust toward Blackness also aid Lil Dicky to sow confusion about his comedic intentions, and thus keep white male backlash palatable. "Professional Rapper"[82] exemplifies this ambivalence: on one hand, Dicky depicts Snoop Dogg as running the rap industry, and he desires Snoop to validate his rap authenticity. On the other, Dicky fears and disdains all the video's Black gentile men: one shot even positions Snoop in the role of the Black rapist, looming over a naked Lil Dicky in the bathroom. As in "Professional Rapper," rap is always the crucial vehicle for Dicky's vicarious Jewface because it (1) allows Dicky to constantly juxtapose his Jewfaced emasculation against tropes of Black gentile hypermasculinity, and (2) to thus rail against Black men's ostensible physical, sexual, and social power, while (3) constantly tapping blackface's contradictory desire and hatred toward Blackness.

Jewfacing the Manosphere: Jewish Incels, White Stacys, and Black Chads

When "Ex-Boyfriend" casts Lil Dicky as the emasculated victim of a frigid-yet-promiscuous white gentile woman and a hypermasculine Black gentile man, it mirrors tropes from the *manosphere*. Media scholar Debbie Ging describes the manosphere as a "loose confederacy" of far-right online groups mainly comprising white, straight men, who claim that feminists have twisted America into a gynocentric society that oppresses men.[83] Prominent manospheric subgroups include "men's rights activists," "pick-up artists," "traditional Christian conservatives," and elements of gamer/geek culture.[84] This manosphere entwines with white nationalist communities like the alt-right by sharing adherents, platforms (like 8chan, Reddit, Gab, and Parler), and extreme racism and sexism. For instance, both manospheric and white nationalist communities often endorse "gender realism" and "race realism,"[85] the far-right's new lingo for old bigotry: these ideologies claim that it is biologically right and necessary for men to dominate women and for white gentiles to dominate Jews and people of color.

In "Ex-Boyfriend," Lil Dicky's Jewface character mirrors the manospheric notion of the "cuck" (cuckold), "a weak man whose girlfriend cheats on him, usually with Black men."[86] His role also mirrors the manospheric subculture of *incels* ("involuntary celibates"). Incels are mainly white, straight, middle-class men who claim that, despite their

supposed intelligence and sensitivity, their lack of conventional masculinity biologically precludes them from achieving sex with women.[87]
This ideology vilifies women as cruel abusers, whom evolution has allegedly hardwired to choose brutish musclemen over "nice guys." This
dogma fuels incels' aggrieved entitlement primarily against beautiful
women (derided as *Stacys*) and secondarily against more masculine men
(derided as *Chads*), who supposedly monopolize "Stacys."[88] Both cucks
and incels fit within the wider manospheric category of *betas*: men who
claim they are disenfranchised because they are unathletic, nerdy, or
crushed by America's supposedly man-hating culture.[89]

Dicky's "comedic" reflection of beta beliefs is so worrisome because
manospheric dogma, like white nationalism, fuels violence. For instance, incel ideology promotes an "incel rebellion" to "liberate" incels
from the "Stacys and Chads" who "wrong" them, and this directive motivated almost fifty murders during the 2010s.[90] The deadliest incel attack saw twenty-five-year-old Alek Minassian murder ten pedestrians
with his van in Toronto in April 2018. Beforehand, Minassian defined
himself on social media as a "recruit" to the "Incel Rebellion" "infan-
try."[91] Minassian's militaristic fantasy mirrors those of hypermasculine
alt-right subcultures like the Proud Boys, who militarize themselves
"in defense" against feminists, Jews, LGBTQ+ people, and/or people of
color.[92] This synchrony seems unexpected, since many incels disdain
masculine "Chads." However, like all white male victim narratives, beta
ideologies claim victimization only to justify violently reasserting power.
Thus, like Lil Dicky's rap, beta ideologies exemplify abject hegemony.

It's no fluke that "Ex-Boyfriend" mirrors incel and cuck identities.
While reflecting widespread sexist and racist backlash, Lil Dicky's
Jewface comedy most precisely matches the manosphere's grievances,
tropes, tones, and digital networks. This match between manospheric
dogma and Lil Dicky's Jewface comedy is uncanny because it seems truly
unplanned: Dicky has never publicly mentioned the manosphere nor its
lingo like "incel" or "race realism." And whereas manospheric and white
nationalist ideologies often deify Donald Trump, Dicky decried then
candidate Trump as a "supervillain" in 2016 and urged Twitter followers
to vote out Trump in 2020.[93] Although Dicky seems unfamiliar with the
manosphere and even opposed to its political goals, his comedy channels near-identical white male backlash for near-identical audiences on

some of the same platforms, like YouTube and Reddit. This unplanned match is possible because far-right ideology is just a more explicit, detailed, and openly violent version of mainstream misbeliefs that mislabel white men today "the low man on the totem pole." Dicky's ostensible distaste for far-right hate communities does not disqualify him or his Dickheads from sympathy for hate groups' underlying grievances. Indeed, his stardom exemplifies the widespread parallels between mainstream and extremist white male victim narratives.

Like "Ex-Boyfriend," Dicky's comedy usually puts a racial twist on the manospheric trinity of the incel, the "Stacy," and the "Chad," without using those terms. Casting Dicky's Jewfaced body as the incel, his comedy positions white gentile women as "Stacys," the temptresses who sexually deprive him. Meanwhile, Dicky uses racist tropes to cast *Black* gentile men as "Chads," the "brutish" men whose masculine sex appeal overshadows him—like Dicky's (allegedly Black) hunky rival in "Ex-Boyfriend." This conflation mirrors incels' racism: many incels feel particularly wronged when "a man lower down the racist social hierarchy gain[s] sexual and emotional access to a white woman."[94] Dicky's depiction of Black "Chads" helps him simultaneously channel incel fury at being "dispossessed" by stronger and/or darker men *and* channel general white male resentment at being "dispossessed" by people of color.

Unlike gentile Black "Chads" and white "Stacys," Black gentile women do not clearly match manospheric bogeymen in Lil Dicky's comedy. Dicky therefore depicts Black gentile women less frequently and less prominently, as titillating-but-intimidating background characters. For instance, during his audition for Snoop Dogg in "Professional Rapper,"[95] Dicky gets sexually overwhelmed by Snoop's loud, voluptuous, neck-rolling Black secretary, Juanita. As her massive bosom looms over Dicky, Juanita casually offers "head" (fellatio) as a hospitality service. Dicky nervously stammers, "D-Did you just say 'head?,'" prompting Juanita to laugh, "You ain't never got no head before?" This exchange positions Juanita as a déclassé sex worker whom Dicky objectifies, *and* an emasculating powerhouse who mocks Dicky while her mountainous curves threaten to engulf him. This image of Black women as neck-rolling, hypersexual whores reflects America's wider misogynoir, a term coined by feminist scholar Moya Bailey to name how racism and sexism jointly degrade Black women.[96] Dicky extends this degradation by casually fetishizing and fearing Black women, but he does not depict them as the primary antagonists guilty of "dethroning" white-privileged men.

Lil Dicky's narratives about gentile white "Stacys," Black "Chads," and Black "whores" mirror the topmost *grievances* and *narrative formats* of the manosphere. Building on the work of political scientist Zizi Papacharissi and media scholar Mark Andrejevic, Debbie Ging explains that today's manosphere constitutes an *affective public*: a community linked by intense emotions co-experienced through digital networks.[97] As an affective public, the manosphere differs from pre-Internet "men's rights activists" that aimed to rationally lobby against policies that purportedly oppress men, like divorce law that allegedly favors mothers for child custody.[98] Instead, the manosphere's method to "dismantle perceived threats" to white male power is to circulate "emotionally charged claims to victimhood," often through "personal storytelling."[99] To inflame this furor, manospheric storytelling often labels men victims of "politically correct" censorship, in which nasty minorities allegedly rob men of individual opportunity and fun—like when women critique misogynist video games. Manospheric devotees likewise deem themselves victims of feminism,[100] which has supposedly freed cruel, filthy women to emasculate, exploit, and sexually deprive men. Meanwhile, incels also deem themselves "wronged" by stronger men, who ostensibly monopolize women. And in manospheric thinking, this personal "victimization" requires viciously punishing the villains who have "wronged" you, as incel "infantryman" Alek Minassian did.[101]

Mirroring these manospheric trends, Lil Dicky performs comedic personal vignettes that channel white men's rage at (ostensibly) being sexually deprived or sexually overwhelmed by powerful women, gagged by political correctness, or excluded from cool Black masculinity. Dicky's comedic struggle to get laid in "Ex-Boyfriend" and to win Snoop Dogg's patronage in "Professional Rapper" exemplify such vignettes. But rather than openly threatening sexist or racist violence, or openly promoting hateful ideologies, Dicky's Jewface humor submerges manospheric ideas within palatable narratives for mainstream viewers. If manospheric adherents claim victimhood in order to violently reaffirm white male power, then Dicky's Jewface persona offers listeners an ideal "beta" body for stoking-yet-concealing this desire, even from themselves: this vicarious beta body is a racially emasculated Jew, so feeble that his aggression appears like harmless comedy.

"Redpill Me on Lil Dicky": "Soft" Deplorable Satire

In 2016, one Redditor highlighted the fit between Lil Dicky's comedy and manospheric dogma by writing that "Lil Dicky understands some red pill teachings, definitely."[102] The term *red pill* riffs on the 1999 sci-fi hit *The Matrix*: the hero frees himself from a computerized mind-prison by taking a red pill, which enables him to battle his robotic jailers.[103] He also refuses a tranquilizing blue pill that would reestablish his comfortable mind-prison. From this origin, "to redpill" means opening someone's eyes to a secret truth,[104] while taking "the blue pill" means accepting soothing but oppressive delusions.[105] This terminology is most strongly associated with manospheric and white nationalist communities. Just as *The Matrix*'s red pill enlightens its protagonist to hard truths, far-right adherents aim to redpill "normies" (uninitiated readers) by awakening them to the "secret truth" that white gentile men are oppressed by a cabal of Jews, feminists, Muslims, people of color, and/or LGBTQ+ people.[106] Conversely, this rhetoric accuses Jews of orchestrating "the blue pill," meaning the media misinformation that allegedly conceals white gentile men's oppression.[107]

The parallels between Lil Dicky's comedy and "red pill teachings" are what make his stardom so dangerous: although Dicky has no intentional far-right associations, his work may still help to "redpill" audiences into manospheric and white nationalist ideology by palatably packaging that extremism as humor. A comment beneath Dicky's 2014 music video "Lemme Freak"[108] evokes this risk, when one viewer writes, "redpill me on Lil Dicky." Although this phrase may simply mean "I'm excited to discover Lil Dicky," it also highlights that Dicky's comedy might "redpill" listeners toward far-right extremism, which always tends toward violence in the name of white men's "liberation." And regardless of whether Dicky's audiences ever find far-right communities, his appeal always depends on encouraging viewers to embrace, intensify, and enjoy the most rageful white male victim narratives.

By packaging far-right white male victim narratives as harmless self-satire that may "redpill normies" toward extremism, Lil Dicky mirrors one of the far-right's top recruitment methods: *deplorable satire*. First named by the media scholar Viveca Greene, deplorable satire disguises deadly serious prejudice and fury as edgy ironic humor to radicalize new recruits.[109] Like other white nationalist and manospheric content, deplorable satire often circulates in the same digital networks as Dicky's music videos.[110] Both Dicky's rap and far-right deplorable satire are presented as "hammily outrageous"[111] humor that provocatively pushes the limits of publicly acceptable bigotry. This "edgy" branding helps such content go viral even in a hypersaturated media landscape, and it particularly entices "young white men" by "exploit[ing] their rebellion and dislike of 'political correctness.'"[112] In turn, deplorable satire helps far-right propogandists to discredit any critics as humorless fools for taking their "jokes" seriously.[113] Mocking critics makes deplorable satire even more alluring to young men: these men can toast themselves for being clever and free-thinking enough to understand the provocative humor that uptight liberals want to censor . . . when in fact, they are unwittingly consuming earnest Nazism.

Most deplorable satire comes from far-right propagandists who deliberately promote inequality and violence, and deliberately conceal this dogma as ironic comedy to "redpill normies."[114] Andrew Anglin, founder of the *Daily Stormer* neo-Nazi website, details these tactics in "The Normie's Guide to the Alt-Right," a leaked manual for his blog's contributors.[115] Anglin explains that "[p]acking our message inside of existing cultural memes and humor can be viewed as a delivery method. Something like adding cherry flavor to children's medicine."[116] In other words, deplorable satire's "irony and the coy misdirection are all in service of tricking people into following [Anglin] on his path toward a white supremacist state."[117] For instance, this humor can help lure a reader along a spectrum from the (sadly mainstream) misconception that "everybody else is above the white man" in America today to the extremist belief that Jews are conspiring to commit "white genocide." Just like Lil Dicky, then, the far right uses outrageous comedy to coyly package earnest white male rage, racism, and misogyny as harmless self-satire.

While all deplorable satire stokes extreme bigotry in publicly acceptable guises, several factors make Lil Dicky's deplorable satire especially *soft*: especially nebulous, self-contradictory, outrageous, deniable, and thus palatable. First, since most deplorable satire comes from far-right communities that label Jews "race enemies," Dicky's Jewface distances him from far-right deplorable satirists. For instance, although Dicky enumerates his white male privileges in the 2013 rap "White Dude,"[118] one YouTube commenter named "Fashmaster" ("fascist master") jeers below it, "He's not white. He's a fucking Jew."[119] Dicky's vulnerability to this type of racial antisemitism makes it harder to confront how his own lyrics echo white male supremacist dogma. Dicky's artistic collaborations with Black gentile men like Snoop Dogg (co-star of "Professional Rapper" in 2015), Chris Brown (co-star of "Freaky Friday" in 2018), and Kevin Hart (co-executive producer of *Dave* in 2020–2023) similarly soften his deplorable satire.

Lil Dicky's deplorable satire is also softer because his political messages are inconsistent and often apparently unintentional. Although he has made few public comments about misogyny, he has denounced white male supremacists' darling, Donald Trump, and has issued sharply contradictory statements on racism. This inconsistency became vivid during the antiracist protests that followed George Floyd's murder by Minneapolis police in May 2020, when Dicky entreated his Instagram followers to combat racism. His post condemns racism as the "horrifying foundation of our country," a "legitimately evil" problem that he learned about by seeing Black rap colleagues wrongfully harassed.[120] Dicky also urges fans who "grew up like me" in a "suburban white bubble" to move beyond "passively observing racism" and actively challenge it. His post ends with the hashtag #BlackLivesMatter. This post never acknowledges that Dicky has *not* "passively observed racism": since 2013, his stardom has depended on stoking racist stereotypes and resentments camouflaged as harmless satire.

This inconsistency suggests that Dicky *lacks* political intentions, that his bigoted messages express implicit biases rather than purposeful propaganda, and that he voices these biases only to chase viral popularity. This effect highlights how deplorable satire inflicts real harm even when unintentional. In fact, Dicky's soft deplorable satire may inflict harm *precisely because it is uncalculated* (as far-right deplorable satire *pretends* to be), and therefore harder to confront. This ambivalence also aligns Dicky with postmodern minstrelsy more broadly: we have seen that postmodern minstrels often camouflage or even *lack* political intentions.[121] In turn, this ambiguity is marketable because it helps minstrels like Dicky to thrill audiences with ambivalent and deniable meanings.

However, the most vital factor that softens Lil Dicky's deplorable satire is the way he wields antisemitic racial stigmas through vicarious Jewface. Tropes of grotesque Jewish emasculation are the tools that best help Dicky to market white male rage as harmless comedy. In turn, the "softness" of his deplorable satire aids him to stoke both mainstream and far-right white male grievances in plain sight, potentially enticing "normies" toward violent extremism. Past scholarship on deplorable satire incisively examines how far-right propagandists manipulate phrasing and digital platforms.[122] However, Lil Dicky highlights how deplorable satirists can wield their own *bodies* to masquerade white male backlash as ironic satire.

Dicky also thus embodies an oppressive *fusion* of deplorable satire with "open TV." Media scholar A.J. Christian theorizes open TV as a liberatory phenomenon, in which minoritized artists (like Issa Rae, a Black gentile woman) harness social media to assert their voices.[123] This liberatory effect inverts the way white gentile male supremacists harness social media to "redpill" new bigots. Yet Lil Dicky blends these trends by wielding digital media to flaunt his Jewishness in once-taboo ways and using that flamboyant Jewishness to stoke white male backlash. Further, his success illustrates how deplorable satire can comprise an appalling *by-product* of implicit bias and of chasing viral open TV stardom, rather than a deliberate radicalization tactic. Like all practices that inflict racial, gendered, and sexual harm, deplorable satire can emerge from everyday people who deem themselves unbigoted or even liberal.

"Lemme Freak," the rap video that attracted the comment "redpill me on Lil Dicky," epitomizes how Dicky's vicarious Jewface fuels "soft" deplorable satire, and how this satire beckons mainstream audiences into manospheric dogma. With 94 million YouTube views, "Lemme Freak" also illustrates how his self-degrading Jewface comedy makes extremism *appealing* to mainstream audiences. "Lemme Freak" mocks Dicky's struggle to get laid throughout his lifelong marriage to a beautiful but sexually "withholding" white woman.[124] The video opens by reapplying his grotesquely emasculated cinematographic Jewface: a close-up stresses his greasy skin, dingy facial scruff, oily brown curls, and arched nose (in profile) as he raps that it's been "two months since I fucked a lady."[125] The video then derides Dicky's inept flirting when he encounters a beautiful white woman by a club: trying to show his rap videos, he accidentally shows his porn searches. While reemphasizing Dicky's Jewish sexual perversion and failure, this gag mirrors incel rhetoric about being inherently unable to attract women. Against expectation, Dicky and the beautiful woman end up married until old age, but "this bitch" always turns him down when he begs her to "lemme freak" (penetrate her). Thus, even while married, Dicky embodies incels' supposed deprivation and their aggrieved rage.

"Lemme Freak" also mirrors the manosphere's misogynist evolutionary theories, which claim that "women are children: mentally, behaviorally, evolutionarily," who cannot stop themselves from financially exploiting and sexually depriving the beta "gentlemen" who would really make supportive mates.[126] "Lemme Freak" makes Dicky's sexual deprivation look unjust because he is so "well-behaved," patiently helping his wife draft work emails as she hysterically melts down at him. The video further infantilizes his wife through her film preferences: when Dicky angrily lists his sacrifices in pursuit of sex, these include watching the animated children's films that his wife enjoys. His tirade ends with the demand that his wife reward his supportive behavior by letting him "freak."

"Lemme Freak" also uses Dicky's Jewfaced body to flaunt-and-dismiss the threat of rape. When he first approaches his wife-to-be at the club, her friends ask her "if everything is okay." Dicky retorts, "Nah, this a rape. You can't tell? Give me a break. Now please, get the hell away." This sarcasm asserts that others should read Dicky's Jewfaced body as self-evidently harmless. Together, his words and body reflect the burning resentment of many American men who accuse feminists of victimizing men by exaggerating claims of sexual violence. These male victim narratives encompass streams of the manosphere that deny rape is a problem or even celebrate rape,[127] but also pervade mainstream media. The *Wall Street Journal* exemplified these claims in 2017 with an article titled "Witch Hunt on the Quad," alleging that college rape-prevention initiatives comprise a baseless "moral panic," fueled by feminists who "grossly inflate" rape statistics to violate the due process of the (mostly male) students accused of rape.[128] Such narratives gained legal force that year: then secretary of education Betsy DeVos rolled back Obama-era regulations intended to reduce campus rape and shield survivors from retaliation, claiming that these regulations disenfranchised students accused of sexual violence.[129] Throughout "Lemme Freak," Dicky uses his Jewfaced body to endorse this cultural and legal backlash against rape survivors.

Even while dismissing America's rape problem, "Lemme Freak" celebrates a manospheric rape fantasy called "going caveman": unleashing men's allegedly primal urge to sexually dominate women.[130] Although many white-privileged Americans stigmatize Black men for their ostensibly animalistic lust, the manosphere's mostly white men claim the right to impose their *own* animalistic lust on women. Dicky's "comedic" version of going caveman appears when he first propositions his wife-to-be at the club: he lunges at her, grabs his crotch, and rips open his shirt, while rapping, "This is me coming at you as a man right now / Lemme freak / Lemme freak . . . It's all I need." By making Dicky's sexual "needs" look explosively vulgar, this sequence cuts two ways. From one perspective, Dick's crudity paints him as a repulsive man who can only blame himself for his sexual starvation. From this angle, the video satirically deflates incel-ish narratives that vilify women for "wrongfully withholding" sex. Yet Dicky's explosive desires also celebrate manospheric fantasies of "going caveman," while denying that such aggression could really harm women. For instance, a massive bouncer separates Dicky from his wife-to-be. Although this bouncer deems Dicky threatening, the bouncer's size just reinforces how puny Dicky is. Further, as Lil Dicky's stage name, his Jewface, and his many prior videos had established by 2014, the Jewish dick that he thrusts at this woman is impotent and tiny. Supposedly too weak to inflict harm, Dicky can enact incel-ish violence as "unobjectionable" comedy—and invites viewers to root for that violence.

By casting Lil Dicky as a harmless and cruelly deprived underdog, "Lemme Freak" sets up one of the most disturbing scenes of his career, in which he "comedically" rapes his wife. This "humorous" climax fast-forwards to 2074, with the couple in old-age makeup, a time leap that helps to frame this scene as unthreatening fantasy. The elderly Dicky pops a Viagra-like pill to induce an erection (which he disparages as "little"), then strives to force himself on his wife even though her dementia has left her comatose and frightened. This montage even shows Dicky lying atop her unresponsive body and dipping down for a kiss, but the camera softens this image by cutting away before his lips land. Finally, his wife offers under duress to perform fellatio, a coerced surrender that not all viewers may recognize as rape. Dicky's Jewface persona frames this rape not just as harmless, but also *justified* and *triumphant*, by implying that a long-suffering underdog is receiving his due—precisely how incels view themselves. By inviting audiences to relish this incel-ish rape as both innocent comedy and righteous revenge, "Lemme Freak" exemplifies how Dicky's vicarious Jewface always fuels soft deplorable satire that can "redpill" audiences toward extremism.

Grotesque Aggressor and Victim: "Comedic" Manospheric Misogyny

While "Lemme Freak" uses comedy to directly normalize sexual assault against women, Lil Dicky's soft deplorable satire also expresses manospheric misogyny through more symbolic means. For instance, when his "Stacy"-ish girlfriend in "Ex-Boyfriend" finally beds him, Dicky concludes their sex by rapping that "I pulled out and nutted all over her left thigh."[131] This grotesque lyric softly echoes a common pornographic trope, in which men ejaculate on women's bodies (especially faces) to express disdain. This practice holds special salience in manospheric fantasies: in manospheric rhetoric, "recurrent themes" include "ejaculating in women's faces, eyes and other orifices," and "vomiting, spitting, ejaculating and urinating on women."[132] Unlike these openly violent fantasies, Dicky keeps his aggression stealthier in "Ex-Boyfriend" by ejaculating on his girlfriend's thigh rather than face. And like all Dicky's Jewface comedy, his grotesque ejaculation comes off as harmless by degrading himself, too. On one hand, this lyric mirrors manospheric and mainstream misogynist fantasies to punish the "Stacy" who has "withheld" sex from Dicky. On the other, it extends Dicky's self-degrading Jewface persona as a grotesque, leaky, sexually impotent body.

This ambivalent cum joke exemplifies how an "aesthetics of the grotesque" always aids Lil Dicky to perform comedic abject hegemony: to both embody white male "victimhood" and unleash white male rage in humorous guise. Kathleen Rowe has coined "aesthetics of the grotesque" to describe how women comedians can weaponize raunchy physical transgressions to shatter the social limits of submissive femininity—for instance, asserting women's right to gleefully guzzle, flatulate, and fuck.[133] Conversely, Lil Dicky practices an *anti-feminist* aesthetics of the grotesque that comedically stigmatizes and punishes women. To this end, he self-consciously links his Jewface with orifices and excreta that symbolize contamination. For instance, in "Grimy as a Gooch" (2013),[134] Dicky compares his Jewfaced body to a "gooch," slang for the skin between the testes and anus, where sexual sweat and fecal residue comingle. The lyrics proclaim that he enjoys "[l]ickin' grease off of that pizza," that his "sack" (scrotum) smells "appalling," and that he commonly falls "asleep before I brush my teeth." This grotesque imagery invokes historical hysteria about the polluting power of Jewish bodily fluids and orifices.

By packaging his Jewfaced body as grotesque (reeking, oozing, grimy), Lil Dicky can better unleash-and-absolve straight white-privileged men's backlash fantasies. First, his grotesquery functions similarly to the bloody brutality of *Fight Club*: it misrepresents Dicky (and any white-privileged man who identifies with him) as a wretched victim. Further, Dicky's extreme grotesquery casts his vignettes as ridiculous fantasies too absurd to take seriously. For example, when freestyling to impress a Black gentile rapper in *Dave*'s pilot, Dicky raps that "I menstruate,"[135] echoing (however inadvertently) the medieval myth that Jewish men-struate as punishment for crucifying Jesus.[136] Exemplifying how stigmas of Jews' and women's filth overlap, this myth enhanced the wider image of Jewish men as grotesquely feminized, perverse, unnatural bodies. In Dicky's lyrics, this image sounds so bizarre and so wildly repulsive that it casts his comedy as meaningless nonsense. This impression pulls a veil of absurdity even over his most misogynist and racist ethical transgres-sions, like raping his wife in "Lemme Freak." Additionally, Dicky *pivots* the presumed target of Jewish filth. Antisemites (like the aforementioned neo-Nazi Chris Cantwell) have historically accused Jews of contaminat-ing and perverting all white gentiles. Instead, Dicky's grotesque fluids "comedically" aggress against women on behalf of all white-privileged men, like when he "nuts" on his girlfriend in "Ex-Boyfriend."

Moreover, to "comedically" demonize and punish women, Lil Dicky casts himself as the frightened victim of women's allegedly grotesque, polluting bodies. In Dicky's work, male sexual filth is "good" because it transmits misogynist aggression, while women's supposed sexual filth is "bad" because it symbolizes the threat of unrestricted, dominant, masculinized women. And Dicky's grotesque rhetoric about women's bodies mirrors the manosphere's. Just as manospheric slang obsesses about ejaculating, urinating, and defecating on women, this slang fixates on the fear of "engorged, deformed or putrid female genitalia," with special disgust for "unshaven female genitalia."[137] These themes arise in Dicky's first hit, "Ex-Boyfriend," when he calls his girlfriend "hot as hell," partly because her "vagina [is] shaven and it don't smell."[138] This praise invokes the threatening specter of a monstrously hairy and smelly vagina, unrestrained by men's preferences.

When using grotesquery to demonize women, Lil Dicky also mirrors manospheric rage against women who pursue sex.[139] This disgust for sexually active women may seem to contradict manospheric rage against "withholding" women—but both attitudes vilify women for controlling their own sexuality. To comedically vilify sexually active women, Dicky sometimes pairs tropes of neurotic Jewish emasculation with rhetoric about women's "polluting" (grotesque) bodies. For instance, the same *Newsweek* article that dubs him "The Jerry Seinfeld of Rap" quotes Dicky as stating that he is "very, very, very concerned with STDs."[140] This fear of sexual contamination helps Dicky cast himself as an overwhelmed victim while actually slut-shaming women: when telling *Newsweek* that he refuses sexual offers from female fans, he calls two such women "disgusting" and wonders "what kind of STDs does a girl like that have?" This slut-shaming translates the manosphere's blatant rage about women's sexual autonomy into palatable comedy about Dicky's neurotic Jewish fear of sex. Like Dicky's narratives about sexual aggression, though, these narratives about fearing sex weaponize grotesquery to convey misogynist rage and terror.

"He Cannot Say It": "Black Privilege," "Political Correctness," and Black Masculinity

While Lil Dicky's soft deplorable satire casts white gentile women as "Stacys" who sexually threaten or deprive him, it casts Black gentile men as "Chads" who disenfranchise him from full masculinity. Although incels disdain "Chads" as brutes, many incels also envy Chads' masculinity and covet Chads' supposed sexual monopoly over women. Using vicarious Jewface, Dicky's soft deplorable satire synthesizes these incel resentments with America's racist narratives that disdain-yet-envy Black men's alleged hypermasculinity. By channeling this resentment against Black men as Chads, Dicky stokes the broader myth of "Black privilege," without using that phrase. This myth, popularized by conservative Internet pundits in the 2010s, claims that Blackness has become a "tremendous asset" while "whites struggle daily against the indignities heaped upon them because of their skin color."[141]

When Dicky channels this "Black privilege" myth, he mirrors two of the strongest bridges that link the manosphere with mainstream American society: shared grievances about "political correctness" and about Black hypermasculinity. Dicky often conveys both grievances by lamenting his "exclusion" from saying the N-word. Online "Black Privilege Checklists" often bewail that "Blacks can call white people 'honky' and 'cracker,' but whites cannot use the N-word."[142] This grievance ignores how the N-word crystallizes white Americans' racist power over Black Americans. It also extends the wider myth that any effort to reduce public bigotry constitutes "politically correct" censorship that wrongfully muzzles free speech.[143] While this misplaced resentment against "political correctness" permeates American society, it is especially central to manospheric and white nationalist ideologies: lambasting "politically correct censorship" is a primary method by which these communities label themselves "dispossessed."[144] Dicky's soft deplorable satire wavers between ridiculing and endorsing this white outrage about "political correctness" in general and about how Black people "monopolize" the N-word in particular. His rap "All K" (2013) exemplifies this mixed message by (satirically?) lamenting that "the N word is the most commonly uttered noun in hip hop. But he cannot say it."[145] This line resonates with Dicky's self-description as "the voice of the voiceless" in "Really Scared" (2014),[146] which further evokes the myth that political correctness is unjustly censoring (straight white men's) free speech. And in "All K," this supposed censorship interlaces with Dicky's "exclusion" from Black masculinity. Right after lamenting that "he cannot say" the N-Word, the video laments that this inability heightens his "struggle for acceptance" as a "mild-mannered Jewish boy" in "a rap landscape littered with hardened criminals, hypermasculinity, and irrational swagger." As this example suggests, Lil Dicky's narratives about "Black privilege" express aggrieved envy not just about the *words* that Black people supposedly monopolize, but also the *physical traits*: cool, sexy, tough hypermasculinity. Yet Dicky simultaneously conveys disdain, fear, and outrage for the "criminal" Black men who allegedly monopolize rap stardom. His depictions of "Black privilege" thus fuse incels' envy and disdain for brutish "Chads" with white-privileged Americans' widespread envy and disdain for Black masculinity.

This envy-and-disdain for the "privileges" of Black speech and masculinity fuel an even more sensationalized plotline in Dicky's most popular single to date: the 2018 video "Freaky Friday,"[147] which boasts 745 million YouTube views. In turn, "Freaky Friday" illustrates how mainstream envy of/disdain for Black masculinity reflect the same ideologies that have fueled past and present racist violence. The video takes its title from a twice-remade comedy film (1976/1995/2003) in which a white gentile mother and daughter swap bodies via enchanted fortune cookies. Dicky's racier version shows him swap bodies with Chris Brown, a Black gentile pop star who enjoys great success despite infamously abusing fellow pop star Rihanna in 2009. Dicky thus enacts what critical race scholar Lauren Michele Jackson has termed "digital blackface,"[148] while Chris Brown enacts digital Jewface. When analyzing "Freaky Friday," Leonard Stein has written that this body swap enables Dicky to "enjoy the various cultural privileges of Blackness," like using the N-word.[149] However, this phrasing inadvertently affirms the myth of "Black privilege." Instead, I clarify that Dicky's body swap channels white men's enraged envy about *imaginary* "Black privilege," Black hypermasculinity, and "political correctness."

As we have seen, "Freaky Friday" opens with a butch white gentile Dickhead (Jimmy Tatro) embarrassing Lil Dicky in a Chinese restaurant, by praising him as a "funny rapper" who "raps about how small his dick is." Since Tatro's character is a prototypical "Chad" who humiliates Dicky, he seems a natural target for Dicky's incel-ish resentment—but Dicky reroutes his resentment toward *Black* gentile men instead. Gazing at TV coverage of Chris Brown, Dicky laments, "Dude, everybody else in hip hop is so much cooler than me." As the TV depicts Chris Brown dancing and revealing his tattoos, Dicky continues, "People are so good at dancing, or they've got the sickest tattoos. Sometimes, I really wish I could be somebody else." Echoing past performances like

"All K," these lines convey that Dicky specifically wants to be *Black*, which would supposedly grant him coolness and dance skills. By yearning for Black people's alleged dance prowess, Dicky echoes the long racist history of white Americans who objectify or impersonate Black people as lively entertainment while abusing them offstage. For instance, Dicky's lament presages dialogue from Spike Lee's 2018 drama *BlacKkKlansman*, which premiered two months later. In *BlacKkKlansman*, as three Klansmen plot violence against "n****rs," one laughs, "I'll say this, though, they can *dance*."[150] In other words, he hates Black people but enjoys having them dance for his entertainment. And since the Klansmen accuse Black men of (in their words) "savagely raping" white women, *BlacKkKlansman* highlights how the primitivistic tropes that cast Black people as exuberant dancers also cast them as dangerous savages, thus "justifying" Black violability.[151] In "Freaky Friday," Lil Dicky articulates these very sentiments, but in a seemingly harmless comedic plot about his own Jewfaced emasculation. And Dicky obtains his racist desire when Chris Brown mentions on the restaurant's TV that he also wishes to "be somebody else for a day." Granting both wishes, the Chinese restaurant owner magically body-swaps the stars, so that Dicky awakes the next morning in Chris Brown's body.

This digital blackface exhilarates Lil Dicky by finally granting him the free speech and hypermasculinity that Black "Chads" allegedly monopolize. Upon entering Chris Brown's body, Dicky-in-Chris (played by Chris Brown) admires his tattooed brown arms and the gorgeous white women snoozing on his bed, while rapping (in Chris Brown's voice), "I woke up Chris Breezy / Oh my god, I'm the man!" Experimentally boogying in the mirror, he continues, "I'm so fly and I can dance!" Dicky-in-Chris next thrills to discover lots of "hoes in my DMs" (women messaging him on Twitter) and that "I can sing so well!" Dicky-in-Chris luxuriates in Chris's well-known dance moves, as if test-driving a sports car. He also gleefully looks down his pants to declare, "It's my dream dick!" This plot implies that if only Dicky were a Black "Chad" like Chris Brown, he'd possess ideal masculinity *and* an ideal sex life, with endless Stacy-ish white "hoes." Yet while exploring Brown's house, Dicky-in-Chris gets comedically scared when he discovers a gun. Thus, even when fetishizing Black men as hypermasculine dancers and sex partners, the video fears and disdains Black men as criminals.

Although Lil Dicky delights to access a Black man's penis, dance moves, and white "hoes" in "Freaky Friday," he seems most ecstatic about accessing the N-word. Dicky-in-Chris wonders, "Wait, can I really say the N-word?!" Then, with a euphoric grin, he calls everyone he meets by the N-word and shouts it triumphantly into the sky, repeating the N-word eleven times in eleven seconds. Dicky-in-Chris thus shouts the same slur as *BlacKkKlansman*'s Klansmen and as white nationalists across the Internet, but within an absurdist, upbeat music video about escaping his Jewfaced emasculation. And while *BlacKkKlansman*'s villains explicitly state that they use "n****r" to reassert racial dominance, "Freaky Friday" ignores the slur's abusive function. Instead, Dicky depicts "n***a" (a slightly softened form of the slur)[152] alongside great dancing, hot sex, and large penises as just another fun masculine power that Black men allegedly withhold from white-privileged men—a power that Dicky, on behalf of all white-privileged men, can now freely relish.

"Incredibly Gay": Weaponizing Gayness

When Lil Dicky exclaims in "Freaky Friday" that Chris Brown's penis is "my dream dick!," does he dream of *having* a Black penis or *having sex* with one? This deliberate ambivalence between jealousy and homoeroticism has pervaded Dicky's comedy since his 2013 "Ex-Boyfriend" debut. In that video, after discovering that his (allegedly Black) rival has a massive penis, Dicky kneels to gape in envy, fear, and desire, as though preparing to fellate him.[153] Dicky's ambivalent envy of/lust for Black masculinity has also specifically targeted his fellow millennial Jewish star, Drake. One example comes from Dicky's semi-autobiographical sitcom, *Dave* (2020–2023). In that series, Dicky displays a poster of Drake in his bedroom (suggesting that he desires to be *like* Drake), but also makes eye contact with this poster when orgasming (suggesting that he desires to be *with* Drake).[154]

Across many performances, Dicky's ambivalent homoeroticism helps to camouflage white male victim narratives as harmless comedy. While some straight white male victim narratives vilify LGBTQ+ people,[155] Dicky never presents LGBTQ+ villains. Instead, he constantly links himself with gayness in ways that mirror manospheric contradictions. In the manosphere, "[w]hile homophobic language is rife, the culture is generally accepting of homosexuality, as it is of any sexual expressions that are perceived as transgressive."[156] Evoking similar ambivalence, Dicky vacillates between using "gay" or "faggot" as insults; calling himself "gay" and expressing homoerotic desires; and voicing heterosexual desires. For instance, he raps in "Famous Dude" (2013) that "I'm tryna make the move / From gay, lame, dateless Jew to famous dude."[157] Using "gay" as a synonym for "uncool," this lyric links Dicky's "gay" loser status with Jewishness and (heterosexual) romantic failure. Conversely, on *Funny or Die* in 2016, Dicky nearly expresses gay desire by saying, "I love gay people, I'd be the very first person to admit if I was gay," and then claiming that he obsessively views gay porn just to be sure he's not.[158]

Lil Dicky's disorienting approach to gayness dovetails with his vicarious Jewface to soften his deplorable satire, by sowing further confusion about his intentions. His rap battle against Hitler in "Jewish Flow" (2013)[159] exemplifies how Dicky wields gayness for comedic misdirection. Despite objectifying white gentile "German bitches" as sexual pawns in his battle against Hitler, Dicky repeatedly appears in a shirt that says "Incredibly Gay," with pink triangles like the patches that marked gay prisoners in Nazi concentration camps. By evoking Jewish men's and gay men's shared Holocaust suffering and shared stereotypes (like effeminacy), these pink triangles help Dicky to recruit homophobic stigmas into his emasculated Jewface persona. Further, his gay references in "Jewish Flow" *soften his misogyny*: his self-mockery as "incredibly gay" contradicts his fantasies about impregnating "German bitches" as pawns in his racial contest against Hitler. Throughout Dicky's career, his contradictory gay references similarly distract from his misogyny. These contradictions fuel his image as a perverse yet harmlessly emasculated Jew whose filthy comedy is too absurd to threaten anyone.

Homoeroticism likewise aids Lil Dicky to "comedically" aggress against gentile men of color. Although his homoerotic racial lust and envy look light-hearted in "Freaky Friday," they turn grisly in his series, *Dave*. The first season finale, which Dicky screenwrote, opens with a ten-minute sequence in which he seduces a male Mexican prison inmate—only to chomp off his penis and bloodily spit it out.[160] The episode narratively ties Dicky's anti-Mexican sexual violence to his envy, fear, and desire for Black men: this sexual encounter results from Dicky's failure to win masculine acceptance from Black inmates. This narrative begins when Dicky flashes his scrotum to concertgoers who happen to include teens, landing him in prison for indecent exposure to minors. As Dicky arrives in prison, a guard confirms that he'll likely get raped, and his Black gentile cellmate links this sexual vulnerability to Jewishness: this cellmate rhetorically Jewfaces Dicky by warning that he won't find protection from the white inmates, since they are white supremacists who would "see that you're Jewish, it's evident." Dicky consequently uses his basketball skills (a stereotypical marker of Black masculinity) to bond with Black inmates for protection.

Yet Lil Dicky's masculine success, safety, and access to Blackness vanish when a tough-looking Mexican inmate exaggerates Dicky's crime: he proclaims that Dicky "raped some kids." All the Black and Mexican inmates then unite in brutalizing Dicky, a scene that feels orgiastic as point-of-view-shots show him gazing up from below at a circle of tough brown men. No white supremacist inmates join this violence: as always, Dicky's Jewface distinguishes him from white gentiles only to channel white-privileged men's fear, envy, and desire toward men of color. Realizing that all prisoners now have "the green light" to rape him, Dicky formulates a self-emasculating plan to "offer willing head." However, the only inmate shown accepting this offer is the Mexican man who labeled him a pedophile. Dicky beckons this man into the bathroom, tells him "I'm into it" and kisses him on the neck before pulling out the man's penis, which Dicky links with Blackness by describing it as "so big" and "darker than I expected." In pornographic slow motion, this Mexican inmate grips Dicky's curly Jewish hair and pushes Dicky's head down toward his cock—and only then does *Dave* reveal that this whole ordeal has been an absurdist fantasy: a video concept that Dicky is pitching to his record label. Downplaying this prison plot as an imaginary escapade gives *Dave* permission to show its gruesome climax: Dicky bloodily bites off and spits out his Mexican rapist's penis, which arcs in gory slow motion across the screen.

In this climactic shot of *Dave*'s first season, Lil Dicky eagerly pleasures and inhales a "dark" penis, yet also mutilates and spits out that penis. This bloody homoerotic fantasy crystallizes the ambivalent envy, lust, disdain, fear, and hatred that Dicky has channeled toward Black "Chads" throughout his career. This gore also nearly exposes the historical violence that underlies white-privileged Americans' fixation on

Black penises, including Dicky's lyric in "Freaky Friday" about obtaining a Black "dream dick." Like the Klansmen in *BlacKkKlansman*, white Americans have often "justified" lynching by depicting Black men as animalistic rapists, and lynching often involved sexual torture: between 1890 and 1940, one in three male lynching victims suffered the removal of his penis and/or testicles.[161] Lynchers also harvested their victims' body parts, including penises, as trophies.[162] This grisly violence was white men's long-running technique for possessing the Black penises that they feared and fetishized, as Dicky "dreams" of doing. But by pairing Jewface with grotesque homoerotic humor, *Dave*'s prison sequence manages to repackage this gory sadism as unthreatening self-satire.

Conclusion

By fetishizing, fearing, and bloodily castrating men of color in a tale about Lil Dicky's own Jewfaced emasculation, Dicky's prison fantasy captures the key to his soft deplorable satire. Dicky differentiates his body from white gentile men's by exaggerating antisemitic racial stigmas of emasculation, neurosis, filth, and perversion—but only to better embody all white-privileged men's alleged victimhood in twenty-first-century America. In turn, Dicky vicariously voices straight white-privileged men's resentment, fear, lust, envy, and aggression toward the minoritized people who allegedly wrong them. This vicarious Jewface specifically bridges the manosphere's grievances, tones, and tropes with mainstream white male backlash. Dicky's soft deplorable satire thus amplifies beliefs that fuel real-world violence, and it may specifically "redpill" audiences toward far-right dogma. Yet this ideological labor depends precisely on the antisemitic stigmas that cause far-right extremists to violently target Jews like Dicky himself.

The next chapter turns to Lil Dicky's fellow millennial Jewish YouTubers-turned-network-TV-stars, Abbi Jacobson and Ilana Glazer. Although they cameo in Dicky's 2015 rap video "$ave Dat Money,"[163] Jacobson and Glazer usually invert Dicky's comedy by striving to promote feminist, queer, and antiracist liberation.

3

Ecstatic Jewessface

Blending Feminist, Queer, and Racist/Antiracist
Fantasies with Abbi Jacobson and Ilana Glazer

"Two Jewesses Tryin' to Make a Buck"

"We're just two Jewesses tryin' to make a buck."[1] So declare Abbi Jacobson (b. 1984) and Ilana Glazer (b. 1987) in the 2014 pilot of *Broad City*, their prime time debut.[2] On *Broad City*, this comedy duo plays alter egos called "Abbi Abrams" (Abbi Jacobson) and "Ilana Wexler" (Ilana Glazer), whom the stars describe as "15% exaggerations of themselves."[3] Loosely based on their creators, these leading "Jewesses" are underemployed, sexually fluid, politically progressive, conditionally white Jewish millennial stoner best friends in their mid-twenties, romping around New York City. To mark the faint line between actors and characters, I distinguish the stars by surname and their madcap alter egos by first name. Jacobson and Glazer, like the millennial Jewish rapper Lil Dicky, are "open TV"[4] stars who proved their marketability on social media before approaching industry gatekeepers. The duo initiated *Broad City* with homemade webisodes on YouTube and Facebook in 2009–2011, charming veteran comedian Amy Poehler.[5] When Poehler brought the show to Comedy Central in 2014, *Broad City* instantly "attracted blazing devotees"[6] and ran strong for five seasons. It also drew A-list guest stars like then presidential candidate Hillary Clinton and millennial Jewish film star Seth Rogen. This success elevated Jacobson and Glazer from digital underdogs to industry insiders, even winning them contracts to produce three new Comedy Central series.[7] And although *Broad City* has ended, it continues to define the duo's star texts as their first, longest, best-known work.

Figure 3.1. *Judith and the Head of Holofernes* (Gustav Klimt, 1901), analysis beginning on p. 128. Image from www.Gustav-Klimt.com.

Figure 3.2. *Salomé* (Henri Regnault, 1870), analysis
beginning on p. 131.
Image from the website of the Metropolitan Museum
of Art.

From *Broad City*'s first moments, "Jewess" identity proved queerly
(oddly) central to the pair's self-marketing: when Abbi and Ilana need
quick cash for concert tickets in the pilot episode, Ilana advertises semi-
nude housekeeping on Craigslist with the aforementioned headline
about "Two Jewesses Tryin' to Make a Buck."[8] Since this header can describe Jacobson and Glazer's hustle to create *Broad City* as much as their
characters' hustle for cash, it markets the stars (not just their alter egos)
as *Jewesses*. This "Jewess" self-marketing startles because the word is so
outdated that few today even remember it. It also startles because Jewish

Figure 3.3. Ilana Glazer on *Broad City*, 2019. Image analyzed below.
Screenshot from *Broad City*, season 5, episode 8, "Sleep No More," aired March 14, 2019, on Comedy Central. Pulled from Amazon.com.

performers historically face pressure to keep Jewish identity discreet, to avoid alienating white gentile audiences.[9]

Indeed, self-marketing as "Jewesses" sharply distances Jacobson and Glazer from America's long lineage of Jewish "unruly women."[10] The term "unruly women," coined by feminist media scholar Kathleen Rowe,[11] describes comedic women stars and characters who shatter restrictive, dainty, passive models of femininity. To reject those social limitations, unruly women flaunt a bawdy "aesthetics of the grotesque": rather than silencing, starving, and submitting themselves for men's pleasure, they gleefully guzzle, cackle, fuck, and/or defecate.[12] Earlier unruly Jewish women like Fanny Brice, Sophie Tucker, Joan Rivers, Barbra Streisand, Gilda Radner, Fran Drescher, and Sarah Silverman almost never self-marketed as "Jewesses." The few who have touched this word did so fleetingly rather than making it their hallmark, such as when Gilda Radner used "Jewess" in a single, obscure 1980 *Saturday Night Live* sketch.[13] Meanwhile, Jacobson and Glazer's most direct sitcom foremother faced pressure to erase Jewishness onscreen, foreclosing the sensationally Jewish term "Jewess." We have seen that when Fran Drescher launched *The Nanny* (1993–1999), America's first sitcom starring an openly Jewish woman New Yorker, sponsors pressured her to restyle the protagonist as Italian.[14] Although Drescher refused, *The Nanny* still often "double-coded"[15] Jewishness, using clichéd mannerisms to imply Jewishness without actually saying "Jew/Jewish."

Self-labeling as "Jewesses" even distances Jacobson and Glazer from fellow millennial Jewish unruly women like Rachel Bloom, Lena Dunham, Amy Schumer, Jenny Slate, Natasha Lyonne, and Julie Klausner. On one hand, the scholars Shaina Hammerman and Samantha Pickette have each classified these stars (including Jacobson and Glazer) as part of an unprecedented cohort of unapologetically Jewish and rebellious women comedians.[16] This Jewish cohort extends a multiethnic wave of unruly women who unabashedly asserted their minoritized identities in the 2010s, including Issa Rae, Mindy Kaling, and Awkwafina. Yet even Jacobson and Glazer's millennial Jewish peers use only *present-day* terminology to forefront Jewishness, such as when Rachel Bloom (Glazer's former roommate)[17] raps about being a "Jewish American Princess."[18] Only Jacobson and Glazer flourish the sensational and archaic term "Jewess."

Ecstatic "Jewessface"

Although this outdated and flamboyantly Jewish label seems bound to alienate viewers, it actually fuels Jacobson and Glazer's allure on *Broad City*. Their marketability depends on a new form of racial minstrelsy that I term *Jewessface*, an especially elusive type of subliminal postmodern minstrelsy. This elusiveness reflects the slippery and salacious stigmas that historically smolder around Jewish women. As we have seen, European and American Christian cultures from the thirteenth to the early twentieth century often fetishized Jewish women through a stock figure known as "the beautiful Jewess."[19] By the 19th century, this beautiful Jewess often appeared as a racially exotic temptress who might conceal perverse masculinity behind her hyperfeminine façade.[20] Below we will see how this beautiful Jewess trope historically flickered between masculine and feminine, seductive and repulsive, and white and nonwhite. For now, the point is that this elusive, exotic, mesmerizing image is precisely what Jacobson and Glazer capture through Jewessface.

Because it channels such an elusive trope, Jewessface stays more ethereal than its better-known brother, Jewface. Jewface is an androcentric stage tradition that caricatures Jewishness through concrete physical traits like false noses and beards.[21] Jewface thus reflects antisemitic racial stigmas that despise Jewish men as blatantly uglier than white Christian men.[22] As we have seen, Lil Dicky's subliminal postmodern Jewface subtly extends this tradition: Dicky wields only camera angles and minimal cosmetics to accentuate his beaked nose, greasy brown curls, and oily skin. But even Dicky's subtle minstrelsy still depicts Jewishness as an unequivocally revolting difference, located in tangible traits like a hooked nose. Although women can perform Jewface (like by wearing a fake nose), Jewessface is far harder to pin down. Rather than encrusting Jacobson and Glazer in a greasy Jewface mask, Jewessface swathes them in a *glimmering aura: an iridescent sheen that tickles the eye precisely by eluding crisp coherence.*

In turn, Jacobson and Glazer mirror-yet-invert Lil Dicky's "vicarious Jewface" by offering *vicarious Jewessface* on their sitcom: they style "Abbi and Ilana" as exoticized, seductive-yet-masculinized Jewesses, and vicariously offer this Jewessface to viewers. This vicarious Jewessface exhilarates audiences by providing two self-contradictory fantasies that reflect the beautiful Jewess's historical ambivalence between masculine and feminine, seductive and repulsive, white and nonwhite. First is *the liberatory dream of reconciling "masculine," "filthy," or "perverse" freedoms with glamorous femininity.* Through this synthesis, Jewessface channels the liberatory desire of progressive straight women, queer women, and queer men to break free from misogynist and heteronormative restrictions without being labeled disgusting. American society often accuses these groups of monstrous and filthy masculinity for breaking social norms. For instance, consider the common stigmas that feminists, lesbians, or any assertive women are revoltingly "masculine" (hairy, ugly, and aggressive)[23] or that gay men are filthy by association with anal sex.[24] To defuse these stigmas, Jewessface harnesses the tropes that cast Jewesses as externally seductive no matter what dirty blood, masculine aggression, or perverse sexuality lurks invisibly within. For instance, we will see how Jewessface helps Abbi appear gorgeously feminine even while she dons a dildo to anally penetrate her male partner, thereby glamorizing a stereotypically "masculine," "dirty," and "gay" sexual role. By making liberation look so lovely, Jacobson and Glazer become alluring avatars who invite straight women, queer women, and queer men to joyfully uncensor their own bodies. They thus invert Lil Dicky's anti-feminist Jewface comedy, which vilifies sexually autonomous women.

But Jewessface enmeshes this liberatory gendered and sexual fantasy with a subtly oppressive racial fantasy. This racial fantasy involves *achieving guilt-free antiracist identity while retaining white privilege and retaining unacknowledged racist pleasures,* like sexually fetishizing people of color and appropriating their cultures. This second fantasy depends on the way Jewessface fuses whiteness with nonwhiteness. This fantasy channels the oppressive desire of white-privileged progressive audiences to achieve a pleasurably guiltless but unearned antiracist identity.

Together, these two fantasies invite viewers to fuse subtle racist pleasures with the self-perception of perfect antiracist allyship, perfect feminist liberation, and perfect queer liberation. Jewessface thus offers white-privileged progressive viewers *ecstatic liberation from misogyny, from queerphobia, from white guilt, and supposedly (but not actually) from their own racism.* This ideological labor is what makes the obscure, flamboyantly Jewish term "Jewess" so unexpectedly alluring, fueling Jacobson and Glazer's queer (counterintuitive, gender-bending, and sexually transgressive) glamor on *Broad City.* In turn, this dynamic exemplifies how all forms of subliminal postmodern minstrelsy thrill audiences by helping them to reconcile contradictory fantasies about disrupting/sustaining straight white gentile male supremacy.

And like many forms of subliminal postmodern minstrelsy, Jewessface is so marketably elusive partly because it is *inadvertent.* Jacobson and Glazer seem neither to intend nor to recognize their Jewessface: they have never stated why they use the word "Jewess" nor indicated that they even know the history of "beautiful Jewess" imagery, though we will see how closely they mirror that imagery on *Broad City.* Ideologically, Jewessface seems unintentional because it ambivalently serves/scuttles the duo's stated political aims. Jewessface's liberatory gender and sexual messages affirm the pair's claim that "we're feminists . . . [and] the people who work on the show are feminists."[25] However, Jewessface's racist effects undermine Jacobson's statement that they "really want [*Broad City*] to be extremely inclusive—so we're trying to always have the backs of especially disenfranchised groups."[26] This disconnect puts a twist on the tendency for all postmodern minstrels to camouflage or even *lack* political intentions.[27] As we have seen, such nebulous intentions help to delight audiences by producing ambivalent and deniable messages. Jacobson and Glazer produce even more potent yet palatable contradictions because they *explicitly state* liberatory political goals, but they partly undercut these goals with minstrelsy that they *don't mean* to perform at all. Thanks to these contradictions, Jewessface can even more smoothly help viewers to blend subtly racist pleasures with the pleasures of antiracist allyship, feminist liberation, and queer liberation.

Racialized and Racist/Antiracist Unruly Womanhood

Deciphering Jacobson and Glazer's Jewessface compels new dialogues across scholarship on racism, unruly womanhood, Jewish women's comedy, and female masculinity. For all these fields, Jewessface offers new insights on *racialized unruly womanhood*—my term for comedy in which racially minoritized women harness their own racial stigmas to raunchily disrupt misogynist restrictions. When Kathleen Rowe coined "unruly womanhood" in 1995, she presented the Jewish comedian Roseanne Barr as an exemplar,[28] but did not mention how antisemitic tropes like the seductive-yet-masculinized Jewess might shape Barr's unruliness. Nor did Rowe consider how any racially queer tropes (the nonnormative gender and sexuality projected onto racial outgroups) may shape unruly womanhood.[29] Newer work reveals how racially queer tropes like the "angry Black woman," "fiery Latina," or cunning "Asian tiger mom" fuel distinct types of unruly womanhood—for example, in Wanda Sykes's comedy.[30] However, this work still rarely addresses Jewishness[31] and fully overlooks the beautiful Jewess trope.[32] Inverse silences shape scholarship on Jewish women's comedy. For instance, both Roberta Mock and Hannah Schwadron rightly note how Euro-American Jewish women comedians can harness their racial position between white and nonwhite to perform grotesque gender styles that reject dainty, submissive femininity.[33] Yet neither links this technique with the wider pattern of unruly women who weaponize grotesquery to shatter misogyny. And while Samantha Pickette rightly applies the term "unruly woman" to many millennial Jewish comedians,[34] her focus is not on the way that different racial statuses enable different varieties of unruliness. I newly clarify that *"Jewess" identity produces a racially specific brand of unruly womanhood, uniquely suited to collapsing dichotomies like masculine/feminine, lovely/revolting, white/nonwhite, and racist/antiracist in marketable ways.*

By dissolving these dichotomies, Jewessface newly illustrates an ambivalent relationship between racialized, *racist*, and *antiracist* unruly womanhood. Past scholarship emphasizes how unruly women perform liberatory gender and sexual transgressions. I coin *racist unruly womanhood* to describe how this gendered and sexual liberation can coexist with (or even depend upon) unruly women's oppressive racial transgressions. For example, we will see that Ilana Glazer's sexually liberated Jewessface persona partly depends on objectifying Black men. Yet I will also show that Jewessface fuses such racist transgressions with antiracist critiques, thereby enmeshing racist unruly womanhood with *antiracist unruly womanhood*: unruly women's comedy that challenges racism. This fusion helps white-privileged viewers to *feel* guiltlessly antiracist even while indulging racist pleasures. And this marketable blend of racism/antiracism depends precisely on Jacobson and Glazer's status as racialized unruly women who dissolve the border between white and nonwhite.

Because Jewessface also dissolves the border between masculine/feminine, it likewise illuminates new connections between unruly womanhood and *female masculinity*. Female masculinity is a queer (nonnormative) gender style, first named by Jack Halberstam, in which female bodies enact speech, clothing, grooming, and body language that connote masculinity.[35] Although unruly women in general and Jewesses in particular violate the masculine/feminine binary, scholarship on these figures has not yet integrated Halberstam's lens of female masculinity. Meanwhile, studies on female masculinity usually examine butch women *or* women who strategically flip between butch and femme—such as Gladys Bentley, a Black lesbian Harlem Renaissance star.[36] Conversely, Jewessface packages Jacobson and Glazer as racialized unruly women who *seamlessly blend* "masculine" aggression, filth, and freedom *into* exotic and glamorous femininity.

By clarifying how Jewessface fuses masculinity with femininity and fuses racialized, racist, and antiracist unruly womanhood, I also complicate Hannah Schwadron's scholarship on "sexy Jewess" comedy. Schwadron applies the term "sexy Jewesses" to a recent cohort of Jewish women who harness their ambivalent position inside/outside whiteness to fuel transgressive humor.[37] Within this cohort, Schwadron groups Jacobson and Glazer alongside Sarah Silverman, Sandra Bernhard, Natalie Portman, Mila Kunis, and porn star Joanna Angel. Yet in this cohort, *only* Jacobson and Glazer consistently label themselves "Jewesses" and style their bodies to match historical "Jewess" imagery. Therefore, Jacobson and Glazer simultaneously resonate with fellow "sexy Jewesses" *and* stand apart as twenty-first-century America's sole Jewessface minstrels. This difference leads me to label the duo's minstrelsy differently than Schwadron. When describing how Jacobson, Glazer, and their peers strategically embody antisemitic stigmas, Schwadron deems them all Jewface performers.[38] However, as detailed above, I find that "*Jewess-face*" better describes how Jacobson and Glazer weave "beautiful Jewess" tropes into a shimmering minstrel aura.

In turn, I emphasize how Jewessface reconciles themes that Schwadron deems contradictory. Schwadron writes that "sexy Jewesses" comedically *pivot* between opposite tropes which cast them as lovely white women or revolting nonwhite women.[39] For instance, past scholarship analyzes how Sarah Silverman seesaws between mocking herself as a masculinized and grotesque "hairy Jew" or a "cute white girl."[40] Instead, Jacobson and Glazer's Jewessface *unifies* these poles: they portray the masculinized, aggressive, dirty Jewess as gorgeous, glamorous, and having a blast! Meanwhile, Schwadron writes that sexy Jewesses often use their racial in-betweenness to vacillate between challenging injustice (whether racial, classed, gendered, or sexual) and indulging "the guilty pleasures of whiteness," like cultural appropriation.[41] I clarify how Jacobson and Glazer's Jewessface helps audiences to experience the "guilty pleasures of whiteness" as *guiltlessly compatible* with challenging injustice. This knack for *fusing* (not just wavering between) opposite racial, gendered, and sexual effects is what makes Jewessface so alluring.

Lastly, by analyzing how Jewessface dissolves these dichotomies, I complicate recent scholarship by Taylor Nygaard and Jorie Lagerwey on "horrible white people" comedies (HWPs).[42] "HWPs" describes comedy series from the 2010s that star liberal white people (usually women) who disrupt misogyny and heteronormativity but remain complicit with white supremacy, even while self-critiquing that complicity.[43] In other words, HWPs' women exemplify ambivalently racist/antiracist unruly womanhood. The dozens of HWPs that Nygaard and Lagerwey identify include Jacobson and Glazer's *Broad City*.[44] Despite mentioning that Jewishness complicates whiteness in *Broad City*,[45] the authors never note how Jacobson and Glazer invoke the archaic racial term, "Jewess." By overlooking "Jewessness," Nygaard and Lagerway oversimplify the racial sources and effects of Jacobson and Glazer's unruliness. Though these authors rightly observe that *Broad City*'s protagonists are unruly women who look uncommonly lovable while committing raunchy and/or racist transgressions,[46] Nygaard and Lagerway never link this lovability with Jewessness. Meanwhile, the authors also write that HWPs sometimes play up Jewish outsiderness to downplay white privilege.[47] Instead, we will see that Jewessface's racial ambiguity aids Jacobson and Glazer to *bitingly critique* white privilege, yet to reconcile these critiques with unacknowledged racist pleasures. Nygaard and Lagerwey hint at this effect when noting that *Broad City* outstrips most HWPs in urging viewers to "actively critique" the protagonists' racist missteps.[48] I clarify that *Broad City*'s earnest antiracism often helps to camouflage inadvertent racism, and that this racist/antiracist fusion depends on the stars' racially ambiguous Jewessface. Thus, within Jewessface, racist unruly womanhood paradoxically *relies upon* antiracist unruly womanhood and both rely upon racialized unruly womanhood.

Meeting the Beautiful Jewess

Understanding how Jewessface can fuse so many opposite racial, gendered, and sexual elements first requires better understanding the tantalizing "beautiful Jewess" trope. We have seen that this figure was first recorded circa 1292 in Iberian tales of a Christian king who becomes sexually entranced by a Jewish woman, possibly ensnared by "spells and love magic that she knew."[49] From these early roots, the trope spread across Europe and North America, reaching peak popularity between the eighteenth and early twentieth centuries: it permeated art, literature, theater, opera, and even early Hollywood films like *Romance of a Jewess* (1908).[50] However, "beautiful Jewess" imagery faded from American imaginations across the twentieth century as America reclassified Euro-American Jews from exotic "Orientals" to people usually deemed white.[51] This Jewish re-racialization partly reflected American horror that the Nazis had cited American racial "science" to help justify the

Holocaust.[52] Overnight, American scientific journals that had labeled Jews a "Semitic race" in the 1930s pivoted to preach that all Europeans constitute one white race. Likely due to this re-racialization, the word "Jewess" faded from American usage across the 1940s.[53] And by the 1960s, archetypes of the domineering-but-desexualized "Jewish mother" and "Jewish American Princess" reconfigured the Jewess's improper assertiveness without her dusky exoticism.[54]

During the nineteenth-century peak of "beautiful Jewess" images, this figure flickered thrillingly between masculinity and femininity, seduction and repulsion, whiteness and darkness. This image often took inspiration from, and was retroactively projected onto, biblical characters like Judith, whose name *means* Jewess.[55] As we have seen, Judith famously seduces the enemy general Holofernes only to behead him. She thus reveals "masculine" aggression, deceit, and swordsmanship behind her feminine façade. This seductive-but-masculinized reputation came to characterize many "beautiful Jewess" figures in the nineteenth century. While some beautiful Jewesses appeared as tragic victims awaiting salvation by white gentile heroes,[56] others were threatening "*juives fatales*"[57] who lured Christian men to ruin. These seductive Jewesses stood accused of possessing an exaggerated femininity that was "all show," masking their true masculine "sexual aggressiveness and deceit."[58] Ann Pellegrini thus writes that the "hyperbolic femininity of the beautiful Jewess conceals her perverse masculinity."[59]

This gendered and sexual ambivalence were inseparable from the Jewess's *racial* ambivalence between white and nonwhite. While the thirteenth-century "beautiful Jewess" embodied religious transgression with her sinful-but-sexy "love magic," this trope later merged with new racial stigmas that alienated Jews as "Semites," "Asiatics," or "Orientals." For instance, when the Austrian playwright Franz Grillparzer adapted the original Jewess tale into his 1872 play, *The Jewess of Toledo*, he compared Jewesses' sexuality to an "oriental" plant, "locked up in the hot-house of a harem."[60] This fantasy exemplifies how "beautiful Jewesses" of the eighteenth to early twentieth century often embodied "Eastern exoticism," appearing with "stereotypically dark hair and black eyes" and "serpentine" sexual allure that provoked both desire and revulsion.[61] Gustav Klimt captured this exotic, seductive-but-revolting fantasy in his 1901 painting of the murderous biblical Judith (figure 3.1).[62] Crowned by brown curls, bejeweled with an exotic golden choker and serpentine golden scales, Judith gazes out with post-orgasmic bliss as her breasts peek through translucent gold-embroidered silk—but this titillating siren also brandishes Holofernes's grisly head to one side. Like this painting, the "beautiful Jewess" often seamlessly blended dangerous aggression and nauseating filth with tantalizing, exotic, glittering hyperfemininity.

In fact, the beautiful Jewess's shimmer often *signaled* her thrilling racial ambiguity, and this shimmer shapes Jacobson and Glazer's Jewessface. Like Klimt's painting, Jewess imagery often paired concrete physical traits (like dark curly hair) with an ethereal *shimmer*, an external sheen connoting *internal* racial exoticism. Art historian Carol Ockman explains that European painters created this sheen by swathing Jewesses in "sumptuous color, glittering jewels, and iridescent fabrics" that would have been "shocking" on white gentile women of respectable classes.[63] And this tantalizing sheen could also shine from Jewesses' hair, eyes, and skin. For example, the literary scholar Bryan Cheyette analyzes this intoxicating luster in the 1869 novel, *Phineas Finn*,[64] by Anthony Trollope. One plotline follows a Jewess, Madame Goesler, who seduces a white gentile British duke.[65] The duke's infatuation with Goesler depends on fantasies of placeless racial exoticism that appear in her elusive glossiness: he imagines a "mystery in the very blackness and gloss and abundance of her hair, as though her beauty was the beauty of some world which he had not yet known."[66] But the otherworldly beauty that enthralls the duke horrifies one of his fellow aristocrats, who fears that the couple will spawn a "half-monkey baby, with black, brown and yellow skin."[67] This fear exemplifies how the Jewess's ambivalent blackness/glossiness conveys racial difference that is vivid but imprecise, enthralling yet disgusting.

In the twenty-first century, Jacobson and Glazer's appeal depends on using Jewessface to "disidentify with"[68] (creatively reinhabit) this beautiful Jewess trope: to resurrect and *flip* her from a fetishized object to a riotously laughing subject.

Shimmering Stars: Weaving Gossamer Jewessface through "Jewessface Pedagogy"

Just as Jewessface is more visually and ideologically elusive than Jewface, it also requires greater *instructional labor* in twenty-first-century

America. Because androcentric tropes about emasculated, hook-nosed Jewish men remain well-known, the Jewface rapper Lil Dicky need only teach audiences to envision these tropes on his body. Instead, Jacobson and Glazer address audiences who have largely forgotten the name and image of the beautiful Jewess. This duo must therefore conduct *Jewess-face pedagogy* that reteaches what Jewessness entails *and* teaches viewers to envision Jewessness on the stars' bodies. This pedagogy instructs viewers to perceive "Jewessness" as a self-evident physical trait emanating from Abbi and Ilana's dark hair, slightly olive skin, unladylike antics, and sexual appetites.

Yet to stay marketable, Jewessface pedagogy must ambivalently flaunt-and-*minimize* the racial difference that it constructs. On one hand, Jacobson and Glazer craft Jewessface by amplifying the racial stigmas that historically divide "Jewesses" from white gentile women. But they must also minimize this racial division to attract non-Jewish and assimilated Jewish audiences, who might struggle to identify with such an outdated and vividly Jewish image. By flaunting-and-minimizing Jewess difference this way, Jacobson and Glazer partly mirror Lil Dicky: Dicky crafts his emasculated Jewface from the racial stigmas that historically degrade European Jewish men beneath white gentile men, but he offers that image to all white-privileged men (both Jewish and gentile) as an avatar for their alleged victimhood.

However, this paradoxical offer is smoother for Jacobson and Glazer because the racial stigmas on "beautiful Jewesses" are so *slippery, diaphanous, and evanescent*. When Lil Dicky calls his Jewface persona "white," he is working *against* his sharply caricatured, beak-nosed, greasy, frail, and hunched Jewish male image. Conversely, in white gentile art and literature, "beautiful Jewesses" appear so titillating because their bodily difference is so vivid-yet-*elusive*, like Madame Goesler's ethereal "glossiness." Likewise, Jewessface paints Jewessness as an entrancing-but-slippery iridescence that *never definitively separates* Abbi and Ilana from white gentiles. This opaline aura always simultaneously aligns the duo with Jewess tropes *and* makes those tropes vicariously available to (white) gentile audiences. We will see that Jewessface's elusive gleam is often literal, but can also be metaphorical: the slippery sensation that this duo emanates Jewessness as a physical but unfixed difference.

To produce this gossamer racial aura, Jewessface pedagogy always stays *tacit*: Jacobson and Glazer never acknowledge the historical Jewess imagery that their hair, makeup, clothing, and erotic antics so closely mirror. As noted earlier, they may not even know about this historical imagery. A useful contrast is the vampire mockumentary series *What We Do in the Shadows* (2019–present), which debuted as *Broad City* concluded. *What We Do in the Shadows* directly uses Jewess art to mark its leading vampiress as seductive-but-deadly: the opening credits always superimpose her face onto Henri Regnault's 1870 painting of Salomé,[69] another lethal Jewess temptress from the bible (figure 3.2). Because this painting has resided in New York's Metropolitan Museum of Art since 1916,[70] it could potentially appear in *Broad City*. However, Abbi and Ilana's misadventures around the city never pose them alongside Salomé, nor any such historical imagery that racially divided Jewesses from white gentile women. Whether the duo doesn't know about or just doesn't reference such images, this erasure makes Jewessface more accessible for white and/or gentile viewers to identify with.

To produce Jewessface without referencing historical images, Jewessface pedagogy takes an implicit and two-pronged approach. First, Jacobson and Glazer *rhetorically Jewessface* their characters simply by calling Abbi and Ilana "Jewesses," and by interspersing this word with constant other Jewish references, like quipping about Ilana's rabbi. Second, to reteach what Jewessness *entails*, they *tacitly link the word "Jewess" and their own bodies with present-day symbols of racial exoticism, perverse masculinity, hyperfemininity, hypersexuality, and/or filth*. This tacit Jewessface pedagogy instantly begins in *Broad City*'s pilot. As mentioned above, Ilana pursues quick cash for concert tickets by advertising seminude housekeeping on Craigslist with the salacious headline, "We're Just Two Jewesses Tryin' to Make a Buck."[71] By instructing the audience to perceive Abbi and Ilana as "Jewesses," this startling anachronism inaugurates their rhetorical Jewessface. And by reteaching this word within a smutty sex-work ad, this Craigslist post instantly revives the Jewess's image as a titillating but dirty temptress. However, white gentile men historically objectified Jewesses as fantastical seductresses to excite *themselves*. Instead, Ilana seizes self-authorship to wield Jewessness for her own pleasure (snagging concert tickets). This self-assertion depends on reviving the sense that Jewesses conceal "masculinized" power and aggression behind their seductive façades, an image that makes Abbi and Ilana into liberatory comedic avatars for some women viewers. For example, when their Craigslist john refuses to pay after an hour of semi-nude cleaning, the Jewesses trash his apartment, they seize alcohol and clothing in payment, and finish by riotously laughing at him. In a society that often punishes women for "withholding" the sexual or domestic labor to which men feel entitled,[72] *Broad City*'s Jewesses violently seize compensation for their labor and gleefully refuse men's authority. Thus, by the pilot's conclusion, *Broad City* tutors viewers to perceive Abbi and Ilana as delightfully autonomous Jewesses, whose exoticized, seductive-but-masculinized, filthy and aggressive image serves their own pleasure.

Alongside props like the Craigslist post, Jewessface pedagogy also deploys subtle cosmetics. Ilana's signature look includes wild brown curls that (like Lil Dicky's) reflect cosmetic enhancement. When Jacobson and Glazer initiated *Broad City* as a homemade webseries in 2009, that webseries presented Glazer's hair in flat waves. By contrast, just as the 2014 Comedy Central pilot inaugurated their use of the word "Jewess," it also inaugurated Ilana's cloudlike curls, which constitute cosmetic Jewessface. *Broad City* later fuses cosmetic with rhetorical Jewessface by verbally instructing viewers to link Ilana's curls with Jewishness. For instance, Ilana quips in season 4 that "I look like a true Jew if I don't straighten" my hair.[73]

Accentuating this cosmetic and rhetorical Jewessface, Jewessface pedagogy also sometimes deploys *vestiary* Jewessface: costumes that mirror the golden, sheer, flickering fashions that served to Orientalize Jewesses in historical paintings like Regnault's *Salomé*. This vestiary Jewessface jointly radiates a *literal* and *metaphorical* Jewessface aura—it makes the leading ladies literally shimmer like nineteenth-century Jewess characters, and this shimmer metaphorically evokes the beautiful Jewess's entrancing racial difference. For example, the 2019 episode "Sleep No More" costumes Ilana in a translucent plastic coat with golden scales flickering beneath (figure 3.3), which mirrors the translucent silks and golden scales of Gustav Klimt's 1901 Judith portrait.[74] This costume makes Ilana literally gleam gold while swathing her in the beautiful Jewess's titillating, serpentine, Orientalized allure.

It's no fluke that these cosmetic and vestiary Jewessface examples spotlight Ilana rather than Abbi. To magnetize viewers by flaunting-and-minimizing Jewessface, each "Jewess" performs slightly different versions of Jewessface. These differences produce a *doubling* effect that intensifies the duo's overall Jewessface aura, while keeping that Jewessface relatable to gentile audiences.

Doubling, Flaunting, and Minimizing Jewessface

This doubling effect always positions Abbi as the slightly staider straight-woman because her Jewessface stays subtler. This difference accentuates Ilana's Jewessface, but also positions Abbi as a relatable midpoint with whom viewers can identify. This doubling effect begins in the first seconds of *Broad City*'s 2014 pilot. Abbi first appears holding a massive vibrator labeled "7AM," implying that she takes masturbation seriously enough to schedule it.[75] As a sexually autonomous woman with straight brown hair, faintly olive skin, and her own (plastic) penis, Abbi subtly invokes imagery of seductive-yet-masculinized Jewesses—but Ilana instantly extremifies that imagery. Ilana Skypes Abbi mid-coitus to invite her to the concert that will soon prompt Ilana's "Jewess" ad. As Ilana gyrates, her brown curls tickle her bare olive-toned shoulders, her skin a shade darker than Abbi's. Thus, especially when juxtaposed against Abbi, Ilana uncannily matches historical depictions of the dusky, serpentine Jewess with curly black or "brown hair flowing over her naked shoulders."[76]

While this doubling effect sharpens Ilana's Jewessface, it also makes Abbi a relatable conduit through whom viewers can embrace the more outrageous Ilana. Indeed, during the pair's first Skype call, Abbi provides the more relatable eyes through which viewers first experience Ilana's extreme Jewessness. Ilana initially seems just to be dancing as they chat, until the Skype camera dips to reveal her partner Lincoln's stomach between her thighs. Viewers experience this revelation through a point-of-view shot from Abbi's perspective, as if seeing Ilana on our own Skype screens, before Abbi gasps, "Oh my *god!* Is that Lincoln?! Is he *inside* you?!" The camera thus positions viewers *as* Abbi, and viewers are sucked alongside her into Ilana's wild antics. Minutes later, when Ilana's "Jewess" Craigslist ad rhetorically Jewessfaces Abbi, it invites into vicarious Jewessface the viewers who find Abbi more relatable because she's slightly less lewd and less visibly Jewish. Indeed,

Abbi's rhetorical Jewessface is always passive: she never speaks the word "Jewess," but several times gets labeled such by others. Like her straighter hair, lighter skin, and slightly staider sexual decorum, Abbi's passive rhetorical Jewessface always makes her a conduit through which to identify with Ilana's more extravagant rhetorical, cosmetic, and vestiary Jewessface.

The duo's doubling effect also helps to paint them as *racially protean* (ever shifting), thus *intensifying* their elusive Jewessface aura while keeping that aura *accessible* to white gentile viewers. As we have seen, racial proteanism differs from Drake's "racial chameleonism," which entails switching between many different minstrel personae. Instead, racial proteanism entails crafting one single minstrel persona that appears racially liquid, multiple, and elusive,[77] such as when Lil Dicky unpredictably labels his Jewface character a (nonwhite) greasy kike, a (conditionally white) neurotic Jewish boy, or a generic white boy. Abbi Jacobson and Ilana Glazer's Jewessface proves even more vividly, dizzyingly, and multidirectionally protean.

To produce this racial proteanism, Jacobson and Glazer first erratically depict their characters as visibly Jewish or visibly white. For instance, in one episode, a bowling alley manager visually pegs Abbi and Ilana as "you! The Jews!" but soon after mocks them as "white trash."[78] He thus reminds viewers to paradoxically perceive the Jewesses as visibly Jewish *and* visibly white. This paradoxical racialization resonates with the way that Lil Dicky ambivalently labels himself a "white boy"/"kike boy."[79]

Jacobson and Glazer further enhance their racial proteanism through their doubling effect: to intensify their racial elusiveness, they kaleidoscopically *align and divide* their two racial statuses. For example, the aforementioned bowling alley scene aligns both Jewesses as equally racially protean, since they flow together between whiteness and nonwhiteness. Conversely, the series sometimes racially *juxtaposes* Abbi against Ilana to create confusion about what traits "should" make Jewessness visible, rendering the pair even more racially protean. On one hand, Ilana repeatedly deems Abbi's nose too small for a "full Jew," while tapping her own nose for contrast.[80] Thus, Ilana sometimes rhetorically excludes Abbi from Jewessface to rhetorically Jewessface herself. However, *both women actually have small, straight noses* that contradict antisemitic stereotypes. *Broad City* thus disorientingly activates-and-undercuts stereotypes for spotting Jewishness. Similar contradictions encircle both Jewesses' skin and hair. Regarding skin tone, Ilana's complexion unpredictably appears identical to or a shade darker than Abbi's, fueling ambiguity about whether the two share one racial status and about whether Jewesses are visually distinct from white women. Further, although Abbi and Ilana both embody tropes of dark brown Jewish hair, only Ilana's hair bears cosmetic and rhetorical Jewessface: as mentioned above, *Broad City* optimizes her curls and verbally equates them with Jewishness. However, Abbi's straight brown hair destabilizes this link between curliness and Jewessness, implying that Jewesses might be indistinguishable from white gentile women. This racial proteanism makes the duo's Jewessface aura even more vivid-yet-elusive, and thus more widely accessible.

To make the duo even more racially protean, and thus make their Jewessface more intense-but-nebulous, *Broad City* sometimes *inverts* its reading of Abbi: it contradicts Ilana's claim that Abbi is less visibly Jewish and it links Abbi with placeless racial ambiguity. For example, Ilana herself rhetorically Jewessfaces Abbi in the pilot by dubbing them *both* "Jewesses" on Craigslist.[81] Further, other characters (like the aforementioned bowling alley manager) visually peg both as Jewish. And *Broad City* spotlights Abbi's racial ambiguity when she visits a dermatologist (Korean American actress Greta Lee), who brags that "I can make you whiter."[82] The camera then literalizes Abbi's racial in-betweenness as she nervously glances left to skin-lightening ads for Black and Latina women, glances right to a creepy image of white blond twins, and finally looks straight on at her Asian American doctor to decline. Refusing to cement her whiteness, Abbi instead sits between white, brown, black, and "yellow" racial categories, just like Trollope's Madame Goesler.[83] By highlighting Abbi's slightly olive complexion and the conflicting racial narratives about Jewishness, this sequence rhetorically and cinematographically Jewessfaces her. And by contradicting Abbi's typical "whiter" image, this effect further blurs the boundary between Jewessness and gentile whiteness. Such proteanism always makes the duo's pearlescent Jewessface aura more intense yet more accessible to white and/or gentile viewers.

However, just because wide-ranging audiences *can* identify with Abbi and Ilana's Jewessface doesn't explain why so many viewers would *crave* and *enjoy* that identification so passionately.

Ecstatic Feminist and Queer Liberation

As previewed above, Jewessface elates some audiences by offering a thrilling model of gendered and sexual liberation for straight women, queer women, and queer men: *a model that reconciles "masculine," "filthy," or "perverse" freedoms with gorgeous femininity*. A prime example of how Jewessface glamorizes gender and sexual liberation is the aforementioned episode in which Abbi straps on a dildo to anally penetrate her male neighbor, Jeremy,[84] a sex act known as "pegging." This scene provocatively confronts viewers with Abbi's female masculinity: her dildo dangles before the camera in a risqué close-up (figure 3.4). Abbi's pegging thus capsizes heteronormative narratives that define penises and penetration as men's exclusive domain and as "proof" that men are biologically opposite from and superior to women.[85] Because pegging disrupts heteronormativity, many Americans might judge Abbi's actions not only "masculine," but also "unnatural" or "disgusting"—yet Jewessface reframes Abbi's penetrative anal sex act as lovely and lovable.

To beautify pegging through Jewessface, this plotline interweaves with a narrative about the shiva (Jewish mourning ceremony) for Ilana's late Grandma Esther. Esther's name links her with the biblical Jewess *Queen Esther*, who famously uses her beauty to gain sexual and political sway over a non-Jewish king. *Broad City* explicitly ties Abbi's pegging to the legacy of Grandma Esther, and thus tacitly to the legacy of the Jewess Queen Esther. For example, Ilana urges Abbi to peg in Grandma Esther's memory: she reminds Abbi that "we are going to my grandmother's shiva!" today, and then asks, "You wanna go to the grave dreaming of Jeremy's hairy, adorable little butthole? Or do you wanna die knowing you brought him pleasure by *plowin' it like a queen?*" (my emphasis). This rant about Grandma Esther rhetorically reconciles Abbi's masculine "plowing" of a "hairy butthole" with "queenly" femininity, an adjective that further evokes the Jewess Queen Esther. Ilana thereby presents Abbi as Queen Esther's erotic heir: seductive

Figure 3.4. A close-up of Abbi's dildo confronts viewers with her female masculinity in the episode "Knockoffs" (2014).
Screenshot from *Broad City*, season 2, episode 4, "Knockoffs," aired February 4, 2015, on Comedy Central. Pulled from Amazon.com.

and glamorous even while wearing a plastic penis. And this rhetorical Jewessface renders Abbi not just lovely but *lovable* because Ilana calls Jeremy's anus "adorable," thereby reframing anal sex from grotesque to sweet.

Jewessface further glamorizes Abbi's masculinized, queer-coded, and "dirty" sex act when Abbi reaches the shiva post-pegging. Ilana's mother praises Abbi as a "high-class Jewess" for her lovely purse (a classic feminine symbol) even while holding Abbi's dildo in her other hand. This combination Jewessfaces Abbi as a glamorous figure who seamlessly blends crass, perverse, masculine freedoms with classy femininity. The ensuing dialogue also spotlights the gay male connotations of Abbi's transgression, and it disrupts heteronormative judgments. When Ilana's father ponders that pegging sounds like "more of a gay thing," Ilana joins her gay brother in edifying their father, the shiva guests, and the audience that "straight men and gay men alike both enjoy prostate stimulation." This shiva sequence thus aligns the Jewesses with gay men as people who may not only relish forbidden anal sex, but also actively destigmatize it. Thus, even as the connotations of gay anal sex embellish

Abbi's Jewessface (by marking her as filthy and perversely masculinized), her Jewessface also glamorizes and affirms that transgressive gay masculinity.

This knack for making gender and sexual transgression look so lovely is always a key reason why Jewessface thrills straight women, queer women, and queer men viewers. And Jewessface's vivid-but-elusive nature helps audiences to digest this exhilarating model of liberation without noticing, or feeling alienated by, Jewessface itself. The *New Yorker's* Emily Nussbaum captures this tendency to adore the duo for making gendered and sexual liberation look so lovely, yet to overlook how this synthesis depends on Jewessface. Nussbaum praises *Broad City* as "sweetly liberatory" thanks to Jacobson and Glazer's "compassionate take on shit and sex, [their] insistence that bodies out of control are hilarious and lovely, not dirty and grotesque."[86] Despite this gender- and race-neutral phrasing, the duo actually wields *Jewessface* to present uncontrolled *women's* and/or *queer* bodies as "hilarious and lovely" even when unleashing masculinized, non-heteronormative antics like "shit and sex."

While Nussbaum intellectually appreciates this synthesis, many think pieces convey how it *viscerally exhilarates* viewers and invites them to vicariously identify with Abbi and Ilana. One exemplar is the 2019 *Vulture* think piece "*Broad City* Encouraged Women to Be Their Grossest, Truest Selves,"[87] by the millennial conditionally white Jewish author Caitlin Wolper. Linking sordid "grossness" with lofty "truth," this title frames Jacobson and Glazer's filthiest antics as lovely invitations to women's liberation. Making this theme explicit, Wolper writes that "by brashly delight[ing] in all things icky," the duo encouraged women to "live life freely" rather than anxiously censoring their bodies into sanitized "sexual objects" for men. Most strikingly, Wolper writes of Abbi and Ilana that women "*peer into their toilet bowls and see ourselves reflected in the water*" (my emphasis). This quip transmutes foul toilet water into an alluring magic mirror that vicariously links women viewers with Jacobson and Glazer, thus freeing women to "delight" in their "truest selves." Wolper thus imitates the way Jacobson and Glazer synthesize "vulgar" freedoms with gorgeous glamor—and that synthesis always depends on their Jewessface.

Just as Wolper adores Jacobson and Glazer as avatars who free women from misogyny, many embrace them as avatars who free queer women and queer men from heteronormativity. Although only Jacobson came out as bisexual during *Broad City*'s run,[88] Glazer's more erotically adventurous character has become a bisexual icon. For example, *Huffington Post*'s Jenavieve Hatch (a white-privileged woman) writes that "Ilana from *Broad City* Taught Me to Be Unapologetically Bi," that "Ilana has *become my community*," and that she "has helped me to see the absolute *beauty* in my identity" (my emphasis).[89] Meanwhile, Mike Albo (a white gentile gay man) has effusively praised *Broad City* in *Out*, America's widest-read LGBTQ+ magazine. In 2016, Albo proclaimed *Broad City* "the greatest show on television" and deemed Jacobson and Glazer "candid, over-the-top, bold but vulnerable, and sex-positive—the kind of women gay men tend to relate to because their lives *seem to mirror our own*" (my emphasis).[90] Both think pieces capture how white-privileged queer men and women (including gentile ones) counterintuitively see themselves in *Broad City*'s Jewesses, and adore Jacobson and Glazer for this affirming reflection.

All these accolades reveal how Jewessface serves as a magic mirror that bestows gorgeous, joyful, unbridled self-actualization on straight women, queer women, and queer men. However, Jewessface also offers a funhouse mirror to white-privileged progressive audiences: it helps these viewers to inaccurately see themselves as guiltless antiracists while retaining white privilege and unacknowledged racist pleasures.

"Hyper-whiteguiltiness" and Ecstatic Racist/Antiracist Self-Actualization

Jewessface offers this racist/antiracist self-actualization to white-privileged viewers by curing both white guilt and what I call *white meta-guilt*. White guilt is guilt for receiving and perpetuating white privilege.[91] White *meta-guilt* is guilt for yearning to *shuck* white guilt rather than productively *confront* racism. This meta-guilt is rife among white-privileged antiracists who are too knowledgeable about racism to deny their white privilege. A perfect example of white meta-guilt appeared in the *New York Times* advice column in 2018, in a letter titled "How Can I Cure My White Guilt?"[92] Under the pseudonym "Whitey," the college-aged author writes that "I'm riddled with shame. White shame. *This isn't helpful to me or to anyone, especially people of color.* . . . I consider myself an ally. . . . *I take courses that will further educate me.* I donated to Black Lives Matter. Yet I fear that nothing is enough" (my emphasis). This letter reveals a well-informed, proactive antiracist who nevertheless self-criticizes for experiencing white guilt that "isn't helpful to anyone." "Whitey" thus captures the way white-privileged antiracists often waver between desiring to shed white guilt and despising that very desire. The latter self-disdain is white meta-guilt. For white-privileged antiracists who do-and-don't yearn to cure their white guilt, Jacobson and Glazer's racially exotic Jewessface offers to absolve both guilts, without giving up white privilege or racist pleasures.

This contradictory cure entails packaging Ilana, the more vividly Jew-essfaced character, as both an *exotic aspirational figure* and a *white butt of derision*. Hannah Schwadron has observed that Ilana often appears idiotic for cluelessly fetishizing and appropriating from people of color.[93] However, this self-mockery is only half the picture. We will soon see how Ilana's microaggressions vitally enhance her racially protean, ex-oticized, seductive-but-masculinized Jewessface persona. In these moments, *Broad City* invites viewers to *feel wiser than Ilana by condemning the racist processes that assist her Jewessface* (to mock Ilana as a white butt of derision), *yet still to relish the gorgeous, exoticized Jewessface product* that these racist processes generate (to idealize Ilana as an exotic aspirational figure). As we will see, this exoticized Jewessfaced product feels so easy to relish because it *fuses racist pleasures (like fetishizing Black men) with ecstatic gendered and sexual freedoms (like women's right to erotic pleasure)*. In other words, this effect fuses racist and antiracist unruly womanhood. Further, Ilana's role as an exotic aspirational figure invites white-privileged viewers to *indulge-and-deny fantasies of becoming less white, and therefore less white-guilty*. However, since Ilana always jointly serves as a white butt of derision, she helps viewers to feel guiltless by *fusing trenchant antiracist critiques with their own unacknowledged racist pleasures and their own unacknowledged desires to shuck white guilt*.

To make Ilana a white butt of derision, the series packages her as a *hyper-whiteguilty* character who flagrantly commits *liberal racism*. That is, Ilana presents the cringey spectacle of a white-privileged woman who is overwhelmed by white guilt but lacks white meta-guilt; who therefore desperately strives to shuck her white guilt rather than productively challenge racism; and who thereby accidentally but egregiously

microaggresses against people of color. For instance, when trying to express solidarity with her Asian beautician through a generous tip, Ilana
stereotypes her as (in Ilana's words) an "exploited salon worker."[94] When
the livid beautician reveals that "I am the owner," Ilana awkwardly sings,
"White guilt, white guilt, white guilt." This exchange urges viewers to
notice how Ilana's racist microaggression stems from her self-centered
desperation to relieve white guilt. As this example suggests, "liberal racism" here names *self-serving antiracist ardor that flows from white guilt,
and therefore crosses into microaggressing against people of color, fetishizing people of color, speaking for people of color, and appropriating their
cultures.* This definition invokes the insights of Jewish feminist Melanie
Kaye/Kantrowitz, who observes that white-privileged people often strive
to prove themselves "innocent" of racism and win approval from people
of color rather than challenging racist oppression.[95] Such self-centered
impulses can fuel misguided approaches to antiracism, like when Ilana
stereotypes and microaggresses against the Asian beautician that she
aims to support. Ilana's cartoonishly extreme white guilt and liberal racism make her a "hyper-whiteguilty" butt of derision.

By coining the term "hyper-whiteguilty," I clarify how Ilana mirrors-
yet-inverts the phenomenon of "hyperwhite" antagonists who help white
audiences feel racially guiltless. This concept of hyperwhite antagonists
comes from the film scholars Gretchen Bakke and Russell Meeuf,[96]
who build on Richard Dyer's broader analysis of whiteness in film.[97]
Per this scholarship, hyperwhite antagonists are villains who embody
the worst physical and ethical stereotypes of whiteness: pallid, greedy,
cruel, shallow, conformist, elitist, bloodthirsty, and/or blatantly racist.[98]
Examples range from the ravenous, ashen vampires in *Blade* (1998)[99] to
the platinum-blond, racist aristocrat Draco Malfoy in the *Harry Potter*
films (2001–2011).[100] Although vilifying hyperwhite antagonists seems
to critique white supremacy, Russell Meeuf observes that such villains
often just help white-privileged viewers to feel innocent by comparison.[101] Further, by seeing hyperwhite characters slaughtered or chastised, white-privileged viewers can fantasize about purging the openly
nasty parts of whiteness, and thus feel guilt-free about subtler white
privilege.[102]

At first glance, the Jewessfaced Ilana inverts hyperwhiteness: she
is not pale but dusky, not cold but exuberant, not elitist but ashamed

of her privilege, and not a villain but a beloved protagonist. However, Ilana mirrors hyperwhite antagonists by serving as a cartoonish outlier who helps white-privileged viewers to disavow their own subtler racism. Ilana's hyper-whiteguiltiness especially helps her to cure the white guilt and meta-guilt of progressive white-privileged viewers. As a hyper-whiteguilty woman, *Ilana takes liberal racism to cartoonish extremes that progressive white-privileged viewers can easily recognize and mock.* Further, like hyperwhite characters, the hyper-whiteguilty Ilana often suffers chastisement for her transgressions. For instance, when Ilana proclaims that she prefers "Black dick" over "pink dick" (and thus crosses from valuing to objectifying Black men), Abbi replies, "You're so antiracist sometimes that you're actually really racist."[103] Optimistically, watching Ilana's hyper-whiteguilty transgressions may truly educate progressive white-privileged viewers into being better antiracists. However, similar to hyperwhite antagonists, the hyper-whiteguilty Ilana may simply help viewers feel wise and innocent by comparison. For instance, white-privileged viewers who share Ilana's fetishization of Black men can pat themselves on the back for never voicing this racist fetish so gauchely. Additionally, seeing Ilana chastised for her liberal racism may fuel the fantasy that progressive white-privileged people are collectively purged of their most embarrassing missteps.

Broad City's first moments exemplify how Ilana's Jewessface depends on racist microaggressions; demonstrate how these microaggressions simultaneously shame Ilana as a white butt of derision *and* glamorize her as an exotic aspirational figure; and illustrate how this fusion aids progressive white-privileged viewers to reconcile racist pleasures with antiracist identity. This opening also epitomizes how Ilana's role as an exotic aspirational figure often *blends racist pleasures into euphoric gendered and sexual liberation,* thereby helping audiences to guiltlessly relish this racism.

Blending Racist Pleasures with Euphoric Gendered and Sexual Liberation

When the pilot introduces Ilana on a mid-coitus Skype call,[104] her Jewessface pedagogy depends on fusing ecstatic sexual liberation with cringeworthy racial appropriation and fetishization. The docile man on whom Ilana undulates is Black: her "sex friend" Lincoln, whose name evokes Abraham Lincoln and thus America's history of enslavement. The scene strongly implies that Ilana objectifies Lincoln as a symbol of Black masculinity and Black cultural authenticity—while riding Lincoln, Ilana is listening to rap by Lil Wayne, one of America's best-known Black male rappers and a self-described "gangster."[105] *Broad City* deepens this impression that Ilana is objectifying Lincoln when, still lying beneath her with his penis inside her, Lincoln asks "are we dating?" and Ilana replies that "this is purely physical." Ilana thus extends long racist traditions of objectifying Black men as walking penises.[106] This opening makes Ilana's racist transgressions even more blatant through her fixation on Lil Wayne: she not only listens to Lil Wayne's music while riding Lincoln, but invites Abbi to a Lil Wayne concert. This invitation also reveals that Ilana fetishizes Lil Wayne as a conduit to gritty cultural authenticity, powerful womanhood, and sexual adventure. For example, Ilana tells Abbi that attending Lil Wayne's concert will help them become "boss bitches" (cool and impressive women), a phrase appropriated from African American Vernacular English. Likewise, Ilana later delusionally claims that "I'm gonna fuck him! [Lil Wayne]." In fact, Ilana *first introduces the word "Jewess" specifically to pursue Lil Wayne's Black subcultural and sexual cachet*: her "Jewess" Craigslist ad aims to raise money for his concert. This origin previews how Jewessface always partly serves to facilitate racial appropriation.

On one hand, this outrageous introduction positions Ilana as a white butt of derision, who helps white-privileged audiences to feel racially enlightened by contrast. For instance, Ilana's over-the-top behavior (like dabbling in prostitution and delusionally shouting that "I'm gonna fuck [Lil Wayne]!") invites viewers to notice, critique, and cringe at how she fetishizes Blackness. Further, the pilot contextualizes Ilana's fetishization of Lincoln and Lil Wayne as part of her wider liberal racism: the way she flees white guilt in self-centered ways that cause her to speak for and microaggress against people of color. For example, upon hearing Louis Armstrong's 1967 song "What a Wonderful World," Ilana incorrectly exclaims, "Ugh! This is a *slave song*! . . . It's . . . widely known by the black community," prompting Abbi to retort, "I totally forgot that you're like, the voice of the whole Black community." Overhearing, a Black cashier contemptuously shakes her head at the Jewesses, briskly serves them, then tersely asks, "Can you leave?" This exchange critiques Ilana as a white butt of derision whose ill-informed efforts at antiracism actually microaggress against people of color.

However, this sequence simultaneously *glamorizes* Ilana as an exotic aspirational figure whose Jewessface blends racism with euphoric gendered and sexual liberation. Even while the pilot critiques Ilana's liberal racism, it also *recruits Lincoln's body (especially penis) and Lil Wayne's rap into Ilana's Jewessface* alongside her olive skin, brown curls, masculinized slang, and brazen sexuality. First, staying physically and emotionally atop Lincoln (sexually dominating him) enhances Ilana's seductive-yet-masculinized Jewessface. Second, the racially dark, dirty, and hypersexual connotations of Black masculinity (both Lincoln's and Lil Wayne's) enhance Ilana's racially exotic, dirty, and hypersexual Jewessface. Incorporating Blackness into her body on these unequal terms embellishes Ilana's Jewessfaced image of exotic beauty, unbridled pleasure, and powerful womanhood. By fusing racism with women's sexual liberation, the pilot thus *invites audiences to virtuously critique Ilana's racist microaggression* (how she fetishizes Lincoln and Lil Wayne) *yet relish her scintillating Jewessface* (which forms partly by fetishizing Lincoln and Lil Wayne).

Just as countless think pieces celebrate the way Jacobson and Glazer blend masculinized freedoms with gorgeous femininity, many white-privileged bloggers tacitly convey how the duo helps them reconcile antiracist identity with unacknowledged racist pleasures. These think pieces often underline how Jewessface synthesizes racist microaggressions with women's sexual liberation and with antiracist critiques. The conditionally white Jewish author Arielle Bernstein exemplifies this synthesis in her 2016 *Salon* article "Joy Is a Feminist (Comedy) Act."[107] At first, Bernstein positions Ilana as a white butt of derision and tacitly acknowledges Ilana's hyper-whiteguiltiness, briefly critiquing Ilana for being "so wrapped up in her own 'woke' identity that she often says racially and culturally insensitive things." Likewise, Bernstein praises *Broad City* for "smartly call[ing] attention to" Ilana's "foolish" racial missteps. However, Bernstein primarily aims to convey that "[o]ne of the greatest pleasures of viewing *Broad City*" is watching the "bold, beautiful" Ilana as she "enjoys the hell out of being a woman in her 20s."

Importantly, Bernstein never recognizes that the sexual and gendered antics that most delight her entail *racial appropriation*. In turn, this enjoyment spotlights how viewers who virtuously critique Ilana's racist microaggressions can simultaneously relish the exotic, sexually powerful Jewessface product that those microaggressions produce. For example, Bernstein joyfully recounts how Ilana "twerks" with excitement about Abbi's sex life, and how Ilana "cries . . . YAS, KWEEN" (meaning, "go, girl!") to "exalt powerful women" like Hillary Clinton. Twerking is a dance strongly associated with Afro-Caribbean women like Nicki Minaj, and widely perceived as hypersexual. When Ilana twerks to fête Abbi's sexcapades, she extends a long legacy of white-privileged women's appropriating Black styles of dance and gesture to express their own sexual liberation, a form of blackface minstrelsy.[108] Importantly, Ilana twerks during the aforementioned episode about her grandmother's shiva. By reminding audiences of Ilana's "Jewess" identity while she twerks, this plotline recruits twerking into her racially exotic, hypersexual Jewessface. The fact that Bernstein can guiltlessly relish Ilana's twerking is especially striking, because twerking is the well-known cardinal sin in American debates about appropriation: the phrase "cultural appropriation" entered mainstream American vocabularies after a much-criticized 2013 twerking performance by the white gentile pop star Miley Cyrus.[109] Meanwhile, Ilana's catchphrase of "yas, kween" (also spelled "yas, queen") originated in Harlem in the 1980s within ballroom culture, a performance community of Black and Latinx drag queens, gay men, and trans women.[110] Although *Out* credits Ilana for mainstreaming "yas, kween!,"[111] others have critiqued this linguistic transmission as cultural appropriation, and Glazer herself has since apologized for this appropriation.[112] Like twerking, the phrase "yas, kween!" enhances Ilana's Jewessface with connotations of racially exotic, transgressive, and exuberant sexuality. Thus, even as Bernstein establishes her own antiracist identity by critiquing Ilana's racist missteps, she celebrates those same racist behaviors as key ingredients in Ilana's "bold," "beautiful," "joyful" womanhood. And whether viewers recognize it or not, Ilana's ecstatic model of womanhood always constitutes Jewessface. The inconsistencies in Bernstein's praise reveal how Jewessface aids many white-privileged viewers to reconcile the pleasure of guilt-free antiracist identity with racist pleasures like appropriation, by fusing those racist pleasures with antiracist critiques and with euphoric gendered and sexual rebellions.

However, Ilana's Jewessface does more than help white-privileged viewers tacitly enjoy racist transgressions as ingredients within sexual and gender liberation. Her dual role as an exotic aspirational figure and white butt of derision also provides another paradoxical pleasure: Ilana invites white-privileged viewers to pleasurably *reimagine their own racial status* as a less-culpable form of whiteness, even while denying any such desire and while priding themselves on antiracist self-awareness.

Craving (Deniable) Racial Mobility, "Appropriative License," and Blackfishing

As an exotic aspirational figure, Ilana (and to a lesser extent, Abbi) offers white-privileged viewers an *exoticized whiteness* that *feels further from white privilege without actually denying it*, but which can also *more guiltlessly microaggress against people of color because it stands closer to them*.

This exoticized whiteness highlights how tropes of Jewess racial ambiguity overlap with and differ from tropes of Latina racial ambiguity. Hannah Schwadron's work on "sexy Jewesses" and Priscilla Peña Ovalle's work on Latina stars both stress how these women embody racial "in-betweenness."[113] For example, Ovalle writes that Euro-Latina stars like Jennifer Lopez offer white women "exotic sameness": a look that can "be read as 'ethnic' yet remain[s] familiar enough for white women to appropriate through hair coloring, tanning, fashion, and makeup."[114] Jewessface offers an even more accessible "exotic sameness" that is not just *near* whiteness, but ambivalently *is* white. After all, Euro-American "Jewesses" are a group now commonly deemed white, even though that whiteness remains conditional. Further, even at the height of racial antisemitism, the "beautiful Jewess" was a flamboyant but indefinable racial outsider who rarely landed in any specific color or place. Trollope's Madame Goesler exemplifies this imprecision with her mysterious blackness/gloss and her ambiguous position between white, "black, brown, and yellow."[115] Likewise, as analyzed above, Jacobson and Glazer constantly offer this vivid-but-placeless racial exoticism to white-privileged viewers by erratically dubbing themselves white women/Jewesses, and by depicting Jewessness as an elusive racial aura.

In turn, these different shades of racial in-betweenness enable different types of racial *mobility*. As we have seen, Ovalle coined "racial mobility" to describe how Euro-Latina stars can maneuver themselves closer to Blackness or whiteness onscreen through different costumes, hairstyles, and choreography.[116] Instead, Jewessface vicariously offers to white-privileged *viewers* a *deniable* form of racial mobility that soothes white guilt and meta-guilt. This elusively exotic Jewessface feels *compatible with, but less guilt-inducing than, viewers' own whiteness*. Therefore, white-privileged viewers who identify with Abbi and Ilana can fantasize about maneuvering away from whiteness and white guilt *without acknowledging* that fantasy.

To embody this less-guilty racial status and vicariously offer it to white-privileged viewers, Jacobson and Glazer often contrast their dusky Jewessfaced characters against *gentile hyperwhite antagonists*. A prime example is the duo's pale, blond, WASPy, stick-thin, snobby former coworker Morgan, in the episode "Destination: Wedding" (2014).[117] The episode links Morgan's pallid skin with racism: she complains with aggrieved disbelief that she's still single even though "this year, I opened myself up to minorities, and *still* nothing!" (original emphasis). Morgan thus implies that dating men of color is an awful concession, and that such men should treasure her reluctant attention. In fact, the episode reveals that Morgan's sexual taste is so racist and classist that she only beds her own brother(!), thus hinting that her own sallow body may reflect inbreeding. Morgan's repulsive (incestuous, ashen, unhealthily thin, openly racist) gentile hyperwhiteness urges viewers to instead identify with the olive-skinned, brunette, curvaceous Jewesses who grow increasingly annoyed by her, and who eventually reject her inbred hyperwhiteness when Abbi derisively yells, "Go fuck your brother!" This climax invites white-privileged audiences to feel that they, too, have rejected racism by vicariously rebuking Morgan's hyperwhiteness. In turn, Abbi and Ilana's visual contrast against the hyperwhite gentile Morgan *accentuates their dusky Jewessface*. This heavier Jewessface invites white-privileged audiences to identify with them as exoticized avatars who seem farther from white privilege and racism without disingenuously denying either—the perfect balm to white guilt *and* white meta-guilt.

Yet this alluring contrast against Morgan disavows how Abbi and Ilana's exotic Jewessface (especially Ilana's) partly *depends* on racist microaggressions. It's significant that Ilana's Black "sex friend," Lincoln, accompanies Ilana and Abbi on their misadventure with the hyperwhite Morgan—and unlike usual, Ilana makes no objectifying comments toward him. Although consistent viewers may recall how Ilana fetishizes Lincoln's Blackness, this racist fetishization appears slighter and sweeter when contrasted against Morgan's overt disdain for men of color. And yet, the plot *does* objectify Lincoln: his presence tacitly embellishes Ilana's Jewessface by highlighting her emotional and sexual proximity to Blackness. A circular effect thus emerges: Lincoln's presence helps to Jewessface Ilana as an exoticized alternative to the hyperwhite gentile Morgan, and Morgan's hyperwhiteness excuses the racial appropriations that exotically Jewessface Ilana.

If Jewessface offers an exoticized whiteness that can less guiltily microaggress against people of color, then popular reviews capture how this effect enchants white-privileged audiences. Just as the *New Yorker's* Emily Nussbaum notes how Abbi and Ilana remain oddly lovely at their crassest moments, she notes that Ilana's racist microaggressions seem oddly sweet. Nussbaum writes that Ilana's fetishization of Black people (including Lincoln and Lil Wayne) should make Ilana "a nightmare of cultural appropriation," but somehow doesn't.[118] Instead, "Ilana's fascination with blackness has a warmer feeling," in part because Ilana seems truly "awed" by the people of color who obsess her. In other words, Ilana makes liberal racism look counterintuitively lovable, even to the television critic calling her out. And though Nussbaum doesn't note it, this "warmth" often depends precisely on contrasting the well-meaning, Jewessfaced Ilana against hyperwhite gentile antagonists like Morgan.

If Jacobson and Glazer's less-white Jewessface personae help to reconcile racist microaggressions with antiracist identity, one of the most vital microaggressions that they normalize is cultural appropriation. Cultural appropriation (like Ilana's aforementioned twerking and usage of "yas, kween!") enhances the duo's exotic Jewessface, but then gets retroactively rendered less-guilty by that very Jewessface, since Jewessface moves the duo closer to women of color. Tracing this loop extends one of Hannah Schwadron's points about all "sexy Jewess" performers: these stars often invoke Jewessness as *comic appropriative license*,[119] meaning an excuse to comedically appropriate from more marginalized cultures. Jewessness can serve as appropriative license by implying that Euro-American Jewish women and people of color share common forms of outsiderness and/or share specific stigmas like exotic-but-dirty sexuality. However, even as exotic Jewessface helps Jacobson and Glazer to seem blameless while committing appropriation, their proximity to whiteness also *vicariously offers this appropriative license* to gentile and Jewish white-privileged viewers offscreen. When these viewers fantasize about copying (or actually *do* copy) the Jewesses' appropriative behaviors—like saying "yas, kween!"—viewers can imagine that they are harmlessly imitating fellow white people rather than oppressively appropriating from people of color. This effect helps white-privileged viewers to reconcile their fantasized or actual racial appropriations with guiltless antiracist identity.

Indeed, the plot arc that most sharply critiques Ilana's liberal racism also most seductively invites white-privileged viewers to relish cultural appropriation, and even to relish *blackfishing*. As we have seen, blackfishing is a form of appropriation so extreme that it crosses into minstrelsy by *impersonating* people of color.[120] *Broad City*'s invitation to blackfishing depends on the way Jewessface offers an exoticized whiteness that feels further from white privilege without actually denying it, and which can more guiltlessly microaggress against people of color because it stands closer to them.

This racist/antiracist plot arc about blackfishing concerns Ilana's penchant for gold-hoop earrings, a style associated with Black and Latina femininities. Season 2 (2015) reveals that Ilana's elaborate masturbation ritual includes donning gold-hoop earrings that say "Latina" in curly script,[121] and she later wears these earrings around the city.[122] By combining her "Latina" earrings with her (naturally) olive skin and (cosmetically optimized) curly brown hair, Ilana invites passerby to misread her as Latina. By weaving tropes of "spicy," exoticized, racially ambiguous Latinidad into Ilana's image, these scenes enhance her racially protean, exotic, hypersexual Jewessface.

When she passes as Latina in order to self-exoticize, Ilana exemplifies blackfishing, even though this plotline aired three years before the word "blackfishing" was coined to name such behavior.[123] Ilana's gold hoops especially align her with other white women stars who blackfish by pairing cosmetics or costumes with preexisting traits that connote racial in-betweenness, like the Spanish-sounding (but actually Italian) name "Ariana Grande."[124] Likewise, this performance aligns Ilana Glazer with Drake: we have seen how Drake often pairs his North American biracial Jewish body with Afro-Latino music and fashions to craft an exoticized "Dominican Drake" persona.[125] And like all blackfishing, Ilana's performance harmfully silences the people whom she impersonates: when this non-Latina Jewess passes as Latina, she erases America's actual community of Latinx Jews,[126] such as the millennial Jewish Venezuelan-American comedian Joanna Hausmann.

On one hand, *Broad City* invites viewers to feel that they are virtuously critiquing Ilana's blackfishing, thus making her a white butt of derision. In season 3, Ilana's Latino roommate, Jaime, calls her out for cultural appropriation. In Jaime's words, "You're stealing the identity from people who fought hard against colonial structures, so in a way, it's almost like you are the colonist."[127] And indeed, Ilana stops wearing those earrings. Further, Glazer has stated that this plot arc intentionally aimed "to point out" why "[c]ultural appropriation is . . . not cool."[128]

However, this antiracist lesson quickly gives way to plotlines that *glamorize* blackfishing and reframe Ilana as an exotic aspirational figure. This twist invites white-privileged viewers to fantasize about committing the very transgression they have just critiqued. And this glamorization partly depends on Abbi and Ilana's long-established personae as dusky "Jewesses," personae embellished by Ilana's blackfishing. Just three episodes after Jaime's antiracist intervention, Abbi and Ilana actively misrepresent themselves as Latina to sneak into an exclusive nightclub with a private party named "Hernández."[129] To this end, they restyle their shirts into crop tops (a common blackfishing technique),[130] and Ilana even dons a faux-Latina accent and stereotypically "sassy" body-language to trick the bouncer. This deception illustrates that Ilana has learned nothing: she continues to use her racially exotic Jewessface to appropriate from people of color. Yet this Jewessface also softens the effect of her transgression. If performed by a white gentile star, or even a lighter-complected Jewish star like Amy Schumer, this racial deceit and caricature would seem blatantly unethical. However, Jacobson and Glazer's Latina blackfish personae appear less obviously unethical because they closely approximate the duo's long-running and racially protean Jewessface personae.

Additionally, the series *narratively* glamorizes Abbi and Ilana's black-fishing adventure in the club. Although this plotline constitutes Abbi and Ilana's most deliberate, deceitful, and racially caricatured appropriation of Latinidad, the duo receives no chastisement this time. Instead, *their Jewessface helps their blackfishing to appear joyfully liberating for all involved*, including for the people of color that Abbi and Ilana mislead. Thus, both women (especially Ilana) reemerge as exotic aspirational figures while blackfishing. This aspirational appeal depends on the way Jewessface blends racist pleasures with euphoric gendered and sexual rebellions. On one hand, this sequence should come off as ethically disturbing because blackfishing helps Ilana to sexually access the men of color whom she fetishizes: while blackfishing in the club, Ilana meets and beds the Haitian American basketball star Blake Griffin, played by himself. However, Griffin never suggests that Ilana's racial masquerade has sexually and emotionally violated his trust. Instead, at Ilana's suggestion, the pair unleash a long montage of kinky sexual games that appear ecstatically pleasurable for both. Thus, just three episodes after inviting white-privileged viewers to virtuously critique Ilana's blackfishing, *Broad City* invites them to idealize her as an exotic aspirational figure and vicariously relish her blackfishing.

While this club adventure fuses racist blackfishing with gendered and sexual liberation, a later plot twist fuses racist blackfishing with *antiracist liberation*. Through Jewessface, *Broad City* eventually implies that Ilana's blackfishing techniques no longer constitute cultural appropriation at all, but instead constitute a liberatory expression of Jewish pride and antiracist self-awareness. Although her roommate's intervention ends Ilana's "Latina" earrings, Ilana later receives identical gold hoops that spell "Jewess" in the same curly script.[131] Significantly, these new earrings are a gift from her Black "sex friend," Lincoln. Because these new "Jewess" hoops come from a Black man and because they declare Ilana's true identity, they symbolize her antiracist growth and they seem praiseworthy compared to her bombastically blackfishy "Latina" earrings. But this contrast downplays the reality that Ilana's new "Jewess" hoops still appropriate Latina styles. In fact, these new earrings *even more effectively recruit the exoticized connotations of Latina femininity into vestiary Jewessface*, by packaging the word "Jewess" and the Jewess's golden shimmer within a Latina cultural symbol.

These "Jewess" hoops thus spotlight how Jewessface offers an *especially plausible pretext to commit-and-disavow blackfishing,* aiding white-privileged viewers to burnish their antiracist self-image while relishing unacknowledged racist pleasures. The media scholar Lauren Michele Jackson observes that blackfishing depends on a paradoxical disavowal: visually encouraging others to misread you as a person of color until someone criticizes you, then declaiming in faux shock that "I've never claimed not to be white!"[132] But Jackson adds that such disavowals are often laughably implausible, as exemplified by the white gentile Swedish model Emma Hallberg: Hallberg routinely misrepresented herself on Instagram with wavy black wigs and brown-painted skin until confronted. She then absurdly claimed that a natural suntan (not wigs or cosmetics) had produced her Black appearance.[133] Unlike Hallberg's implausible denial, Ilana's new "Jewess" hoops plausibly disavow their own blackfishing by symbolizing a liberatory story arc about critiquing racial appropriation, listening to people of color, and embracing one's own Jewishness.

Further, Ilana's blend of Jewessface with blackfishing invites progressive white-privileged people to *actively commit* the same transgressions *in real life,* while still feeling pleasurably guiltless: her "Jewess" hoops have inspired real-world jewelry like the Etsy product in figure 3.5,[134] which directly encourages Jewish women to mimic Ilana's blackfishy style.

The blogosphere's applause for Ilana's gold hoop plotline exemplifies how seamlessly Jewessface can reconcile antiracist identity with unacknowledged racist pleasures. One vivid example of this applause is the 2019 blog post "My Intersectional Feminist Queen, Ilana Wexler."[135] This post's racial contradictions are striking because it comes from an author and organization that thoughtfully pursue social justice. The post was published by the Jewish Women's Archive (JWA), a national organization that "collect[s] and promote[s] . . . Jewish women's stories to excite people to see themselves as agents of change."[136] The post's author is Lily Drazin, a conditionally white Jewish high school student who published four JWA think pieces between 2018 and 2019, all astutely addressing feminism, social justice, and Jewish identity.[137] When analyzing *Broad City*'s gold hoop saga, Drazin illustrates how Ilana's Jewessface invites even proactive antiracists to guiltlessly

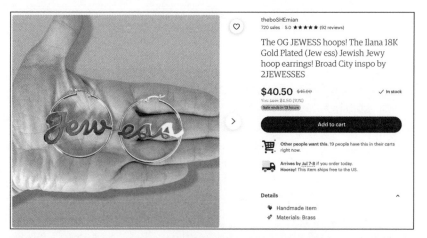

theboSHEmian
720 sales 5.0 ★★★★★ (92 reviews)

The OG JEWESS hoops! The Ilana 18K
Gold Plated (Jew ess) Jewish Jewy
hoop earrings! Broad City inspo by
2JEWESSES

$40.50 ~~$45.00~~   ✓ In stock
You save $4.50 (10%)
Sale ends in 13 hours

> [Add to cart]

🛒 Other people want this. 19 people have this in their carts
   right now.

🚚 Arrives by Jul 7-8 if you order today.
   Hooray! This item ships free to the US.

Details   ^

👐 Handmade item
✦ Materials: Brass

Figure 3.5. These Etsy earrings exemplify how Ilana's "Jewess" hoops from *Broad City* invite Jewish women to mimic her blackfishy style. The ad even appropriates AAVE ("OG" for "original gangster") to market these symbols of Jewish pride.
Earrings by "theboSHEmian" shop on Etsy. Image from Etsy.com.

mimic racist microaggressions. Like many other think pieces that analyze Ilana's earrings,[138] this one asserts that Ilana "immediately recogniz[es] that she's wrong" once her roommate chastises her for appropriating Latinidad—a claim that ignores Ilana's unethical passing as Latina three episodes later, and ignores Ilana's "Jewess" hoops in season 5. Further, Drazin writes that Ilana's contrition "*teaches us that being imperfect is acceptable, but that it's also necessary to recognize our mistakes, and change our ways.*" This description counterintuitively identifies with Ilana as a fabulous "intersectional feminist queen" who models personal growth toward ideal antiracist allyship. Yet by echoing *Broad City*'s appropriative use of the word "queen," (as in, "yas, queen!"), Drazin's post repeats Ilana's own racial appropriations. Thus, while Arielle Bernstein (cited above) tacitly enjoys Ilana's racial appropriations as ingredients in gendered or sexual liberation, Drazin tacitly enjoys Ilana's racial appropriations *while praising and imitating Ilana's antiracism.* This contradiction epitomizes how Jewessface aids white-privileged viewers to pleasurably envision themselves as principled antiracists even while continuing to enjoy unacknowledged racist microaggressions.

Conclusion

By simultaneously identifying with Ilana as an intersectional feminist hero *and* echoing Ilana's racist microaggressions, Drazin exemplifies the ideological contradictions that make Jacobson and Glazer's Jewessface so alluring. Just as the historical "beautiful Jewess" trope flickers between masculine and feminine, seductive and repulsive, and white and nonwhite, Jewessface helps viewers to reconcile many contradictory desires into cohesive fantasies of freedom. On a liberatory note, Jewessface seamlessly reconciles "masculine," "perverse," "filthy" freedoms with gorgeous femininity, offering many women and queer men a glamorous vision of liberation. Yet on an oppressive note, Jewessface blends racist microaggressions with pleasurably guiltless antiracist identity, offering many white-privileged antiracists an unearned release from white guilt. In fact, this smooth blend of racism with antiracism often underpins the gorgeous femininity that makes the duo's gender and sexual rebellions look so lovable.

While Jacobson and Glazer's Jewessface often appears seductive, their millennial Jewish peer Seth Rogen cultivates a less eroticized cuteness. For instance, when guest-starring on *Broad City*, Rogen plays a sweet but pudgy date who comedically passes out during sex.[139] The next chapter analyzes why Rogen's visually unsexy persona makes him so ideologically alluring.

4

Boys Just Want to Have Fun?

Seth Rogen's Beta Male Patriarchy, Post-Meninist Violence, and Fun Fatherhood

Cuddly Domination: Seth Rogen's "Gently Messy Jewish Man-Baby"

Seth Rogen (b. 1982) soars among Hollywood's top comedic stars. Hailing from a conditionally white Jewish Canadian family, at age sixteen Rogen placed second in Vancouver's 1998 amateur stand-up comedy contest.[1] He then joined the American high school dramedy series *Freaks and Geeks* (1999–2000),[2] his first collaboration with the conditionally white Jewish American director/producer Judd Apatow. Apatow later provided Rogen's breakout role in the 2007 hit comedy *Knocked Up*.[3]

In *Knocked Up*, Rogen played his first leading man—albeit a queer (odd, emasculated, and homoerotic) one. Hollywood's leading men are historically trim, tough, mature, and strictly straight white gentile men, like Daniel Craig as James Bond. Conversely, *Knocked Up* cast Rogen as a pudgy, unemployed, childish, explicitly Jewish loser, "Ben Stone," who is supposedly straight but relishes deep homoerotic bonds with other men. The opening scene finds Ben sharing a fetid bachelor pad with fellow infantile stoners, wasting their days with endless pot, roller coasters, and jokes about gay sex. Yet fate forces this Jewish loser to straighten out and grow up when he accidentally impregnates a woman who seems his opposite: a thin, gorgeous, ambitious white gentile news anchor played by blond bombshell Katherine Heigl. Against expectation, the pair deepens their hookup into monogamous courtship, planning to wed and co-parent. To this end, Ben fumbles toward a more adult, clean, and breadwinning masculinity. By the finale (the baby's birth), he lands a web-design job so he can afford to exit his swarming bachelor pad and rent a tidy apartment fit for a middle-class man, wife, and child.

This messy journey toward adult straight white middle-class masculinity landed on *Rolling Stone*'s list of the year's top films[4] and elevated Rogen into a household name. Since *Knocked Up*, he has found blockbuster success playing near-identical childish, pudgy, emasculated, homoerotic, explicitly Jewish losers in *Pineapple Express* (2008), *Funny People* (2009), *The Guilt Trip* (2012), *This Is the End* (2013), *Neighbors* (2014), *The Interview* (2014), *The Night Before* (2015), *Neighbors 2* (2016), *Sausage Party* (2016), and *An American Pickle* (2020). These roles have made Rogen one of Hollywood's highest-earning stars, illustrated by his $17 million paycheck for *The Interview*.[5] This marketably pathetic persona has also shaped Rogen's smaller roles post-2007. For instance, in 2015 he guest-starred on *Broad City* as Abbi Jacobson's chubby, passive boyfriend, with the feminized name "Stacey."[6] Rogen's success also includes co-writing, co-producing, and co-directing many of his own loserish roles and other films starring similar characters, often in collaboration with Judd Apatow. For example, Rogen mined his own youthful misadventures to co-write the 2007 comedy *Superbad* (produced by Apatow), about immature and homoerotic high school boys.[7] Along the way, Rogen has occasionally dabbled in gentile characters, masculinized characters, and darker storylines. For instance, in 2022 he played a white gentile carpenter turned pornographer in Hulu's darkly comedic biographical miniseries *Pam & Tommy*.[8] So far, though, Rogen remains best-known for writing, producing, and starring in lighthearted romps about lovably emasculated Jewish losers.

Responses to Rogen's comedies often fall into two camps. The first deems his films sweet, goofy, even uplifting commentaries on twenty-first-century life. For instance, the crowdsourced review site Rotten Tomatoes declares *Knocked Up* "a hilarious, poignant and refreshing look at the rigors of courtship and child-rearing."[9] The second camp critiques oppressive themes in Rogen's films, but implies that these themes contradict his gentle image. For example, in 2021 *The Times of London* critiqued Rogen's early work as "eye-wateringly misogynistic," partly because his character in *Knocked Up* objectifies women through pornography.[10] Nevertheless, the author valorizes Rogen's characters as "charmingly idiotic, directionless, but lovable man-children." She also conflates Rogen with his lovable characters by writing that he "looks like a big smiley bear." Thus, while Rotten Tomatoes reads *Knocked Up* as harmless and endearing fun, *The Times* spots oppressive themes in it—but deems those themes to be at odds with Rogen's teddy bear-ish image.

Whether overlooking oppressive themes in Rogen's comedy or implying that such themes contradict his childish charm, both commentaries inadvertently reflect the ideological labor that has fueled Rogen's stardom since *Knocked Up*. Since 2007, Rogen's success has depended on embodying an especially *cuddly model of straight white-privileged male power and procreation*: a model that appears fun, innocent, and lovable, rather than appearing dreary, unethical, or unlikable to straight white-privileged male viewers, and rather than appearing noxious to minoritized viewers. And while *The Times* critiques Rogen's childish characters for viewing porn, his cuddliness has camouflaged far harsher abuses. To dominate white women, women of color, and men of color, Rogen's characters sometimes even commit rape or murder—for instance, shooting an Asian adversary point-blank in *Pineapple Express* (2008).[11] Yet no matter what oppressive violence Rogen's characters commit, they still come off as "lovable man-children." Rogen's man-child image is marketable precisely because it helps these abuses to seem palatable, and even (per Rotten Tomatoes) to seem "hilarious, poignant, and refreshing."

Although *The Times* overlooks Jewishness when describing Rogen's lovable man-child persona, this persona vitally depends on antisemitic racial tropes. In *Knocked Up*, Rogen inaugurated a new relationship to the racial stigmas that historically mark Jewish men as repulsively emasculated, perverse, and filthy. "Disidentifying"[12] with those stigmas (creatively repurposing them), Rogen initiated a subliminal postmodern Jewface persona that I call *the gently messy Jewish man-baby*, which has remained his hallmark ever since. This subtle Jewface packages Rogen's fat body as *babyishly soft, cute, helpless, innocent, guileless, clumsy, and therefore lovable*. Although Rogen's Canadian identity can also connote wholesomeness, his minstrel persona forefronts Jewishness instead. To capture Rogen's infantile Jewface, I dub him a man-*baby* rather than "man-child." I also use the babyish term "messy" to describe Rogen's comedic grotesquery, which features untidy bodies (flabby, leaky, dirty) and unseemly conduct (drugs, sex, homoeroticism, and violence). His brand of messiness depends on this babyishly soft, clumsy, guileless image. These traits help Rogen to produce filth and chaos that appear blameless and endearing, but which actually serve to subordinate minoritized people. To convey how Rogen's Jewface fuses fatness with cuteness and lovable-looking chaos, I also describe his bulk with the toddlerish term "roly-poly." "Roly-poly" evokes huggable, hapless, wriggly, and silly softness like a puppy's. *Like a puppy, Rogen's roly-poly Jewface appears endlessly innocent and adorable even when it poops, vomits, humps—or bites.*

Below we will see how Rogen builds this babyish Jewface and how it helps straight white-privileged male power and procreation to appear both lovable and fun. Yet this analysis first requires grasping how Rogen's Jewface looks, how it inverts his earlier roles, how it links him with fellow Jewish comedians, and how it thrills diverse audiences. Rogen's babyish Jewface first appeared in a widely circulated publicity poster for *Knocked Up*,[13] which previews the Jewface techniques we will examine later (figure 4.3, on p. 160). This poster poofs his hair into curls that the film explicitly equates with Jewishness, as we will soon see. Yet the poster fuses this Jewish imagery with the sensuous style that embellished Christian cherubs in eighteenth-century Rococo art. Warm, creamy light graces

Figure 4.1. Rogen's violent white gentile villain in *Donnie Darko* (2001). Analysis beginning on p. 161. Screenshot from *Donnie Darko*, 2001. Pulled from Amazon.com.

Figure 4.2. Rogen's tattooed, greasy, sexually jaded Jewish side-character in *The 40-Year-Old Virgin* (2005). Analysis beginning on p. 161.
Screenshot from *The 40-Year-Old Virgin*, 2005. Pulled from Amazon.com.

Rogen with a faint halo, softens his bulk into gentle plumpness, lavishes his curly hair with a luxuriant shimmer, and gifts his lips a pillowy allure. Alongside this cinematographic softness, Rogen's facial expression conveys emotional softness: his wide eyes, raised eyebrows, and small bemused smile emote helpless startlement. The effect packages Rogen as huggably soft, sweet, and earnest.

Viewers today may misperceive this babyish persona as an automatic result of Rogen's plump Jewish body. This misperception emerges because he has played so many similar Jewish man-babies since 2007. Further, he has framed this earnest and infantile Jewface persona as his unscripted self. For example, when testifying before Congress in 2014 about his charitable work for Alzheimer's care, Rogen explained this activism by calling himself a "mensch," a Yiddish term that connotes kind,

Figure 4.3. This publicity poster for *Knocked Up* (2007) reframes Rogen's fat Jewish body as soft, cute, and innocent. Analyzed above on p. 158.
Image pulled from www.ImpAwards.com.

responsible manhood.[14] Yet he concluded by asking Congress to fund Alzheimer's care themselves, so that "I can go back to being the lazy, self-involved man-child I was meant to be." This conclusion implies that Rogen simply *is* a sweet Jewish man-baby.

Whether or not Rogen's Jewish man-baby persona approximates his private identity, it did not automatically become his marketable *public* image. Indeed, his pre-2007 roles vividly denaturalize his present image. For example, *Donnie Darko* (2001)[15] casts Rogen as a white gentile villain (Ricky Danforth) whose physical strength, precision, and cruelty make his fatness look menacing. Ricky comes off as gentile partly by default: although his identity goes unmentioned, America's Christo-normative[16] social conventions presume nearly everyone to be gentile until actively marked otherwise by clothing, accent, appearance, name, or self-declaration. Additionally, Seth Rogen and his real-world Jewish identity were too little known in 2001 to link his character with Jewishness. Further, *Donnie Darko* accentuates Ricky's gentility with the stereotypically gentile surname "Danforth" and with a stereotypically un-Jewish style of powerful, violent masculinity that equates his size with frightening strength. For example, in the film's violent climax, Ricky chillingly stalks the protagonists at knifepoint, sneers at their terror, and brutally beats the sensitive male lead (fellow millennial Jewish star Jake Gyllenhaal). Worse, Ricky lethally forces the female lead (Jena Malone) into oncoming traffic. Ricky's costume further equates his large body with threatening masculinity: he wears a black shirt and cutoff jean-jacket that evoke biker gangs, plus a stocking head-covering to obscure his identity, which signals premeditated criminality (figure 4.1). This cruel, calculating, and well-coordinated white gentile villain smashes today's impression that Rogen's body "self-evidently" looks Jewish, gentle, guileless, or bumbling. Instead, Rogen has had to actively cultivate his current roly-poly Jewface, which casts his violence as blameless and even lovable.

Rogen's next prominent role, a sleazy sidekick in Judd Apatow's *The 40-Year-Old Virgin* (2005),[17] further denaturalizes his later infantile Jewface. Featuring Rogen's first explicitly Jewish character, "Cal," this film illustrates how Rogen experimented with different performances of Jewish masculinity before reaching his babyish Jewface. Although less violent than Rogen's white gentile villain in *Donnie Darko*, Cal remains aggressive and repulsive: he embodies vulgar masculinity with an oily goatee and large tattoos (figure 4.2). Cal also links Jewishness with perverse sexuality: he introduces his Jewishness by mentioning that "I touched a guy's balls once in Hebrew school." This disclosure begins Cal's filmlong stream of aggressively sexual vignettes, which include describing "a woman fucking a horse" at a Tijuana sex show.[18] The film also links Cal's sexual depravity with repulsive appearance and narrative marginality, as noted by film scholar Casey Ryan Kelly. For example, Cal calls himself "ugly as fuck" and eventually pairs with a woman who is stigmatized as too sexually "freaky" for the wholesome male lead, Andy (Steve Carrell).[19] Importantly, this wholesome leading man is gentile by default, since he is never marked otherwise and since he is played by a gentile actor who was already well-known by 2007. The film thus constructs an implicit dichotomy between the clean, appealing gentile Andy and vulgar, unattractive Jewish Cal. This dichotomy serves to further equate Rogen's Jewishness with irredeemable physical and ethical ugliness that foreclose maturity or domesticity.

Departing from this repulsive Jewish image, *Knocked Up* instated the gently messy Jewish man-baby persona that alchemized Rogen into an A-list star and remains his hallmark today. Rogen has explicitly linked his babyish Jewish characters to Hollywood's lineage of self-deprecating conditionally white Jewish men like Eddie Cantor, Jerry Seinfeld, and Adam Sandler. For instance, the semi-autobiographical film *Funny People* (2009) casts Rogen as a young stand-up comic who aspires to "be like Seinfeld," and befriends a jaded older Jewish stand-up comic played by Sandler.[20] These links emphasize how Rogen, like past Jewish comedians, harnesses tropes about racially queer (nonnormative) Jewish masculinity. And although Rogen's roly-poly Jewface inverts Hollywood's typical steely white gentile heroes, his success proves that his pathetic persona queerly (oddly) thrills audiences.

Cute Abject Hegemony

Since 2007, Rogen's many Jewface comedies have generated this queer glamor by stoking-and-resolving two ideological anxieties about the role of white-privileged men (both Jewish and gentile) in sustaining straight white male supremacy. These films convey the worries that (1) *millennial straight, white-privileged middle-class men don't want to commit the racist, sexist, or homophobic abuses that would maintain their power over other groups,* and that (2) *these millennial men don't want the restrictive responsibility or restrictive social life of married fatherhood, and therefore won't reproduce white-privileged babies.* In turn, by modeling a cuddly version of straight white-privileged male power and procreation, Rogen's Jewface persona offers these men the dream of retaining social and demographic dominance in *fun, guiltless, lovable ways.* By suggesting that such men will dutifully reproduce straight white male supremacy and reproduce the white population, and by suggesting that white male supremacy is harmless, Rogen's infantile Jewface also soothes *everyone* who partly benefits from current inequalities—including many middle-class white-privileged straight women and gay men who may identify as progressive.

Just as Rogen's babyish Jewface helps straight, white-privileged, male, and/or middle-class viewers to enjoy-but-disavow oppressive fantasies, this cuddly camouflage also keeps Rogen marketable to more minoritized viewers. Vancouver journalist Stephanie Ip, as an Asian woman, illustrated this broad appeal in 2018. When Vancouver needed a new celebrity voice to record public transit messages, Ip proposed the hometown hero, Rogen: she tweeted that "I would happily listen to him announce my transit stops all day," partly thanks to his braying laughter, which Ip describes as "THE LAUGH."[21] Ip's enthusiasm is striking because Rogen's films consistently feature both misogynist and anti-Asian violence, like the aforementioned bloody murder in *Pineapple Express*. By asking to hear Rogen's laugh all day, Ip highlights that some minoritized audiences can easily enjoy his racist and sexist comedy as lovable mirth. For all audiences, this misreading depends on Rogen's babyish Jewface.

Rogen thus mirrors-yet-inverts the millennial Jewface rapper Lil Dicky by performing an aesthetically cuter, ideologically sweeter, more widely marketable version of *abject hegemony*. As we have seen, "abject hegemony" describes how dominant groups can feign weakness to stealthily reassert power by embracing traits they usually despise, expel, and project onto marginalized groups.[22] For example, historically, many straight white gentile men have claimed superiority by contrasting themselves against "pathetic" feminized, homoerotic, soft, dirty, nonwhite, and/or Jewish bodies like Rogen's and Dicky's. However, Dicky and Rogen have built mass appeal precisely by flaunting these allegedly pitiful and revolting traits. By vicariously identifying with Rogen's and Dicky's weak Jewface personae, any straight white-privileged men can falsely imagine themselves as underdogs to (1) disavow their privilege, (2) justify discrimination and violence as "self-defense" against "aggressive" minorities, and (3) deem their own violence "harmless," since they are allegedly too weak to inflict real damage.

Despite these similarities between Dicky and Rogen, Rogen illustrates that abject hegemony can look more *aesthetically appealing* than past scholarship acknowledges. When first coining the term "abject hegemony," Claire Sisco King emphasized how it requires dominant groups to depict their bodies as aesthetically *repulsive*.[23] For instance, Lil Dicky invites white-privileged viewers to identify with a Jewface persona that is both weak and *foul*: grimy, reeking, and greasy. Conversely, Rogen's roly-poly Jewface reframes his filthiest antics as endearing, helping him look *adorably* pathetic. He thus offers an avatar of abject hegemony that *aesthetically* charms many audiences. This aesthetic appeal is one reason why Rogen can enthuse many women and/or people of color like Stephanie Ip, while Dicky's most fervent fans are near-exclusively young, straight, white-privileged, middle-class men.

Rogen can also charm wider audiences than Dicky because Rogen's version of abject hegemony appears *ideologically sweeter*. Specifically, Rogen's model more distantly echoes far-right ideology by more fully disavowing its own resentment, sadism, and power lust, and by upholding respectable middle-class monogamy and procreation. We have seen that Lil Dicky inadvertently echoes the *manosphere*, a web of far-right online communities for (mainly young, straight, white) men who believe themselves "dispossessed" by white women, women of color, and men of color.[24] Deeply entwined with the alt-right, the manosphere stokes young straight white men's resentment against the outgroups who have "wronged" them, and it promotes violent revenge that can encompass rape and murder.[25] This far-right ideology is just a more explicit, detailed, and openly violent version of mainstream misbeliefs which claim that straight white men are now America's disenfranchised victims.[26] This overlap between extremist and mainstream white male victim narratives explains how stars with no apparent knowledge of the manosphere can produce media that echo far-right beliefs. For example, neither Dicky nor Rogen has ever referenced the manosphere. Indeed, Rogen's breakout role in *Knocked Up* came two years before the word "manosphere" entered circulation.[27] Nevertheless, both Dicky and Rogen's emasculated Jewface personae uncannily mirror manospheric *beta* identities: the umbrella of manospheric communities who claim they are disenfranchised because they are unathletic, nerdy, gay, or crushed by America's supposedly man-hating culture.[28] However, Rogen and Dicky differently mirror betas' fantasies of reclaiming their "lost" power. We have seen how Dicky specifically echoes the manospheric beta subcommunity of *incels*: men who claim that women "unjustly" deny them sex due to their lack of conventional masculinity, and who therefore fantasize violent revenge against these "withholding" women.[29] For example, we have seen how Dicky concludes his 2014 music video "Lemme Freak"

by raping his "withholding" wife after decades of "wrongful" deprivation. Like in "Lemme Freak," Dicky often flaunts incel-ish power lust,
misogyny, and sadism behind the thinnest plausible veneer of satire.

Rogen's babyish Jewface packages similarly oppressive fantasies in
far more wholesome-looking form, thereby fueling his stardom. For instance, although *Knocked Up* could have launched its accidental pregnancy plot with a broken condom, it instead uses-but-disavows one
of the manosphere's favorite weapons: a form of rape called *stealthing*,
which means secretly removing a condom during sex.[30] When first
drawing legal attention to stealthing in 2017, the attorney Alexandra
Brodsky noted that some manospheric forums promote stealthing because they claim that it expresses their "natural" right to "spread their
seed"—a right that women allegedly should never deny.[31] Significantly
for *Knocked Up*'s pregnancy plot, manospheric stealthers often aim to
control women's bodies by *impregnating* them, claiming that women
who have sex "deserve to be impregnated."[32] Although *Knocked Up*
premiered a decade before the word "stealthing" caught America's national attention, the film presages this manospheric violence when
Ben (Rogen) removes his condom without Alison's (Heigl's) knowledge, thereby impregnating her.[33] We will see how this stealthing scene
uses Rogen's hapless Jewface to echo-yet-repress the same oppressive
fantasies that motivate manospheric stealthers. On one hand, Rogen's
softness frames him as a disrespected victim who "deserves" revenge
against shrewish women, just as manospheric betas view themselves. Yet
Rogen's babyishness casts his stealthing as an innocent, hilarious, even
sweet mistake. By deeply denying its own misogynist revenge fantasies,
Knocked Up stays more palatable than manospheric dogma that openly
relishes harming and controlling women. *Knocked Up* thus exemplifies how Rogen's babyish Jewface always helps straight white-privileged
men's violent backlash to look sweet and wholesome.

Knocked Up also illustrates how Rogen's Jewface comedies uphold
respectable middle-class white monogamy and procreation, thereby
staying more palatable than manospheric dogma and Lil Dicky's humor.
Manospheric ideologies often vilify women as irrational, cruel abusers who are allegedly hardwired by evolution to exploit men.[34] Viewing women as irredeemable, such ideologies often dismiss loving
partnership (or even mutually joyful sex) between men and women as

impossible. Instead, manospheric dogma often conceives sex solely as a weapon in this supposed battle of the sexes. Lil Dicky's comedy often mirrors this rejection of heteronormative marriage. For instance, we have seen how "Lemme Freak"[35] not only glorifies rape-as-revenge, but also scorns marriage as a miserable concession to women.

Conversely, Rogen's Jewface comedies idealize heteronormative marriage and procreation because these films depict "bad" women as *redeemable*, so long as these women submit to men. *Knocked Up* exemplifies this more "wholesome"-seeming backlash narrative: it wields Rogen's "accidental," "sweet" stealthing to punish-yet-*rehabilitate* Alison by taming her into motherly and wifely femininity. This process pulls both protagonists into wholesome-looking monogamous white-privileged parenthood. Alison begins as a haughty, ambitious reporter who disdains Ben's slackerish, unkempt emasculation—yet once pregnancy binds them, she slowly "loosens up" to appreciate his comedic charms. *Knocked Up* explicitly spotlights how this unplanned pregnancy reroutes Alison into traditional gender roles: Alison tells Ben that "I really had never even thought about having a baby" until their hookup, and that "if this hadn't happened" (meaning, *if he hadn't stealthed her*) she wouldn't have wanted children for "another ten years, at least!"[36] Despite Alison's initial objections to motherhood and to Ben, the climactic ending finds her tearfully exclaiming to Ben that "I love you so much!" as she clasps their newborn to her breast. This ending implies that Alison had forgotten her "proper" maternal role until Ben's stealthing happily reminded her, restoring "natural" femininity that Alison comes to enjoy. In turn, punishing and domesticating Alison elevates Ben from pathetic loser to respectable husband-and father-to-be, as he exits his filthy group bachelor pad and lands a white-collar job. Ben's "accidental" stealthing thus advances an idealized fantasy of straight white-privileged romance and procreation. When Rotten Tomatoes praises this rape-based plotline as "a hilarious, poignant and refreshing look at the rigors of courtship and child-rearing,"[37] it illustrates just how sweet Rogen's abject hegemony can seem.

(Jewish) Beta Male Comedies and "Proto-Betas in Denial"

The similarities between Rogen and Lil Dicky reveal unacknowledged overlaps between manospheric "betas" and cinematic *beta males*, an unexpectedly marketable group identified by the film scholar David Greven.[38] Greven defines "beta male comedies" as a subgenre that emerged in the 2000s, pioneered by Judd Apatow and often starring Seth Rogen. Indeed, Greven spotlights Rogen as a "beta male star par excellence."[39] Like *Knocked Up*, beta male comedies often star "out of shape" straight white-privileged middle-class men who invert Hollywood's typical leading men by initially "refus[ing] to grow up" into breadwinners, homeowners, husbands, and fathers.[40] Alongside *Knocked Up*, prominent beta male comedies include *The 40-Year-Old Virgin* (2005), *Superbad* (2007), and *Pineapple Express* (2008), which all star or feature Rogen.[41] Matching my analysis of *Knocked Up*, the film scholar Casey Ryan Kelly notes that beta male comedies often strive "to tame female sexual agency" and enforce "neotraditional romance"[42] that includes heterosexual monogamy and/or procreation.

The similarities between Seth Rogen and Lil Dicky highlight how beta male comedies not only enforce conservative gender and sexual norms, but specifically echo far-right dogma in gentler form. If Rogen is a "beta male star par excellence," he illustrates that cinematic beta males are *proto-betas in denial*: cinematic beta males display embryonic versions of the fears, resentments, and fantasies of manospheric betas, yet deny their own aggression more completely and stay more invested in respectable straight domesticity and procreation. And although beta male comedies emerged earlier in the 2000s than manospheric betas, beta male comedies now coexist with the manosphere in America's spectrum of straight white-privileged male backlash narratives. Rogen's beta male comedy thus promotes real harm by helping mainstream audiences to palatably consume the myth that straight white-privileged men are now America's dispossessed victims and to palatably entertain fantasies of vengefully reasserting power. *This ideological labor invites all straight white-privileged men to become "proto-betas in denial"*: to believe themselves blameless or even progressive while embracing beta-ish resentments that make them ripe targets for the manosphere's radicalization campaigns.[43] Even for viewers who never encounter manospheric memes, the myth of white male victimhood makes it harder to recognize America's real inequalities.

Rogen's own apparently sincere progressivism helps him sell these oppressive resentments within beta male comedies, by appealing to self-identified liberal straight white-privileged men who similarly dis-avow such feelings. *The Times* reports that Rogen "has always considered himself a left-wing, feminist progressive."[44] He has illustrated this pro-gressivism through high-profile social media conflicts with Republican leaders—for instance, tweeting at hyper-conservative senator Ted Cruz, "Fuck off you fascist" in January 2021.[45] Alongside such Twitter state-ments, Rogen has expressed his progressivism in slightly more concrete terms than his more openly oppressive (but still self-declared liberal) contemporary, Lil Dicky. Although Lil Dicky has endorsed #BlackLives-Matter on social media,[46] he constantly normalizes anti-Black violence by depicting Black men as threatening criminals. Conversely, Rogen has taken modest but tangible action against the misogynist violence that his films sometimes normalize: despite his close friendship with James Franco, Rogen discontinued their professional collaborations in May 2021 due to growing #MeToo allegations against Franco.[47] Al-though it hardly constitutes groundbreaking advocacy, this step conveys Rogen's desire to see himself and be seen as genuinely progressive. No matter how sincere, this progressive image helps to further deny (and thus to make more palatable) the oppressive messages in his beta male comedies.

While illuminating how cinematic beta males share resentments with manospheric betas, I also clarify that tropes of Jewish emascula-tion are more central to the beta male subgenre than previously rec-ognized. When first identifying beta male comedies, David Greven briefly observes that "issues of Jewish masculinity are an intriguing . . . aspect of [beta male] films."[48] This understatement obscures the reality that nearly all beta male stars are Jewish and invoke tropes of Jewish emasculation. Indeed, film scholar Nathan Abrams notes that most beta male films recycle the same small cohort of conditionally white Jewish men dubbed the "Jew-Tang Clan" (punning on the iconic Black gentile hip hop group, the Wu-Tang Clan), including Rogen, Paul Rudd, Jason Segal, Jonah Hill, and James Franco.[49] Even this cohort's two white gentile actors, Michael Cera and Jay Baruchel, fit tropes of Jewish emasculation with shrimpy frames and brunette complex-ions. This Jewish and "Jewish-looking" cohort illustrates that tropes of Jewish emasculation fuel the beta male subgenre more centrally than Greven suggests.

I also flip Greven's analysis of how Rogen, as a "beta male star par excellence," performs Jewish masculinity. When briefly discussing Jewish masculinity, Greven calls Rogen a "striking rebuttal of Jewish stereotypes" who allegedly inverts emasculated predecessors like "Woody Allen and Jerry Seinfeld."[50] Greven instead attributes to Rogen a "non-neurotic" masculinity, with a "husky physicality and . . . aggressivity." This reading overlooks how Rogen actively aligns himself with self-emasculating Jewish predecessors, such as when his character in *Funny People* aspires to "be like Seinfeld."[51] Indeed, Rogen's beta male stardom depends on *emphasizing* (not rebutting) racial tropes of Jewish emasculation to *negate* his own "husky physicality and aggressivity." By packaging his bulk as roly-poly, Rogen's babyish Jewface casts him as innocent even when he violently enforces dominance, like by stealthing in *Knocked Up*. This Jewfaced emasculation is precisely what makes Rogen an effective "proto-beta in denial" and thus a compelling beta male star.

Beta Male Patriarchy, Post-Meninism, and Fun Fatherhood

Indeed, if Rogen's babyish Jewface embodies a "cuddly" (allegedly fun, guiltless, and lovable) model of straight white-privileged male domination and procreation, then a more precise name for this model is *beta male patriarchy*. The payoff of beta male patriarchy is that straight white-privileged men (both Jewish and gentile) can sustain their power and population without sacrificing their soothing self-image as harmless nice guys, and allegedly without sacrificing any youthful fun. Rogen's character in *Knocked Up*, Ben, exemplifies this fantasy: Ben is an affable stoner without the ambition or efficacy to dominate a prickly career woman. Yet Ben blamelessly and effortlessly reroutes his leading lady, Alison (Katherine Heigl), into subservient, motherly femininity by accidentally impregnating her. Heigl herself has criticized *Knocked Up* in terms that expose this misogynist domestication plot. Shortly after the film debuted, Heigl critiqued it as sexist because it "paints the women as *shrews*, as humorless and uptight, and it paints the men as lovable, goofy, fun-loving guys" (my emphasis).[52] Her word-choice evokes Shakespeare's *The Taming of the Shrew* (approximately 1590), which celebrates an aggressive male suitor as he breaks a "shrew" into a docile bride.[53] *Knocked Up* echoes yet inverts Shakespeare's "comedic" play to produce beta male patriarchy. Shakespeare's male protagonist deliberately asserts patriarchal power: he conspires with other men to crush the "shrew" via torments like food deprivation, and the play applauds this abuse for restoring "natural" gender inequalities.[54] Instead, *Knocked Up* disavows Ben's desire for patriarchal power and his aggression toward Alison, always depicting Ben as "lovable" and "goofy." Yet the film still celebrates Ben for domesticating an independent, acerbic woman into a sweetly supportive girlfriend and mother.

By enabling beta male patriarchy, Rogen's babyish Jewface resolves ideological tensions that past scholars deem paradoxical in beta male comedies. David Greven writes that beta male films invite viewers to empathize with their leading losers' struggles, but "leave almost completely unexamined the gender and racial privilege" on which these schlubby stars depend—including their entitlement to "be misogynistic, racist, and homophobic."[55] Although this phrasing treats privilege and pathetic-ness as contradictory, they are actually *complementary* within beta male comedies: Rogen's beta male stardom depends partly on using infantile Jewish emasculation to render straight white-privileged male power innocent-looking and thereby palatable to straight, white-privileged middle-class men themselves.

If beta male patriarchy includes guiltless power, then Rogen's Jewface characters achieve this guiltless power through a technique I call *post-meninism*: the fantasy that straight white-privileged middle-class men can *violently punish* minoritized people who challenge their power, but in ways that feel *accidental, unmalicious, and apolitical.* The ostensibly innocent stealthing in *Knocked Up*, which impregnates and tames the leading lady, exemplifies this post-meninist violence. Terming this technique "post-meninism" crystallizes how Rogen's comedy blends two better-known forms of anti-feminist backlash, "post-feminism" and "meninism." While feminism urges women to challenge institutional oppression (like abortion bans), post-feminism dismisses such large-scale inequalities as "over" and stigmatizes feminists as "shrill" or passé. In turn, as analyzed by Susan Douglas and Diane Negra,[56] post-feminism urges women to pursue only "fun," individualized, consumption-based liberation that won't trouble men and may even please them, such as buying an "empowering" red lipstick. Meanwhile, "meninism" is one term for "men's rights activism," an anti-feminist backlash movement born in the 1970s.[57] Meninists often bill themselves as respectable advocates, such as when contesting child-custody laws that allegedly favor mothers.[58] However, meninism's true engine is violent rage from men who resent the slightest reduction of their privilege and yearn to reassert their "rightful" power. This meninist violence first grabbed headlines in 1989 when a white male Canadian gunman attacked an engineering class in the Montreal Massacre: ordering men out of the room, he shouted, "I hate feminists!" before murdering the women.[59]

Rogen's post-meninist comedy disavows such openly rageful and violent meninism. Just as post-feminism urges women to pursue "empowerment" through depoliticized individual fun, Rogen's post-meninism reassures straight white-privileged men that they can punish and block rebellious outgroups through individualized, depoliticized, guilt-free fun. Indeed, Rogen's frequent colleague Judd Apatow has illustrated how deeply this post-meninism helps men disavow their own aggression. In a 2017 interview, Apatow described all his beta male protagonists as "terrified boys" who are "not aggressors in any way."[60] Apatow is dead wrong: beta males (including Rogen's characters) routinely commit racist and sexist aggression to protect privileges that they're "terrified" of losing. However, beta male films *laboriously construct* that aggression as apolitical, harmless, accidental, and unmalicious (post-meninist). And in all Rogen's beta male films, his roly-poly Jewface vitally helps to construct such "blameless" and "endearing" violence.

By "guiltlessly" reproducing straight white male dominance, post-meninism upholds one facet of beta male patriarchy. The second component of beta male patriarchy entails reproducing *white-privileged babies* without the restrictive responsibility or restrictive social life of married fatherhood. To model this stress-free procreation, Rogen's babyish Jewface also embodies a fantasy that I call *fun fatherhood*: the fantasy that straight white-privileged middle-class men can "have it all" by balancing fun, youthful, even homoerotic male camaraderie with respectable straight fatherhood. David Greven observes that beta male comedies often feature close male friends who blur homosocial (platonic) with homoerotic (sexual) bonds, as signaled by beta male titles like *I Love You, Man* (2009).[61] This pattern leads film scholar John Alberti to label beta male films *bromances*: films centering around "confused homosocial/homoerotic relationships between putatively straight male characters," even when these films ostensibly constitute straight rom-coms.[62] However, calling beta male films erotically "confused" implies a clash between homoeroticism and heterosexuality. Instead, Rogen's Jewfaced beta males neutralize this clash into an erotic *balance*, modeling how straight men can pleasurably weave homoeroticism into their straight-privileged lives as husbands and fathers.

For instance, *Knocked Up* shows Rogen's character (Ben) balance straight fatherhood with the gaiety (in every sense) of warm relations with his juvenile male housemates. On one hand, Ben's unplanned fatherhood distances him from these friends as he courts Alison and rents his own apartment.[63] Yet in the climactic birth scene, Ben's ex-housemates flood the hospital to celebrate with him, rejoicing, "We got a daughter! Mazel tov!" This exclamation conjures a queer (nonnormative and homoerotic) vision of many co-fathers: it implies that these ex-roommates will contribute helpful labor, boyish exuberance, and homoerotic intimacy to Ben's new life as a straight father. And by pairing this homoerotic premise with the Hebrew congratulation "Mazel tov!", Ben's ex-roommates link this fun fatherhood with Jewishness. As we will see, Rogen's babyish Jewface underpins his fun fatherhood by enabling an especially *nonthreatening* version of homoeroticism that does not disrupt heterosexual relationships.

By modeling fun fatherhood, Rogen defuses a dilemma famously observed by the Jewish queer theorist Eve Sedgwick in *Between Men* (1985).[64] Sedgwick notes that patriarchal societies encourage men to bond primarily with fellow men as friends and mentors. These homosocial networks (platonic bonds between men) maintain men's political and economic power, as the phrase "old boys' club" implies. But even while promoting this *homosocial* world, patriarchy historically pressures men to deny *homoerotic* feelings in their close bonds, since same-sex desire disrupts the rigid gender and sexual norms that "justify" patriarchal inequalities. Yet Rogen's fun fatherhood defangs homoeroticism into a pleasure that straight white-privileged middle-class male friends can openly relish without sacrificing their privilege. Thus, rather than destigmatizing LGBTQ+ characters (who rarely appear in his films), Rogen normalizes homoeroticism to offer *straight* white-privileged men a more fun, anxiety-free, emotionally fulfilling version of the respectable fatherhood that reproduces their privilege and population.

By blending youthful homoeroticism into straight fatherhood, Rogen's bromances put an androcentric twist on the ideological aim of most romantic comedies: to help straight domesticity look endlessly thrilling. Past scholarship affirms that Hollywood rom-coms emerged in the 1930s in response to dipping marriage rates and rising divorce rates, trends that reflected new conflicts over women's autonomy.[65] Linda Mizejewski specifies that rom-coms strove to *reconcile* women's autonomy with conventional monogamy and procreation: many rom-coms imply that spunky women can find contentment by using their assertiveness to *initiate* zany, scintillating straight relationships that culminate in marriage.[66] While conventional rom-coms still often ponder what women want and how to reconcile these desires with conventional gender roles, film scholar John Alberti observes that bromances (including Rogen's films) pivot to ask what twenty-first-century *men* want.[67] I add that these films strive to reassure men that straight procreative monogamy can remain endlessly fun and fulfilling. To this end, just as conventional rom-com heroines assure women that they can sustain plucky autonomy into straight marriage, Rogen's Jewish bromantic man-babies assure men that they can sustain youthful homoerotic gaiety and intimacy into straight fatherhood.

And if Rogen's techniques of fun fatherhood (effortless procreation) and post-meninism (guiltless domination) jointly produce beta male patriarchy, then these techniques depend on his gently messy Jewish man-baby persona.

Labradoodle: Building the Gently Messy Jewish Man-Baby

In turn, Rogen's Jewface persona depends on four techniques that start with *subtle cosmetic Jewface*. While Rogen's brutal white gentile bully in *Donnie Darko* has short straight hair (figure 4.1), later roles usually poof his hair into fluffy curls. *The 40-Year-Old Virgin* initiated this shift by presenting Rogen's first explicitly Jewish character, complete with short curls (figure 4.2). *Knocked Up* amplified this cosmetic transformation by volumizing his curls in publicity posters (like figure 4.3) and in the film itself.

Further, *Knocked Up* introduced Rogen's strategy of pairing cosmetic Jewface with *rhetorical Jewface*: dialogue that instructs viewers to perceive his hair, face, and body as self-evidently Jewish. Rhetorical Jewface begins in *Knocked Up* when Rogen's character (Ben) meets Katherine Heigl's (Alison) at a nightclub. When Alison enthuses that "I love your curly hair" and asks what styling product Ben uses, he chuckles, "I use Jew!,"[68] implying that his curls biologically signal Jewishness. Fusing rhetorical and cosmetic Jewface this way aligns Rogen with Lil Dicky and with the millennial Jewish comedian Ilana Glazer, who similarly accentuate their curls to embody Jewish racial tropes. Also like Glazer, Rogen sometimes rhetorically Jewfaces his features that do *not* fit antisemitic racial tropes. For example, although Rogen's straight nose has helped him play white gentile roles, he denies this passing potential in *Funny People* (2009). In the trailer, his semi-autobiographical character muses that "I don't think I can hide [my Jewishness]" because "my face is circumcised,"[69] implying that Jewishness is self-evidently carved onto his face. In such moments, rhetorical Jewface overrides physical appearance to intensify Rogen's overall Jewface.

Alongside rhetorical and cosmetic Jewface, Rogen's minstrel persona requires a third strategy of *narrative Jewface*: plotlines tying his emasculated, inept, filthy, or homoerotic image with Jewishness. This narrative Jewface turns spectacular during a mental breakdown in the 2015 Christmas comedy *The Night Before*.[70] Rogen's Jewish protagonist ("Isaac Greenberg") spends the film overcoming fears of fatherhood with his pregnant white, blond Catholic wife. These fears peak when Isaac—despite being high on mushrooms and sporting a blue Star of David sweater that declares him Jewish—unwisely joins his wife's prim white family for Christmas Eve Mass. There, Isaac hallucinates that an infant is heckling him (exaggerating his fears of fatherhood) and that a crucifixion statue is glaring at him (exaggerating his Jewish sense of outsiderness). This psychedelic fusion of masculine and Jewish anxieties launches Isaac into a tailspin that raunchily disrupts the Mass (figure 4.4). He sweats profusely, chants loudly in Hebrew, vomits prolifically in the center aisle, and finally yells that "we did not kill Jesus!" before fleeing. This scene depicts Rogen's Jewish body as wildly incompatible with the cathedral *and* with competent fatherhood. By making Rogen's Jewishness sensationally visible through

Figure 4.4. Rogen performs narrative Jewface during Christmas Eve Mass in *The Night Before* (2015), when his character loses control of his emotions, face, and body. Screenshot from *The Night Before*, 2015. Pulled from Amazon.com.

his sweater and dialogue, and by linking this Jewishness with Isaac's emasculation, sweat, vomit, and hysteria, this sequence exemplifies narrative Jewface.

However, Rogen's filthy, perverse, and emasculated Jewface always appears lovable thanks to his fourth technique: rhetorical, narrative, kinetic, and cinematographic *softness*. Rogen's Jewface always merges with dialogue, plotlines, and camera angles that depict his fat Jewish body as babyishly cute rather than menacing or repulsive. *Knocked Up* introduced this fusion of Jewface with cute softness in its publicity posters. As analyzed above, these posters employ lighting and cosmetics to make Rogen's curly Jewish hair look sumptuous; make his face look invitingly soft; and make his personality look adorably hapless. Further, when the film itself first rhetorically Jewfaces his curly hair, it links these Jewish curls to both physical and emotional softness. First, Katherine Heigl's character spotlights Ben's hair by exclaiming, "I love your curly hair!" and sinking her fingers into it, as though finding it delightfully soft.[71] Next, when Ben explains that "I use Jew" (not hair products) to create those curls, this reply links his Jewfaced hair to guileless cuteness. Whereas Rogen's greasy Jewish character from *The 40-Year-Old Virgin* was a slick player with slick hair, Ben is an artlessly adorable Jew.

In addition to rhetorically fusing Jewface with lovable softness, Rogen performs a *vestiary* fusion through costumes like his fuzzy blue Star of David sweater in *The Night Before* (figure 4.4). As Rogen's character melts down in a Catholic cathedral, his sweater links his Jewishness with his sweatiness, vomit, and hysteria. But even at his messiest, this sweater makes him look like an oversized toddler ready for cheesy holiday photos. This warm-and-fuzzy image inverts Rogen's image in prior films, like his tattooed arms in *The 40-Year-Old Virgin* (figure 4.2) or his biker-gang outfit from *Donnie Darko* (figure 4.1). Contrasting these earlier costumes against his adorable sweater in *The Night Before* reveals how, in post-2007 roles, fashion recodes Rogen's fat Jewfaced body as "self-evidently" soft.

Contrasting *Donnie Darko* against Rogen's later roles also highlights that his post-2007 Jewface wields *kinetic softness*: wobbly facial expressions and body language that cast him as adorably inept and guileless. In *Donnie Darko*, Rogen's white gentile villain appears menacing due not only to his criminal costume, but also his precise, premeditated, sadistic violence. Conversely, during Rogen's cathedral meltdown in *The Night Before*, his eyes, mouth, arms, and legs wobble like an infant's as his anxieties overwhelm him (figure 4.4). This infantile body language exemplifies how kinetic softness helps Rogen to recruit tropes of neurotic, filthy Jewish emasculation into a cute (not revolting) man-baby persona.

Yet even while crafting his adorable Jewface from antisemitic racial tropes, Rogen must invite *all* white-privileged men to embrace this image as their avatar of innocent victimhood. This paradoxical invitation aligns Rogen with his contemporaries Lil Dicky, Abbi Jacobson, and Ilana Glazer, who similarly craft their images from antisemitic racial stigmas, but vicariously offer those personae to wider white-privileged audiences. Also like these peers, Rogen extends his paradoxical invitation partly by performing racial proteanism. As we have seen, racial proteanism means crafting a single minstrel persona that appears racially multiple and elusive.[72] In Rogen's case, he achieves this proteanism by ambivalently depicting Jewishness as inside/outside whiteness, and by describing his own Jewfaced body as visibly Jewish or generically white.

This technique—wielding racial proteanism to make his babyish Jewface more accessible to all white-privileged men—is especially salient in *Neighbors 2* (2016). When Rogen's character begs a college dean to evict a rowdy sorority from his block, the dean (a white gentile woman) initially mocks him as a sexist "Mr. White Man" trying to restrict women.[73] Rogen protests, "Hey, don't talk to me like that, because I am Jewish,

I *am* a minority"—to which the dean dismissively replies, "Well, less of you. *Like labradoodles*" (my emphasis). This exchange spotlights the ambivalent way that America envisions conditionally white Jews as wavering between dominant white majority and marginalized nonwhite minority. On one hand, the dean states that Euro-American Jews are "less" of a minority (perhaps in comparison to people of color). On the other, her "labradoodle" quip condenses many antisemitic racial tropes to rhetorically Jewface Rogen: this quip envisions his Jewishness as a *biological, mongrelized*, and *animalized* difference that manifests in *curly brown hair*. However, the accusation that Jews embody or promote racial mixing usually marks Jews as threatening "race enemies" in white supremacist ideology.[74] Instead, labradoodles are a trendy designer mix costing up to $4,000.[75] Dubbing Rogen a "labradoodle" thus puts an appealing twist on his racial position between white majority and nonwhite minority, inviting all white-privileged men to embrace him as an avatar of lovable victimhood. When a powerful white woman dismisses Rogen's fears about other aggressive women, and then mocks him as "Mr. White Man," but also tacitly targets him with antisemitic tropes, this Jewish labradoodle can channel the resentment of any white-privileged man who feels victimized by "uppity" women.

While Rogen's racial proteanism aligns him with fellow millennial Jewish stars, he is the only millennial Jewish star to harness *marriage and procreation* as tools that offer his racially specific Jewface persona to all white-privileged men. Rogen's beta male film courtships always pair him with white gentile actresses who embody visual tropes of gentility, like small noses, blond hair, and/or slim physiques. Examples include Katherine Heigl in *Knocked Up* (2007), Rose Byrne in *Neighbors* (2014), and Jillian Bell in *The Night Before* (2015).[76] Further, Rogen's procreative films never discuss plans to raise the children Jewish. Indeed, Jillian Bell's pregnant character in *The Night Before* signals her commitment to Catholicism by attending Christmas Eve Mass. Thus, despite actively Jewfacing Rogen's body to racially distinguish him from white gentiles, these procreative films imply that his "mixed" children will seamlessly enter gentile whiteness. This contradiction (the way his films racially Jewface his body, but show him biologically fusing with gentile whiteness) may convey Jewish fantasies of fully assimilating into white gentile privilege. Yet this contradiction can also assist white-privileged men (both Jewish and gentile) to fantasize about *making their privilege more fun- and innocent-looking.* By constructing Jewishness as a racial difference that can fully fade into gentile whiteness, these films invite all white-privileged men to identify with Rogen's soft, lovable Jewface.

To intensify this invitation, Rogen's procreative plotlines suggest that his Jewishness will do even better than fading into gentile whiteness: it will *embellish* that whiteness by leaving faint and appealing traces of his cuddly Jewface. While white nationalists demonize Jews as "race enemies" and accuse Jews of orchestrating racial mixing to biologically pollute whiteness,[77] Rogen's procreative films send the opposite message. These films imply that pairing goofy conditionally white Jewish men with prim white gentile women can enliven a more lovable whiteness: *a whiteness that is gentler, more relaxed, and ever-so-slightly diversified— but still thin, beautiful, and brightly white-skinned.* This utopic fantasy further invites all white-privileged men to identify with Rogen's Jewface persona. And this fantasy depends on another Jewface tactic inaugurated in *Knocked Up*: pitting Rogen's Jewish man-babies against "hyperwhite shrews."

"Hyperwhite Shrews"

Rogen's gently messy Jewish man-baby persona depends not only on Jewfacing his own body, but also *contrasting* that Jewfaced body against unlikable women whom I term *hyperwhite shrews*. This term riffs on Katherine Heigl's critique of *Knocked Up* for vilifying women as "shrewish."[78] The phrase "hyperwhite shrew" also emphasizes how women in Rogen's comedies (including Heigl's character) put a misogynist twist on the wider phenomenon of "hyperwhiteness."[79] As we have seen, "hyperwhite" characters embody the worst stereotypes of whiteness: pallid, greedy, cruel, conformist, elitist, bloodthirsty, and/or blatantly racist. They thus help white-privileged viewers to feel racially innocent by comparison.[80] And by seeing hyperwhite characters punished, white-privileged viewers can imagine purging the nastiest parts of whiteness, and thus feel guilt-free about white supremacy.[81]

However, past scholarship overlooks how hyperwhite *women* characters can simultaneously convey white liberal anxieties (about wanting to virtuously critique white privilege without losing it) *and* convey misogynist anxieties about feminism. To fill this gap and illuminate Rogen's comedy, I define *"hyperwhite shrews" as women who fuse tropes of "nasty" hyperwhiteness with misogynist tropes about "nasty" independent women.* This fusion makes hyperwhite shrews into scapegoats for the supposed indignities that feminism inflicts on men *and* for the real injustices of white supremacy. To this end, hyperwhite shrews contradict the scholarly assumption that hyperwhiteness must look ugly. Instead, hyperwhite shrews combine *beautiful* thin, blond white gentile femininity with *social power* and with *sour, elitist, humorless, mean-spirited behavior.* In Rogen's comedies, these hyperwhite shrews serve as foils who enhance his lovable, babyish, hapless Jewface, including his physical appearance and his social distance from white abusive behavior. Likewise, these shrewish foils *invite all white-privileged men to identify with Rogen's Jewish emasculation* and *invite all audiences to justify his characters' hostility toward women.*

One hyperwhite shrew who exemplifies these effects is the aforementioned dean in *Neighbors 2.*[82] This dean is a slim, beautiful, blond, straight-haired, straight-nosed, and green-eyed white gentile woman.[83] This beautiful white gentile woman wields her institutional power to expose men to ill-treatment by fellow women: she refuses to help Rogen's character (Mac Radner) curb the rowdy sorority upending his family's life. Alongside this gendered malice, the dean doubly disdains Mac as a Jew: her "labradoodle" quip both animalizes Jews *and* trivializes antisemitism. Together with her prim white blond femininity, this misconduct makes the dean a symbol for spiteful women *and* spiteful white gentiles. Further, the "labradoodle" comment that helps to vilify this dean as a hyperwhite shrew simultaneously Jewfaces Rogen, by equating his Jewishness with adorable roly-poly emasculation. Alongside this rhetorical Jewface, the hyperwhite shrewish dean visually accentuates Rogen's babyish Jewface: her thin, pale, blond body, her confident body language, and her disdainful facial expressions all accentuate Rogen's doughy body, light brown hair, flailing gestures, and bewildered facial expressions.

While vilifying a white gentile man would risk alienating white gentile male viewers, hyperwhite shrews like this dean offer a "common enemy" to Rogen and all white-privileged men, and perhaps to viewers of color. Further, when hyperwhite shrews belittle Rogen's helpless

Jewish man-babies, they *frame Rogen's aggressive reactions as natural self-defense or well-deserved payback*, thereby "justifying" white male backlash against women. Even more insidiously, hyperwhite shrews help audiences *to sheathe this sexist aggression inside an antiracist veneer*: these antagonists make it difficult for audiences to distinguish between yearning to vengefully punish "uppity" women or to virtuously rebuke elitist white people. In all these ways, hyperwhite shrews enhance Rogen's cute abject hegemony, post-meninist backlash, and beta male patriarchy by helping him look more *harmless*; yet also look more *justified* in committing misogynist harm; and look more benevolent, blameless, and lovable when he achieves power.

This ideological labor grows even more complex and disturbing in the procreative films like *Knocked Up* that cast hyperwhite shrews *as leading ladies*. These plots offer an additional promise: that *Rogen's goofy Jewface can make gentile whiteness more lovable, both by thawing hyperwhite shrews and by begetting gentler white daughters*. This rosy message obscures how these films actually enable straight white-privileged men to dominate "their" women while feeling blamelessly benevolent. This promise of taming hyperwhite shrews and siring lovable whiteness is especially central in *Knocked Up*. Just as that film inaugurated Rogen's babyish Jewface, it introduced "hyperwhite shrews" as handmaidens to his ideological labor.

Jewish/Gentile "War of the Sexes"

Indeed, *Knocked Up* tacitly stages a racialized "war of the sexes" between goofy conditionally white Jewish man-babies and humorless gentile hyperwhite shrews. Members of the Jew-Tang Clan play nearly all the male roles: Seth Rogen plays the leading loser (Ben), Paul Rudd plays his future brother-in-law (Pete), and Jason Segal, Jonah Hill, and Jay Baruchel play Ben's childish Jewish housemates. Against these jubilant Jewish slobs, *Knocked Up* pits three slim, gorgeous, radiantly blond gentile hyperwhite shrews: the leading lady Alison (Katherine Heigl), her sister Debbie (played by Judd Apatow's wife, Leslie Mann, who self-describes as "WASPy"),[84] and their mother (Joanna Kerns). This racialized clash underpins Rogen's post-meninist violence in the film: his stealthing that appears "justified"-yet-accidental. In turn, his post-meninist violence appears even more benign because its ripple effect *resolves* this racialized war of the sexes, producing a "happier" world that is less hyperwhite and more beta-patriarchal.

As *Knocked Up*'s leading hyperwhite shrew, Alison initially seems pleasant but tacitly threatens straight white-privileged middle-class men. After all, Alison is a career woman in the historically male-dominated field of journalism. Indeed, when she first meets Rogen's character (Ben) at a nightclub, Alison is celebrating her recent promotion.[85] Thus, like the women engineering students murdered in the Montreal Massacre, Alison embodies the threat that ambitious women will weaken men's monopoly on prestigious high-paying careers. Ben—a rudderless unemployed loser—embodies the hapless men "marginalized" by women's ascent. Further, Alison's hyperwhiteness accentuates Ben's babyish Jewface during their first meeting, amplifying the sense that she socially outranks him. Ben is pudgy, with light-brown curly hair that he rhetorically links to Jewishness, and he wears a black shirt that darkens his complexion. Conversely, Alison is slim, gorgeous, and radiantly white: her straight blond hair, gold earrings, and white blouse all literally glow. This contrast amplifies the sense that Alison socially outranks Ben and all the white-privileged men who identify with him. Further, Alison represents the misogynist fear that autonomous women will "selfishly" assert their erotic desires in ways that intimidate men.[86] After all, Alison is a beautiful woman confidently chatting up Ben at the club, and when he asks if "you wanna get out of here?" she matter-of-factly invites him home. Alison's sexual, economic, and professional empowerment thus exemplify the traits that misogynists fear in women.

The subtle power differentials and resentments in this exposition turn blatant in *Knocked Up*'s key stealthing scene, which more harshly vilifies Alison as a hyperwhite shrew, and thus accentuates Ben's lovable Jewfaced emasculation. In turn, this contrast stokes-and-disavows the audience's hunger for misogynist revenge against Alison. In bed, Ben sweetly self-deprecates while trying to please Alison. He exclaims that "you're prettier than I am!," obliquely referencing her hyperwhite (thin, blond) femininity; he apologizes for "sweating on you"; and he declares after two seconds that "I just doubled my record time [before ejaculating]!" These comments depict Ben's body as childishly messy in accidental, endearing ways. But Alison answers Ben's puppyish vulnerability with scorn, especially when he fumbles with his condom, a struggle that exemplifies his emasculation and sexual incompetence. Given Ben's ever-present puffy brown curls, his condom struggles serve as narrative Jewface that enhances his hapless Jewish man-baby persona. The hyperwhite gentile Alison has no patience for this sweetly inept Jewish man-baby: she first snaps, "Hurry up," then demands, "What are you doing?" before scornfully hissing, "Oh god, just do it already!" Alison thus embodies the "uppity" women that manospheric misogynists urge each other to punish with stealthing, and that many men beyond the manosphere also yearn to see punished.

This contrast between the hyperwhite shrewish Alison and babyish Jewfaced Ben enables *Knocked Up*'s central post-meninist violence, which I term *sweet stealthing*: stealthing that offers viewers the pleasure of misogynist revenge, yet utterly disavows this revenge as a sweet, earnest, hilarious mistake. When Alison orders him to "just do it," Ben's surprised expression implies that he has misinterpreted her command, thinking she *wants* him to proceed without a condom. Obediently replying, "Oh, great, okay," he drops the condom before mounting Alison. Like all his motions, Ben moves clumsily when dropping the condom, like a wobbly baby that can't control its limbs, thereby reinforcing his hapless Jewface persona. Thus, Ben unintentionally places Alison in a situation in which she believes a condom protects her from STIs, HIV, and pregnancy, but she actually remains vulnerable to all three. Ben thereby gives audiences the satisfaction of seeing Alison stealthed, but he stealths her by accident *and at her own command*, even thinking he has pleased her. This "sweet stealthing" thus appears earnestly blameless and well-intentioned.

Like its stealthing scene, all of *Knocked Up* elaborately denies that Ben's transgression constituted misogynist revenge, but also implies that Alison "deserved" stealthing as punishment for being a hyperwhite shrew. For example, the morning after this stealthing, the first shots of Ben show his naked, roly-poly body snoozing face down, including a close-up of his plump pink buttocks. These shots frame him as an oversized infant whose brown curls relink his babyish softness to Jewishness. Meanwhile, the golden-blond Alison frowns sourly down at this fat Jewfaced man-baby (figure 4.5). Thus, as Ben's infantile Jewish image reinforces his harmlessness, Alison's haughty frown reinforces her image

Figure 4.5. Alison appears as a "hyperwhite shrew" in *Knocked Up* (2007), sourly judging the Jewish man-baby in her bed.
Screenshot from *Knocked Up*, 2007. Pulled from Amazon.com.

as a hyperwhite shrew who "deserves" punishment for disdaining goofy, lovable Jewish "nice guys" like Ben. The scene's humor recruits the audience's knowing gaze: Alison's haughty regret about bedding Ben is "funny" because viewers know that this hyperwhite shrew will soon get knocked off her high horse. She is already pregnant with Ben's child, and must learn to appreciate the Jewish man-baby she scorns.

Contrasting Ben (the Jewish man-baby) against Alison (the hyperwhite shrew) not only helps to justify-but-disavow Ben's vengeful stealthing; this racialized contrast also helps the stealthing plot *to produce beta male patriarchy*. The stealthing's ripple effect combines with Ben's roly-poly Jewface to reassert traditional gender norms and inequalities in ways that advantage Ben, but which look unmalicious, unintended, and lovable. For example, Ben's babyish Jewface not only helps to excuse the stealthing, but also underpins Alison's decision to keep the baby and begin courting Ben. For comparison, no rom-com would envision Alison partnering with Rogen's sexually jaded, "ugly as fuck" Jewish character from *The 40-Year-Old Virgin* or his brutal white gentile character from *Donnie Darko*. Indeed, Alison hints at the importance of Ben's softness on their second date by asking, "You're a sweet guy, right?"

And if Ben's "sweet" Jewface encourages Alison to keep the baby that he stealthed into her, this sweetness grows appealing *by contrast against* another hyperwhite foil: Alison's egregiously hyperwhite shrewish mother, who urges abortion. This mother combines icy blue eyes, porcelain skin, and blond hair with large white pearls that signal WASPy wealth. She thus looks even more hyperwhite than Alison, who has brown eyes and dresses less ostentatiously. In the mother's single appearance, she also outstrips Alison's shrewishness by displaying cartoonish frigidity. When urging Alison to "take care of it" (get an abortion), this hyperwhite mother never addresses the agonizing emotional, financial, medical, or professional decisions that lead many women to seek abortions. Instead, she reflects the misogynist myth that only callous monsters could condone abortion. For instance, she pressures Alison to wait for "a real baby" later, a shocking phrase which implies that she disrespects human life rather than fears for her daughter's future. Yet this hyperwhite shrewishness makes the mother so odious that she drives Alison *toward* Ben and motherhood: as her mother reaches peak frigidity, Alison's face sets with determination to remain pregnant, marking Alison's first step toward "likable" domestication.

To thaw Alison from hyperwhite shrew to likable white woman, Ben not only reroutes her priorities from career to motherhood: he also claims her sexual labor, emotional labor, and respect. The film's central romance (rooted in "sweet stealthing") thus implies that immature uncouth men deserve more esteem from gorgeous, ambitious, self-possessed women. This misogynist message grows especially clear—and plays especially hard on the contrast between Jewishness and hyperwhiteness—in a scene featuring Alison's sister and fellow hyperwhite shrew, Debbie. In this pivotal scene, the sisters watch Ben playing with Debbie's young daughters and getting stuck inside their pink-and-purple play castle. This fat joke stresses Ben's immaturity and emasculation, but also highlights his willingness to meet children at their level, suggesting that his childishness will make him a warm father.

Alison and Debbie's opposite reactions to Ben's play castle snafu illustrate Alison's newfound affection for Ben. In turn, this affection reframes Alison from hyperwhite shrew to "lovable" woman. As Ben struggles out of the play castle, Debbie judgmentally calls Ben "overweight" and muses that he must have "bad genes." Although this judgment ostensibly just targets Ben's fatness, Debbie's hyperwhiteness tacitly links it to eugenicist rhetoric about white gentile racial purity. Conversely, this is the moment when Alison starts valorizing Ben's conventionally unattractive traits: she warmly affirms that "he's funny," then orders Debbie to "give him a break." Alison thus displaces the stigma of hyperwhite shrewishness onto her sister by proving her own ability to appreciate (even desire!) a schlubby, underachieving Jewish man. Juxtaposing Alison against Debbie this way accentuates the message that "good" women should appreciate immature and unambitious men.

And while Ben's beta male patriarchy includes domesticating Alison, it also includes "lovably" enforcing more direct patriarchal power over her hyperwhite sister, Debbie. The film's climactic birth scene sees Debbie try to dismiss Ben from the delivery room, but he angrily claims the room (and implicitly, the woman and infant within it) as his territory, forcefully exclaiming, "That's my room now, back the fuck off!" Rather than taking offense, Debbie interprets this hostility as proof of *loving and responsible* (not aggressive) masculinity: she concludes that "he's gonna be a good dad." David Greven interprets this odd reaction as evidence that beta male films desire their leading losers to "man up" toward conventional masculine behaviors and power abuses.[87] I concur but emphasize how Rogen's gently messy Jewish man-baby persona enables *beta male patriarchy* that disavows the power it seeks. A brutal white gentile bully like his character from *Donnie Darko* would seem villainous if trying to territorially claim his lover or separate her from her sister. Instead, Rogen's emasculated Jewface in *Knocked Up* makes him seem (yet again) a lovable victim to a hyperwhite shrew who wrongfully disdains him. In turn, his speech comes off as dignified self-defense rather than menacing abuse. In fact, this disavowed aggression positions Ben as a *loving caretaker* for the woman and baby in "his" room: the perfect beta male patriarch.

In addition to "guiltlessly" taming the hyperwhite shrews Alison and Debbie, Ben models beta male patriarchy by promising *to make whiteness itself look more lovable*. This promise of lovable whiteness depends not only on softening Alison and Debbie, but also on siring children who embody a slight and appealing racialized diversity. Since this racial message depends on the daughter that Ben sired through stealthing, it further valorizes Ben's stealthing as wholesome. This promise of birthing a more lovable whiteness emerges through Ben and Alison's foils: Alison's hyperwhite sister, Debbie, and Debbie's Jewish-coded husband, Pete (Paul Rudd). Pete is Jewish-coded because he is played by a well-known Jewish actor and is a proxy for the film's Jewish director, Judd Apatow: Rudd shares Apatow's dark hair and pairs with Apatow's real-life wife in *Knocked Up*. Further, Pete and Debbie's young daughters in *Knocked Up* are played by Apatow and Mann's own children, Maude and Iris Apatow. Maude and Iris bring to the film not only their mixed Jewish/gentile ancestry, but also physical appearances which symbolize the promise that Jewish ancestry can revitalize whiteness. In contrast to their mother's straight blond hair (which connotes hyperwhiteness), Maude and Iris embody the barest hints of stereotypically dark and curly Jewish hair: Maude's hair is light-brown but straight, while Iris's is bright blond but curly. And in contrast to their mother's sour facial expressions, the girls joyfully play with the rolypoly Jewish Ben. Yet both girls share their mother's thinness, radiant white skin, and button noses. The girls thus visually imply that when their aunt Alison bears Ben's baby, this "mixed" child (conceived by stealthing) will similarly repackage the privileges of beautiful whiteness in more lovable form. Thus, if *Knocked Up* stages a racialized war of the sexes between lovable Jewish goofballs and hateful hyperwhite shrews, then this war wields post-meninist violence ("sweet stealthing") to produce a "utopic" ending in which beta male patriarchs affably rule a more likable white future.

Post-Meninist Racial Violence

Even as Ben's babyish Jewface in *Knocked Up* defuses hyperwhiteness, this Jewface also helps him to commit post-meninist racial aggression that "guiltlessly" dominates people of color. And although this racist aggression appears mild in *Knocked Up*, it presages how Rogen's later roles commit-and-disavow grislier racist violence to enforce beta male patriarchy.

After dominating Debbie (his hyperwhite, shrewish future sister-in-law), Ben also dominates a surly Asian male obstetrician. This Asian man, Dr. Kuni (Ken Jeong), is an undesired substitute: Alison's usual white-privileged doctor is out of town for a bar mitzvah.[88] This bar

mitzvah snafu not only refreshes the theme of Jewish masculinity during Alison's labor, but enables Ben to "man up" as Alison's (Jewish) male
protector. When Dr. Kuni disrespects Alison's autonomy by demanding
to medically induce labor, Ben sternly requests to "talk outside in the
hall." He then schools Dr. Kuni on empathizing with Alison's distress,
concluding that "you can be as big a dick to me as you want, just be
nice to her, man." This lecture persuades Dr. Kuni to apologize to both
Ben and Alison. Ben thus disciplines a man of color *into being a better
agent of white-privileged reproduction,* but Ben achieves this dominance
in a way that appears utterly loving toward Alison. Further, this lovable
act of racial dominance prompts Alison to tearfully proclaim, *"I just
never thought . . . that the guy who got me pregnant would actually be the
right guy for me."* This line reemphasizes how Ben's cutely soft Jewish
image enables him to dominate white women and/or people of color in
lovable-looking ways.

While *Knocked Up* (2007) limits Ben's post-meninist racial aggression
to stern words, *Pineapple Express* (2008) shows Rogen shoot an Asian
man point-blank and *still* appear adorably innocent.[89] This "blameless,"
"cute" violence depends on depicting Rogen's Jewish man-baby (Dale
Denton) as a hapless bystander in a racialized struggle between two rival
drug cartels. Dale and his pot dealer, Saul (James Franco), are mellow
Jewish stoners caught between an invading gang called "the Asians" (led
by Ken Jeong, from *Knocked Up*) and an established multiracial gang
(led by white gentile actor Gary Cole and Afro-Latina actress Rosie
Perez). This plot about an Asian invasion mirrors white-privileged
Americans' anxieties about being displaced by Asian immigrants (and
nonwhite immigrants generally). Within this racial conflict, *Knocked Up*
helps Dale and Saul to evade culpability for white abuses, but they still
channel white anxiety and white revenge fantasies. On one hand, these
Jewish losers look harmless and distant from white male power when
contrasted against the film's bloodthirsty white gentile drug lord (Gary
Cole), who embodies a form of hyperwhiteness. When this hyperwhite
druglord targets them, Dale and Saul appear as bumbling Jewish man-
boys incapable of white male cruelty, power lust, or physical strength.
They confirm this harmless image by using violence only in self-defense
and doing so ineptly, such as when Dale klutzily drops the first gun he
ever holds.

Yet the harmless image that helps Dale and Saul to disavow white male privilege when fleeing Gary Cole also makes them perfect symbols for white male victimhood when fleeing Rosie Perez or "the Asians." When facing death from people of color, the hapless Jewish beta males easily symbolize the myths that (1) people of color are displacing and harming white-privileged Americans, and (2) these white-privileged Americans are innocent of any racist aggression. This symbolism becomes clearest through Perez's role. Although Perez rose to prominence in Spike Lee's *Do the Right Thing* (1989),[90] about white police violence against young Black men, *Pineapple Express* flips Perez's legacy to endorse white male victim narratives: Perez plays a crooked cop turned cartel henchwoman who ruthlessly hunts Dale and Saul. This plotline bizarrely implies that white-privileged men now suffer state violence from women of color. *Pineapple Express* even winks at this racial reversal when Saul yells at Perez, "Fuck the police!" He thus misappropriates a protest slogan from the 1988 hip hop album *Straight Outta Compton*[91] by the Black gentile group N.W.A., a slogan that now widely serves to condemn racist police violence.[92]

The same babyish Jewish image that helps Dale and Saul to embody white male victimhood in *Pineapple Express* also lets them unleash hor-rifying post-meninist racist violence—violence that appears "justified" as self-defense *and* hilariously "harmless" because it comes from weak Jewish losers. Dale's point-blank murder of an Asian man epitomizes this post-meninist racist violence: when one of "the Asians" seizes him from behind, Dale flails wildly before shooting him, then makes a car-toonishly panicked expression before galumphing away. This babyish body language and emotion vividly contrast against Rogen's murderous white gentile character from *Donnie Darko*, who executed violence with precision and relish. To further excuse Dale and Saul's violence, *Pineap-ple Express* also displaces most killing blows onto other characters. For example, the leader of "the Asians" inadvertently explodes himself, his Asian crew, the hyperwhite gentile male drug lord, and his Afro-Latina henchwoman.

By blamelessly decimating the hyperwhite, Asian, Afro-Latina, and/or female "bad guys," this post-meninist violence frees the two Jewish beta males and their white gentile male friend (Danny McBride) to achieve blissful beta male patriarchy. The final scene shows this trio celebrating their homoerotic friendship over a tasty brunch, during which the man-boys exclaim that "I love you guys," imagine sharing heart-shaped necklaces, and envision "moving in together." Even as they tend wounds from their recent violence, this dialogue implies that (straight white-privileged) boys just want to have fun, not hurt anyone. This innocent aura grows clearer and more strongly linked to Jewishness when Saul's bubbe (Yiddish for grandmother) picks them up, like children from school. Yet by providing their transportation, Bubbe illustrates how this new beta male utopia depends on women's unpaid labor to sustain men's carefree fun. Indeed, Bubbe never appears onscreen: she matters only as invisible labor for the beta males. Thus, *Pineapple Express*'s happy ending depends on preserving only the minoritized people who pleasingly serve beta male patriarchy, while using post-meninist violence to "guiltlessly" eliminate any others.

However, the three straight white-privileged stoners at the end of *Pineapple Express* all remain happily unwed and childless. Conversely, many of Rogen's Jewish beta male protagonists specifically struggle to balance youthful male camaraderie with mature monogamous father-hood. This struggle pervades *Knocked Up* (2007), *Neighbors* (2014), *The Night Before* (2015), and *Neighbors 2* (2016). Through these struggles, Rogen models fun fatherhood: the promise that men can sustain endless youthful fun while wedding white-privileged women and reproducing white-privileged babies. Alongside the promise of guiltless domination, this promise of fun white procreation completes the fantasy of beta male patriarchy.

Queer Time for the Straight Guy: Homoeroticism, Chrononormativity, and Fun Fatherhood

Time travel makes a queer (unexpected and homoerotic) appearance halfway through *Knocked Up*, disrupting the star's progress toward straight monogamous fatherhood. The topic arises just when Ben (Rogen) seems to be exiting his eternal adolescence in a homoerotic group bachelor pad and entering his new life as a straight monogamous father with Alison. Illustrating this transition, Ben and Alison attend a swanky double date with their older foils: Alison's sister, Debbie, and brother-in-law, Pete.[93] Yet under the influence of their elegant drinks,

Ben and Pete turn suddenly bitter about straight monogamous fatherhood, turn nostalgic for their carefree youth, and turn lustful for each other—and these disruptive feelings coalesce around the metaphor of time travel.

Pete initiates this rebellion against straight monogamous fatherhood by asking, "Isn't it weird though, when you have a kid, and all your dreams and hopes go right out the window?" Ben eagerly agrees, sharing his fantasy of fleeing Alison's pregnancy to remain "free." Ben specifically fantasizes about using the time-traveling DeLorean car from the sci-fi classic *Back to the Future* (1985) to undo Alison's pregnancy. These insensitive comments lead Debbie to snap at the men, "Why don't the two of you get in your time machine, go back in time, and fuck each other?" Rather than apologizing, the men embrace this homoerotic fantasy: Pete gazes lustfully at Ben and sultrily asks, "Who needs a time machine?," implying that he's ready to "fuck" Ben now. Pete then evokes the bodice-ripping style of romance novels by describing how he'd ravish Ben: in a barely joking tone, Pete throatily proclaims that "I'm gonna throw you in my DeLorean and gun it to '88." Ben returns this homoeroticism by enthusing, "Look at his face, I just wanna kiss it! I think he's cute!" Ben then concludes, "This is the most fun I've had in a really long time." This claim is striking because Ben has recently been courting Alison and escorting her to obstetricians. Ben thus implies that his homoerotic banter with Pete about recapturing youthful freedom is more enjoyable than heterosexual romance or fatherhood.

When Ben and Pete fantasize about trysting in a time machine, their sci-fi reference exposes the temporal anxieties that pervade Rogen's films about fatherhood. These anxieties concern *chrononormativity* and *queer time*. The term "chrononormativity" comes from queer theorist Elizabeth Freeman, who builds on work by the fellow queer theorist Dana Luciano.[94] Chrononormativity describes socially approved timelines for a "normal" life which urge individuals "toward maximum productivity," including interlaced expectations about economic, gendered, and sexual productivity.[95] For instance, chrononormativity sets expected timetables for marrying, building wealth, procreating, and rearing children to meet those milestones in turn.[96] To promote this life schedule, chrononormativity also more broadly prescribes timelines for "proper" gendered and sexual maturation. For example, consider the present-day

American expectation that straight white-privileged middle-class men should progress from raucous fraternity parties in college to wholesome marriage, fatherhood, and homeownership in the decade after. People who disobey chrononormativity enter "queer time," a term coined by Jack Halberstam. Rather than simply describing homoeroticism, "queer time" names any behavior that disrupts chrononormative and hetero-normative timelines of maturation, matrimony, procreation, and gender performance.[97] For example, when David Greven writes that beta male characters "refuse to grow up, get jobs, get out of their parents' house, get wives,"[98] he pinpoints how these men refuse chrononormative progress and thus enter queer time. Although these beta males are heterosexual, their temporal disobedience stigmatizes their masculinity as queer (strange and deficient).

If Rogen's films often convey the fear that young straight white-privileged middle-class men will refuse marriage or procreation, this fear reflects two contradictory anxieties about chrononormativity. First, that such men will *fail* at chrononormativity and get stuck in queer time. Second, that chrononormativity is *inherently undesirable*, and must compromise with queer time to tempt heterosexual men back into marriage and procreation. *Knocked Up* exemplifies these conflicting anxieties through Ben's Jewish male foils. On one hand, Ben's childish housemates embody the threat that young straight white-privileged middle-class men will fail at chrononormativity and get stuck in queer time. To stigmatize their eternal adolescence, the film makes their immaturity look nauseating. For example, all but Ben contract the oozing and toddlerish ailment pink eye by (in their words) "farting" on each other's pillows, which spreads contagious "poo particles." Yet even while stigmatizing these squalid homoerotic man-boys, the film endows them with desirable *gaiety* (jubilance and closeness). For instance, the film opens by depicting these man-boys exuberantly play-fighting and dancing together. Inverting these joyful-but-pathetic losers is Ben's sad-but-respectable future brother-in-law, Pete, who embodies the anxiety that chrononormativity is inherently undesirable. This worry takes center screen when Ben first meets Pete, who appears glamorously adult but unfulfilled. As a handsome man in business casual escorting his young daughters from their spacious suburban home to their pristine SUV, Pete presents every marker of adult straight white-privileged middle-class masculinity. Yet as Ben and Alison emerge from the guesthouse (where their fateful hookup has just occurred), Pete gazes at Ben's rumpled T-shirt and sighs, "Ah, to be young." Thus, long before Pete voices his time machine fantasy, he explicitly yearns to reexperience youth (to enter queer time).

Pete's plotline soon reveals another pervasive assumption in Rogen's films: that queer time is alluring specifically because it *offers homoeroticism*. More specifically, these films imply (1) that what straight white-privileged middle-class heterosexual men truly miss about their youth is *homoerotic intimacy with their male friends*. Likewise, (2) what these men truly fear in monogamous fatherhood is social isolation with a wife who cannot meet their homoerotic needs. Therefore, (3) such men will never fully embrace chrononormativity—never commit to white middle-class marriage or procreation—until those heteronormative institutions loosen their chrononormativity to accommodate moderate doses of youthful homoerotic camaraderie. These assumptions about homoeroticism are striking because queer time does not inherently require homoeroticism: if a man yearned simply to reenact the more casual clothing and lighter responsibilities of his youth, this behavior too would constitute queer time. Indeed, these youthful pleasures initially seem to be what tempt Pete in *Knocked Up*, since he reminisces about "being young" while watching Ben emerge from a straight hookup late in the morning in rumpled clothing. However, the film soon clarifies that what Pete really misses about "being young" is male camaraderie: after hinting that Pete is cheating on his wife, *Knocked Up* reveals that he's actually sneaking out at night to attend an all-male fantasy baseball league. And although this pastime appears platonic, Ben and Pete's time-travel discussion makes clear that both men also crave homoerotic intimacy.

In turn, Rogen's model of fun fatherhood offers straight men the promise that they can "have it all" by reconciling chrononormativity (maturing into respectable straight monogamous fatherhood) with queer time (eternally sustaining youthful and homoerotic gaiety). In other words, Rogen's Jewish beta male comedies offer *queer time for the straight guy*: they accessorize heteronormative institutions and privileges with queer (nonnormative) time that includes openly queer (homoerotic) pleasures. Rogen's comedy thus aids straight white-privileged men to render their own supremacy more pleasurable.

In order to produce fun fatherhood that blends youthful homoeroticism with straight monogamous procreation, Rogen's Jewface *desexualizes* him. Just as Rogen's emasculated, fat, babyish Jewish image casts him as innately weak and hapless, it also casts him as innately incapable of *feeling or inciting strong sexual desires*. This fatphobic assumption defuses even Rogen's most graphic homoerotic performances by casting them as "self-evidently" comical, implausible, or just unsexy. This deflection helps viewers to relish but discount homoerotic exchanges onscreen, and it reduces the risk that straight male viewers may find *themselves* uncomfortably aroused by Rogen's homoeroticism. Thus, Rogen's babyish Jewface offers straight men the fantasy of openly embracing homoeroticism without destabilizing straight identity or privilege. This knack for flaunting-and-defusing homoeroticism is especially clear during Ben and Pete's time-travel repartee in *Knocked Up*, because Rogen's desexualization counterbalances Pete's serious sex appeal and serious lust. Pete is played by Paul Rudd, one of the only conventionally handsome actors in the Jew-Tang Clan. Further, Pete's speech, intonation, and facial expression all convey smoldering homoerotic desire behind the thinnest veneer of humor (*"I'm gonna throw you in my DeLorean"*). Yet by addressing Rogen's babyish Jewfaced character, Pete's sultry fantasy loses its edge. Pete's hot-and-heavy speech would raise more threatening possibilities if addressing one of Rogen's earlier incarnations, like the aggressively sexual Jewish character Cal from *The 40-Year-Old Virgin*. Pete's lust would also land differently if targeting a conventionally handsome millennial Jewish man like James Franco or Jake Gyllenhaal, especially since Gyllenhaal had just starred in the breakthrough gay drama *Brokeback Mountain* (2005). Instead, Rogen's pudgy, emasculated Jewface image defuses the possibility that Pete's attraction might be real or that the men might actually fuck onscreen. And this soothing effect grows when Ben returns Pete's homoerotic interest: Ben transposes this homoeroticism from the linguistic register of softcore porn to the register of desexualized cuteness. When Ben answers, "Look at his face, I just want to kiss it. I think he's cute," he adopts a baby-talking tone often addressed to pets or toddlers. This tone, alongside Ben's desexualized word-choice ("cute"), makes him sound more like a grandmother preparing to peck her grandbaby's cheek than a grown man salivating over his future brother-in-law. Ben thus uses his babyish Jewface to embrace-but-defuse Pete's homoeroticism.

By embracing-but-defusing this homoeroticism, Ben previews how *Knocked Up* narratively produces fun fatherhood. The film's happy ending pulls Ben and all his Jewish foils to a new sweet spot that balances homoerotic queer time with chrononormative straight monogamous fatherhood. This balance emerges during the climactic birth scene that marks Ben's chrononormative entry into fatherhood. As mentioned above, Ben's squalid-but-exuberant roommates proclaim that "we got a daughter!," thereby implying that their labor, gaiety, and homoeroticism will enliven Ben's new life. Rather than trapping Ben in eternal homoerotic adolescence, these friends now *embellish* his straight monogamous fatherhood, making this fatherhood more appealing to Ben and to male viewers. Pete joins this new balance by celebrating the birth with a warm kiss to Ben's forehead. Lasting a full second, Pete's kiss conveys tender affection without his former sultriness. And this affection is further desexualized because the men's bodies stay physically separated by Pete's wife, Debbie, past whom he leans to kiss Ben. Through this staging, the kiss implies that Ben and Pete will henceforth share just enough homoerotic intimacy to *warm* (but not burn down) their lives as straight monogamous fathers.

This happy ending exemplifies how Rogen's babyish Jewface persona safely weaves homoerotic queer time into chrononormative straight monogamous fatherhood, producing fun fatherhood. By softening chrononormativity, this compromise offers straight white-privileged middle-class men the privileges of monogamous fatherhood (including women's sexual and domestic labor) alongside the homoerotic pleasures and intimacies of youth. It thus *strengthens* white heteronormative institutions by enticing straight white-privileged men to reproduce white babies.

Conclusion

By using Rogen's babyish Jewface to fuel fun fatherhood and post-meninist violence that co-produce beta male patriarchy, *Knocked Up* exemplifies the key to his success. Like public-service announcements about social change, Rogen's films acknowledge that many straight white-privileged middle-class men may be questioning established models for reproducing their own privilege and population—that some men may find these models both unethical and unenjoyable. Yet Rogen's comedy reassuringly invites these men into a fun, guiltless, lovable-looking model of power and procreation. Rogen thus offers a brand of comedy that feels profoundly innocent, and even *benevolent*, but which actually renaturalizes straight white male supremacy.

The final chapter turns to Rogen's co-star from *Neighbors*, the sandy-haired Jewish muscleman Zac Efron, who wields a very different Jewish body to similar ends.

From Blue-Eyed Demon to Nice Jew-ish Goy

Zac Efron's "Goyface" as Sexy Abject Hegemony

Getting *Goyfaced*

"Here's a bombshell: I'm Jewish."[1] This "bombshell" came in 2014 from the brawny, blue-eyed, button-nosed, sandy-haired film star Zac Efron (b. 1987). Until then, Efron had exclusively played white gentile roles that reflected his stereotypically gentile beauty—but his career was faltering by 2014. Efron had first achieved stardom in 2006 as the leading heartthrob in Disney's megahit television film *High School Musical*.[2] Extending this teen-idol success, he co-starred in *High School Musical*'s two sequels (2007–2008) and the 2007 *Hairspray* remake.[3] However, when slated to star in the 2011 *Footloose* remake, Efron withdrew to prevent further typecasting as a musical teen pretty boy.[4] He then unsuccessfully tackled more dramatic, masculine, and adult white gentile roles: when he played a grief-stricken athlete in *Charlie St. Cloud* (2010), a lovelorn marine in *The Lucky One* (2012), and an aspiring racecar driver in *At Any Price* (2012), these films all earned mixed to poor reviews.[5] Declaring himself Jewish in 2014 helped Efron to pivot from these unmarketable dramas about straight white gentile masculinity to *raunchy slapstick comedies* about that masculinity, hitting a nerve in America's culture wars.

Specifically, proclaiming his Jewishness revitalized Efron's career by enabling him to perform comedic *goyface*. I define "goyface" as racial minstrelsy in which openly Jewish actors caricature white gentiles' appearance and conduct, thereby exposing white gentile privilege and critiquing the way this privilege can fuel ignorance, arrogance, or incompetence. "Goyface" aptly names this caricature, since "goy" is a dismissive Yiddish term for gentiles. By specifying that goyface *lampoons* gentile whiteness, I differ from past scholarship that has variously applied "goyface" to any Jew playing gentile, to a Jew earnestly exploring gentile perspectives by playing one, and to Jewish performers who downplay Jewishness in their public images.[6] For instance, I do *not* deem Efron's pre-2014 gentile roles goyface, because his Jewishness was lesser-known and his films never mocked white gentile masculinity. Only in 2014 did he pivot from semi-closeted Jewishness to goyface—and specifically, *subliminal postmodern goyface*. Although blatant goyface can wield blond wigs and chalky makeup, we will soon see how Efron's subliminal postmodern goyface operates more subtly.

Efron inaugurated this goyface in the step from his Jewish "bombshell" to his very next film, the slapstick comedy *Neighbors* (2014).[7] Efron announced his Jewishness while promoting *Neighbors* alongside his famously Jewish co-star, Seth Rogen. For publicity, Efron and Rogen guest-starred in a YouTube minisode of the sitcom *Workaholics* (2011–2017), during which Efron spoke the line, "Here's a bombshell: I'm Jewish."[8] And right after declaring himself Jewish, in *Neighbors* Efron played his first goyfaced stooge: a belligerent white gentile fraternity president, Teddy, whose raucous pranks terrorize the married couple next door. *Neighbors* is Efron's first film to spotlight his character's gentility and link this gentility with boorishness. For instance, when spotting Hebrew text, Teddy ignorantly exclaims that it's written "in Jewish!" He thus echoes common microaggressions in which gentiles show ignorance about Jewish culture by mislabeling Hebrew "Jewish" (i.e., "Do you speak Jewish?"). Teddy's gaffe extends a broader Jewish/gentile conflict, since his next-door nemeses include a sweet Jewish husband (Rogen). This lovable Jewish foil accentuates Teddy's gentility and links it with his destructiveness. When Efron played this cartoonish white gentile hooligan in *Neighbors* right after proclaiming his Jewishness in *Workaholics*, he exemplified goyface.

Yet Teddy elicits more sympathy in *Neighbors 2* (2016), when his misconduct leaves him friendless, jobless, and homeless post-college.[9] Newly vulnerable, Teddy confesses to his Jewish nemesis that "I just want to be valued." By yearning to regain his lost social value, Teddy pinpoints why Efron's goyface proves so marketable: it fuels *redemptive goyface comedies*.

Redemptive Goyface Comedies

Efron's redemptive goyface comedies are slapstick films that initially deride straight white gentile middle-class millennial American men— but only to *rehabilitate* them, thereby *bolstering* their privilege by helping it look *more benign* and *better deserved*. Efron performed this ideological labor in a cycle of four redemptive goyface comedies after "coming out" as Jewish in 2014: *Neighbors* (2014), *Neighbors 2* (2016), *Mike and Dave Need Wedding Dates* (2016), and *Baywatch* (2017). Despite earning mediocre to negative reviews like Efron's earlier dramas, these goyface comedies proved commercially successful and reenergized his career. The Golden Raspberry Awards ("Razzies," parody awards for terrible films) illustrated this new momentum. In 2018, the Razzies nominated Efron for Worst Actor for starring in *Baywatch*, but also nominated *Baywatch* for the Razzie Nominee So Rotten You Loved It.[10] This ambivalent scorn/praise illustrates how even negative reviews kept Efron high-profile and how audiences found his goyface comedies oddly appealing. Indeed, before the 2018 Razzies even arrived, Efron's goyface cycle had granted him enough momentum to leave goyface behind. Starting with *The Greatest Showman* (December 2017),[11] Efron successfully progressed from goyface to uncaricatured white gentile adult roles, and has since let Jewishness fade again from his image.

Efron's redemptive goyface comedies thrill audiences by defusing what I call a *double shock of being seen* for straight white gentile middle-class millennial men. The philosopher Jean-Paul Sartre notes that "the white man has [historically] enjoyed the privilege of seeing without being seen"—producing pseudoscience, literature, and art that belittle others, without worrying how minoritized people view him in return.[12] Therefore, as minoritized people gain freedom of expression, Sartre observes that some white men face "the shock of being seen": an epiphany that others view them as nasty or ridiculous.[13] This effect shapes twenty-first-century US media, as noted by the film scholars George Yang and Tracey Ann Ryser.[14] In news media, #BlackLivesMatter (founded in 2013) and #MeToo (founded in 2006 and revitalized in 2017) have forced many people who are white and/or men to recognize that others fear them as predators. In popular media, minoritized artists have gained greater autonomy to mock straightness, whiteness, gentility, and toxic masculinity. For instance, Efron's millennial Jewish peers Abbi Jacobson and Ilana Glazer often caricature straight white gentile men as bungling bosses and crude catcallers. Indeed, the shock of being seen has grown common enough that US media now routinely depict straight, white, gentile, and/or male characters confronting it. For example, Efron hyperbolizes this shock in *Neighbors 2*, when a sorority informs Teddy the frat boy that all his past party themes (like "Pimps & Hos") were sexist.[15] As Teddy newly notices his own sexism—and notices that women are *scrutinizing* his sexism—he gasps, "Oh no! Oh God!" in horror (figure 5.1). Like Teddy, many straight white gentile American men today experience the shock of being seen.

A *double* shock of being seen emerges when well-founded critiques of straight white gentile male privilege dovetail with *unfounded* millennial-bashing. Since the 2008 recession, countless headlines have scorned millennials as, in the words of one *Time* magazine cover, "lazy, entitled narcissists who still live with their parents."[16] Downplaying economic hardships, these headlines disparage millennials as simply too spoiled and childish to "properly" mature into white-collar jobs, homes, cars, and marriages. This rhetoric also vilifies millennials as economic threats,

Oh, no. Oh, God!

Figure 5.1. Teddy faces "the shock of being seen" in *Neighbors 2* (2016). Screenshot from *Neighbors 2*, 2016. Pulled from Amazon.com.

whose "improper" earning and spending have allegedly "killed" everything from cars to wine to McDonald's.[17] This misconceived millennial-bashing can dovetail with well-conceived feminist, queer, and antiracist critiques of straight white gentile middle-class male privilege. Together, these critiques jointly reimagine straight white gentile middle-class millennial men from wholesome citizens to objects of national scrutiny, suspected of being immature, entitled, or destructive.

Rather than denying these criticisms, Efron's goyface *exaggerates* and then *transcends* them. His redemptive goyface comedies stoke-and-resolve four scaffolded anxieties about straight white gentile middle-class millennial men. These anxieties include that (1) such men may be badly out of step with feminist values, multicultural values, and post-2008 economic realities, and also (2) that such men may be objectively dysfunctional and destructive (not just behind the times). Based on these anxieties, the films also worry (3) that straight white gentile middle-class millennial men may menace American society. Yet these comedies chiefly fear (4) that such men may *sabotage their own futures*, by getting stigmatized as *bad feminist and multicultural citizens* and by *failing at adult masculinity*.

However, redemptive goyface comedies ultimately assure viewers that straight white gentile middle-class millennial men can mature into good citizens of feminist, multicultural, post-recession America *without sacrificing any privilege*. This message defuses the double shock of being seen by seeming to admit and atone for these men's perceived transgressions. Efron's redemptive goyface comedies may thus soothe straight white gentile middle-class millennial men anxious about their public image and economic prospects. His comedies may also soothe other audiences who partly benefit from present inequalities—for instance, white-privileged viewers (both Jewish and gentile) who are older adults, millennial straight women, and millennial gay men. By critiquing-and-bolstering straight white male privilege this way, Efron's goyface exemplifies how all subliminal postmodern minstrelsy aids audiences to reconcile contradictory fantasies about disrupting/upholding straight white gentile male supremacy.

To deride-and-redeem straight white gentile middle-class millennial American masculinity, Efron's redemptive goyface comedies share key strategies. First, his goyface characters mirror *real-world groups or individuals* known for sexy-but-delinquent straight white gentile middle-class millennial American masculinity. Efron easily channels these men, as a beautiful star who has personally overcome behaviors connoting reckless and unhealthy masculinity. For instance, Efron's highly publicized recovery from alcoholism in 2013–2014[18] positions him to channel other men known for overdrinking. By jointly invoking his and other high-profile men's real histories, Efron's goyface characters easily symbolize straight white gentile middle-class millennial men's struggle with "the shock of being seen" as harmful or pathetic.

Efron first mirrored other sexy-but-delinquent straight white gentile middle-class millennial men when playing Teddy the fraternity president in *Neighbors* and *Neighbors 2*.[19] The "frat boy" is one American ideal of handsome, muscular, straight white gentile masculinity, but fraternities also constantly grab headlines for promoting toxic masculinity, overdrinking, and rape. For instance, 2010 headlines exposed one Yale fraternity for instructing pledges to chant, "No means yes! Yes means anal!"[20] Since fraternities publicly symbolize the best and worst of young straight white gentile middle-class men, Teddy in *Neighbors* and *Neighbors 2* easily symbolizes this demographic. Teddy spotlights this symbolism while harassing his Jewish neighbor: Teddy gloats that even after he graduates, "there's gonna be *hundreds and thousands of Teddies* living next door to you for all time. Because *'Teddy' is just an idea*" (my emphasis). This line packages Teddy as an allegory for all frat boys, and thus for all young straight white gentile middle-class American men.

While Teddy mirrors frat boys as a group, Efron's other goyface roles mirror *infamous individuals* who symbolize sexy-but-delinquent straight white gentile middle-class millennial masculinity. When co-starring in *Mike and Dave Need Wedding Dates*,[21] Efron exaggerates the real 2013 escapades of Mike and Dave Stangle, brothers who went viral for posting a bawdy Craigslist ad to seek dates for a wedding. Their ad marketed the Stangles as sexy but ill-behaved young straight white gentile men: "In our 20s, single, dashingly tall, *Anglo-Saxon* . . . love to party . . . clean up nice . . . but still *bad boys*" (my emphasis).[22] While Efron explicitly plays Dave Stangle in *Mike and Dave*, he tacitly channels the Olympian Ryan Lochte in *Baywatch*. Lochte is a straight white gentile American swimmer who shares Efron's blue eyes, sandy hair, square jaw, and chiseled muscles. He was infamously expelled from the 2016

Rio Olympics for falsely claiming that he'd been robbed at gunpoint during a drunken night out.[23] Mirroring Lochte, in *Baywatch* Efron plays a disgraced Olympic swimmer who gets booted from Rio after overdrinking makes him vomit mid-race.[24] This role fuses an abstract symbol of American masculinity (a male Olympian) with a specific scandal about one out-of-control straight white gentile middle-class millennial man. It thus exemplifies how Efron's goyface characters symbolize all straight white gentile middle-class millennial American men.

To deride-and-redeem this demographic, Efron's goyface characters all undertake slapstick journeys from caricatured *antagonist* to lovable *protagonist*, guided by minoritized peers. Initially, each goyface character embodies disturbingly extreme white gentile masculine beauty. *Baywatch* spotlights this unsettling beauty when Efron's character gets nicknamed "blue-eyed demon."[25] Alongside this unnerving appearance, each goyface character performs wild misconduct that threatens his community, sabotages his path toward adult masculinity, and/or violates twenty-first-century feminist, multicultural, and post-recession norms. However, minoritized co-stars soon humble and reform Efron's character through comedic punishments, such as the sorority in *Neighbors 2* that shames Teddy for his sexism. While this growth reforms Efron's character into a better feminist, multicultural, and post-recession citizen, it *enhances* his privilege by making him more lovable, employable, and respectable. This arc thus repackages straight white gentile masculinity and privilege as more *genteel* (polite, mature, likable). To embody this new genteel masculinity, Efron's goyface eventually *softens* to reveal a less caricatured white gentile hero. By revealing a lovable white gentile character (not a snickering Jewish performer) beneath the goyface mask, each film ultimately models guiltless straight white gentile male privilege. And this resolution looks especially alluring by fusing guiltless privilege with stereotypically gentile *masculine sex appeal*, ensured by Efron's muscular, fair, blue-eyed beauty.

Sexy Abject Hegemony, Hyperwhite Hypermasculinity, and Genteel Jews

By reforming from "blue-eyed demons" to genteel heroes via comedic punishment from minoritized people, Efron's goyface characters fuse two strategies for stealthy domination: *abject hegemony* and *hyper-whiteness*. These two strategies both typically wield repulsive-looking characters, but in opposite ways, as we will soon see. However, Efron *blends and beautifies* these strategies to produce what I call *sexy abject hegemony*. This sexy abject hegemony offers an especially palatable method for dominant audiences to purge both their *guilt* about holding privilege and their *anxiety* about losing privilege. In turn, Efron's sexy abject hegemony reveals unexamined overlaps between hyperwhiteness and abject hegemony, while revealing that both can look surprisingly gorgeous. As detailed below, this ideological labor requires Efron to appear simultaneously hypermasculinized/feminized, straight/queer, seductive/repulsive, scary/pathetic, and Jewish/gentile. It thus endows Efron with a glamor that is "queer" (strange, feminized, and homo-erotic) in myriad ways.

We have seen that "abject hegemony" describes how dominant groups can feign weakness to stealthily reassert power, by embracing traits they usually despise, expel, and project onto minoritized people.[26] We have also seen how this concept builds on Julia Kristeva's theory of "the abject": anything that threatens the boundary between self and other; which individuals must therefore *reject* to delineate their coherent self; and which therefore provokes *disdain, fear, and revul-sion*.[27] For instance, the abject includes excreta like vomit that blur the body's boundaries. It also includes traits that blur *social* boundar-ies between dominant and marginalized groups. For example, straight white gentile men have historically claimed superiority by contrasting themselves against "pathetic" feminized, homoerotic, nonwhite, and/or Jewish bodies. Such men may anxiously deny any "taint" of feminin-ity, homoeroticism, or racial impurity in themselves, since these abject traits threaten to unravel their identities. However, dominant groups sometimes strategically *embrace* abject traits and excreta to *enhance* their privilege by camouflaging it, producing "abject hegemony." For instance, we have seen how this strategy shaped the 1999 hit *Fight Club*: by wallowing in images of bloody, mutilated straight white gentile male bodies, *Fight Club* misrepresents such men as dispossessed victims who "deserve" to reclaim power.[28]

Until now, scholarship on abject hegemony has remained sepa-rate from scholarship on hyperwhiteness. As previously discussed, "hyperwhite" antagonists are characters who embody the worst physical and ethical stereotypes of whiteness,[29] and who help white-privileged viewers feel racially innocent by comparison.[30] By seeing hyperwhite characters punished, white-privileged viewers can imagine purging the nastiest parts of whiteness, and thus feel guilt-free about white supremacy.[31] Further, film scholar Russell Meeuf specifies that American films often *burden characters of color* with the labor of excising hyperwhiteness and thus refreshing "regular" whiteness.[32] This labor is why white-privileged audiences often happily identify with characters of color who butcher hyperwhite villains (like Wesley Snipes as a Black vampire-hunter in *Blade*),[33] or identify with swarthier white-privileged protagonists who defeat hyperwhite villains (like Draco Malfoy's nemesis, the brunette Harry Potter). While seeming to punish whiteness, these nonwhite and less-white characters actually labor to *beautify* it.

When analyzing how hyperwhite antagonists evoke disgust and help white audiences feel guiltless, past scholarship overlooks Kristeva's concept of abjection. I note that one variety of hyperwhite villain is the hyperwhite supernatural monster (such as zombies), and these hyperwhite monsters often embody nauseating abjection. For instance, half-decayed zombies and bloodthirsty vampires violate the self/other boundary by guzzling or oozing excreta. By wielding abjection, these supernatural hyperwhite monsters aid white viewers to disavow their own complicity with racism. Audiences who feel viscerally nauseated by a rotting zombie can imagine that they have viscerally rejected the white supremacist greed, violence, and conformity that the pallid, insatiable, mindless zombie symbolizes.

Thus, supernatural monstrous hyperwhiteness and abject hegemony both *wield abjection to help dominant audiences deny and guiltlessly reassert their own dominance.* But to reach this shared goal, each strategy wields abjection to *evoke opposite identifications.* Supernatural monstrous hyperwhiteness wields abjection to urge dominant audiences into rejecting villains who symbolize the ugliest parts of themselves. Conversely, abject hegemony wields abjection to invite dominant audiences into embracing protagonists who disguise their dominance as sympathetic victimhood. Yet these opposite strategies both typically require *permanent* abjection. Just as zombies must look incurably putrid to embody hyperwhiteness, privileged characters often must look incurably weakened or disfigured to achieve abject hegemony. Media scholar Claire Sisco King emphasized this permanence when she first coined the term "abject hegemony" and used *Fight Club* to exemplify it. Regarding *Fight Club*, King specifies that the narrator's path to abject hegemony includes nonfatally shooting himself in the mouth, creating "a conspicuous scar" that "will *forever* herald the Narrator's fragility, vulnerability, and instability"[34] (my emphasis).

Unlike this mutilated narrator or a putrid zombie, Efron illustrates that just *brief and comedic abjection* can deliver the ideological rewards of abject hegemony and abject hyperwhiteness, while making both more palatable, thereby producing sexy abject hegemony. We will soon see how Efron's goyface persona embodies a form of hyperwhiteness that I dub *hyperwhite hypermasculinity*: straight white gentile masculine beauty so extreme that it slips into abject monstrosity, femininity, homoeroticism, and filth. But his hyperwhite hypermasculine goyface characters stay redeemable because their abjection is funny and fleeting. If their beauty is so extreme that it slips into abjection, so can their abjection easily slip off to reveal stainless, sexy, strong white gentile masculinity. And this visual beautification grows permanent as Efron's characters grow more socially genteel, redeemed via comedic punishment by minoritized characters. Jointly belittled and perfected, his characters thus achieve sexy abject hegemony.

By using self-mockery to reach sexy abject hegemony, Efron mirrors-yet-inverts his millennial Jewish peers Lil Dicky and Seth Rogen. The rapper Lil Dicky illustrates that self-mockery, like self-mutilation, can produce abject hegemony which looks irreversibly weak and revolting. We have seen how Dicky comedically degrades himself with tropes of Jewish racial queerness: the eight-century antisemitic lineage that stigmatizes Jewish men as swarthy, emasculated, hook-nosed, greasy, and perverse. Wielding these stigmas, Dicky crafts an incurably feeble and foul Jewface persona. By vicariously offering this Jewfaced abjection to straight white-privileged men, Dicky helps them disavow their privilege, validate their resentment against "threatening" minorities, and guiltlessly unleash their revenge fantasies. Meanwhile, we have seen how Seth Rogen's model of abject hegemony offers similar rewards in cuter—but still incurably weak—form. Harnessing the same antisemitic racial tropes as Dicky, Rogen weaves these stigmas into a sweetly emasculated and babyish Jewface persona. This roly-poly Jewface helps Rogen's characters to look harmlessly adorable even as they violently dominate gentile white women, women of color, and men of color. Rogen's "cute abject hegemony" illustrates that abject hegemony can look more *aesthetically alluring* than previously recognized. However, this cute abject hegemony still requires viewers to identify with permanently emasculated, weak, unsexy Jewish protagonists.

Instead, Efron's sexy abject hegemony avoids sacrificing *any* strength, beauty, or white gentile privilege, yet still achieves the benefits of feigning victimhood and of vilifying hyperwhiteness. Efron thus helps white-privileged viewers to achieve guiltless privilege without embracing ugly or pathetic avatars, nor rejecting any part of whiteness as irredeemable. Further, unlike Rogen and Lil Dicky, Efron never obliges gentile viewers to identify with Jewish characters in exchange for abject hegemony. Additionally, typical hyperwhite villains must meet death or defeat by minoritized people to expiate white-privileged audiences. Instead, Efron's hyperwhite hypermasculine goyface characters are *themselves* redeemed and restored to full privilege through the minoritized labor that seems to punish them. This redemption implies that dominant audiences can easily shed the guiltiest excesses of their power, and easily win love from minoritized people without ceding power.

Efron's sexy abject hegemony also appears more ethically attractive than typical abject hegemony, because his version looks *self-aware* and *egalitarian*. Typical abject hegemony depicts straight white-privileged men as innocent victims of minoritized people. It thereby helps such men deny their own privilege, while guiltlessly fantasizing revenge against any who threaten that privilege. Seth Rogen's and Lil Dicky's comedy exemplifies this effect. Instead, Efron offers dominant audiences the fantasy of *atoning* for their privilege, *learning* good egalitarian twenty-first-century citizenship, and having their goodness *validated* by minoritized people— while actually renewing their privilege. This atonement fantasy mirrors-yet-inverts the ideological labor of Abbi Jacobson and Ilana Glazer. That duo sometimes uses their dusky, seductive Jewessface to help white-privileged straight women, queer women, and queer men feel sincerely progressive without ceding white privilege. Similarly, Efron uses his blazingly white, muscular, sexy goyface to help straight white-privileged men feel sincerely progressive without ceding *any* privilege.

Efron offers this faux self-awareness because, by blending hyper-whiteness with abject hegemony, he positions straight white gentile men simultaneously *as overprivileged jerks* and *downtrodden underdogs*. On one hand, his comedies imply that his hyperwhite hypermasculine goyface characters *deserve punishment* from minoritized people. Thus, dominant audiences who laugh at this suffering can self-congratulate for critiquing their own privilege. Yet when Efron's goyface characters suffer, they also mirror common backlash narratives claiming that minoritized people seek domination (not equity), and that these minoritized people have *already dispossessed* straight, white, gentile, and/or male Americans. Thus, even as dominant audiences appear to virtuously critique their own privilege, they can misperceive that privilege as *already lost*, and guiltlessly yearn to *regain* it. Further, if dominant audiences ambivalently crave to reject and renew their privilege, they satisfy both cravings by seeing Efron's goyface characters "learn their lesson" (get both humbled and enlightened). This learning only *seems* to make his characters shed their privilege, but actually helps them refresh it in more genteel guise.

Although Efron's image differs sharply from Rogen's and Lil Dicky's, his sexy abject hegemony does not simply reject stigmas of ugly, weak Jewish emasculation. After all, abject hegemony always requires dominant groups to selectively embrace traits that they usually expel. I deliberately spotlight this tactic when labeling Efron's reformed protagonists "genteel." It seems unfitting that a Jewish star like Efron could help gentile men look more genteel, because genteelness historically *excludes* Jews: we have seen that both "genteel" and "gentile" share a root with "gentle," which "initially meant well-behaved because 'well-born.'"[35] All three words thus originally imply that white gentile bodies are inherently better behaved than (allegedly vulgar, perverse, dirty) Jewish bodies. Shakespeare exemplified this thinking in *The Merchant of Venice* by using "gentle Jew" as an oxymoron.[36] However, many twenty-first-century Americans now critique traditional straight white gentile masculinity as noxious rather than princely, producing "the shock of being seen."

To re-ennoble straight white gentile men through sexy abject hegemony, Efron's redemptive goyface comedies ambivalently depict Jewish emasculation as a *pathetic inferior opposite*, a *threatening superior opposite*, and a *helpful, integrable resource* to white gentile masculinity. This ambivalence often helps Efron's hyperwhite hypermasculine goy-face characters to become what I call *nice Jew-ish goys*: white gentile men who absorb the most lovable and invisible stereotypes about emasculated Jewish behavior, while displacing the weakest, unsexiest, and most visible stereotypes about emasculated Jewish bodies onto Jewish characters. This "nice Jew-ish goy" effect aids Efron's characters to soften into genteel heroes, thereby achieving sexy abject hegemony and enabling Efron's queer glamor.

And if Efron's sexy abject hegemony depends on paradoxically expelling and absorbing Jewish emasculation into white gentile masculinity, then this performance depends on Efron's own Jewish but gentile-looking body.

Ready-Made Redeemable Goyface: Efron's "Doubly Impossible Body"

To achieve sexy abject hegemony, Efron's redemptive goyface comedies recruit what I call his *doubly impossible body* and its ambivalently ideal/abject masculinity. Efron exemplifies star studies' typical definition of "impossible bodies": stars with unbelievably extreme appearances.[37] Efron is specifically famous for superhuman *white gentile* beauty (fair, blue-eyed, muscular, and fine-featured); as detailed below, commenters often deem his beauty so intense that it tacitly turns unsettling and/or unmanly, evoking ridicule and disgust. Therefore, Efron's superhuman image has always wavered between ideal and abject (feminized, queer, unnatural, repugnant) masculinity. However, even his abject connotations sharply invert antisemitic racial tropes. Rather than casting Efron as an ugly emasculated Jew, commenters often imply that *Efron extremifies white gentile male beauty until it turns disquieting and feminized.* By spectacularly inverting tropes of Jewish racial queerness, Efron's body becomes impossible in a second way, which I call *impossibly Jewish*: a body that audiences cannot believe Jewish because it breaks racial assumptions about Jews. Efron thus mirrors-yet-inverts the rapper Drake, who "impossibly" holds Jewishness, Blackness, and muscularity in one body. Further, Efron's doubly impossibly body provides *ready-made redeemable goyface*. That is, his Jewish but extremely gentile-looking body needs only subtle cosmetic enhancement to both caricature *and* idealize straight white gentile masculinity.

This doubly impossible image and its ideal/abject masculinity emerged years before Efron declared himself Jewish or began performing hyperwhite hypermasculine goyface. For example, in 2008 *Elle* magazine gushed about Efron's "courtly beauty—with his creamy complexion, thick-lashed blue eyes, and dimpled chin."[38] *Elle* later added that Efron looks "like a live-action prince drawn in a Walt Disney fever dream," with a "heavy brow, Technicolor-blue upturned eyes, black curling lashes, a *linear nose*, bowed lips. His smile, so ultrabrightly perfect, makes you wonder, 'Are those his real teeth?'" (my emphasis).[39] On one hand, this praise assigns Efron ideal white gentile masculinity as a "courtly" "Disney prince," evoking European Christian royalty. Yet this praise also feminizes Efron by emphasizing his "beauty" rather than "handsomeness," and by spotlighting his delicately "creamy" skin and "curling lashes." Further, *Elle* deems his beauty so extreme that it sounds unnatural and unnerving: like a "Disney fever dream," this prince has "Technicolor-blue" eyes and "ultrabright" teeth that barely seem "real." Yet mentioning Efron's "linear nose" illustrates how even these feminizing and unsettling descriptions invert racial tropes about repulsive Jewish emasculation.

Although Efron's body changed during the 2010s, commentators have continued to assign him supernatural white masculine beauty that appears ambivalently ideal or abject, with "abject" including both "feminized" and "monstrous." Likewise, even when casting Efron as abject, these commenters have continued to envision his body sharply at odds with antisemitic racial tropes. Like Drake, Efron labored toward an extraordinarily muscular body in the early 2010s, and by 2016, *Men's Fitness* magazine lauded Efron for transforming from "Pretty Boy Teen Idol" to "Shredded Human Ken Doll."[40] In this ambivalent description, the slang term "shredded" praises Efron's extreme muscles, but tacitly casts this hypermasculinity as abject mutilation rather than ideal power or beauty. Yet even while idealizing/abjecting Efron as *hypermasculine* and *mutilated*, the magazine also conversely idealizes/abjects him as *beautiful* and *feminized*: "Ken dolls" are (stereotypically) girls' toys that epitomize fine-featured white gentile beauty. And whether deeming Efron too masculine, feminine, beautiful, or mutilated, this headline equates him with an unnatural plastic doll. Yet all this ambivalently ideal/abject imagery inverts antisemitic tropes of greasy, smelly, swarthy, hook-nosed, perversely emasculated Jewish men.

Until 2014, Efron's hyper-gentile beauty kept his Jewishness *unbelievable* (not unknown). Ever since *High School Musical* (2006), fan blogs and Jewish newspapers have sporadically noted Efron's Jewish ancestry, which descends from his paternal grandfather.[41] This lineage makes Efron's Jewishness tenuous, because most Jewish denominations define Jewishness matrilineally and because he was raised agnostic in the distinctly non-Jewish town of Arroyo Grande, California.[42] Yet rather than questioning Efron's ancestry or upbringing, audiences often question his Jewishness due to his *appearance*. MTV exemplified this pattern in a 2012 listicle, "20 Movie Stars You Didn't Know Were Jewish."[43] Efron's entry proclaims, "This *elven-faced heartthrob's* last name actually means 'lark' in Hebrew. And yet, with all the evidence in, it's still *really, really, really hard to believe* [that he's Jewish], right?" (my emphasis). This elven metaphor is striking: from Keebler cookie ads to Tolkien films, popular media often envision elves as luminously white and ultra-delicately lovely. And MTV finds this impossible (mythical) white beauty doubly impossible to reconcile with Jewishness: Efron's very existence as a Jewish "elven-faced heartthrob" seems "really, really, really hard to believe."

Despite such coverage, Efron's Jewish ancestry and the public disbelief about it long remained minor murmurs, because Efron never publicly mentioned either. Only in his 2014 *Workaholics* minisode did he newly forefront his Jewishness. We will also see how this sketch newly harnessed the impression that Jewishness racially "mismatches" Efron's body. This shift would soon help him juxtapose his Jewish identity against his supernaturally gentile appearance to perform hyperwhite hypermasculine goyface.

Efron's doubly impossible body not only provides ready-made resources for *visually* crafting goyface, but also for *narratively* inflicting brief comedic abjection on his goyface characters. Historically, his abject (queer, feminized, unsettling) reputation has drawn ridicule even during his peak successes. For instance, Efron's appeal as a straight heartthrob helped to make *High School Musical 2* (2007) "the most watched event ever broadcast on basic cable" at that time, with 17.2 million viewers.[44] Yet 2007–2009 also saw dozens of derisive entries about Efron in the crowdsourced website Urban Dictionary. Like the endless memes that feminize Drake, Urban Dictionary's entries often feminize and queer Efron, such as when labeling him "a fag that has no talent" and "the biggest pansy ever."[45] Efron's redemptive goyface comedies alchemize this stigma into an asset that assists sexy abject hegemony, fueling his queer glamor. Since his image always wavers between ideal and abject masculinity, Efron easily embodies the fear that all straight white gentile middle-class millennial men may be disturbing or pathetic. Yet he also easily embodies the hope of *redeeming* this demographic as strong, sexy, and lovable.

Just as Efron's impossible (extreme) white gentile beauty provides ready-made tools for redeemable goyface, so does his impossible (unbelievable) Jewishness. Efron wields his doubly impossible body to *flaunt-and-minimize* Jewishness even more delicately than this book's other stars. On one hand, by declaring his Jewishness in 2014, Efron framed his forthcoming goyface characters as deliberate caricatures. This impression helps his redemptive goyface comedies seem to self-consciously critique and purge white gentile masculinity's worst excesses. While spotlighting his Jewishness helps Efron to mock white gentile masculinity, downplaying Jewishness helps him to *redeem* that masculinity. As previewed above, his characters' goyface always softens to reveal a genteel white gentile hero (not a sardonic Jewish performer) beneath. If Efron's image grew "too" Jewish, he could no longer convincingly play "regular" white gentiles. Efron's Jewish but gentile-looking body perfectly positions him to flaunt-and-minimize Jewishness so finely.

Enabling Goyface: Becoming Explicitly-but-*Barely* Jewish

To begin flaunting-and-minimizing Jewishness and thus to enable his redemptive goyface comedies, Efron had to do more than simply confirm his Jewishness. Instead, on *Workaholics* in 2014, he repackaged himself as explicitly-but-*barely* Jewish. An instructive foil here is Drake: although Drake avoids embodying Jewish emasculation, he has prominently performed Jewish religious and cultural difference, such as restaging his bar mitzvah on *Saturday Night Live*.[46] Conversely, Efron's explicitly-but-barely Jewish image casts him as *just nominally Jewish*, with *no* religious, cultural, or bodily difference. This barely-Jewish image is aided but not assured by his gentile appearance, agonistic upbringing, and ongoing distance from Jewish culture. For instance, Efron has assisted this image since *Workaholics* by never again calling himself Jewish or playing a Jewish character. Likewise, he has never publicly attended Jewish events or challenged antisemitism. He thus sharply differs from Drake, Seth Rogen, Lil Dicky, Ilana Glazer, and Abbi Jacobson. Regardless of how Efron personally experiences Jewishness, his choice to *just once* publicly signal Jewishness enhances his explicitly-but-barely Jewish branding.

Further, Efron's passive silence about Jewish culture and antisemitism contrasts against his active engagement with antisemitic *bodily* stigmas. Like Drake, Efron "counteridentifies"[47] with racial stigmas of Jewish emasculation—proactively rebuffs those tropes by crafting an opposite image. Rather than debunking antisemitic tropes, this strategy "counter*determines*"[48] them: accentuates them, validates them, and displaces them onto more stigmatized Jewish foils, while elevating Efron as a spectacular exception. Displacing Jewish bodily stigmas has mattered even more than dissociating from Jewish culture for his explicitly-but-barely Jewish image.

Efron initiated this counteridentification, and thus initiated his explicitly-but-barely Jewish image, on *Workaholics* in 2014. This minisode also illustrated how his new image could help straight white *gentile* men to defuse critiques of their privilege. *Workaholics* follows three straight white gentile millennial men who barely perform their telemarketing jobs. In the 2014 minisode "The Workaholics Guys Find a New Cubicle Mate," Efron and Seth Rogen guest-star as themselves, interviewing for one spot in the protagonists' cubicle.[49] This plotline initially critiques straight white gentile men's workplace privilege by mocking the white gentile protagonists' unprofessionalism. For instance, when pondering "who's qualified to work here," the gentile protagonists blatantly disregard office skills. Instead, they praise Efron's "hard" body, "superhandsome" face, "blue" eyes, and skill at "plowin' chicks," and they proclaim him perfect for their cubicle's "vibe": its climate of (straight white gentile male) camaraderie. Conversely, they tell Rogen—already famous for his pudgy, emasculated Jewface—that he "fuckin' sucks." This dialogue invites viewers to question why straight, white, gentile, and/or male Americans should enjoy greater access to stable white collar work, enjoy greater leeway for unprofessionalism in that work, and enjoy greater gatekeeping power over that work than do other groups.

However, the minisode quickly reverses to *vilify* diversification efforts like affirmative action that might unseat straight white gentile men. This reversal begins when Rogen urges the white gentile protagonists to hire him because "if you had a Jewish person you could probably be more edgy, *because you'd have a minority*" (my emphasis).[50] This comment evokes the accusation that diversity initiatives constitute "reverse discrimination" against straight white gentile men. Since Rogen states that hiring "a minority" would make the cubicle "edgy" (not "equitable"), he also implies that employers who seek diversity just want to look trendy rather than challenge inequality. Rogen's pitch sounds especially dubious because he is a conditionally white Jew: although such Jews can experience racial violence (such as in the Pittsburgh synagogue shooting) and workplace microaggressions in America today, they are well-represented in white-collar employment.[51] Together, Rogen's identity and rhetoric stoke the myth that *any* minoritized candidate who challenges straight white gentile men's workplace privilege is just exploiting liberal fashions for special treatment.

To defuse such "threatening" diversification efforts, Efron discloses his own minoritized identity with the aforementioned line, "Here's a bombshell: I'm Jewish." This revelation *thrills* the straight white gentile male protagonists, who emote startled delight as one exclaims, "*Get the fuck out! . . .* So you're handsome *and* Jewish?!*" (original emphasis).[52] This news specifically thrills the interviewers by making Efron a perfect "diversity hire": he technically possesses a minoritized identity, but conforms to "ideal" straight white gentile male appearance and conduct. Thus, the straight white gentile leads can now *seem* pro-diversity while actually hiring the candidate most like themselves. Efron's Jewish bombshell thus insulates himself and the white gentile protagonists from critiques of their privilege.

However, Efron's revelation can only preserve this privilege because he is explicitly-but-*barely* Jewish. If he represented any bodily, religious, or cultural Jewish difference, he might suffer the same rejection as Rogen. In turn, *Workaholics'* straight white gentile male protagonists might find a "more Jewish" candidate inconvenient. Embracing the barely-Jewish Efron enables these straight white gentile male protagonists to *effortlessly* perform "good" multicultural citizenship while sustaining their own comfort and power. Thus, while Rogen's salient Jewishness *threatens* straight white gentile male supremacy in this narrative, Efron's explicit-but-minimal Jewishness offers a *helpful, integrable resource* to that supremacy.

To ensure that Efron's Jewishness remains substanceless, *Workaholics* hastily helps him counteridentify with racial tropes of Jewish emascula-tion. This counteridentification wields a key symbol in both masculin-ist and antisemitic ideologies: the penis. American culture often deems penis size the ultimate masculine metric, outweighing handsomeness or musculature. Further, before circumcision became common in America during the 1920s,[53] antisemitic ideologies often equated circumcision with castration.[54] Depicting Jewish men as castrated freaks, this rheto-ric helped to "prove" Jewish racial difference. These racial and mascu-line histories underpin the *Workaholics* climax, when Rogen demands to inspect Efron's circumcised "Jewish dick" to verify his Jewishness. This inspection threatens to disrupt Efron's barely-Jewish image: if he revealed a small or ugly penis, it could outweigh his "shredded" muscles, "Technicolor-blue" eyes, and "linear" nose as proof that he actually em-bodies Jewish emasculation.

Instead, to keep Efron barely-Jewish and ideally masculine, this cli-max shows him expel antisemitic racial stigmas onto Rogen's penis. Although viewers never see Efron's penis, the other characters deem it unbelievably big and beautiful. One white gentile interviewer exclaims, "*Holy fucking shit!*" while Rogen gasps, "Did Leonardo DaVinci circum-cise you? It's *beautiful*" (original emphases).[55] Rogen's question con-firms that Efron is Jewish (circumcised), but idealizes his Jewish penis as Renaissance artwork. Rogen thus echoes commentaries that assign Efron superhuman gentile beauty as a "Disney Prince" or "Human Ken Doll." To cement Efron's image as an exceptionally gorgeous and mas-culine Jew, the skit then displaces antisemitic racial stigmas onto Rogen. Desperately competing with Efron, Rogen reveals his own penis—but evokes horror, mockery, and pity. One white gentile protagonist calls Rogen's penis "a rejected Sesame Street monster" (small, soft, and ugly). Meanwhile, Efron gasps, grimaces, and leans away in horror, distanc-ing his barely-Jewish body from Rogen's "more-Jewish" body. This scene exemplifies how Efron's barely-Jewish persona always requires "counteridentifying" with antisemitic racial stigmas (rebuffing them) and thus "counterdetermining" those stigmas (validating and displacing them onto other Jewish men).

In turn, *Workaholics* previews how Efron's explicitly-but-barely Jewish persona would soon help him to model sexy abject hegemony for straight white gentile middle-class millennial men in redemptive goyface comedies. This new image would soon position Efron's goyfaced characters as deliberate caricatures of straight white gentile masculinity, yet also help those characters believably grow into uncaricatured white gentile heroes. Further, although Seth Rogen's Jewfaced model of abject hegemony often thrills both Jewish and gentile white-privileged men, *Workaholics* illustrates the risk that some white gentile men may find Rogen's Jewface unrelatable. Instead, Efron's explicitly-but-barely Jewish image makes him an even more relatable proxy for white gentile men. Additionally, *Workaholics* previews how his barely-Jewish image fuses "the best" of majoritarian and minoritarian experience: in Efron and his characters, straight white gentile men can find the sexiest version of themselves *and* the version least accountable for his privilege.

Yet to reach sexy abject hegemony, Efron's goyface characters must first suffer derision by exaggerating the ugliest, nastiest, most pathetic stereotypes about straight white gentile middle-class millennial masculinity. To achieve this fleeting comedic abjection, Efron harnesses his doubly impossible body to perform hyperwhite hypermasculine goyface.

Sculpting (and Then Softening) Hyperwhite Hypermasculine Goyface

To sculpt hyperwhite hypermasculine goyface, Efron's redemptive goyface comedies extend the public discourse that deems his masculine beauty ambivalently ideal/abject. Further, when emphasizing abjection, his goyface techniques mirror public discourse by ambivalently depicting Efron as *powerfully monstrous* yet *pathetically feminized*. All this ambivalence helps his hyperwhite hypermasculine goyface characters to briefly dabble in abjection, providing bodies that white-privileged viewers can initially love to hate—but ultimately just love.

If Efron's doubly impossible body provides ready-made resources for hyperwhite hypermasculine goyface, then his first technique for tapping these resources is what I call *exhibitionist goyface*. Just as *Men's Fitness* labeled Efron a "shredded Ken doll,"[56] his exhibitionist goyface spotlights his superhuman musculature: it reveals skin stretched so tightly over his muscles that he appears disturbingly desiccated and robotic. Although racial minstrelsy typically masks performers in heavy makeup or wigs, exhibitionist goyface *exposes* Efron's flesh: his goyface characters constantly appear shirtless or in tank tops to exhibit their "shredded" arms, chest, and abs. *Baywatch* exemplifies this exhibitionist goyface when Efron's shirtless character navigates a gymnastics course: his quivering muscles look so hard and his skin so leathery that they evoke a cockroach's carapace (figure 5.2).[57] Likewise, his exhibitionist goyface always frames his hyperwhite hypermasculine body as supernaturally strong, potentially sexy, yet disturbing.

Baywatch's gymnastics scene also exemplifies how Efron's exhibitionist goyface dovetails with *rubescent goyface*: my term for techniques that make his exposed flesh *glow red*. Rubescent goyface can entail cosmetic methods like tanning—Efron reports that his *Baywatch* preparations included "*lots* of fake tans" (original emphasis).[58] Rubescent goyface can also redden Efron via onscreen exercise, like *Baywatch*'s gymnastics course. Further, rubescent goyface can dovetail with *emotive goyface*: clownishly idiotic or rageful facial expressions that caricature "meatheaded" straight white gentile masculinity, making Efron's face blaze red. This emotive goyface is sharpest in the climax of *Neighbors*, when Teddy the frat boy (Efron) unleashes slapstick violence on his Jewish neighbor.[59] As Teddy attacks, his face burns red, his blue eyes bulge, and his mouth animalistically snarls, looking truly demonic (figure 5.3). This scene exemplifies how Efron's rubescent goyface can depict him as downright monstrous, like hyperwhite zombies or vampires. Efron's redness thus symbolizes the anxiety that all straight white gentile middle-class millennial men may conceal some monstrous internal dysfunction, always threatening to blaze outward.

Complementing these visual techniques, *rhetorical goyface* sharpens Efron's hyperwhite hypermasculinity. Rhetorical goyface is dialogue that echoes public rhetoric about Efron's impossible body, which thereby presents his body as ambivalently ideal/abject, and which ambivalently casts his abject side as powerfully monstrous yet pathetically feminized. For instance, when first seeing Teddy in *Neighbors*, Seth Rogen's

Figure 5.2. Efron's exhibitionist and rubescent goyface in *Baywatch* (2017). Screenshot from *Baywatch*, 2017. Image pulled from Amazon.com.

Figure 5.3. Efron's exhibitionist, rubescent, and emotive goyface in *Neighbors* (2014). Screenshot from *Neighbors*, 2014. Image pulled from Amazon.com.

character exclaims that he's "the sexiest guy I've ever seen. He looks like *something a gay guy designed in a laboratory!*" with arms like "two giant veiny dicks" (my emphasis).[60] Invoking Frankenstein's monster, this line extends public commentaries that envision Efron as a "shredded Ken doll" too beautiful to be natural. Yet even while idealizing Efron, this line abjects him by comparing him to a hideous undead monster. But while Frankenstein's monster connotes powerful and frightening abjection, Rogen's line also invokes pathetic abjection: deeming Efron a *gay* man's fantasy, it links him with (supposedly weak) femininity and queerness. Similar ambivalence arises in *Baywatch*: Efron's goyface character not only receives the aforementioned nickname "blue-eyed demon," but also "Little Mermaid."[61] Both monikers serve as rhetorical goyface, accentuating his uncanny white beauty. These nicknames ambivalently cast Efron's beauty as ideal/abject, while ambivalently casting his abjection as powerfully monstrous/pathetically feminized.

However, the techniques that build Efron's hyperwhite hypermasculine goyface and make it look abject also keep his visual abjection *fleeting*. First, rhetorical goyface simply vanishes once his goyface characters mature. For instance, although *Baywatch* barrages Efron's character (Matt) with abject nicknames like "blue-eyed demon" and "Little Mermaid," this rhetorical goyface ceases once Matt learns teamwork and responsibility. *Baywatch* explicitly spotlights this shift: when Matt's boss finally calls him "Matt" instead of some abject nickname, Matt rejoices that "you just said my real name!"[62]

Just as rhetorical goyface easily evaporates, Efron's exhibitionist, rubescent, and emotive goyface easily *soften* into genteel beauty with a change of mood, lighting, costume, or dialogue. *Neighbors* illustrates how swift this visual softening can be, once the fraternity president Teddy (Efron) gets humbled by his Jewish neighbor Mac (Rogen). As pictured above, Teddy appears monstrously muscular, red, and rageful during the film's climactic slapstick battle (figure 5.3).[63] But ten minutes later, after Mac successfully shuts down Teddy's fraternity, the chastened Teddy reemerges in lovelier form. Mac spots Teddy working as a shirtless model for Abercrombie, a brand infamous for hiring only the whitest and sexiest models.[64] Although this job emphasizes Teddy's white gentile privilege, it also reframes him as unequivocally attractive. To aid this reframing, Teddy's exhibitionist, rubescent, and emotive goyface have all softened: although he is shirtless, his muscles no longer bristle aggressively, but instead look somehow slender. Likewise, his ruddy skin has softened from demonically red and leathery to sun-kissed and silky. And rather than diabolically snarling, Teddy now sweetly smiles while maturely acknowledging that his earlier misbehavior "escalated very quickly." This dénouement exemplifies how the same goyface tactics that vilify Efron as an abject hyperwhite hypermasculine monster easily soften to idealize him as a gorgeous genteel protagonist.

By softening Efron's goyface once his characters get humbled, *Neighbors* and *Baywatch* illustrate a key connection. Efron's visual arc from sharper to softer goyface, and thus from abject to ideal white gentile masculinity, always assists narratives about taming hyperwhite hyper-masculine *misconduct.*

Bad Boy: Hyperwhite Hypermasculine Misconduct

Like typical hyperwhite antagonists, Efron's goyface characters fuse physical monstrosity with monstrous misbehavior. Their hyperwhite hypermasculine misconduct conveys the anxiety that straight white gentile middle-class millennial men may be inherently dysfunctional and/or badly out of touch with feminist, multicultural, and post-recession norms, and may therefore menace twenty-first-century American society. Yet even when Efron's goyface characters misbehave monstrously, this narrative abjection (like their visual and rhetorical abjection) remains funny and fleeting.

To convey the fear that straight white gentile middle-class millennial men may be inherently destructive, Efron's hyperwhite hypermasculine goyface characters often violently disrupt other people's straight white middle-class domesticity, reproduction, and financial security. In *Neighbors*, this threat begins when Teddy's (Efron's) fraternity moves in next to a suburban family comprising the conditionally white Jewish Mac Radner (Seth Rogen), his white gentile wife, Kelly (Rose Byrne), and their baby, Stella.[65] Although the Radners have sunk "every penny we have" into their suburban house, the frat's arrival undercuts its value. This financial strain evokes post-recession anxieties about millennials' alleged failure or refusal to become homeowners. While the Radners represent "good" millennials striving for heteronormative middle-class adulthood, Teddy's "bad" hyperwhite hypermasculinity menaces this idealized goal.

Teddy's hyperwhite hypermasculinity also *erotically* threatens straight white-privileged middle-class domesticity. When Mac deems Teddy "the sexiest guy I've ever seen," he implies that Teddy's white gentile beauty tempts Mac outside marriage, and even outside heterosexuality. More ominously, to intimidate the Radners, Teddy tells them that baby Stella will grow up under his fraternity's desiring eyes. This sexual threat turns concrete when Teddy's frat brothers (whom he commands) leave an open condom in the Radners' yard, which Stella promptly eats. When the Radners rush Stella to the hospital, the doctor facetiously claims,

"Your baby has HIV." Invoking a deadly epidemic associated with gay men, this "joke" positions Teddy as a monstrous saboteur, infecting wholesome straight white middle-class domesticity with abject sexual perversion, disease, and excreta (semen). And like Teddy's economic menace, his erotic menace symbolizes the fear that straight white gentile middle-class millennial men may be inherently destructive.

While monstrously disrupting other people's heteronormative adulthood, Efron's hyperwhite hypermasculine goyface characters also monstrously threaten other people's *multicultural coexistence*. Specifically, his goyface protagonists undercut models of multiculturalism that would let other white gentile characters (and audiences who identify with them) feel racially innocent without challenging white supremacy. These storylines convey anxiety that straight white gentile middle-class millennial men may be badly out of touch with feminist and multicultural values.

This theme of disrupting multiculturalism began subtly in *Neighbors* and *Neighbors 2*. The family that Teddy disrupts represents minor forms of multiculturalism that barely challenge white privilege, since Mac Radner is a conditionally white Jewish American man and Kelly Radner is a white gentile Australian woman. Yet in *Mike and Dave Need Wedding Dates*, Efron overtly threatens multiculturalism. Efron's character (Dave) and his brother (Mike) are infamous for wild party antics that threaten to ruin their sister's wedding—to a Black man.[66] This fiancé is the only Black main character, whose family barely appears. The wedding will thus let Dave's family induct a Black token without questioning their own white privilege or closely engaging their Black in-laws. This union thus symbolizes white fantasies of *easily* performing virtuous, nonracist whiteness—but Dave's (Efron's) hyperwhite hypermasculinity threatens to derail this feel-good fantasy.

Meanwhile, Efron's hyperwhite hypermasculine goyface character in *Baywatch*—the disgraced Olympian, Matt—most directly threatens multiculturalism. Matt begins the film by accepting the only job that will take him: lifeguarding with a Florida beach town's elite "Baywatch" corps.[67] This corps symbolizes a multicultural and gender-egalitarian utopia. For instance, its leaders are a biracial man and woman: Lt. Mitch (played by Dwayne "the Rock" Johnson, of Black and Samoan ancestry) and his second-in-command, Steph (Ilfenesh Hadera, of Ethiopian and European ancestry).[68] Extending this diversity, the

Baywatch's other members are two white gentile women and a conditionally white Jewish man. Yet this egalitarianism remains comfortable for dominant audiences because the Baywatch ultimately reports to a straight white gentile male superior, Captain Thorpe. However, Matt's arrival disturbs this "unthreatening" egalitarianism. First, Matt lands this job through Captain Thorpe's nepotism, thereby exposing both Thorpe's and Matt's privilege as destructive. This threat becomes sharper when, thanks to the captain's favoritism and his own fame, Matt demands to skip the Baywatch's meritocratic tryouts. During this demand, Matt disrespectfully orders the team's biracial leaders to "figure out who the fuck I am." This confrontation conveys the anxiety that straight white gentile middle-class millennial men may threaten twenty-first-century American society by acting too behind-the-times (disrespectful to women and people of color) and too downright dysfunctional (delusionally arrogant).

However, just as Efron's hyperwhite hypermasculine goyface characters easily shed visual abjection, so can they easily shed narrative abjection. Unlike bloodthirsty hyperwhite vampires, Efron's goyface protagonists often appear just minorly and comedically destructive. For instance, Teddy's idiotic line in *Neighbors* about a letter written "in Jewish"[69] marks him in a small humorous way as a bad multicultural citizen. Further, Efron's redemptive goyface comedies use slapstick to frame even severe violence as ridiculous, harmless, and thus forgivable. *Neighbors* exemplifies this effect in the final battle between Teddy and his Jewish neighbor, Mac, when the nemeses absurdly beat each other with pale white dildoes. Teddy eventually shoves his pale dildo down Mac's throat and pinches Mac's nose, literally choking Mac with hyperwhite hypermasculinity in a potentially lethal way. Yet the dildoes make this murder attempt look ridiculous, humorously homoerotic, and thus harmless. Also crucial, Mac breaks free. This escape highlights another reason why Efron's hyperwhite hypermasculine goyface characters stay narratively redeemable: their comedic violence never kills fellow protagonists.

Another key reason why narrative abjection easily slips off Efron's hyperwhite hypermasculine goyface characters is that their abjection evokes dual responses. Although his abjection can incite *disgust*, it can also invite *pity*, keeping his characters sympathetic.

Sad Boy: Pitying the Goyfaced Pariah and Man-Baby

Efron's redemptive goyface comedies imply that his characters deserve pity because their hyperwhite hypermasculine misconduct allegedly *sabotages themselves* as much as (or more than) it victimizes others. Thus, the misconduct that makes his characters menacingly abject (powerfully monstrous) also makes them pitiably abject (pathetically failed and weak). By jointly inflicting and suffering from their own hyperwhiteness, these characters *fuse the roles of hyperwhite antagonist and sympathetic protagonist*. In turn, these self-sabotaging plotlines reveal the true priorities of redemptive goyface comedies: even when worrying that straight white gentile middle-class millennial men may harm others, these films primarily worry that such men will *sabotage their own success* in twenty-first-century America. This effect urges audiences to cheer for such men's moral and economic redemption.

Two forms of self-sabotage frame Efron's goyface characters as sympathetic victims of their own hyperwhite hypermasculine misconduct, producing pitiable but curable abjection. First, these characters debase themselves into destitute, friendless, even homeless *pariahs*. For instance, *Baywatch* paints the disgraced swimmer Matt Brody (Efron) as a sympathetic outcast, victimized by his own misbehavior: the film's first night finds Matt homeless beneath a boardwalk, phone-scrolling through articles that mock his fall from "American hero to pool-boy zero."[70] This rare tender moment in the slapstick *Baywatch* exemplifies how Efron's redemptive goyface comedies invite viewers to jointly scorn and *pity* his goyface characters for their hyperwhite hypermasculine transgressions.

While reducing themselves to pariahs, Efron's goyface characters also reduce themselves to *pathetic man-babies* unequipped for adult careers in post-recession America. Babyishness may sound antithetical to Efron's hyper-muscular goyface, which sharply inverts Seth Rogen's infantile roly-poly Jewface. But hypermasculinity actually infantilizes Efron's goyface characters by making them violate *chrononormativity*. We have seen that "chrononormativity" describes social timelines for a "normal" and "properly" productive life, including expected schedules for marrying, growing wealth, and conceiving children,[71] and more broadly including customary timetables for gendered and sexual maturation. For instance, chrononormativity in America today dictates that straight white middle-class men should progress from raucous fraternity parties in college to respectable careers and marriages post-graduation. Efron's goyface characters convey anxiety that straight white gentile middle-class millennial men will *overcommit* to youthful models of masculinity and thereby *foreclose* adult models.

An arc from *Neighbors* to *Neighbors 2* crystallizes this anxiety that hypermasculinity will make straight white gentile middle-class millennial men regress into pitiable man-babies. This arc also exemplifies how "man-baby" status and "pariah" status often entwine in redemptive goyface comedies. This arc begins halfway through *Neighbors*, when the fraternity president Teddy (Efron) pauses from terrorizing his neighbors to attend a job fair.[72] There, Teddy realizes that he lacks post-graduation prospects because he has wasted his college years on hypermasculine fraternity fun rather than studying. As the rejected Teddy exits, he sticks a lollipop (an iconically childish candy) into his mouth. This lollipop hints that Teddy will not only fail at adult white-collar masculinity, but also regress toward infancy. And Teddy's emerging man-baby image interweaves with his emerging pariah image. For instance, Teddy's rude awakening about his unemployability comes from a nerdy Asian male recruiter, who informs Teddy that "you're too dumb" to work at AT&T, then snidely wishes him "good luck, *bro*" (original emphasis). This rejection implies that straight white gentile middle-class "bros" like Teddy will soon become scorned and impoverished outcasts, displaced by minorities who are allegedly weaker but savvier about twenty-first-century realities.

After *Neighbors* previews this fear that straight white gentile middle-class millennial men may devolve into pathetic man-babies and pariahs, *Neighbors 2* places these anxieties center stage. Post-college, Teddy finds himself relegated to retail jobs where he reports to teenaged managers, and then finds himself jobless altogether, while his more studious peers pursue prestigious careers like architecture.[73] Worse, Teddy loses his housing with his friend Pete by failing to understand adult middle-class domesticity. Pete exemplifies "homonormative"[74] gayness, meaning that he obeys white middle-class norms of professionalism, domesticity, and chrononormativity. Therefore, when Pete's boyfriend proposes, the new fiancés promptly evict Teddy to convert his room into an office and eventually a nursery. This eviction blindsides Teddy, who childishly parrots fairytales by lamenting that "I thought you two would move into your room and I would live in my room, for *happily ever after*" (my emphasis). Here, Teddy's immaturity does more than make him homeless: it specifically excludes him from a monogamous white-collar gay household that symbolizes progress, diversity, professionalism, and maturity. Like in this case, Efron's pariah/man-baby status always conveys anxiety that straight white gentile middle-class millennial men are unprepared to succeed financially or culturally in twenty-first-century America.

Although Teddy's failures can evoke scorn, they also evoke sympathy—even from characters who previously found Teddy monstrous. In fact, the homeless, jobless, friendless Teddy finds shelter with his former nemeses, the Radners (Seth Rogen and Rose Byrne). Moreover, Teddy becomes their *surrogate baby*: he slurps baby food before napping in fetal position on a cot in their toddler's room. As Teddy sleeps, the Radners gaze parentally down and observe that he has "tuckered himself out,"[75] an expression typically reserved for toddlers. By reevaluating Teddy from monstrous threat to pitiable baby, the Radners illustrate how Efron's hyperwhite hypermasculine goyface characters always embody dual forms of abjection (scary monster and pathetic manbaby or pariah) that invite both censure and sympathy.

Further, when appearing as pariahs and man-babies, Efron's hyperwhite hypermasculine goyface characters easily invite sympathy because their pitiable narrative abjection (like their visual goyface) stays so *cleansable*. When Teddy in *Neighbors 2* sleeps on a baby cot and Matt in *Baywatch* sleeps under a boardwalk, both occupy physically low positions that symbolize disempowerment—but without physically marring Efron's body. Unlike *Fight Club*'s self-mutilating white gentile narrator or *Neighbors'* doughy, Jewish Mac Radner (Rogen), Efron's goyface characters can shed their metaphorical weakness simply by standing back up.

Killing 'Em with Kindness: Minoritized Labor for the Goyfaced Antagonist

It is significant that when Teddy hits rock bottom in *Neighbors 2*, his former nemeses, the Radners, become his surrogate parents. Battling and nurturing Teddy are two sides of one coin: in Efron's redemptive goyface comedies, like all films about hyperwhiteness, the minoritized labor that seems to punish whiteness actually redeems it by trimming its worst excesses. And since Efron's goyface characters suffer from their own hyperwhiteness, they directly benefit from the minoritized labor which pummels away that hyperwhiteness. Indeed, after punishing Efron's character in ways that actually improve him, most minoritized characters openly become his helpful mentors, lovers, or friends, like the Radners do. Further, even harsh punishments from these minoritized peers impose just fleeting comedic abjection that keeps Efron's characters redeemable.

Baywatch exemplifies this palatable path to purging hyperwhiteness, and how this path enlists minoritized labor. As we have seen, *Baywatch* initially positions the disgraced Olympian Matt (Efron) as a hyperwhite hypermasculine goyface stooge. However, Matt literally gets trained into a better person and colleague by the minoritized Baywatch lifeguards (a biracial gentile man, biracial gentile woman, two white gentile women, and a conditionally white Jewish man), until Matt eventually co-leads the team. For instance, the biracial co-leaders Mitch and Steph edify Matt about meritocratic success: when Matt demands to skip tryouts, Mitch and Steph retort that they "don't give a fuck" about his fame, and that "if you wanna be on this team, you gotta earn it" through egalitarian competition.[76] Next, these biracial leaders unleash comedic insults at Matt. On one hand, these insults constitute rhetorical goyface that exaggerates Matt's hyperwhite hypermasculinity while abjecting him as weak, feminized, and queer. Yet by mocking Matt's hyperwhiteness, these insults also begin pressuring him to shed it, thereby improving him. For instance, Mitch and Steph link Matt's origin in Iowa (a stereotypically white and gentile state) to overdelicate beauty: they claim that Iowa produces "cocky pretty boys" accustomed to "little fucking pond[s]" but unready for Florida's ocean, which has "riptides that will tear your little *man-gina* in two" (my emphasis). Disturbingly, these insults mask misogyny and queerphobia behind antiracism and feminism—audiences can relish watching an arrogant straight white gentile man humbled, *and* relish watching a man shamed for his alleged femininity. While these jibes harmfully normalize misogyny and queerphobia, they *benefit* Matt by humbling him without physically injuring him. Indeed, rather than brutalizing this hyperwhite hypermasculine antagonist, the Baywatch team blends mockery with serious *caregiving*: just as the Radners in *Neighbors 2* shelter the homeless Teddy, Lt. Mitch in *Baywatch* takes in the homeless Matt.

When humbling Matt into a better teammate, the Baywatch team blends rhetorical abjection with cleansable visual abjection. This funny and fleeting visual abjection peaks when they sneak into a morgue to investigate recent drug violence. When narco-traffickers arrive, the lifeguards all hide in cadaver drawers—but only Matt ends up lying beneath a corpse. The team then mocks Matt for panicking when the cadaver drips fat into his face and mouth. This cadaverous slime, which epitomizes abject excreta, makes Matt look sickening in ways that resonate with putrid hyperwhite zombies. However, while zombies incurably guzzle and ooze gore, Matt proves more redeemable: he comedically bursts from the drawer, spits out the fat, and gargles hand sanitizer. Even his most nauseating abjection thus proves brief, funny, and cleansable.

And although Matt's morgue mishap distresses him, this type of comedic abjection ultimately *helps* him by reforming him from an arrogant hyperwhite hypermasculine antagonist into a genteel protagonist. By making Matt more lovable, employable, and respectable, his minoritized colleagues thus restore his social and financial status, while helping this privilege look benign. Matt's genteel new image and its subtle power crystallize when the Baywatch confronts a nefarious Indian immigrant drug queenpin, Victoria. To neutralize the meddlesome Baywatch, Victoria bribes the white gentile Captain Thorpe to appoint Matt (who seems inept) as team leader. This promotion constitutes Matt's second nepotistic boost from Captain Thorpe, drawing negative attention to both men's straight white gentile male privilege. Yet Matt's privilege now appears more benign and deserved because he has grown humbler, more competent, and more team-spirited. Rather than commanding the Baywatch to recognize "who the fuck I am," Matt now modestly demurs that "I'm not ready" to lead. He only accepts leadership once Lt. Mitch assures him that the other lifeguards "need you" in this tough time, reframing Matt from usurper to benevolent shepherd. And Matt's power looks especially benevolent because he wields it for justice: against Captain Thorpe's orders, Matt leads the Baywatch in destroying Victoria's cartel. In the process, Matt sides with his minoritized teammates against straight white gentile male power, by punching the corrupt Captain Thorpe. Yet rejecting Thorpe protects Matt's *own* straight white gentile male privilege (his new leadership role) by helping it look better-deserved.

Further, Matt's new egalitarian image enables egregious violence against women of color, violence that safeguards straight white gentile male privilege. The villainess Victoria, played by Bollywood icon Priyanka Chopra, is a gorgeous elite Indian woman drug lord who threatens wholesome Americans and often seduces men to advance her business. She thus fuses stereotypes about brainy Indian immigrants, violent Latinx narco-traffickers, assertive businesswomen, and sexually liberated women—groups all commonly imagined to threaten straight white gentile American men's dominance. Victoria even literalizes this threat by holding Matt at gunpoint in their final confrontation. But thanks to Matt's genteel new masculinity, his minoritized teammates do the dirty work of saving him and thus symbolically defending straight white gentile male privilege. If Matt's "nice" reformed masculinity convinces his teammates to join his mission against Victoria, then this mission ends in gory murder: to defeat Victoria and rescue Matt, Matt's team explodes Victoria with a firework that evokes patriotic fourth of July celebrations. Despite reducing an immigrant woman of color to bloody chunks that graphically land onscreen, this murder comes off as a *multicultural victory* because it is co-executed by the biracial Mitch, by a white gentile woman lifeguard, and by a conditionally white Jewish male lifeguard. Further, although Matt has commanded the mission that leads to Victoria's murder, and although he benefits most directly from her death, he comes off as her *victim* and an innocent bystander in her demise. This murder thus exemplifies what I have called *post-meninist violence* in the previous chapter: violence that reasserts straight white male power but which appears unmalicious, apolitical, and/or accidental. In turn, this post-meninist murder exemplifies how Efron's redemptive goyface comedies reassert straight white gentile male domination in genteel guise.

Moreover, while Victoria symbolizes the fear that minoritized people might dominate, exclude, or even kill straight white gentile men, the Baywatch team offers a seemingly egalitarian utopia in which these men still receive respect, emotional labor, and sexual labor from minoritized people. *Baywatch*'s dénouement finds Matt happily sharing a meal with the diverse Baywatch lifeguards. Although Mitch (Dwayne Johnson) has reclaimed leadership, he now warmly applauds Matt rather than belittling him. As mentioned above, Mitch also stops rhetorically goyfacing

Matt with nicknames like "Little Mermaid." Further, although Matt's earlier hyperwhite hypermasculine misconduct repulsed his beautiful white gentile coworker, Summer, she now awards the reformed Matt a kiss. This kiss holds extra significance because Summer witnessed Matt's most nauseating abjection, when cadaverous fat dripped into his mouth. By now kissing that mouth, Summer emphasizes that Matt has utterly shed his abjection. In turn, this ending assures audiences that straight white gentile middle-class millennial men like Matt can shed their dysfunctional or outdated behaviors to mature into successful, beloved citizens of twenty-first-century America, yet retain their privilege. This ending thus exemplifies how Efron's redemptive goyface comedies model sexy abject hegemony that defuses the "double shock of being seen" for straight white gentile middle-class men.

Nice Jew-ish Goy: Scorning, Fearing, and Embracing Jewish Softness

Although many minoritized people help to deride-and-redeem Efron's hyperwhite hypermasculine goyface characters, this labor falls in especially complex ways on conditionally white Jewish men. Three of Efron's four redemptive goyface comedies juxtapose his hyperwhite hypermasculine goyface characters against fat emasculated Jewish foils: the neighbor Mac Radner in *Neighbors* and *Neighbors 2* (Seth Rogen) and the lifeguard Ronnie Greenbaum in *Baywatch* (Jewish actor Jon Bass).[77] Through these foils, Jewishness appears simultaneously as an excluded Other of white gentile masculinity *and* a solution to its problems. This effect reemphasizes how Efron's sexy abject hegemony always depends on his own Jewish but superhumanly gentile-looking body.

To help deride-and-redeem Efron's goyface characters, his Jewish foils restyle the "nice Jewish boy" trope and its deeper antisemitic roots. We have seen that racial antisemitism historically stigmatizes Jewish men's bodies and behavior as emasculated; envisions this emasculation as purely abject; and depicts this abjection as jointly weak, repulsive, and menacing.[78] For instance, Nazi propaganda depicted Jewish men as fat, dark, greasy, hook-nosed, and ugly weaklings who eschewed honest work or honorable romance.[79] Further, this propaganda accused Jewish men of conniving to steal German wealth and to sexually ensnare

German women and children.[80] Although such blatant racial antisemitism still circulates, subtler versions often shape today's mainstream American "common sense" about Jewish emasculation. For example, since the mid-twentieth century, the "nice Jewish boy" stereotype has reconfigured older stigmas about Jewish men into *unthreatening* emasculation, which includes *pathetic bodily softness* and ambivalently *appealing behavioral softness*. Bodily, the "nice Jewish boy" often appears scrawny, short, and neurotic. He may also have a beaked nose, and he presumably has a small penis. Behaviorally, the "nice Jewish boy" is pathetically neurotic and overattached to his mother, but also appealingly smart, devoted, and responsible.[81] Thus, the nice Jewish boy's bodily emasculation typically appears unattractive, but his behavioral emasculation wavers between weak and sweet.

In Efron's redemptive goyface comedies, the Jewish characters Mac and Ronnie sharpen this split between pathetic bodily softness and appealing behavioral softness: Mac and Ronnie are fat, weak, and unsexy, but kind, smart, and responsible, and therefore successful in twenty-first-century America. On a bodily level, these Jews thus serve as *pathetic inferior opposites* who visually accentuate Efron's hyperwhite hypermasculine goyface and its potential sexiness. This juxtaposition previews how Efron's goyface characters will reemerge as gorgeous genteel heroes. Since Mac and Ronnie are *pudgier* than typical nice Jewish boy characters, they contrast more sharply against Efron's hypermuscular body, accentuating his exhibitionist goyface. For example, *Baywatch* juxtaposes Matt's (Efron's) oiled, shining, impossibly muscular body (figure 5.4) against Ronnie Greenbaum's flabby, unpleasantly hairy body (figure 5.5).[82] Ronnie's first shirtless shot even uses slow motion to exaggerate his jiggling chest, belly, and arms. The same shot reveals blatantly fake dark-brown fur circling his nipples and straggling down his chest. Evoking repulsive Jewish emasculation, this fur throws Efron's smooth golden muscles into sharper relief. Similar gags contrast Teddy's (Efron's) and Mac's (Rogen's) shirtless torsos throughout *Neighbors* and *Neighbors 2*. And while Efron's exhibitionist goyface often looks disturbingly extreme, it looks sexy by contrast against Mac and Ronnie's flabby Jewish torsos. Further, since Ronnie has dark unruly hair and an arched nose, he accentuates Efron's superfine face and fair hair. Meanwhile, Mac's small Jewish penis accentuates Teddy's large gentile penis: when Mac expresses jealousy about a large dildo molded from Teddy's penis, Mac's wife comforts him that "I'm not sizeist."[83] In these examples, Mac and Ronnie echo Seth Rogen's role in the 2014 *Workaholics* minisode that initiated Efron's explicitly-but-barely Jewish star image. In that minisode, Rogen's pudgy and emasculated Jewface persona helps Efron to counteridentify with stigmas of Jewish racial queerness. Similarly, Mac and Ronnie serve as weak, unsexy, soft Jewish bodies that throw Efron's goyface characters into sexier relief.

However, just as Mac and Ronnie sharpen the ideal bodily traits of Efron's goyface, they also sharpen goyface's abject behavioral traits. Behaviorally, these lovable and successful Jews serve as *threatening superior opposites* who accentuate Efron's hyperwhite hypermasculine misconduct. This juxtaposition helps to cast white gentile men as both monstrously destructive and pitiably dispossessed. While Nazi propaganda depicted fat devious Jewish weaklings who steal German wealth and ensnare German women, Mac and Ronnie are *sweet* Jewish weaklings who *honestly* attract white gentile women, and honestly achieve greater professional success than white gentile men. These characters thus imply that Jewish men may *supplant* white gentile men as more successful citizens of America's feminist, multicultural, post-recession future. This anxiety reconfigures today's far-right American rhetoric. On one hand, Efron's redemptive goyface comedies softly echo far-right conspiracy theories about "the great replacement," which accuse Euro-American Jews of conspiring with feminists and people of color to dispossess and even exterminate white Christians.[84] Yet Efron's films restyle this myth with more ambivalent villains and victims, reflecting Efron's fusion of hyperwhiteness with abject hegemony: his hyperwhite hypermasculine goyface characters (not their Jewish foils) menace American society, implying that sweet Jewish men are *right* to challenge straight white gentile men's privilege. But precisely through this good deed, Mac and Ronnie subtly confirm the impression that Jews have dispossessed white gentile men.

This narrative clash between Jewish and gentile behavior is sharpest in *Neighbors* and *Neighbors 2*, which both frame Mac (Rogen) as Teddy's (Efron's) primary nemesis.[85] Mac, respectably employed and married to a beautiful white gentile woman, appears far more lovable and successful than the wild frat boy Teddy. Also unlike Teddy, Mac looks admirable

Figures 5.4 and 5.5. These images from *Baywatch* (2017) depict Zac Efron's goyfaced protagonist (figure 5.4) and his pudgy Jewish teammate, Ronnie Greenbaum (figure 5.5). Throughout the film, Ronnie's flubby Jewish body serves as a pathetic visual foil, which accentuates and beautifies Efron's exhibitionist goyface.

Screenshots from *Baywatch*, 2017. Images pulled from Amazon.com.

because he cares for others and earnestly *strives* to perform adult masculinity, even when he fails. On one hand, Mac does appear childishly overdependent on his Jewish mother: when he suggests asking his mother for lactation advice, his wife snaps, "You Jews and your fucking mothers!" However, Mac only wants his mother's advice to relieve his wife's lactation pain. Thus, even this childish moment positions Mac as a loving adult Jewish husband and father, far preferable to the unlovable Teddy. Further, just as Rogen questions straight white gentile male privilege in *Workaholics*, so does Mac lead the battle to restrict Teddy's raucous fraternity, for the well-being of Mac's family and his whole block. Mac ultimately wins this battle by getting the fraternity shut down, thereby stripping Teddy's power and fun as fraternity president. Thus, in contrast to the Jewish Mac, the gentile Teddy appears both more pernicious and more deprived.

While *Neighbors* pits Teddy against a Jewish rival, *Baywatch* contrasts Efron's goyface character (Matt) against a Jewish colleague (Ronnie) within a broader multicultural ensemble.[86] Yet this juxtaposition still narratively accentuates Matt's hyperwhite hypermasculine misconduct, making him appear both more harmful and more downtrodden. Although physically unsexy, Ronnie is a robotics and computer whiz who outstrips Matt's intelligence. Further, Ronnie's wit, sweetness, and devotion make the multicultural Baywatch team prefer him over Matt: minutes after mocking Matt as a "cocky pretty boy" from Iowa, the biracial Lt. Mitch warmly welcomes Ronnie into the Baywatch "because you have heart." Moreover, Ronnie's Jewish emasculation makes him a more *successful* teammate: he saves the day when Matt nearly ruins a scouting mission against the queenpin Victoria. Matt, assigned to tail Victoria, instead gets disastrously drunk and thereby draws contempt from his teammates. Stepping in, Ronnie distracts Victoria with ridiculous dancing that includes iconic choreography from Beyoncé's 2008 hit "Single Ladies,"[87] earning praise from his teammates. Ronnie ties this feminizing dance with Jewishness by explaining that he learned it at "Hebrew school." One of Ronnie's most emasculated and explicitly Jewish moments thus idealizes him as a more devoted, effective, beloved teammate than Matt. In comparison, Matt appears both more destructive (endangering the multicultural team) and downtrodden (disdained by the multicultural team).

However, like all the minoritized people who chastise Efron's hyperwhite hypermasculine goyface characters, Mac and Ronnie ultimately help to *refresh and beautify* straight white gentile male privilege. Mac and Ronnie not only present Jewish emasculation as a pathetic inferior opposite and threatening superior opposite to white gentile masculinity, but also as a *helpful, integrable resource* for reaching sexy abject hegemony. When Mac and Ronnie split "abject" Jewish bodily softness from "ideal" Jewish behavioral softness, they set the stage for Efron's goyface characters to grow into *nice Jew-ish goys*: white gentile men who absorb the most lovable and invisible stereotypes about emasculated Jewish behavior, while displacing the weakest, unsexiest, most visible stereotypes about emasculated Jewish bodies onto their Jewish foils. If Efron's goyface characters and their Jewish foils both appear ambivalently ideal/abject but in opposite ways, then absorbing Jewish behavioral softness lets his goyface characters achieve purely ideal masculinity—a masculinity that looks lovely, acts lovable, and thus achieves guiltless privilege in feminist, multicultural, post-recession America.

In *Baywatch*, this process of embracing and expelling a Jewish foil's softness remains tacit. First, *Baywatch* constantly presents the flubby Jewish Ronnie as an admirable foil to the goyfaced Matt (Efron). Second, the film centrally follows Matt's journey to learn the wit, humility, teamwork, and dedication that Ronnie has shown from the start. Precisely by emulating Ronnie's behavioral softness, Matt regains masculine privilege; this growth lets Matt win respect from Lt. Mitch and win a kiss from Summer. Meanwhile, *Baywatch*'s final shot again contrasts Matt's sculpted torso against Ronnie's jiggly torso. This shot emphasizes that abject Jewish bodily softness remains firmly stuck to Ronnie, freeing Matt to embody both physically gorgeous and ethically genteel masculinity.

Neighbors 2 follows a different path from goyface antagonist to "nice Jew-ish goy." In *Baywatch*, the gentile Matt tacitly learns from the Jewish Ronnie, by absorbing Ronnie's exact behaviors. Instead, *Neighbors* 2 explicitly shows the Jewish Mac mentoring the gentile Teddy, and thereby softening Teddy's behavior into an ideal new form—but a form that *complements* Mac's behavior rather than precisely mirroring it. As mentioned above, Teddy becomes the Radners' surrogate baby after his hypermasculine misconduct sabotages and infantilizes him. Under Mac's tutelage, Teddy matures into a more responsible and employable adult. The film's dénouement illustrates this transformation. For the first time, Teddy ceases his exhibitionist goyface by donning a dapper suit, which he combines with elegantly combed hair. Teddy pairs this genteel new image with a genteel new profession: he has rebranded his immature love of partying to become a gay wedding planner, thereby taming his wild debauchery to serve state-sanctioned monogamy. Thus, rather than becoming a sweet husband and father like Mac, Teddy sweetly helps others to achieve this domesticity. This helpful, mature, and glamorous new profession restores Teddy's financial stability while aligning him with feminist and multicultural values. Further, Teddy's genteel new persona wins him love and *obedience* from the gay couple who previously evicted him, as he orchestrates their wedding onscreen. By showing Teddy literally command gay weddings through his headset, this dénouement promises that straight white gentile men can remain *beloved leaders* in a multicultural future. And Teddy achieves this genteel, guiltless, gorgeous masculinity precisely through the mentorship of his flubby Jewish foil, Mac. While Mac remains sweet but pudgy with a small penis, Teddy becomes a sweet gentile Adonis.

When Efron's goyface characters selectively embrace and expel different kinds of softness from Jewish foils, they highlight how his sexy abject hegemony depends on his own Jewish but gentile-looking body. Efron's real-world image as an explicitly-but-barely Jewish star underpins the premise that his white gentile characters can absorb the "best" invisible qualities of Jewish emasculation without sacrificing any privilege or conventional masculine sex appeal.

Conclusion

This tightrope walk between white gentile masculinity and Jewish emasculation always fuels Efron's queer glamor in his redemptive goyface comedies. By first contrasting against and then selectively embracing elements of Jewish emasculation, his characters seem to earnestly atone for their straight white gentile middle-class male privilege and for their millennial immaturity. But in fact, these characters just camouflage and stealthily reassert their privilege by helping it look more compatible with a feminist, multicultural, post-recession future. This fantasy, rooted in Efron's doubly impossible body, is always what makes his sexy abject hegemony so visually, ethically, and ideologically alluring.

Conclusion

Tools for the Road

Jewish racial contradictions may seem abstract, but as this book has shown, they are really as familiar to many readers as their favorite sitcom or star. Indeed, one of my own (formerly) favorite stars spectacularized those contradictions in early 2022: Whoopi Goldberg. By 2022, Goldberg had been a beloved figure in film, television, and theater for nearly forty years. Her award-winning work has included her role as co-host of the daytime talk show *The View* since 2007, for which she won a Daytime Emmy in 2009.[1] However, Goldberg accidentally unleashed a media firestorm on *The View* on January 31, 2022, while discussing *Maus*, a graphic novel about the Holocaust. This controversy epitomized the difficulties that this book has sought to address: Goldberg illustrated that even well-intentioned Americans (including Jewish ones) often lack the tools to analyze racial antisemitism in either the past or present. Likewise, few have the tools to analyze how antisemitism intersects with white privilege or color-based racism in the US today. Goldberg's fiasco exemplified why it is so vital for us all to demystify the relationships between Jewishness, antisemitism, and race.

Goldberg's debacle grew from a mixture of good intentions and bad information. On one hand, she conveyed a liberatory desire to educate young people about genocide: she was criticizing a Tennessee school board that had banned *Maus*.[2] Despite promoting public education about the Holocaust, she then undercut that goal by misguidedly adding that "the Holocaust *isn't about race*. It's not about race. It's not about race" (my emphasis).[3] When co-host Ana Navarro interjected, "But it's about white supremacists going after Jews," Goldberg replied, "But these are two white groups of people!"[4] These assertions unleashed an uproar from viewers and Jewish community leaders, who rightly observed that the Nazis *did* label Jews a separate inferior race, that this racial classification is precisely what motivated the Holocaust, and that it is dangerous to downplay this racial core of Nazi ideology.[5]

Although Goldberg's misstatement was indeed dangerous, it was not simply a personal error. Instead, as philosopher Kenan Malik has observed, Goldberg illustrates a broader "amnesia" about the way racial categories can vary by context.[6] Few Americans receive education about the social construction of race: the way that racial categories which are allegedly "objective" actually fluctuate across time and space based on social consensus, just as national borders do. This educational gap prevents many Americans from comprehending how any group could experience different racial statuses with different life-or-death consequences in different settings. This gap also prevents many Americans from understanding that not all racial categories in other times and places have primarily depended on skin color as they do in the present-day United States. Together, this lack of conceptual tools can lead anyone (as it led Goldberg) to misbelieve that all societies have always deemed European Jews "white people," and therefore to deny that such Jews could ever experience racism in any time or place. This oversight not only fuels misunderstanding of the Holocaust, but also of America's own racial history. It erases the way nineteenth- and early twentieth-century American media, pseudoscience, legal discourse, and popular "common sense" often stigmatized Euro-American Jews in explicitly racial terms as inferior to white gentiles, even while white skin privileged Euro-American Jews over people of color.[7]

And Goldberg's error went beyond denying the racial past. Soon after her initial misstatement, she proceeded to oversimplify America's racial present as well. This second error came when Goldberg appeared on *The Late Show with Stephen Colbert* to apologize for her previous comments. Although many viewers felt that Goldberg's apology "doubled down"[8] on her original misstep, it may be too simple to say that Goldberg was unremorseful. Instead, she seemed to earnestly struggle to articulate how antisemitism overlaps with and differs from anti-Blackness in America today. Nevertheless, her effort predictably and harmfully lacked nuance, reflecting Americans' lack of education about race in general and about Jewish racial status in particular. Goldberg explained that "I feel, being Black, when we talk about race, it's a very different thing to me. So I said I thought the Holocaust wasn't about race." She continued: "When the

Klan is coming down the street and I'm standing with a Jewish friend—I'm going to run. But if my friend decides not to run, they'll get passed by most times, because you can't tell most times . . . That's what I was trying to explain."[9] On one hand, these new comments accurately emphasize that, in the US today, most people with brown or black skin (whether Jewish or gentile) cannot hide from color-based racism in the way that many Euro-American Jews can hide from antisemitism. However, these comments also repeat Goldberg's initial error of projecting today's racial categories onto the past, inaccurately assuming that Jews in Nazi Germany experienced the same racial status as Euro-American Jews in the twenty-first-century United States.

Most intriguingly, though, Goldberg's (non)apology added a new element: it both implied and denied the racial complexities of present-day American antisemitism. Her words imply but dismiss the possibility that, in the US today, antisemitism *can* be racial and that race itself may operate *beyond* a white/people of color binary. By stating that "you can't tell most times" who's Jewish, Goldberg tacitly acknowledges that sometimes people think they *can* tell. This presumption reflects the long history of artistic, literary, and pseudoscientific antisemitism. This history still widely fuels non-melanin-based racial stereotypes (like beaked noses) about Jewish bodies, even among Americans like Goldberg who do not know that any society ever racially stigmatized Jews. Both Jewish and gentile white-skinned people who fit these antisemitic racial stereotypes can thus never be sure when their white privilege may give way to antisemitic racial mockery, discrimination, or murder. Further, Goldberg tacitly acknowledges that even Jews who can physically pass as white gentiles may still suffer Klan violence if they out themselves—for instance, by "running from" (failing to hide their fear of) Klansmen. Despite tacitly recognizing that Euro-American Jews can experience racial stereotypes and white supremacist violence, Goldberg also paradoxically denies that such antisemitism can ever be "about race." This denial is ironic because the Klan and other white supremacist hate groups explicitly define their antisemitism in racial terms. For example, we have seen how the former KKK grand wizard David Duke articulated this racial animosity in 2016, when he angrily tweeted that "JEWS ARE NOT WHITE!"[10] When Whoopi Goldberg implied-but-dismissed these racial nuances, she illustrated that she (like many Americans) lacks the vocabulary to pinpoint *conditional whiteness*. That is, she cannot articulate the way Euro-American Jews today access many parts of white privilege in many contexts, but may unpredictably lose some of those privileges—including physical safety—if their Jewishness becomes known.

Like Goldberg's misunderstanding of the racial past, her oversimplification of America's racial present is far from unique. Even many scholars, activists, and students who earnestly strive to critique injustice lack the tools to articulate (or even notice) present-day racial contradictions around Jewishness. Further, as Kenan Malik wrote after Whoopi Goldberg's debacle, this inattention to Jewish racial complexities "has led some on the left to become blind to antisemitism" altogether.[11] And because antisemitism is a core framework of white supremacist ideologies, anyone who overlooks antisemitism cannot accurately analyze today's pressing problem of alt-right rhetoric and violence. For example, when Whoopi Goldberg incompletely hypothesized how "my Jewish friend" would experience Klan violence, her error was double: like many well-meaning Americans, she miscomprehended antisemitism in particular *and* far-right ideology in general.

Goldberg's gaffe also spotlit two more conceptual gaps around Jewishness and race, gaps that went unnoticed in the backlash. First, Goldberg illustrated the way that many Americans (both Jewish and gentile) erase Jews of color. For instance, when stating that "my Jewish friend" could stay safe from the Ku Klux Klan by passing as a white gentile, Goldberg implied that all American Jews have white skin. This presumption is especially odd since Goldberg *herself* has publicly identified as a Black Jew. And we will soon see that her Jewish self-identification depends on common, tacitly racial definitions of Jewishness. Therefore, when Goldberg's 2022 comments erased Jews of color and denied that antisemitism can ever be racial, she illustrated a second key problem: even American Jews themselves (both conditionally white Jews and Jews of color) often lack the tools to articulate their own contradictory racial statuses.

This wider difficulty within Jewish communities is especially visible in Goldberg's past and recent statements about Jewishness. For example, although many Americans envision Jewishness as (partly) a religious identity, Goldberg has long illustrated how this religious definition rubs uneasily against tacitly racial definitions; how these racial definitions ambivalently place Jewishness inside/outside whiteness; and how anti-semitism permeates American society. Born Caryn Elaine Johnson in 1955,[12] Goldberg had a Baptist clergyman father,[13] but has stated that her family also included "Jewish, Buddhist, Baptist and Catholic" members.[14] She specifically attributes Jewish ancestry and the surname Goldberg to her mother's family history.[15] However, Goldberg has explained that she follows none of these faiths because "I don't believe in man-made religions."[16] Despite this non-Jewish upbringing and non-Jewish religious philosophy, Goldberg has stated that "I just know I am Jewish" because this identity is "part of my heritage. Just like being Black."[17] This self-description invokes a widespread assumption (both inside and outside Jewish communities) that Jewish ancestry alone can transmit Jewish identity, an assumption that clashes against religious definitions of Jewishness. The Pew Research Center captured this popular view in 2013, finding that 32 percent of millennial American Jews "describe themselves as having no religion and identify as Jewish on the basis of ancestry, ethnicity or culture,"[18] as Goldberg does.

Further, when Goldberg compares Jewishness to Blackness as "part of my heritage" (rather than comparing Jewishness to her family's Buddhist, Catholic, or Baptist roots), she highlights that the concept of Jewish ancestry is tacitly racial: it envisions Jewishness as a heritable biological difference rather than a religious practice, and even implies that Jewish ancestry may supersede religious practice. However, this tacitly racial definition of Jewishness ambivalently coexists with the widespread contemporary American assumption that all Jews are white (or at least look white)—a racial assumption that casts Black Americans like Goldberg as inauthentically Jewish. Indeed, Goldberg has noted that others often skeptically ask, "Come on, are you Jewish?" and that "I always say, 'Would you ask me that if I was white? I bet not.'"[19] In other words, America's contradictory racial definitions of Jewishness both enable and undercut Goldberg's Jewish identity, since these definitions paradoxically deem Jewishness a biological difference from and/or a part of whiteness.

Even while Goldberg has navigated these racial cross-currents to declare herself Jewish, her own stage name has always illustrated how antisemitic conspiracy theories permeate daily American assumptions. Goldberg chose this Jewish stage name because her "mother thought that a Jewish surname would get her further in Hollywood."[20] In other words, no matter whether Jewish ancestry and the name Goldberg truly do appear in her family tree, her choice to *forefront* Jewishness in her stage name reflects an antisemitic conspiracy theory: the myth that "Jews run Hollywood," and more broadly that Jewishness grants power. This motivation for a Jewish stage name is especially ironic, for as we have seen, Jewish performers historically face pressure (even from fellow Jews in the industry) to *downplay* their Jewishness in exchange for casting opportunities. In turn, the myths that motivated Goldberg's stage name exist on a spectrum with the more blatantly hateful rhetoric of media figures like Kanye West. Throughout fall and winter 2022, West infamously ranted against Jews for allegedly controlling the media, puppeteering American society, and greedily hoarding wealth, while he praised Hitler and claimed that America should "stop dissing Nazis."[21] Even though Whoopi Goldberg has condemned Nazism and declared herself Jewish, her reasons for signaling Jewish identity in her stage name actually overlap with Kanye's reasons for extolling Hitler and with the myths that motivate real-world racial violence against American Jews.

And Goldberg made it harder to challenge all types of antisemitism when she publicly proclaimed in 2022 that all Jews look white and that antisemitism could never be racial. Her misstatements flattened the very complexities around Jewishness and race that she herself has long publicly embodied. Even worse, Goldberg extended this self-contradiction throughout 2022 by consistently repeating her misstatements about the Holocaust.[22] This ongoing debacle exemplifies why Jews and gentiles alike need better tools to articulate how Jewishness, antisemitism, racism, and white privilege all interact in daily life.

Demystifying and Challenging Racial Antisemitism

Precisely to expand those tools, this book has clarified a central but little-understood aspect of racial antisemitism in American society. I have argued that queer (strange) masculinity often symbolizes Jewish racial difference in twenty-first-century US media for Jews who are both women and men, black- and white-skinned, across diverse platforms from cinema to YouTube. Emerging from an eight-century lineage of artistic, religious, literary, theatrical, and pseudoscientific antisemitism, these stigmas remain primary tools by which US media racially distinguish Jews from gentiles. In turn, these stigmas of queer Jewish masculinity position Jewishness as a racial difference that is *distinct from* but *intersects with* skin color. Recognizing this effect enables us to better visualize how racial antisemitism intersects with America's white/people of color (white/POC) binary, both onscreen and off.

To elucidate how queer masculinity symbolizes Jewish racial difference in US popular media, we have examined six of America's best-known millennial Jewish stars. These stars make such vivid examples because each provocatively spotlights Jewish identity, Jewish racial contradictions, and antisemitic racial stigmas onscreen, in ways that were taboo for earlier mainstream Jewish performers. When analyzing these millennial Jewish stars, I have argued that Jewish masculinity's racial symbolism appears most sharply when each star wields stigmas of queer Jewish masculinity to perform ideological labor. In particular, each star sculpts antisemitic stigmas into subliminal postmodern minstrel personae that ambivalently challenge and/or renormalize white, straight, Christian male supremacy. For instance, Drake's chameleonic minstrel personae, Lil Dicky's incel-ish Jewface persona, Abbi Jacobson and Ilana Glazer's exotic Jewessface personae, Seth Rogen's babyish Jewface persona, and Zac Efron's clownish goyface persona each differently help viewers to fantasize about challenging oppression, sustaining their own privilege, or both at once. Indeed, each star's career depends on performing this ideological labor to generate queer glamor: an unexpected allure rooted in racial stigmas of queer (odd) Jewish masculinity. But whether disrupting and/or naturalizing inequality, each star's persona utilizes (and thereby exposes) America's commonplace racial assumption that Jews look, speak, move, and lust differently from gentiles. Thus, even stars who harmfully normalize inequality against others simultaneously illustrate the antisemitic racial stigmas that expose Jews to mockery, to microaggressions, and sometimes to murder. Further, when these millennial Jewish stars achieve mass appeal by enlisting popular assumptions about Jewish bodies, they demonstrate that racial antisemitism is not limited to America's past or its far-right extremists. Instead, racial antisemitism widely shapes American racial "common sense," even for Americans who (like Whoopi Goldberg) do not consciously classify Jews as a race and have no idea that any society ever did so.

By clarifying how American popular media racially distinguish Jewish from gentile bodies, this book aims to serve scholars, activists, students, Jewish communities, and all readers who wish to better analyze how race operates in America today. I hope that all these readers may carry away new tools for detecting antisemitism, for deciphering how antisemitism intersects with color-based racism and white privilege, and for better challenging all these forms of injustice. To that end, I also hope that readers will better notice how *gentility* (Christian ancestry) shapes racial categories in America today. Likewise, I hope that readers may better notice how *clashing racial statuses can attach to different parts of one body*, including the body's concrete traits (like skin color and nose shape) and its *racialized ephemera* (like styles of speech and gesture). To enhance all these analyses, I also aspire for this book to help popularize the term *conditional whiteness* in both scholarly and everyday conversations. Although this term is not new, it remains underutilized for articulating how white privilege intersects with racial stigma for Euro-American Jews, as well as for many Arab, Persian, and Latinx Americans (both Jewish and gentile).[23]

As another layer of nuance, I also hope readers will better notice *how straight white gentile male supremacy envisions Jewishness ambivalently as both a threat and resource*. That is, American cultural narratives often appropriate Jewish victimhood to misrepresent straight white gentile men as dispossessed underdogs, but simultaneously accuse Jews of orchestrating white gentiles' dispossession, thereby fueling antisemitic resentment and violence. This paradoxical impulse to appropriate Jewish victimhood while vilifying Jews themselves sometimes appears explicitly and among self-identified white supremacists. For instance, we have seen that far-right conspiracy theories often flip Holocaust history to accuse Jews of orchestrating "white genocide," and thus to imagine white gentiles as "the Jews" (imperiled outcasts) of twenty-first-century America. However, this paradoxical attitude toward Jewishness also subtly permeates mainstream American popular culture and affects viewers who may consider themselves unbigoted or even progressive. For instance, with regard to appropriating Jewish victimhood, I have illustrated how Seth Rogen and Lil Dicky invite white gentile male viewers to vicariously embrace tropes of Jewish emasculation, and thus to imagine themselves as sympathetic victims. And with regard to fearing

Jewishness, we have seen how Zac Efron's comedies (including those that co-star Rogen) softly echo white supremacists' antisemitic paranoia: these comedies subtly mirror the fear that Jewish men are plotting to "replace" white gentile men by seducing white gentile women, by monopolizing economic opportunities, and/or by orchestrating a racially diverse future. Demystifying the way white supremacy appropriates-and-vilifies Jewishness is one helpful step toward grasping the slippery problem of antisemitism.

To support more precise scholarship about race, Jewishness, and antisemitism, I particularly intend this book to spark new dialogues between Jewish cultural studies and queer of color critique. Only by conversing can these fields both achieve their common goal of decoding how race, gender, and sexuality co-shape each other and co-shape notions of citizenship, nationalism, diaspora, immigration, and genocide. Jewish cultural studies must especially grow to better consider Jews who are Latinx, Mizrahi, Sephardi, and/or of color. Likewise, queer of color critique can particularly benefit from noticing its own Jewish roots and analyzing diasporic (not solely Israeli) Jewishness. For both fields, these new directions may benefit from recent scholarship by Bryan K. Roby, Marla Brettschneider, and Noah Tamarkin, who each address how different African Jewish communities navigate global notions of Blackness, Jewishness, diaspora, and nationalism.[24]

Alongside queer of color critique and Jewish cultural studies, media studies is a fruitful site for new analyses of race and Jewishness. For instance, through this book's chapter on Drake, I aim to encourage future scholarship about the emerging wave of media by and about Jews of color, Latinx Jews, Sephardic Jews, and Mizrahi Jews in US popular culture. Key examples of this wave include Tiffany Haddish's Netflix special *Black Mitzvah* (2019), recently analyzed by Samantha Pickette;[25] the Asian-American Jewish webseries *Lunar* (2021–present); the Turkish drama *The Club* (released on Netflix in 2021), which features Sephardic Jewish protagonists; and the Argentine Jewish feminist/queer dramedy *The End of Love* (released on Amazon Prime Video in 2022).

In the process of analyzing racial antisemitism and millennial Jewish stardom, I have also offered new analytical tools that may enhance scholarship on wider topics within media studies, Jewish studies, feminist studies, queer studies, and critical race studies. Many of these tools pin-point recent or understudied forms of racial minstrelsy.

Deciphering New Varieties and Techniques of Racial Minstrelsy

To expose new styles and methods of racial minstrelsy, this book has built on Simon Weaver's concept of postmodern minstrelsy[26] to name *subliminal postmodern minstrelsy*. This new paradigm aims to illuminate a wide range of media performances that presently go unrecognized as synthetic racial caricatures at all, because they are so visually subtle and ideologically nebulous. For example, *Saturday Night Live* (1975–present) abounds with such elusive caricatures.

Naming subliminal postmodern minstrelsy may especially deepen analyses of "whitewashing," a racist media practice that is often rightly critiqued but rarely recognized as minstrelsy. The most straightforward form of whitewashing is not minstrelsy, but nonetheless racist: it entails rewriting a nonwhite character as white. However, a second and slipperier form of whitewashing overlaps with subliminal postmodern minstrelsy: in this version, white actors *semi-plausibly play* non-white characters by pairing *their own natural appearance* with racially loaded names, costumes, gestures, music, plotlines, or locales, but without brown makeup. One infamous case of this whitewashing-as-minstrelsy is the 2015 rom-com *Aloha*, which whitewashed a multiracial protagonist, "Allison Ng."[27] Descending from Chinese, Pacific Islander, and European ancestry, this character theoretically constituted a milestone in representation for multiracial Hawaiians, who made up nearly one-quarter of Hawaii's population in 2015.[28] But rather than letting a multiracial Hawaiian woman control her own representation, the film instead cast Emma Stone, a non-Hawaiian blond white gentile star who happens to have slightly almond-shaped eyes. This racial impersonation depended on pairing Stone's natural eye shape with an Asian surname ("Ng"), a Hawaiian setting, and some brief hula hand-gestures, but without cosmetically darkening her skin or hair. Therefore, although critics rightly lambasted *Aloha* for whitewashing Asian, Indigenous, and multiracial identities, almost none identified this transgression as *yellowface*.[29] Naming this role as subliminal postmodern yellowface can help to make visible how such practices extend long histories of racial minstrelsy. More broadly, recognizing how whitewashing often overlaps with subliminal postmodern minstrelsy can help to clarify how white-washing always serves (regardless of intention) to silence and caricature people of color.

Just as the term "subliminal postmodern minstrelsy" may help to critique whitewashing, this term may also help to expose the way cosmetic-free blackface minstrelsy subtly pervades American popular culture. Media scholar Krin Gabbard has written that twenty-first-century white pop cultural performances constantly depend on a "nuanced channeling of blackness" that descends from more blatant blackface minstrel shows of the past.[30] For just two examples, Gabbard observes that Christina Aguilera's famously soulful vocal riffs and the iconic "swagger of white action heroes" each mimic stereotypes of Black speech, gesture, and sex-uality.[31] Without using cosmetics, these techniques aid white performers to metaphorically "wear" stereotypes of Black sensuality and coolness. Although today's stars and their fans "would strenuously deny" it, these cosmetic-free techniques for wearing Blackness descend directly from historical blackface minstrel shows, in which white performers cosmeti-cally blacked up to caricature Black people and/or to access the thrilling-but-scary primitivism that supposedly characterized Black people.[32] If we recognize that this nebulous channeling of blackness constitutes one type of subliminal postmodern minstrelsy, then it becomes easier to recognize and critique this subtle, omnipresent form of blackface.

By dissecting subliminal postmodern minstrelsy into concrete mechanisms, this book also aims to support wider scholarship about unexpected dimensions of minstrelsy. Conventional wisdom assumes that racial minstrels must shroud their bodies in makeup, prosthetics, wigs, costumes, or props. Instead, my new concept of *exhibitionist goyface* illustrates that some minstrels must *expose* their bare flesh to produce racially caricatured personae. Meanwhile, extending the work of Hannah Schwadron,[33] I have newly pinpointed techniques that allow minstrelsy to extend beyond the face and even beyond the body. For instance, my new concepts of *rhetorical Jewface* and *cinematographic Jewface* clarify that dialogue, lyrics, lighting, and camera angles may instruct viewers to perceive a star in racially caricatured ways, *no matter whether* that star visually presents any racially caricatured facial features, hairstyles, costumes, gestures, or props. Regarding another subtle and unexpected form of racial minstrelsy, my new paradigm of *Jewessface* clarifies that not all racial minstrelsy coheres into a racial mask (whether overt or subliminal). Instead, some minstrelsy diffuses an ethereal racial *aura* that thrills audiences precisely by eluding crisp coherence.

Concerning new dimensions of minstrelsy, the chapter on Drake also strives to open fresh investigations into blackfishing and brownfishing. While past scholarship in these areas has near-exclusively analyzed white women performers such as Ariana Grande, it is also valuable to examine how *male blackfishing* and/or *blackfishing by people of color* help to circulate racist ideologies. Just one popular figure who invites such analysis is the Moroccan American rapper French Montana. Although he is not Latino, French Montana has performed a Dominican alter ego alongside Drake in the music video "No Shopping" (2016).[34] And although French Montana has not self-identified as Black or Afro-Moroccan, he has sometimes donned cornrows that let him pass as Black.[35]

Because all these understudied and unexpected forms of minstrelsy produce such subtle caricatures, they often *aid oppressive narratives to pass as harmless or even liberatory onscreen*. This effect allows even screenwriters, directors, and stars to misunderstand the ideological impact of their own narratives. To further unmask such faux-liberatory narratives, I have also proposed new analytical tools that reach beyond racial minstrelsy.

Unmasking Faux-Liberatory Narratives

For one such tool, I have extended Viveca Greene's model of deplorable satire[36] to name "*soft* deplorable satire." Greene's model exposes the way far-right groups weaponize digital humor to entice new recruits. My new term reveals how the technique can be subtler, less deliberate, and thus even more seductive than previously recognized. This insight can support the growing literature about far-right humor[37] and about the way far-right ideologies are bleeding into mainstream thought.[38] Meanwhile, my term *post-meninism* articulates how some white-privileged men (both onscreen and off) can deem themselves guiltlessly progressive while actually yearning to maintain power. To this end, post-meninist media fantasize about "accidentally," "unmaliciously," "apolitically" punishing any minoritized people who challenge white male privilege.

To further decipher such fantasies of guiltless and lovable straight white gentile male dominance, I have also expanded Claire Sisco King's concept of abject hegemony to recognize *cute abject hegemony* and *sexy abject hegemony*. These new paradigms may illuminate many recent media in which straight white male protagonists keep most of their masculine sex appeal, social power, and/or physical strength, yet still manage to misrepresent themselves as sympathetic victims to "justify" re-dominating minoritized people. For example, the term "sexy abject hegemony" can sharpen scholarship about white male backlash in the hit series *Breaking Bad* (2008–2013): the show stars a cancer-stricken but craggily handsome and ruthlessly violent straight white gentile male druglord, who often battles against Latino narco-traffickers for economic dominance and clashes with his own wife for domestic dominance.[39]

To continue clarifying how popular media can package oppressive narratives as harmless or liberatory, I have also expanded past insights about "unruly womanhood" from Kathleen Rowe[40] and about "hyper-whiteness" from Gretchen Bakke and Russell Meeuf.[41] My new term *racist unruly womanhood* illuminates how rebellious women characters can fuse euphoric gendered and sexual liberation with racist oppression, as when Ilana Glazer asserts sexual independence by objectifying Black men. Such performances invite progressive viewers to excuse or even guiltlessly *relish* racist narratives by misbelieving that they have only relished feminist liberation. And while racist unruly women camouflage racism within feminism, *hyperwhite shrews* camouflage misogyny within antiracism. The new term "hyperwhite shrews" names elitist white women villains who invite the audience to mistake misogynist desires (to punish powerful women) for antiracist desires (to chasten a haughty, cruel, or exploitative white person). This pattern extends far beyond media featuring millennial Jewish stars. For instance, the hit political thriller *House of Cards* (2013–2018) often invoked hyperwhite shrewishness through its icy, cunning, and power-hungry blond white gentile antihero, Claire Underwood.[42] Meanwhile, the new term *hyperwhite hypermasculinity* clarifies how some media help audiences to reconcile their contradictory desires to critique-and-sustain straight white male dominance. To fuse these antithetical desires, hyperwhite hypermasculine characters present a straight white masculine beauty so extreme that it wavers between alluring and monstrous, but ultimately stays redeemable. For example, this insight not only illuminates Zac Efron's clownish goyface bros, but also illuminates Robert Pattinson's lustrously white vampiric heartthrob in the megahit *Twilight* film series (2008–2012).[43] This pearly undead Romeo illustrates a key thread linking hyperwhite hypermasculine protagonists with hyperwhite shrews: both demonstrate that hyperwhiteness need not appear visually repulsive (as past scholarship supposes), but can instead appear intimidatingly *gorgeous*.

Despite this innovation, the terms "hyperwhite hypermasculinity" and "hyperwhite shrew" still mirror conventional hyperwhiteness by describing characters who are overtly threatening and/or elitist. Conversely, my new term *hyper-whiteguiltiness* describes well-meaning characters who are desperately ashamed of their white privilege and earnestly intent on promoting racial justice. Nevertheless, in their misinformed and self-centered efforts at fleeing white guilt, these characters blatantly microaggress against the people of color whom they claim to support. Although this phenomenon might serve to educate progressive white viewers about avoiding similar pitfalls, it may actually just help viewers imagine themselves as already-perfect antiracists by contrast. Hyperwhiteguilty characters can thus serve the same end as all hyperwhite characters: helping white-privileged viewers (both Jewish and gentile) to feel racially guiltless without actually challenging racism or giving up any privilege. These insights about hyper-whiteguiltiness may decode a spate of recent characters on both Black- and white-written comedy series, including the bumbling white student Clifton in *Dear White People* (2017–2021)[44] and the overearnest white schoolteacher Jacob in *Abbott Elementary* (2021–present).[45]

Because all these new analytical tools have emerged from studying millennial Jewish stardom, they highlight why Jewishness and antisemitism constitute key lenses for critical race, media, gender, and queer studies. Firstly, Jewishness and antisemitism are vital concepts to understand in their own right, both onscreen and off. Secondly, Jewishness and antisemitism constitute central but understudied elements in America's broader notions of race, gender, sexuality, and nationhood. When studying these wider themes, anyone who overlooks Jewishness automatically dams up key dialogues, drains away key questions, and thereby funnels their inquiry toward incomplete conclusions. By contrast, pulling Jewishness into the picture opens a floodgate of new insights that freshly enable us to map how stigma, inequality, and identity operate in everyday life. These fuller insights are vital for all of us—both Jewish and gentile—who wish to understand ourselves, to diagnose our society's ills, and to pursue a more humane future.

ACKNOWLEDGMENTS

This book could not exist without the colleagues, friends, and family who have supported me along the way. I especially thank Linda Mizejewski for her warm and insightful mentorship over the past ten years. Special thanks also to Bella Cameron, whose feedback helped me clarify my voice. Likewise, for their generous encouragement and intellectual feedback, I thank Shannon Winnubst, Laura Levitt, M. Joseph Ponce, Treva Lindsey, Lynn Kaye, Lynn Itagaki, Janet Freedman, Marla Brettschneider, Joyce Antler, Carol Siegel, Rich Lowry, Liz Losh, Arthur Knight, Jonathan Boyarin, Caroline Levine, Deborah Starr, Jane Juffer, Susan Stiritz, Guisela Latorre, Cynthia Burack, Wendy Smooth, Rin Reczek, Amy Shuman, Alicia Andrzejewski, Emily Fine, Vineeta Singh, Josh Hubbard, Jody Allen, Amy Limoncelli, Cristina Galmarini, Russell Meeuf, Golan Moskowitz, Melissa Weininger, Jenny Caplan, Samantha Pickette, Grace Overbeke, Rachel Harris, Sarah Imhoff, Olga Gershenson, Nick Underwood, Rachel Silverman, Robin Judd, Laura Leibman, Shaina Hammerman, and Charlotte Fonrobert. For their wonderful skill and support during my years at the Ohio State University, I also thank Jackson Stotlar, Lynaya Elliot, Elysse Jones, Tess Pugsley, and Cynthia Preston. Likewise, thank you to Jennifer Hammer, Veronica Knutson, and the staff at New York University Press for expertly guiding this book to print. I am also grateful for the organizations and awards that helped to fund this project as it matured across a decade. I first envisioned this book during my doctoral program in Women's, Gender, & Sexuality Studies at the Ohio State University. It then grew during my subsequent appointments at the Hadassah-Brandeis Institute as a resident scholar; at the College of William & Mary as a visiting assistant professor of Film & Media Studies and of Gender, Sexuality, & Women's Studies; at Cornell University as a visiting assistant professor of English and Jewish Studies; and at Stanford University as the Eli Reinhard Postdoctoral Fellow at the Taube Center for Jewish Studies.

Throughout this journey, I received funding for research, conference travel, and publication from each of these departments, programs, and centers. I also received funding from the Ohio State University Graduate School in the form of a Presidential Fellowship, as well as from the Association for Jewish Studies, the National Women's Studies Association, and the Society for Cinema & Media Studies. For the warm community that has sustained me across many years and many cities, I also thank Lara Hardy-Smith, Sasha Jontof-Hutter, Sara Rodríguez-Argüelles Riva, Nick Painter, Liz and Jordan Berman, Rachel Richman and Kacie Lindsley, Mason Yang and Monica Guan, Joel Pierzchala, David Kajander, Nick and Tookie May, Júlia Franceschi Guerra Faria and Guilherme Abreu Faria, Thomas Igeme, J. Caroline Toy, S. Jasmine Stork, K. Everstein, Kati Fitzgerald, Abby Buffington, Eleanor Paynter and Gennaro Ditosto, Larissa Andersen, Philip and Malia Womack, Becca Alexander, Madison Rose, Rachael Coe, Krista Benson and Grant Stancliff, Alexandro Hernández, Diana Sencherey, Abeir Shalash, Abby Gondek, Eliza Reisfeld, Jared Shaffer, Katya Rouzina, Lisa Geduldig, Mike Lakin, Bob Rosenberg, Stan Kagin, Steve Kittay, Thaïs Miller and Chad Fusco, Robyn Miles and Crystal Farshchi, Lili Brown and Anna Carlson, Hannah Kober, Jake Daniels, Zach Kagin and Lina García, Jill Toups, Tyler Kearn, Janet Loebach, Linda Shi, Irina Troconis, Begüm Adalet, Denise Green, Danielle Sonnenberg and Nilay Yapici, Andrew Campana and Ed von Aderkas, Debbie Diner and Caleb MacArthur, Chantal Thibout, Martine Rudloff, Carme Mediavilla Farzón, the Lisker-Chernoff family, the Premack family, the B'Bayit book club, and the Feygelkrayz book club. Finally, thank you to my parents, Joyce and Alan Branfman; my brother, Benjamin Branfman; my grandparents, Helen and Leo Wolk and Harold and Jean Branfman; my aunts and uncles, Michael Wolk and Sandra Gillespie, Lorraine Friedman, and Douglas Branfman; and my cousins, Nicole Applebaum Miller, Ted and Nina Liebman, Hanna Dershowitz, and Jerry and Anne Gechter.

NOTES

INTRODUCTION

1 Katie Couric, "Drake: 'I Always Felt Like an Outsider,'" CBS News, YouTube video, 1:29, October 5, 2010, https://www.youtube.com/watch?v=27FSbztRPo8.

2 Peter Baker and Maggie Haberman, "Trump Targets Anti-Semitism and Israeli Boycotts on College Campuses," *New York Times*, December 10, 2019, www.nytimes.com.

3 David Burd, "Lil Dicky—White Dude," YouTube video, April 30, 2013, https://www.youtube.com/watch?v=Erg1UXGBowE&sns=em.

4 Daniel Solomon, "David Duke Says Jews Aren't White—and Jews Clap Back," *Forward*, December 6, 2016, http://forward.com.

5 See David C. Atkinson, "Charlottesville and the Alt-Right: A Turning Point?," *Politics, Groups, Identities* 6, no. 2 (2018): 309–15.

6 *Vice News Tonight*, "Charlottesville: Race & Terror," featuring lead reporter Elle Reeve, aired August 15, 2017, on HBO. https://news.vice.com.

7 Miriam Jordan, "HIAS, the Jewish Agency Criticized by the Shooting Suspect, Has a History of Aiding Refugees," *New York Times*, October 28, 2018, www.nytimes.com.

8 See Alex Dobuzinskis, "US to Seek Death Penalty for Accused Pittsburgh Synagogue Shooter," *Reuters*, August 26, 2019, www.reuters.com; Miriam Jordan, "HIAS, the Jewish Agency."

9 See Samantha Pickette, "The Last Black (Jewish) Unicorn: Tiffany Haddish's *Black Mitzvah* and the Reframing of Jewish Female Identity," *Studies in American Jewish Literature* 41, no. 2 (2022): 165–84.

10 See Evelyn Torton Beck, "The Politics of Jewish Invisibility," *NWSA Journal* 1, no. 1 (1988): 93–102; Jonathan Branfman, "Teaching for Coalition: Dismantling 'Jewish-Progressive Conflict' through Feminist and Queer Pedagogy," *Frontiers* 40, no. 2 (2019): 126–66; Marla Brettschneider, *Jewish Feminism and Intersectionality* (Albany: State University of New York Press, 2016); Melanie Kaye/Kantrowitz, *The Issue Is Power: Essays on Women, Jews, Violence & Resistance* (San Francisco: Aunt Lute Books, 1992); David Schraub, "White Jews: An Intersectional Approach," *Association for Jewish Studies Review* 43, no. 2 (2019): 379–407; Rachel E. Silverman, "Comedy as Correction: Humor as Perspective by Incongruity on Will & Grace and Queer as Folk," *Sexuality & Culture* 17, no. 2 (2013): 260–74.

11 Susan Stanford Friedman, "Beyond White and Other: Relationality and Narratives of Race in Feminist Discourse," *Signs: Journal of Women in Culture and Society* 21, no. 1 (1995): 39.

12 On these accusations of Jewish gender deviance, see Daniel Boyarin, *Unheroic Conduct: The Rise of Heterosexuality and the Invention of the Jewish Man* (Berkeley: University of California Press, 1997); Jennifer Caplan, "Nebbishes, New Jews, and Humor: The Changing Image of American Jewish Masculinity Post-Holocaust," in *Laughter After: Humor and the Holocaust*, ed. David Slucki (Detroit: Wayne State University Press, 2020); Sander Gilman, *The Jew's Body* (New York: Routledge, 1991); Paula Hyman, *Gender and Assimilation in Modern Jewish History: The Roles and Representation of Women* (Seattle: University of Washington Press, 1995). On the accusation that Jewish men menstruate, see Bruce Rosenstock, "Messianism, Machismo, and 'Marranism': The Case of Abraham Miguel Cardoso," in *Queer Theory and the Jewish Question*, ed. Daniel Boyarin, Daniel Itzkovitz, and Ann Pellegrini (New York: Columbia University Press, 2003), 206.

13 Marla Brettschneider, *The Family Flamboyant: Race Politics, Queer Families, Jewish Lives* (Albany: State University of New York Press, 2006), 9; Sarah Imhoff, *Masculinity and the Making of American Judaism* (Bloomington: Indiana University Press, 2017), 3.

14 David Reznik, *New Jews: Race and American Jewish Identity in 21st-Century Film* (New York: Routledge, 2014), 11.

15 Janice Peck, "TV Talk Shows as Therapeutic Discourse: The Ideological Labor of the Televised Talking Cure," *Communication Theory* 5, no. 1 (1995): 64.

16 See Jeremy Butler, *Star Texts: Image and Performance in Film & Television* (Detroit: Wayne State University Press, 1991); Richard Dyer, *Stars* (London: British Film Institute, 1979); Russell Meeuf, Rebellious Bodies: Stardom, Citizenship, and the New Body Politics (Austin: University of Texas Press, 2017), 7-8.

17 For example, see Daniel Boyarin, *Unheroic Conduct*; Sander Gilman, *The Jew's Body*; and Jennifer Caplan, "Nebbishes, New Jews, and Humor."

18 Eric Lott, *Love and Theft: Blackface Minstrelsy and the American Working Class* (Oxford: Oxford University Press, 1993), 5, 21.

19 See Peter Antelyes, "'Haim Afen Range': The Jewish Indian and the Redface Western," *MELUS* 34, no. 3 (2009): 15–42; Krystyn Moon, *Yellowface: Creating the Chinese in American Popular Music and Performance, 1850s-1920s* (New Brunswick, NJ: Rutgers University Press, 2004); Michael Malek Najjar, "Casting Middle Eastern American Theater: Cultural, Academic, and Professional Challenges," in *Casting a Movement: The Welcome Table Initiative*, ed. Claire Syler and Daniel Banks (New York: Routledge, 2019), 72–82; Raúl Pérez, "Brownface Minstrelsy: 'José Jiménez,' the Civil Rights Movement, and the Legacy of Racist Comedy," *Ethnicities* 16, no. 1 (2016): 40–67.

20 Ted Merwin, "Jew-Face: Non-Jews Playing Jews on the American Stage," *Cultural and Social History* 4, no. 2 (2007): 217.

21 Harley Erdman, Staging the Jew: The Performance of an American Ethnicity, 1860-1920 (New Brunswick: Rutgers University Press, 1995), 33.

22 See Michael Rogin, *Blackface, White Noise: Jewish Immigrants in the Hollywood Melting Pot* (Berkeley: University of California Press, 1998).

23 Jody Rosen, "A Century Later, She's Still Red Hot," *New York Times*, August 28, 2009, www.nytimes.com.

24 David Burd, "Lil Dicky—All K (Official Video)," YouTube video, June 12, 2013, https://www.youtube.com/watch?v=TOzIEEwSyxs; David Burd, "Jewish Flow (Official Video)," YouTube video, 5:37, August 14, 2013, https://www.youtube.com/watch?v=BFVtamh2dNU; David Burd, "Lil Dicky feat. Azadeh—Really Scared," YouTube video, 4:59, October 1, 2014, https://www.youtube.com/watch?v=_fVPtBy2ssM.

25 Lauren Michele Jackson, "The Women 'Black-Fishing' on Instagram Aren't Exactly Trying to Be Black," *Slate*, November 29, 2018, https://slate.com.

26 Hannah Schwadron, *The Case of the Sexy Jewess: Dance, Gender & Jewish Joke-Work in US Pop Culture* (Oxford: Oxford University Press, 2017), 15.

27 Simon Weaver, *The Rhetoric of Racist Humour: US, UK and Global Race Joking* (Farnham, UK: Ashgate Publishing, 2011), 158.

28 Ibid., 153, 158.

29 Ibid., 154.

30 Ibid., 149–60.

31 Ibid., 149–54.

32 Ibid., 149–68.

33 Ibid., 158–60.

34 Ibid., 155.

35 Ibid., 158. Weaver labels only the first interpretation (that Cohen is caricaturing Blackness) as postmodern minstrelsy. However, I find that all three interpretations constitute postmodern minstrel personae, respectively caricaturing Black, Asian, and white men.

36 Ibid., 169, 173.

37 David Burd, "Really Scared."

38 *Who Is America?*, season 1, episode 2, directed, written, and performed by Sacha Baron Cohen, aired July 22, 2018, on Showtime. Amazon.com.

39 Richard Crouse, "Baywatch," *IHeartRadio* (blog), May 26, 2017, www.iheartradio.ca.

40 Weaver, *The Rhetoric of Racist Humour,* 169

41 This discussion of "normative" vs. "queer" glamor broadens my earlier definition of "queer glamor" in a prior article. For that earlier usage, see Jonathan Branfman, "'Plow Him Like a Queen!': Jewish Female Masculinity, Queer Glamor, and Racial Commentary in Broad City," *Television and New Media* 21, no. 1 (2020), 3. For the definitions of "classical" and "grotesque" bodies that underpin the present discussion, see Mikhail Bakhtin, *Rabelais and His World*, trans. Helene Iswolsky (Bloomington: Indiana University Press, 1984), 29, 320–21; Kathleen Rowe, *The Unruly Woman: Gender and the Genres of Laughter* (Austin: University of Texas Press, 1995), 32–33.

42 See Mikhail Bakhtin, *Rabelais and His World*, 24–26, 29, 317–18, 320–21; Kathleen Rowe, *The Unruly Woman*, 32–33.

43 Farah Stockman, "Women's March Roiled by Accusations of Anti-Semitism," *New York Times*, December 23, 2018, https://nyti.ms.

44 Bill Hutchinson, "Israel-Hamas conflict: Timeline and Key Developments," *ABC News*, October 19, 2023, https://abcnews.go.com; Jill Filipovic, "Denying the Gender-Based Violence of Oct 7 Helps No One," *New York Times*, December 13, 2023.

45 See Jennifer Medina and Lisa Lerer, "On Israel, Progressive Jews Feel Abandoned by Their Left-Wing Allies," *New York Times*, October 20, 2023, https://nyti.ms; Michelle Goldberg, "The Massacre in Israel and the Need for a Decent Left," *New York Times*, October 12, 2023, https://nyti.ms.

46 See Ibid; Sofia Rubinson, "Cornell Professor 'Exhilarated' by Hamas's Attack Defends Remark," *The Cornell Daily Sun*, October 18, 2023, https://cornellsun.com/.

47 See Ibid; Ezekiel J. Emanuel, "The Moral Deficiencies of a Liberal Education," *New York Times*, October 17, 2023, https://nyti.ms.

48 See Medina and Lerer, "On Israel, Progressive Jews Feel Abandoned."

49 See Kimberly Crenshaw, "Mapping the Margins: Intersectionality, Identity Politics, and Violence Against Women of Color," *Stanford Law Review*, 1991, 1241–99.

50 This discussion of Jewish erasure in feminist, queer, and critical race studies draws on ideas first presented in an earlier article: Jonathan Branfman, "Teaching for Coalition," 126, 130. For more on this erasure, also see Beck, "Politics of Jewish Invisibility," 93; Irena Klepfisz, "Anti-Semitism in the Lesbian/Feminist Movement," in *Nice Jewish Girls: A Lesbian Anthology*, ed. Evelyn Torton Beck (Watertown, MA: Persephone Press, 1982), 45–54.

51 Barbara Ransby et al., "NWSA EC Letter on Charlottesville," email message to NWSA members, August 18, 2017.

52 Branfman, "Teaching for Coalition," 132.

53 For example, see Ella Shohat, "Sephardim in Israel: Zionism from the Standpoint of Its Jewish Victims," in *Dangerous Liaisons: Gender, Nation and Postcolonial Perspectives* (Minneapolis: University of Minnesota Press, 1997), 39–68.

54 See Dyer, *Stars*; Richard Dyer, *Heavenly Bodies: Film Stars & Society*, 2nd edition (New York: Routledge, 2004).

55 Russell Meeuf, *Rebellious Bodies: Stardom, Citizenship, and the New Body Politics* (Austin: University of Texas Press, 2017).

56 Ibid., 70–71.

57 See Linda Mizejewski, *Ziegfeld Girl: Image and Icon in Culture and Cinema* (Durham, NC: Duke University Press, 1999); Linda Mizejewski, *Pretty/Funny: Women Comedians and Body Politics* (Austin: University of Texas Press, 2014).

58 Meeuf, *Rebellious Bodies*, 10.

59 William K. Rashbaum and Ali Winston, "Ilana Glazer Event at Synagogue Is Canceled after Anti-Semitic Graffiti Is Found," *New York Times*, November 2, 2018, www.nytimes.com.

60 Tal Fortgang, "Why I'll Never Apologize for My White Male Privilege," *TIME*, May 14, 2014, http://time.com.

61 *Black Mitzvah*, directed by Lily Mendoza, performed by Tiffany Haddish (Netflix, 2019), Netflix.com.

62 Schraub, "White Jews," 380.

63 See Sigal Samuel, "For Sephardic and Mizrahi Jews, Whiteness Was a Fragile Identity Long before Trump," *Forward*, December 7, 2016, http://forward.com.

64 For instance, Rachel Luft expresses this concern that Euro-American Jews will misuse the topic of antisemitism to sidestep "accountability to whiteness and racial privilege" in her chapter, "Intersectionality and the Risk of Flattening Difference," in *The Intersectional Approach: Transforming the Academy through Race, Class & Gender*, eds. Michele Berger and Kathleen Guidroz (Chapel Hill: University of North Carolina Press, 2009), 111.

65 *Broad City*, season 4, episode 1, "Sliding Doors," directed by Lucia Aniello, aired September 13, 2017, on Comedy Central. Amazon.com.

66 Janet Adelman, "Her Father's Blood: Race, Conversion, and Nation in 'The Merchant of Venice,'" *Representations* 81, no. 1 (2003): 10.

67 Sander Gilman, *The Jew's Body* (New York: Routledge, 1991), 170–77.

68 Ibid., 174.

69 Michael Omi and Howard Winant, *Racial Formation in the United States*, 3rd edition (New York: Routledge, 2015), 7, 15.

70 See Ian Haney-López, "The Social Construction of Race," in *Critical Race Theory: The Cutting Edge*, ed. Richard Delgado (Philadelphia: Temple University Press, 2001), 191–203; Omi and Winant, *Racial Formation*.

71 Omi and Winant, *Racial Formation*, 109.

72 Ibid., 7, 15

73 See ibid., 115; Audrey Smedley and Brian D. Smedley, *Race in North America: Evolution of a Worldview*, 4th Edition (New York: Routledge University Press, 2011); Nancy Stepan, *The Idea of Race in Science: Great Britain 1800–1960* (London: Palgrave Macmillan, 1982).

74 Jonathan Schorsch, *Jews and Blacks in the Early Modern World* (Cambridge: Cambridge University Press, 2004), 204.

75 See Jerome Friedman, "Jewish Conversion, the Spanish Pure Blood Laws and Reformation: A Revisionist View of Racial and Religious Antisemitism," *Sixteenth Century Journal* 18 (1987): 3–29; Yosef Hayim Yerushalmi, "Leo Baeck Memorial Lecture 26, Assimilation & Racial Anti-Semitism: The Iberian and German Models," in *Leo Baeck Memorial Lectures*, ed. Leo Baeck Institute (New York: Leo Baeck Institute, 1975), 3–38.

76 David Nirenberg, "Race and the Middle Ages: The Case of Spain and Its Jews," in *Rereading the Black Legend: The Discourses of Religious and Racial Difference in the Renaissance Empires*, ed. Margaret R. Greer, Walter D. Mignolo, and Maureen Quilligan (Chicago: University of Chicago Press, 2007), 71–87.

77 Geraldine Heng, *The Invention of Race in the European Middle Ages* (Cambridge: Cambridge University Press, 2018).

78 Susanna Drake, *Slandering the Jew: Sexuality & Difference in Early Christian Texts* (Philadelphia: University of Pennsylvania Press, 2013), 104–5.

79 Sara Lipton, *Dark Mirror: The Medieval Origins of Anti-Jewish Iconography* (New York: Metropolitan Books, 2014), 3, 97.

80 Ibid., 107.

81 Ibid., 7–8, 173.

82 Ibid., 173–76.

83 Schorsch, *Jews and Blacks in the Early Modern World*, 179.

84 Lipton, *Dark Mirror*, 3, 109, 182.

85 See Adelman, "Her Father's Blood," 10, 25; Richard Cole, "Kyn / Fólk / Þjóð / Ætt: Proto-Racial Thinking and Its Application to Jews in Old Norse Literature," in *Fear and Loathing in the North*, ed. Cordelia Heß and Richard Adams (Berlin: De Gruyter, 2015), 239–71; Lisa Lampert, *Gender and Jewish Difference from Paul to Shakespeare* (Philadelphia: University of Pennsylvania Press, 2004), 16; "RaceB4Race," Arizona State University, 2020, 4, https://acmrs.asu.edu.

86 Joshua Trachtenberg, *The Devil and the Jews: The Medieval Conception of the Jew and Its Relation to Modern Antisemitism* (New Haven, CT: Yale University Press, 1943), 47–50.

87 James Shapiro, *Shakespeare and the Jews* (New York: Columbia University Press, 1996), 37.

88 Trachtenberg, *The Devil and the Jews*, 49.

89 See Erdman, *Staging the Jew*; Gilman, *The Jew's Body*; Sander Gilman, *Freud, Race & Gender* (Princeton, NJ: Princeton University Press, 2004); Matthew Frye Jacobson, *Whiteness of a Different Color: European Immigrants and the Alchemy of Race* (Cambridge, MA: Harvard University Press, 1999).

90 On the racialization of European immigrants in the mid-nineteenth to early twentieth century, see Jacobson, *Whiteness of a Different Color*; David Roediger, *Working Toward Whiteness: How America's Immigrants Became White: The Strange Journey from Ellis Island to the Suburbs* (New York: Basic Books, 2005). On the racial reclassification of these groups between the 1920s and 1960s, see Jacobson, *Whiteness of a Different Color*, 95, 187.

91 Ibid., 95, 98–102, 111, 115, 187–88.

92 For more on the continuities and disconnections between colonial violence and the Holocaust, see Thomas Kühne, "Colonialism and the Holocaust: Continuities, Causations, and Complexities," *Journal of Genocide Research* 15, no. 3 (2013): 339–62.

93 Jacobson, *Whiteness of a Different Color*, 188–89. *Gentleman's Agreement*, directed by Eliza Kazan (20th Century Fox, 1947), Amazon.com.

94 For instance, see Katya Gibel Azoulay, *Black, Jewish, and Interracial: It's Not the Color of Your Skin but the Race of Your Kin and Other Myths of Identity* (Durham, NC: Duke University Press, 1997).

95 Brettschneider, *Jewish Feminism and Intersectionality*, 145; Silverman, "Comedy as Correction," 265; Rachel E. Silverman, "Jewish Performativity on Sex and the City," *Journal of Religion & Popular Culture* 26, no. 2 (2014): 174.

96 See Abby Ferber, "The Culture of Privilege: Color-Blindness, Postfeminism, and Christonormativity," *Journal of Social Issues* 68, no. 1 (2012): 63–77; Silverman, "Comedy as Correction," 265.

97 Marjorie Garber, *Symptoms of Culture* (New York: Routledge, 2002), 79.

98 Adelman, "Her Father's Blood," 6–10.

99 *The Jazz Singer*, directed by Alan Crossland (Warner Bros. Pictures, 1927), DVD; *Whoopee!*, directed by Thornton Freedman (United Artists, 1930), DVD.

100 Vincent Brook, *Something Ain't Kosher Here: The Rise of the "Jewish" Sitcom* (New Brunswick, NJ: Rutgers University Press, 2003), 45.

101 Ibid., 3, 45.

102 See Christi Carras, "Fran Drescher Says She Had to Fight to Let 'The Nanny' Be Jewish," *LA Times*, April 28, 2020, www.latimes.com; Ben Yakas, "'Too New York, Too Jewish': The 30th Anniversary of 'The Seinfeld Chronicles' Pilot," *Gothamist* (blog), July 5, 2019, https://gothamist.com.

103 See Rosalin Krieger, "Does He Actually Say the Word Jewish?: Jewish Representations in *Seinfeld*," *Journal for Cultural Research* 7, no. 4 (2003): 387–404.

104 Henry Bial, *Acting Jewish: Negotiating Ethnicity on the American Stage and Screen* (Ann Arbor: University of Michigan Press, 2005), 2–3.

105 Judd Apatow, "Funny People—Trailer," YouTube video, 3:33, June 30, 2009, https://www.youtube.com/watch?v=kzciY15Q3BA.

106 Aymar Jean Christian, *Open TV: Innovation beyond Hollywood and the Rise of Web Television* (New York: New York University Press, 2018).

107 Ibid., 64–66.

108 David Burd, "Jewish Flow."

109 Steven F. Kruger, "Racial/Religious and Sexual Queerness in the Middle Ages," *Medieval Feminist Forum* 16, no. 1 (1993): 35.

110 See Cathy Cohen, "Punks, Bulldaggers, and Welfare Queens: The Radical Potential of Queer Politics?," *GLQ: A Journal of Gay and Lesbian Studies* 3, no. 4 (1997): 337–65; Roderick Ferguson, *Aberrations in Black: Toward a Queer of Color Critique* (Minneapolis: University of Minnesota Press, 2004); Patricia Hill Collins, *Black Sexual Politics: African Americans, Gender, and the New Racism* (New York: Routledge, 2005).

111 Kruger, "Racial/Religious and Sexual Queerness," 35.

112 Ibid., 34.

113 Ibid., 33–35; Rosenstock, "Messianism, Machismo, and 'Marranism'" 206.

114 David Nirenberg, "Deviant Politics and Jewish Love: Alfonso VIII and the Jewess of Toledo," *Jewish History* 21 (2007): 16-17.

115 See Nathan Abrams, *The New Jew in Film: Exploring Jewishness and Judaism in Contemporary Film* (New Brunswick, NJ: Rutgers University Press, 2012), 43–67; Erdman, *Staging the Jew*, 55; Ann Pellegrini, "Whiteface Performances: 'Race,' Gender, and Jewish Bodies," in *Jews and Other Differences: The New Jewish Cultural Studies*, ed. Jonathan Boyarin and Daniel Boyarin (Minneapolis: University of Minnesota Press, 1996), 108–49.

116 Pellegrini, "Whiteface Performances," 129.

117 Livia E. Bitton, "Biblical Names of Literary Jewesses," *Names: A Journal of Onomastics* 21, no. 2 (1973): 103–9.

118 Pellegrini, "Whiteface Performances," 129.

119 J. Hoberman and Jeffrey Shandler, "Hollywood's Jewish Question," in *Entertaining America: Jews, Movies, and Broadcasting*, ed. J. Hoberman and Jeffrey Shandler (Princeton, NJ: Princeton University Press, 2003), 51.

120 Julia Kristeva, *Powers of Horror: An Essay on Abjection*, trans. Leon S. Roudiez (New York: Columbia University Press, 1982), 183.

121 Lipton, *Dark Mirror*, 7.

122 Kenneth R. Stow, *Alienated Minority: The Jews in Medieval Latin Europe* (Cambridge, MA: Harvard University Press, 1992), 5, 230–38.

123 Lipton, *Dark Mirror*, 3, 9.

124 William Shakespeare, *The Merchant of Venice*, believed to be written between 1596 and 1598; Lampert, *Gender and Jewish Difference*, 144–64.

125 Erdman, *Staging the Jew*, 21.

126 Ibid., 63–93.

127 See Erdman, *Staging the Jew*, 71; Milton Nobles, *Shop Talk* (Milwaukee: Riverside Printing, 1889).

128 See Neal Gabler, *An Empire of Their Own: How the Jews Invented Hollywood* (New York: Crown Publishers, 1988).

129 Nicholas Sammond and Chandra Mukerji, "What You Are, I Wouldn't Eat: Ethnicity, Whiteness, and Staging 'the Jew' in Hollywood's Golden Age," in *Classic Hollywood, Classic Whiteness*, ed. Daniel Bernardi (Minneapolis: University of Minnesota Press, 2001), 3–30.

130 N. L. Rothman, "The Jew Onscreen," *Jewish Forum*, 1928, 527–28.

131 Erdman, *Staging the Jew*, 5.

132 José Esteban Muñoz, *Disidentifications: Queers of Color and the Performance of Politics* (Minneapolis: University of Minnesota Press, 1999), 11.

133 Ibid.

134 Ibid.

135 Ibid.

136 Ibid., 3.

137 Erdman, *Staging the Jew*, 5.

138 Muñoz, *Disidentifications*, 40–41.

139 See J. A. Mangan, ed., *Shaping the Superman: Fascist Body as Political Icon—Aryan Fascism* (New York: Routledge, 1999).

140 See Moshe Zimmermann, "Muscle Jews versus Nervous Jews," in *Emancipation through Muscles: Jews and Sports in Europe*, ed. Michael Brenner and Gideon Reuveni (Lincoln: University of Nebraska Press, 2006), 13–26.

141 *The Night Before*, directed by Jonathan Levine (Columbia Pictures, 2015), Amazon.com.

142 José Esteban Muñoz, *Cruising Utopia: The Then and There of Queer Futurity* (New York: New York University Press, 2009).

143 Ibid., 65–68.

144 Ibid., 71.

145 *Saturday Night Live*, season 39, episode 11, "Drake," directed by Don Roy King, aired January 18, 2014, on NBC. www.nbc.com.

146 See Marjorie Garber, "Category Crises: The Way of the Cross and the Jewish Star," in *Queer Theory and the Jewish Question*, ed. Jonathan Boyarin, Daniel Itzkovitz, and Ann Pellegrini (New York: Columbia University Press, 2003), 29; Gilman, *The Jew's Body*, 10–37.

147 Gilman, *The Jew's Body*, 21.

148 Garber, *Symptoms of Culture*, 99.

149 Muñoz, *Cruising Utopia*, 42.

150 Ibid., 33.

151 Frederick Douglass, "The Color Line," *North American Review* 132, no. 205 (June 1881): 567–77; W. E. B. DuBois, *The Souls of Black Folk* (Chicago: A. C. McClurg & Co., 1903), v.

152 Matti Bunzl, "Jews, Queers, & Other Symptoms: Recent Work in Jewish Cultural Studies," *QLQ: A Journal of Lesbian and Gay Studies* 6, no. 2 (2000): 321–41.

153 John Efron, *Defenders of the Race: Jewish Doctors and Race Science in Fin-de-Siècle Europe* (New Haven, CT: Yale University Press, 1994), 99.

154 See Ferguson, *Aberrations in Black*.

155 Jasbir Puar and Amit Rai, "Monster, Terrorist, Fag: The War on Terrorism and the Production of Docile Patriots," *Social Text* 20, no. 3 (2002): 117–48.

156 See Karen Brodkin, *How Jews Became White Folks and What That Says about Race in America* (New Brunswick, NJ: Rutgers University Press, 1998); Michael Hames-García, "Queer Theory Revisited," in *Gay Latino Studies: A Critical Reader*, ed. Michael Hames-García and Ernesto Javier Martínez (Durham, NC: Duke University Press, 2011), 19–45.

157 Ann Pellegrini, "Interarticulations: Gender, Race, & the Jewish Woman Question," in *Judaism Since Gender*, ed. Miriam Peskowitz and Laura Levitt (New York: Routledge, 1997), 49.

158 Ferguson, *Aberrations in Black*, 3. This claim emerges through Ferguson's reading of Chandan Reddy, "Home, Houses, Nonidentity: Paris Is Burning," in *Burning Down the House: Recycling Domesticity*, ed. Rosemary Marangoly George (Boulder: Westview Press, 1997), 356–57.

159 Daniel Boyarin, *Unheroic Conduct: The Rise of Heterosexuality and the Invention of the Jewish Man* (Berkeley: University of California Press, 1997), 231.

160 Ferguson, *Aberrations in Black*, 28.

161 See Pellegrini, "Whiteface Performances."

162 See Brodkin, *How Jews Became White Folks*; Jacobson, *Whiteness of a Different Color*.

163 Muñoz, *Disidentifications*, 40–41.

164 See Hélène Cixous, *Portrait of Jacques Derrida as a Young Jewish Saint*, trans. Beverly Bie Brahic (New York: Columbia University Press, 2004).

165 See Ferguson, *Aberrations in Black*, 11; Karl Marx, "On the Jewish Question," in *The Marx-Engels Reader*, ed. Robert Tucker (New York: Norton & Company, 1978), 26–46.

166 Efron, *Defenders of the Race*, 99.

167 Ben Cohen, "'Jew Coup': The Founder of a White House-Accredited Media Outlet's Shocking Antisemitic Rant," *Algemeiner*, November 27, 2019, www.algemeiner.com.

168 Paul Craig Roberts, "Identity Politics vs. White People: Who Will Win?," *Institute for Political Economy* (blog), January 16, 2018, www.paulcraigroberts.org.

169 Alex Amend, "Analyzing a Terrorist's Social Media Manifesto: The Pittsburgh Synagogue Shooter's Posts on Gab," Southern Poverty Law Center, October 28, 2018, www.splcenter.org.

170 See Michael Kimmel, *Angry White Men: American Masculinity at the End of an Era* (New York: Nation Books, 2013).

171 Sally Robinson, *Marked Men: White Masculinity in Crisis* (New York: Columbia University Press, 2000), 3.

CHAPTER 1. DRAKE'S JEWISH PICKLE

1 Dylan Kelly, "Drake Crowned Artist of the Decade at the Billboard Music Awards 2021," *Hypebeast* (blog), May 24, 2021, https://hypebeast.com.

2 Samuel Momodu, "Aubrey Drake Graham, 1984- ," *Blackpast* (blog), August 20, 2017, www.blackpast.çom.

3 See Alexandra Boutros, "The Impossibility of Being Drake: Or, What It Means to Be a Successful (Black) Canadian Rapper," *Global Hip Hop Studies* 1, no. 1 (2020): 101; Abu Mubarik, "'We Were Very Poor, Like Broke' – How Drake Rose to Stardom and Built a $200m Net Worth," *Face2Face Africa* (blog), September 6, 2021, https://face2faceafrica.com

4 Gabe Friedman, "Drake Raps 'I Should Probably Go to Yeshiva' in His New Single," *JTA*, March 8, 2021, www.jpost.com.

5 Aubrey Drake Graham, "Drake—Take Care ft. Rihanna," directed by Yoann Lemoine, produced by Cash Money Records, YouTube video, 4:08, April 23, 2012, https://www.youtube.com/watch?v=-zzP29emgpg.

6 Ammal Hassan, "Drake Sounds Out of Place on Honestly, Nevermind," *Esquire*, June 17, 2022, www.esquire.com.

7 Paul Grein, "After the 2023 Billboard Music Awards, Who Is the All-Time Biggest Winner?" *Billboard* (blog), November 19, 2023, www.billboard.com.

8 "Drake Net Worth (2023)," *Ledger Note* (blog), December 21, 2022, https://ledgernote.com.

9 See Ella Ceron, "When Exactly Did Drake Get So Swoll?," *New York Magazine*, July 18, 2015, http://nymag.com.

10 Uri Dorchin, "Fight for Your Right to Partycipate: Jewish American Rappers," in *Mazal Tov, Amigos! Jews and Popular Music in the Americas*, ed. Amelia Ran and Moshe Morad (Boston: Brill Publishers, 2016), 166.

11 JayTheKid, "I'm a Massive Fa***t," *Rappad* (blog), March 8, 2015, https://muut.com .

12 *Saturday Night Live*, season 39, episode 11, "Drake," directed by Don Roy King, aired January 18, 2014, on NBC. www.nbc.com.

13 Sarah Bunin Benor, "Black and Jewish: Language and Multiple Strategies for Self-Presentation," *American Jewish History* 100, no. 1 (2016): 56.

14 See Marjorie Garber, "Category Crises: The Way of the Cross and the Jewish Star," in *Queer Theory and the Jewish Question*, ed. Jonathan Boyarin, Daniel Itzkovitz, and Ann Pellegrini (New York: Columbia University Press, 2003), 29; Sander Gilman, *The Jew's Body* (New York: Routledge, 1991), 10–37.

15 See Daniel Boyarin, *Unheroic Conduct: The Rise of Heterosexuality and the Invention of the Jewish Man* (Berkeley: University of California Press, 1997); Daniel Boyarin, Daniel Itzkovitz, and Ann Pellegrini, eds., *Queer Theory and the Jewish Question* (New York: Columbia University Press, 2003).

16 *Saturday Night Live*, "Drake," 2014.

17 See Linda Burton et al., "Critical Race Theories, Colorism, and the Decade's Research on Families of Color," *Journal of Marriage and Family* 72, no. 3 (2010): 440–59; Andrew B. Leiter, *In the Shadow of the Black Beast: African American Masculinity in the Harlem and Southern Renaissances* (Baton Rouge: Louisiana State University Press, 2010).

18 See Remi Joseph-Salisbury, *Black Mixed-Race Men: Transatlanticity, Hybridity and "Post-Racial" Resilience* (Bingley, UK: Emerald Publishing Limited, 2018), 53–84; Alyssa Newman, "Desiring the Standard Light Skin: Black Multiracial Boys, Masculinity and Exotification," *Identities* 26, no. 1 (2019): 113.

19 Imani Perry, *Prophets of the Hood: Politics and Poetics in Hip Hop* (Durham, NC: Duke University Press, 2004), 90.

20 Ibid., 42.

21 Ibid.

22 Ibid., 47.

23 Boutros, "Impossibility of Being Drake," 102.

24 Katie Couric, "@katiecouric: Drake," CBS News, YouTube video, 34:28, October 6, 2010, https://www.youtube.com/watch?v=MVX-M0AgUio.

25 See Joyce Antler, *You Never Call! You Never Write! A History of the Jewish Mother* (New York: Oxford University Press, 2013); Barbara Gottfried, "What Do Men Want, Dr. Roth?," in *A Mensch among Men: Explorations in Jewish Masculinity*, ed. Harry Brod (Freedom, CA: Crossing Press, 1988), 37–52.

26 Althea Legaspi, "Drake Addresses Blackface Photo from Pusha-T's 'Story of Adidon,'" *Rolling Stone*, May 31, 2018, www.rollingstone.com.

27 See ibid.

28 *Saturday Night Live*, "Drake," 2014.

29 David Burd, "Jewish Flow (Official Video)," YouTube video, 5:37, August 14, 2013, https://www.youtube.com/watch?v=BFVtamh2dNU; David Burd, "Lil Dicky feat. Azadeh—Really Scared," produced by Mitchell Owens and Dave Gulik, YouTube video, 4:59, October 1, 2014, https://www.youtube.com/watch?v=_fVPtBy2ssM.

30 José Esteban Muñoz, *Disidentifications: Queers of Color and the Performance of Politics* (Minneapolis: University of Minnesota Press, 1999), 11.

31 Henry Bial, *Acting Jewish: Negotiating Ethnicity on the American Stage and Screen* (Ann Arbor: University of Michigan Press, 2005), 2–3.

32 *Saturday Night Live*, "Drake," 2014.

33 Muñoz, *Disidentifications*, 11.

34 Dorchin, "Fight for Your Right to Partycipate," 166.

35 See Dorchin, "Fight for Your Right to Partycipate"; Leonard Stein, "Jewish Flow: Performing Identity in Hip-Hop Music," *Studies in American Jewish Literature* 38, no. 2 (2019): 119–39; Kristy Warren, "Twenty-First Century Jewish Journeys in Music," *Jewish Culture and History* 11, no. 1–2 (2009): 172–83.

36 Richard Majors and Janet Mancini Bilson, *Cool Pose: The Dilemmas of Black Manhood in America* (New York: Lexington Books, 1992), 4.

37 Ibid., 4, 60.

38 On one hand, no studies yet document the racial demographics of *SNL*'s audience. However, popular commentaries routinely highlight the show's majority-white production team and cast, its fit with white cultural sensibilities, and therefore its disproportionate appeal to white audiences. This imbalance is also visible in *SNL*'s weekly studio audiences, which remain consistently majority-white. For popular commentaries on this topic, see Arit John, "The White Audience Is the Worst Part of the Leslie Jones 'SNL' Slavery Skit," *The Atlantic*, May 5, 2014, www.theatlantic.com; Paul Farhi, "As Saturday Night Live Reboots, Questions About Diversity Emerge," *Washington Post*, October 3, 2013, www.washingtonpost.com; Tanner Colby, "SNL's Real Race Problem," *Slate* (blog), January 9, 2014, www.slate.com.

39 Amara Pope, "Musical Artists Capitalizing on Hybrid Identities: A Case Study of Drake the 'Authentic' 'Black' 'Canadian' 'Rapper,'" *STREAM: Culture/Politics/Technology* 9, no. 1 (2016): 3–22.

40 Evelyn Higginbotham, *Righteous Discontent: The Women's Movement in the Black Baptist Church, 1880–1920* (Cambridge, MA: Harvard University Press, 1993).

41 See Mikhail Bakhtin, *Rabelais and His World*, trans. Helene Iswolsky (Bloomington: Indiana University Press, 1984), 24–26, 29, 317–18, 320–21; Kathleen Rowe, *The Unruly Woman: Gender and the Genres of Laughter* (Austin: University of Texas Press, 1995), 32–33.

42 Margaret Hunter, "The Persistent Problem of Colorism: Skin Tone, Status, and Inequality," *Sociology Compass* 1, no. 1 (2007): 231.

43 Tricia Rose, *The Hip Hop Wars: What We Talk about When We Talk about Hip Hop—and Why It Matters* (New York: Civitas, 2008), 5.

44 Treva B. Lindsey, "Post-Ferguson: A 'Herstorical' Approach to Black Violability," *Feminist Studies* 41, no. 1 (2015): 232–37.

45 See Michelle Alexander, *The New Jim Crow: Mass Incarceration in the Age of Colorblindness* (New York: New Press, 2010); Subini Ancy Annamma et al., "Black Girls and School Discipline: The Complexities of Being Overrepresented and Understudied," *Urban Education* 54, no. 2 (2016): 211–42; Aime J. Ellis, *If We Must Die: From Bigger Thomas to Biggie Smalls* (Detroit: Wayne State University Press, 2011); Monique Morris, *Pushout: The Criminalization of Black Girls in Schools* (New York: New Press, 2016); Sherri Williams, "#SayHerName: Using Digital Activism to Document Violence Against Black Women," *Feminist Media Studies*

16 (2016): 922–25; United States Department of Justice Civil Rights Division, "Investigation of the Ferguson Police Department," March 4, 2015.

46 Alexander Jaffe, "Huckabee: Michael Brown Acted Like a 'Thug,'" *CNN*, December 3, 2014, www.cnn.com.

47 Perry, *Prophets of the Hood*, 90.

48 Ibid., 42.

49 *Saturday Night Live*, "Drake," 2014.

50 Larry King, "Beck Bennett Breaks Down 'SNL' Sketch Writing Process," YouTube video, 1:55, October 30, 2017, https://www.youtube.com/watch?v=cF44J49_tzE.

51 Simon Weaver, *The Rhetoric of Racist Humour: US, UK and Global Race Joking* (Farnham, UK: Ashgate Publishing, 2011), 149.

52 Aisha Durham, Brittney C. Cooper, and Susanna M. Morris, "The Stage Hip-Hop Feminism Built: A New Directions Essay," *Signs* 38, no. 3: 721-37.

53 Priscilla Peña Ovalle, *Dance and the Hollywood Latina: Race, Sex, and Stardom* (New Brunswick, NJ: Rutgers University Press, 2010), 4.

54 Ibid., 132–35.

55 Ibid., 1.

56 See Kate Conrad, Travis L. Dixon, and Yuanyuan Zhang, "Controversial Rap Themes, Gender Portrayals and Skin Tone Distortion: A Content Analysis of Rap Music Videos," *Journal of Broadcasting & Electronic Media* 53, no. 1 (2009): 134–56; Vanatta S. Ford, "Color Blocked: A Rhetorical Analysis of Colorism and Its Impact on Rap Lyrics in Hip Hop Music from 2005 to 2010," PhD diss. (Howard University, 2011); Morgan L. Maxwell, Jasmine A. Abrams, and Faye Z. Belgrave, "Redbones and Earth Mothers: The Influence of Rap Music on African American Girls' Perceptions of Skin Color," *Psychology of Music* 44, no. 6 (2016): 1488–99.

57 Ovalle, *Dance and the Hollywood Latina*, 2–4, 8, 10.

58 Ibid., 10.

59 Chris Holmlund, *Impossible Bodies: Femininity & Masculinity at the Movies* (New York: Routledge, 2002), 5.

60 See Russell Meeuf, *Rebellious Bodies: Stardom, Citizenship, and the New Body Politics* (Austin: University of Texas Press, 2017).

61 Boutros, "Impossibility of Being Drake."

62 Ibid., 96.

63 BET News, "Drake Covers Vibe Magazine's 'Race' Issue," *BET News* (blog), December 19, 2013, www.bet.com.

64 See Lennard Davis, "Visualizing the Disabled Body: The Classical Nude and the Fragmented Torso," in *The Body: A Reader*, ed. Mariam Fraser and Monica Greco (New York: Routledge, 2005), 167–81.

65 Ceron, "When Exactly Did Drake Get So Swoll?"

66 See George Elliot Clarke, "White Like Canada," *Transition* 73 (1997): 98–109.

67 *Saturday Night Live*, "Drake," 2014.

68 Nicki Minaj, "Nicki Minaj—Moment 4 Life (MTV Version) Ft. Drake," directed by Chris Robinson, produced by Young Money, Cash Money, and Universal

Motown, YouTube video, 4:41, February 9, 2011, https://www.youtube.com/watch?v=Ks3_kuRAzHs.

69 See Marianne Garvey, Gary Niemiets, and Oli Coleman, "Diddy Punches Drake during Brawl outside Miami Club: Sources," *New York Daily News*, December 9, 2014, www.nydailynews.com; Edgar Sandoval, "Chris Brown Injured after Bar Brawl with Drake," *New York Daily News*, June 15, 2012, www.nydailynews.com.

70 Erika Harwood, "Millie Bobby Brown Won't Be Shamed Out of Her Friendship with Drake," *Vanity Fair*, September 21, 2018, www.vanityfair.com; Allie Jones, "What's Up with Drake Texting Teens?," *VICE* (blog), December 20, 2019, www.vice.com; Lynne Versluys, "People Are Not Happy That Drake Is Texting Billie Eilish," *Blast* (blog), December 2, 2019, https://theblast.com.

71 For instance, see Adam Rosenberg, "Eliza Dushku Says She Was 'Sexually Molested' at Age 12 While Working on *True Lies*," *Mashable* (blog), January 13, 2018, https://mashable.com.

72 See Louis Chilton, "Billie Eilish Defends Drake Text Messages after 'Creepy' Complaints," *Independent* (blog), February 5, 2020, www.independent.co.uk.

73 Aubrey Drake Graham, "HYFR (Hell Ya Fucking Right)," directed by Director X, produced by Cash Money Records, YouTube video, 3:52, April 26, 2012, https://www.youtube.com/watch?v=oKCWqnldEag.

74 *Saturday Night Live*, "Drake," 2014.

75 Aubrey Drake Graham, "Behind the Scenes: Drake (Feat. Lil Wayne)—HYFR [HD]," YouTube video, 10:58, April 16, 2012, https://www.youtube.com/watch?v=haaxzMfy47o.

76 Kim LaCapria, "Lil Wayne to Katie Couric: 'I'm a Gangster, Miss Katie' Part Two," *Inquisitr* (blog), September 13, 2013, www.inquisitr.com.

77 Robyn Rihanna Fenty, "Rihanna—Work (Explicit) Ft. Drake," directed by Director X, produced by Hound Content, Creative Soul, Diktator, YouTube video, 7:34, February 22, 2016, https://www.youtube.com/watch?v=HL1UzIK-flA.

78 Rogin, *Blackface, White Noise*.

79 Jody Rosen, "A Century Later, She's Still Red Hot," *New York Times*, August 28, 2009, www.nytimes.com.

80 *Saturday Night Live*, season 41, episode 20, "Drake," directed by Don Roy King, aired May 14, 2016, on NBC. www.nbc.com.

81 See Sandoval, "Chris Brown Injured."

82 See John, "White Audience Is the Worst Part of the Leslie Jones 'SNL' Slavery Skit."

83 Aubrey Drake Graham, "Drake—Worst Behavior," directed by Director X, produced by Cash Money Records, YouTube video, 4:37, December 11, 2013, https://www.youtube.com/watch?v=CccnAvfLPvE.

84 Kris Singh and Tracy Dale also note this cinematographic strategy in "Assuming Niceness: Private and Public Relationships in Drake's 'Nothing Was the Same,'" *Popular Music* 34, no. 1 (2015): 104.

85 Pusha T, "Story of Adidon," lyrics from Genius, 2018, https://genius.com.

86 C. Vernon Coleman, "Drake Gets His Hair Braided and People Are Confused," *XXL*, March 12, 2022, www.xxlmag.com.

87 FLAMA, "Flama Conspiracies: Drake Is Dominican," YouTube video, 1:59, Apr 8, 2016, https://www.youtube.com/watch?v=6uakBrVPD0Q.

88 Lauren Michele Jackson, "The Women 'Black-Fishing' on Instagram Aren't Exactly Trying to Be Black," *Slate*, November 29, 2018, https://slate.com; Wanna Thompson, "How White Women on Instagram Are Profiting off Black Women," *Paper*, November 14, 2018.

89 Diyora Shadijanova, "Ariana Grande Is a Blackfish and These Are the Receipts," *The Tab* (blog), February 8, 2019, https://thetab.com.

90 Ovalle, *Dance and the Hollywood Latina*.

91 Ibid.

92 Isabelia Herrera, "The Evolution of Dominican Drake," *Remezcla* (blog), September 21, 2015, https://remezcla.com.

93 FLAMA, "Flama Conspiracies."

94 Herrera, "Evolution of Dominican Drake."

95 Romeo Santos and Aubrey Drake Graham, "Romeo Santos—Odio Feat. Drake (Lyric Video)," produced by Erniel Rodriguez, YouTube video, 3:44, January 26, 2014, https://www.youtube.com/watch?v=W8r-eIhp4jo.

96 "BMI Congratulates Its 2015 Billboard Latin Music Award Nominees," *BMI* (blog), February 12, 2015, www.bmi.com.

97 Herrera, "Evolution of Dominican Drake."

98 Boutros, "Impossibility of Being Drake," 104.

99 Aubrey Drake Graham, "Drake—Hotline Bling," directed by Director X, YouTube video, 4:55, October 26, 2015, https://www.youtube.com/watch?v=uxpDa-c-4Mc.

100 Richard Dryden, Nadine White, and Desmond Alphonso, "Toppa Top 10: Drake's Most Dancehall Moments," *LargeUp* (blog), November 19, 2015, www.largeup.com.

101 See Sajae Elder, "Where Did Drake's 'Jamaican' Accent Come From?," *Buzzfeed* (blog), July 28, 2016, www.buzzfeednews.com.

102 See Carlos Waters, "Why Drake Uses a Jamaican Accent," *Vox*, April 6, 2017, www.vox.com.

103 Fenty, "Rihanna—Work (Explicit) Ft. Drake."

104 See Antler, *History of the Jewish Mother*; Erika Duncan, "The Hungry Jewish Mother," in *On Being a Jewish Feminist: A Reader*, ed. Susan Heschel (New York: Schocken Books, 1983), 27–39.

105 Philip Roth, *Portnoy's Complaint* (New York: Random House, 1969).

106 *Saturday Night Live*, "Drake," 2014.

107 Daniela Cabrera, "Who Is Drake's Mom? Sandi Graham Is Very Close to Her Superstar Son," *Bustle* (blog), March 17, 2017, www.bustle.com.

108 "Drake Celebrates His Mother's Birthday with Sweet Message," *Just Jared* (blog), January 29, 2016, www.justjared.com.

109 Perry Kostidakis, "The Best Hip-Hop Songs about Moms," *Complex* (blog), May 13, 2018, www.complex.com.

110 For historical context on this visual trope, see Richard Dyer, *White: Essays on Race and Culture* (New York: Routledge, 1997), 118–27.

111 Aubrey Drake Graham and Tyra Banks, "Drake—Child's Play (Official Video)," directed by Aubrey Drake Graham and Carlos Suarez, YouTube video, 12:07, August 4, 2017, https://www.youtube.com/watch?v=4iDkc3C0-9U.

112 Treva B. Lindsey, "Ain't Nobody Got Time for That: Anti-Black Girl Violence in the Era of #SayHerName," *Urban Education* 53, no. 2 (2018): 163.

113 Gwendolyn P. Pough, *Check It While I Wreck It: Black Womanhood, Hip-Hop Culture, and The Public Sphere* (Boston: Northeastern University Press, 2004), 17; Treva B. Lindsey, "Let Me Blow Your Mind: Hip Hop Feminist Futures in Theory and Praxis," *Urban Education* 50, no. 1 (2015): 57.

114 Aubrey Drake Graham, "HYFR (Hell Ya Fucking Right)."

115 James T. Patterson, *Freedom Is Not Enough: The Moynihan Report and America's Struggle over Black Family Life—From LBJ to Obama* (New York: Basic Books, 2010).

116 Tomi Lahren (@TomiLahren), "We Don't Have a Policing Problem in the USA, We Have a Parenting Problem," Twitter, June 8, 2020, 10:33 a.m., https://twitter.com/tomilahren/status/1270046351833935873?lang=en.

117 Suzanne Marie Enck and Blake A. McDaniel, "Playing with Fire: Cycles of Domestic Violence in Eminem and Rihanna's 'Love the Way You Lie,'" *Communication, Culture & Critique* 5 (2012): 618–44; John Seabrook, "The Horrifying Details of What Allegedly Happened the Night Chris Brown Assaulted Rihanna," *Business Insider*, March 24, 2016, www.businessinsider.com.

118 Enck and McDaniel, "Playing with Fire," 631.

CHAPTER 2. "REDPILL ME ON LIL DICKY"

1 Winston Ross, "Lil Dicky, the Jerry Seinfeld of Rap," *Newsweek*, November 7, 2015, www.newsweek.com.

2 *Dave*, season 1, episode 5, "Hype Man," directed by Tony Yacenda, aired March 25, 2020, on FX. Hulu.com.

3 David Burd, "Lil Dicky—Professional Rapper (Feat. Snoop Dogg)," directed by Douglas Einar Olsen YouTube video, 5:54, July 31, 2015, https://www.youtube.com/watch?v=LlU4FuIJT2k; *Dave*, "Hype Man."

4 Eric Ducker, "The Viral Comedy Boom Made Lil Dicky Famous," *LA Times*, March 11, 2020, www.latimes.com.

5 David Burd, "Lil Dicky—Ex boyfriend," cinematography by Brian Storm, YouTube video, 4:26, June 18, 2013, https://www.youtube.com/watch?v=DVEeZ7jjHyA.

6 *Sway's Universe*, "Lil Dicky and Sway Calloway, Lil Dicky Talks Judaism, New Music, New Head & Comments on Tom Hanks' Son Using the 'N-Word,'" directed by Sway Calloway, YouTube video, 26:14, June 7, 2015, https://www.youtube.com/watch?v=amP9tfVfVyA.

7 *Sway's Universe*, "Lil Dicky and Sway Calloway."

8 Burd, "Professional Rapper."

9   *XXL*, "Lil Dicky Profile Interview—XXL Freshman 2016," starring David Burd, You-
    Tube video, 3:21, January 24, 2016, https://www.youtube.com/watch?v=hMU011-5P9w.

10 Lesley Goldberg, "Rapper Lil Dicky to Star in FX Comedy from *The League*
    Creator, Kevin Hart," *Hollywood Reporter*, May 31, 2018, www.hollywoodreporter
    .com.

11 Aymar Jean Christian, *Open TV: Innovation beyond Hollywood and the Rise of
    Web Television* (New York: New York University Press, 2018).

12 Henry Bial, *Acting Jewish: Negotiating Ethnicity on the American Stage and Screen*
    (Ann Arbor: University of Michigan Press, 2005), 2-3.

13 Ben Yakas, "'Too New York, Too Jewish': The 30th Anniversary of *The Seinfeld
    Chronicles* Pilot," *Gothamist* (blog), July 5, 2019, https://gothamist.com.

14 Rosalin Krieger, "Does He Actually Say the Word Jewish?: Jewish Representations
    in *Seinfeld*," *Journal for Cultural Research* 7, no. 4 (2003): 387–404.

15 Mark Oppenheimer, "Reclaiming 'Jew,'" *New York Times*, April 22, 2017, www
    .nytimes.com.

16 David Burd, "Lil Dicky—$ave Dat Money feat. Fetty Wap and Rich Homie Quan
    (Official Music Video)," directed by Tony Yacenda, YouTube video, 8:47, Septem-
    ber 17, 2015, https://www.youtube.com/watch?v=yvHYWD29ZNY.

17 David Burd, "Lil Dicky—All K (Official Video)," YouTube video, June 12, 2013,
    https://www.youtube.com/watch?v=TOzIEEwSyxs; David Burd, "Lil Dicky
    feat. Azadeh—Really Scared," produced by Mitchell Owens and Dave Gu-
    lik, YouTube video, 4:59, October 1, 2014, https://www.youtube.com/watch?v
    =_fVPtBy2ssM.

18 David Burd, "Jewish Flow (Official Video)," YouTube video, 5:37, August 14, 2013,
    https://www.youtube.com/watch?v=BFVtamh2dNU.

19 José Esteban Muñoz, *Disidentifications: Queers of Color and the Performance of
    Politics* (Minneapolis: University of Minnesota Press, 1999), 11.

20 See Mikhail Bakhtin, *Rabelais and His World*, trans. Helene Iswolsky (Blooming-
    ton: Indiana University Press, 1984), 29, 320–21; Kathleen Rowe, *The Unruly Woman:
    Gender and the Genres of Laughter* (Austin: University of Texas Press, 1995), 32–33.

21 Muñoz, *Disidentifications*, 11.

22 See Bakhtin, *Rabelais and His World*, 24–26, 29, 317–18, 320–21; Kathleen Rowe,
    The Unruly Woman, 32–33.

23 Emily Wallin, "Lil Dicky Net Worth," *Wealthy Gorilla* (blog), June 30, 2020, https:
    //wealthygorilla.com.

24 See Leonard Stein, "Jewish Flow: Performing Identity in Hip-Hop Music," *Studies
    in American Jewish Literature* 38, no. 2 (2019): 122; Jon Stratton, "The Beastie Boys:
    Jews in Whiteface," *Popular Music* 27, no. 3 (2008): 413–32.

25 Stein, "Jewish Flow," 126.

26 Judah Cohen, "Hip-Hop Judaica: The Politics of Representin' Heebster Heritage,"
    Popular Music 28, no. 1 (2009): 6.

27 Stein, "Jewish Flow," 127.

28 Burd, "Really Scared."

29 Michael Kimmel, *Angry White Men: American Masculinity at the End of an Era* (New York: Nation Books, 2013).

30 Kate Manne, *Entitled: How Male Privilege Hurts Women* (New York: Crown, 2020), 19.

31 Claire Cain Miller, "Republican Men Say It's a Better Time to Be a Woman Than a Man," *New York Times*, January 17, 2017, www.nytimes.com.

32 See Abby Ferber, *White Man Falling: Race, Gender, and White Supremacy* (New York: Rowman & Littlefield, 1999); Sally Robinson, *Marked Men: White Masculinity in Crisis* (New York: Columbia University Press, 2000).

33 Stein, "Jewish Flow," 127.

34 Hannah Schwadron, *The Case of the Sexy Jewess: Dance, Gender & Jewish Joke-Work in US Pop Culture* (Oxford: Oxford University Press, 2017), 15.

35 Harley Erdman, *Staging the Jew: The Performance of an American Ethnicity, 1860–1920* (New Brunswick, NJ: Rutgers University Press, 1995), 33.

36 Ibid.

37 Burd, "Jewish Flow."

38 Burd, "Professional Rapper."

39 See Sara Lipton, *Dark Mirror: The Medieval Origins of Anti-Jewish Iconography* (New York: Metropolitan Books, 2014); Deborah Higgs Strickland, *Saracens, Demons, and Jews: Making Monsters in Medieval Art* (Princeton, NJ: Princeton University Press, 2003).

40 See Ross, "Lil Dicky, the Jerry Seinfeld of Rap."

41 David Burd, "Lil Dicky—Behind the Dick Episode 1," edited by Myles Kramer, YouTube video, 3:10, November 30, 2016, https://www.youtube.com/watch?v=MAIoyvZ-Qng.

42 David Burd, "Lil Dicky—First Shows Ever (Ep. 3)," YouTube video, 9:46, May 14, 2014, https://www.youtube.com/watch?v=cXniQmmEokE.

43 David Burd, "Lil Dicky—Freaky Friday Feat. Chris Brown (Official Music Video)," directed by Tony Yacenda, YouTube video, 5:20, March 15, 2018, https://www.youtube.com/watch?v=aZla1ttZHaw.

44 "Camp Manna," 2018, https://web.archive.org/web/20160331090415/http://campmannamovie.com/about-the-film/.

45 Tricia Rose, *The Hip Hop Wars: What We Talk about When We Talk about Hip Hop—and Why It Matters* (New York: Civitas, 2008), 85; Stein, "Jewish Flow," 123.

46 Jesse Bernstein, "Bieber's Manager Takes Rapper Lil' Dicky under His Wing," *Tablet*, July 22, 2016, www.tabletmag.com.

47 David Burd, "Professional Rapper."

48 Paul Craig Roberts, "Identity Politics vs. White People: Who Will Win?," *Institute for Political Economy* (blog), January 16, 2018, www.paulcraigroberts.org.

49 Ben Cohen, "'Jew Coup': The Founder of a White House-Accredited Media Outlet's Shocking Antisemitic Rant," *Algemeiner*, November 27, 2019, www.algemeiner.com.

50 Muñoz, *Disidentifications*.

51 David Burd, "All K."

52 Claire Sisco King, "It Cuts Both Ways: *Fight Club*, Masculinity, and Abject Hegemony," *Communication and Critical/Cultural Studies* 6, no. 4 (2009): 366–85.

53 Julia Kristeva, *Powers of Horror: An Essay on Abjection*, trans. Leon S. Roudiez (New York: Columbia University Press, 1982).

54 Mary Douglas, *Purity & Danger: An Analysis of Concepts of Pollution and Taboo* (London: Routledge & Keagan Paul, 1966), 104–6, 115, 162.

55 See Bakhtin, *Rabelais and His World*.

56 Kathleen Rowe, *The Unruly Woman: Gender and the Genres of Laughter* (Austin: University of Texas Press, 1995), 42.

57 See Mikhail Bakhtin, *Rabelais and His World*, 24–26, 29, 317–18, 320–21.

58 *Fight Club*, directed by David Fincher (20th Century Fox, 1999), DVD.

59 Rowe, *Unruly Woman*, 196.

60 Ibid., 194–96.

61 Ibid., 195.

62 Eli Bromberg, *Unsettling: Jews, Whiteness, and Incest in American Popular Culture* (New Brunswick, NJ: Rutgers University Press, 2021), 10.

63 Weaver, *Rhetoric of Racist Humour*, 157.

64 David Burd, "Lil Dicky—White Dude," YouTube video, April 30, 2013, https://www.youtube.com/watch?v=Erg1UXGBowE&sns=em.

65 Martha A. Ravits, "The Jewish Mother: Comedy and Controversy in American Popular Culture," *MELUS* 25, no. 1 (2000): 5–6.

66 Burd, "Freaky Friday."

67 Burd, "Jewish Flow."

68 *Vice News Tonight*, "Charlottesville: Race & Terror," featuring lead reporter Elle Reeve, aired August 15, 2017, on HBO. https://news.vice.com.

69 Burd, "Ex-Boyfriend."

70 See Andrew B. Leiter, *In the Shadow of the Black Beast: African American Masculinity in the Harlem and Southern Renaissances* (Baton Rouge: Louisiana State University Press, 2010), 3.

71 See Patricia Hill Collins, *Black Sexual Politics: African Americans, Gender, and the New Racism* (New York: Routledge, 2005), 57.

72 Abby Ferber, "The Construction of Black Masculinity: White Supremacy Now and Then," *Journal of Sport & Social Issues* 31, no. 1 (2007): 18.

73 Ibid.

74 Eric Lott, *Love and Theft: Blackface Minstrelsy and the American Working Class* (Oxford: Oxford University Press, 1993), 5, 21.

75 Jayna Brown, *Babylon Girls: Black Women Performers and the Shaping of the Modern* (Durham, NC: Duke University Press, 2008), 72; Krin Gabbard, *Black Magic: White Hollywood and African American Culture* (New Brunswick, NJ: Rutgers University Press, 2004), 19; Lott, *Love and Theft*, 52.

76 Lott, *Love and Theft*, 3–6.

77 Gabbard, *Black Magic*, 19.

78 Ibid.

79 Lott, *Love and Theft*, 4; Gabbard, *Black Magic*, 21.

80 Gabbard, *Black Magic*, 21.

81 See Michael Rogin, *Blackface, White Noise: Jewish Immigrants in the Hollywood Melting Pot* (Berkeley: University of California Press, 1998); Stratton, "Beastie Boys."

82 Einar Olsen, "Professional Rapper."

83 Debbie Ging, "Alphas, Betas, and Incels: Theorizing the Masculinities of the Manosphere," *Men & Masculinities* 22, no. 4 (2017): 638–57.

84 Ibid., 644.

85 See David C. Atkinson, "Charlottesville and the Alt-Right: A Turning Point?," *Politics, Groups, Identities* 6, no. 2 (2018): 311; Ging, "Alphas, Betas, and Incels," 649–50.

86 Ging, "Alphas, Betas, and Incels," 649.

87 See Ging, "Alphas, Betas, and Incels"; Bruce Hoffman, Jacob Ware, and Ezra Shapiro, "Assessing the Threat of Incel Violence," *Studies in Conflict & Terrorism* 43, no. 7 (2020): 565–87.

88 Ging, "Alphas, Betas, and Incels," 640; Hoffman, Ware, and Shapiro, "Incel Violence," 567.

89 Ging, "Alphas, Betas, and Incels."

90 Hoffman, Ware, and Shapiro, "Incel Violence," 569.

91 Ibid., 570.

92 Alexandra Minn Stern, *Proud Boys and the White Ethnostate: How the Alt-Right Is Warping the American Imagination* (Boston: Beacon Press, 2019).

93 CNN, "Lil Dicky on Political Disinterest, Donald Trump and STDs," YouTube video, 2:21, April 3, 2016, https://www.youtube.com/watch?v=wi6rjOh8TNU; Lil Dicky (@lildickytweets), "Pennsylvania Are You Voting for Biden?," Twitter, November 3, 2020, 10:29 a.m., https://twitter.com/lildickytweets/status/1323693793556586501.

94 Manne, *Entitled*, 24.

95 Burd, "Professional Rapper."

96 Moya Bailey and Trudy, "On Misogynoir: Citation, Erasure, and Plagiarism," *Feminist Media Studies* 18, no. 4 (2018): 762–68.

97 Mark Andrejevic, *Infoglut: How Too Much Information Is Changing the Way We Think and Know* (New York: Routledge, 2013); Ging, "Alphas, Betas, and Incels," 643; Zizi Papacharissi, *Affective Publics: Sentiment, Technology, and Politics* (Oxford: Oxford University Press, 2014).

98 Ging, "Alphas, Betas, and Incels," 639.

99 Ibid., 643.

100 Ibid., 640, 642, 651. On manospheric victim narratives and harassment campaigns that specifically vilify feminist critiques of videogames, see Alice E. Marwick and Robyn Caplan, "Drinking Male Tears: Language, the Manosphere, and Networked Harassment," *Feminist Media Studies* 18, no. 4 (2018), 547.

101 Ibid., 646.

102 "Lil Dicky Understands Some Red Pill Teachings Definitely," *Reddit* (blog), 2016, https://www.reddit.com/r/Hiphopcirclejerk/comments/52ux7k/lil_dicky_understands_some_red_pill_teachings/.

103 *The Matrix*, directed by the Wachowski Sisters (Warner Bros. Pictures, 1999). Amazon.com.

104 Pig-Iron, "Redpill," in *Urban Dictionary*, 2013, www.urbandictionary.com.

105 Ging, "Alphas, Betas, and Incels," 640.

106 Ging, "Alphas, Betas, and Incels"; Viveca Greene, "'Deplorable' Satire: Alt-Right Memes, White Genocide Tweets, and Redpilling Normies," *Studies in American Humor* 5, no. 1 (2019): 31–69.

107 Greene, "'Deplorable' Satire," 65.

108 David Burd, "Lil Dicky—Lemme Freak (Official Video)," directed by Tony Yacenda, YouTube video, 5:04, September 17, 2014, https://www.youtube.com/watch?v=ocGiulPm3IU.

109 Greene, "'Deplorable' Satire."

110 Greene, "'Deplorable' Satire"; Hoffman, Ware, and Shapiro, "Incel Violence."

111 Ashley Feinberg, "This Is the Daily Stormer's Playbook," *Huffington Post* (blog), December 22, 2017, www.huffpost.com.

112 Alice Marwick and Rebecca Lewis, "Media Manipulation and Disinformation Online," Data & Society Research Institute, May 15, 2017, https://datasociety.net.

113 David Neiwart, "What the Kek: Explaining the Alt-Right 'Deity' behind Their 'Meme Magic,'" Southern Poverty Law Center, May 8, 2017, www.splcenter.org.

114 Greene, "'Deplorable' Satire."

115 Ibid., 54.

116 Andrew Anglin, "A Normie's Guide to the Alt-Right," *Daily Stormer* (blog), August 31, 2016, www.dailystormer.com; Greene, "'Deplorable' Satire," 54.

117 Feinberg, "*Daily Stormer*'s Playbook."

118 David Burd, "Lil Dicky—White Dude," YouTube video, April 30, 2013, https://www.youtube.com/watch?v=Erg1UXGBowE&sns=em.

119 David Burd, "Lil Dicky—White Dude (Official Video)," YouTube video, May 22, 2013, https://www.youtube.com/watch?v=3rnFlQAvk8U.

120 Lauren Anderson, "Lil Dicky Speaks Out about George Floyd, Encourages Fans to Take Action against Racism," *Cheat Sheet* (blog), June 2, 2020, www.cheatsheet.com.

121 Simon Weaver, *The Rhetoric of Racist Humour: US, UK and Global Race Joking* (Farnham, UK: Ashgate Publishing, 2011), 149.

122 See Greene, "'Deplorable' Satire"; Viveca Greene and Amber Day, "Asking for It: Rape Myths, Satire, and Feminist Lacunae," *Signs* 45, no. 2 (2020): 449–72; Neiwart, "What the Kek"; Raúl Pérez and Viveca Greene, "Debating Rape Jokes vs. Rape Culture: Framing and Counter-Framing Misogynistic Comedy," *Social Semiotics* 26, no. 3 (2016): 265–82.

123 Christian, *Open TV*.

124 Burd, "Lemme Freak."

125 Ibid.

126 Ging, "Alphas, Betas, and Incels," 649.

127 Ibid., 647.

128 Jennifer Braceras, "Witch Hunt on the Quad," *Wall Street Journal*, January 27, 2017.

129 Stephanie Saul and Kate Taylor, "Betsy DeVos Reverses Obama-Era Policy on Campus Sexual Assault Investigations," *New York Times*, September 22, 2017, www .nytimes.com.S

130 Ging, "Alphas, Betas, and Incels," 649.

131 Burd, "Ex-Boyfriend."

132 Debbie Ging, Theodore Lynn, and Pierangelo Rosati, "Neologising Misogyny: Urban Dictionary's Folksonomies of Sexual Abuse," *New Media and Society* 22, no. 5 (2020): 850.

133 Rowe, *Unruly Woman*, 33.

134 David Burd, "Lil Dicky—Grimy as a Gooch," YouTube video, April 25, 2013, https: //www.youtube.com/watch?v=yoKQIABKvxY.

135 *Dave*, season 1, episode 1, "The Gander," directed by Greg Mottola, aired March 4, 2020, on FX. Hulu.com.

136 Steven F. Kruger, "Racial/Religious and Sexual Queerness in the Middle Ages," *Medieval Feminist Forum* 16, no. 1 (1993): 33–35.

137 Ging, Lynn, and Rosati, "Neologising Misogyny," 850.

138 Burd, "Ex-Boyfriend."

139 See Ging, Lynn, and Rosati, "Neologising Misogyny," 850.

140 Ross, "Lil Dicky, the Jerry Seinfeld of Rap."

141 John Blake, "It's Time to Talk about 'Black Privilege,'" *CNN*, March 31, 2016, www .cnn.com.

142 Ibid.

143 See Moira Weigel, "Political Correctness: How the Right Invented a Phantom Enemy," *The Guardian*, November 30, 2016, www.theguardian.com; John K. Wilson, *The Myth of Political Correctness: The Conservative Attack on Higher Education* (Durham, NC: Duke University Press, 1995).

144 Ging, "Alphas, Betas, and Incels," 651.

145 Burd, "All K."

146 Burd, "Really Scared."

147 Burd, "Freaky Friday."

148 Lauren Michele Jackson, "We Need to Talk about Digital Blackface in Reaction GIFs," *Teen Vogue*, August 2, 2017, www.teenvogue.com.

149 Stein, "Jewish Flow," 129.

150 *BlacKkKlansman*, directed by Spike Lee (2018, Universal City, CA: Focus Features, 2018), DVD.

151 For more on Black violability, see Treva B. Lindsey, "Post-Ferguson: A 'Herstorical' Approach to Black Violability," *Feminist Studies* 41, no. 1 (2015): 232–37.

152 Ibram X. Kendi, *How to Be an Antiracist* (New York: One World, 2019), 137.

153 Burd, "Ex-Boyfriend."

154 See *Dave*, season 1, episode 3, "Hypospadias," directed by Greg Mottola, aired March 11, 2020, on FX. Hulu.com.

155 See Jonathan Branfman, "Unmasking the 'Right to Harm:' The US Supreme Court and the Attack on LGBTQ Lives," *Globe Post*, October 13, 2020, https://theglobepost.com.

156 Ging, "Alphas, Betas, and Incels," 651.

157 David Burd, "Famous Dude," YouTube video, April 25, 2013, https://www.youtube.com/watch?v=cKn85_Im5LU.

158 *Funny Or Die*, "Watch Yo Self Feat. Mystikal, Lil Dicky & Trinidad James," YouTube video, 2:28, April 19, 2016, www.funnyordie.com.

159 Burd, "Jewish Flow."

160 *Dave*, season 1, episode 10, "Jail," written by David Burd, aired April 29, 2020, on FX. Hulu.com.

161 Amy Louise Wood, *Lynching and Spectacle: Witnessing Racial Violence in America, 1890–1940* (Chapel Hill: University of North Carolina Press, 2009), 98.

162 Ibid., 179.

163 Abbi Jacobson, "Lil Dicky—$ave Dat Money," Twitter, September 18, 2015, https://twitter.com/abbijacobson/status/644948976681226240?lang=en.

CHAPTER 3. ECSTATIC JEWESSFACE

1 *Broad City*, season 1, episode 1, "What a Wonderful World," directed by Lucia Aniello, aired January 22, 2014, on Comedy Central. Amazon.com.

2 This chapter draws on ideas first presented in an earlier article: Jonathan Branfman, "'Plow Him Like a Queen!': Jewish Female Masculinity, Queer Glamor, and Racial Commentary in *Broad City*," *Television & New Media* 21, no. 1 (2020): 842–60.

3 Nick Paumgarten, "Id Girls: The Comedy Couple behind *Broad City*," *New Yorker*, June 23, 2014, www.newyorker.com.

4 Aymar Jean Christian, *Open TV: Innovation beyond Hollywood and the Rise of Web Television* (New York: New York University Press, 2018).

5 Anna Carugati et al., "*Broad City*'s Amy Poehler, Ilana Glazer & Abbi Jacobson," YouTube video, 7:01, April 24, 2014, https://www.youtube.com/watch?v=qvkddfn9efo.

6 Emily Nussbaum, "Laverne & Curly: The Slapstick Anarchists of *Broad City*," *New Yorker*, March 7, 2016, www.newyorker.com.

7 Michael Schneider, "*Broad City* Will End after Season 5, as Ilana Glazer and Abbi Jacobson Sign New Deal with Comedy Central," *IndieWire*, April 12, 2018, www.indiewire.com.

8 *Broad City*, "What a Wonderful World."

9 Henry Bial, *Acting Jewish: Negotiating Ethnicity on the American Stage and Screen* (Ann Arbor: University of Michigan Press, 2005), 2–3.

10 For more on this lineage, see Joyce Antler, "One Clove Away from a Pomander Ball: The Subversive Tradition of Jewish Female Comedians," *Studies in American Jewish Literature (1981–)* 29 (2010): 123–38; Jenny Caplan, *Funny, You Don't Look Funny: Judaism and Humor from the Silent Generation to Millennials* (Detroit: Wayne State University Press, 2023); Sarah Blacher Cohen, "The Unkosher

Comediennes: From Sophie Tucker to Joan Rivers," in *Jewish Wry: Essays on Jewish Humor*, ed. Sarah Blacher Cohen (Bloomington: Indiana University Press, 1987), 105–24; Grace Overbeke, "Subversively Sexy: The Jewish 'Red Hot Mamas' Sophie Tucker, Belle Barth and Pearl Williams," *Studies in American Humor* 25 (2012): 33–58; Grace Overbeke, *The First Lady of Laughs: Jean Carroll and the Jewish Female Origins of Stand-Up Comedy* (New York: New York University Press, 2024).

11 Kathleen Rowe, *The Unruly Woman: Gender and the Genres of Laughter* (Austin: University of Texas Press, 1995).

12 Ibid., 33.

13 Gilda Radner, "Rhonda Weiss: Jewess Jeans—SNL," excerpted from *Saturday Night Live*, season 5, episode 11, "Elliot Gould, Gary Numan," directed by Dave Wilson and James Signorelli, aired February 16, 1980, on NBC, accessed as a You-Tube video, 1:30, uploaded to YouTube on October 11, 2013, https://www.youtube.com/watch?v=QZ1Z5TIx4wI.

14 Christi Carras, "Fran Drescher Says She Had to Fight to Let *The Nanny* Be Jewish," *LA Times*, April 28, 2020, www.latimes.com.

15 Bial, *Acting Jewish*, 2-3.

16 Shaina Hammerman, "Dirty Jews: Amy Schumer and Other Vulgar Jewesses," in *From Shtetl to Stardom: Jews and Hollywood*, ed. Michael Renov and Vincent Brook (West Lafayette, IN: Purdue University Press, 2016), 49–72; Samantha Pickette, *Peak TV's Unapologetic Jewish Woman: Exploring Jewish Women's Representation in Contemporary Television Comedy* (Lanham, MD: Rowman & Littlefield, 2022).

17 Dylan Kickham, "Ilana Glazer and Rachel Bloom Used to Be Roommates," *EW*, April 4, 2016, https://ew.com.

18 Rachel Bloom, "JAP Battle (EXPLICIT)—'Crazy Ex-Girlfriend,'" excerpted from *Crazy Ex-Girlfriend*, season 1, episode 6, "Josh and I Go to Los Angeles!," directed by Joanna Kearns, aired November 16, 2015, on the CW, accessed as a YouTube video, 2:57, uploaded to YouTube on March 1, 2016, https://www.youtube.com/watch?v=-TQmo5TvZQY.

19 See David Nirenberg, "Deviant Politics and Jewish Love: Alfonso VIII and the Jewess of Toledo," *Jewish History* 21 (2007): 15–41; Ann Pellegrini, "Whiteface Performances: 'Race,' Gender, and Jewish Bodies," in *Jews and Other Differences: The New Jewish Cultural Studies*, ed. Jonathan Boyarin and Daniel Boyarin (Minneapolis,: University of Minnesota Press, 1996), 108–49.

20 See Pellegrini, "Whiteface Performances," 129.

21 Harley Erdman, *Staging the Jew: The Performance of an American Ethnicity, 1860–1920* (New Brunswick, NJ: Rutgers University Press, 1995), 33.

22 See Sander Gilman, *The Jew's Body* (New York: Routledge, 1991).

23 Penny A. Weiss, "'I'm Not a Feminist, but . . . ,'" in *Conversations with Feminism: Political Theory and Practice* (Lanham, MD: Rowman & Littlefield, 1998), 11–25.

24 Jonathan Branfman and Susan Stiritz, "Teaching Men's Anal Pleasure: Challenging Gender Norms with 'Prostage' Education," *American Journal of Sexuality Education* 7, no. 4 (2012): 404–28.

25 Alanna Vagianos, "*Broad City*'s Ilana Glazer and Abbi Jacobson Are 'Totally Feminists,'" *Huffington Post*, December 6, 2017, www.huffpost.com.

26 Mehera Bonner, "Abbi Jacobson Says Female-Driven Shows Are Judged in a Way Male Shows Just Aren't," *Marie Claire*, October 4, 2017, www.marieclaire.com.

27 Simon Weaver, *The Rhetoric of Racist Humour: US, UK and Global Race Joking* (Farnham, UK: Ashgate Publishing, 2011), 149.

28 Rowe, *Unruly Woman*, 50–93.

29 See this critique in Linda Mizejewski, "Queen Latifah, Unruly Women, and the Bodies of Romantic Comedy," Genders 46, no. 4 (2007).

30 See Jessyka Finley, "Raunch and Redress: Interrogating Pleasure in Black Women's Stand-up Comedy," *Journal of Popular Culture* 49, no. 4 (2016): 780–98; Patricia Hill Collins, *Black Sexual Politics: African Americans, Gender, and the New Racism* (New York: Routledge, 2005); Linda Mizejewski, *Pretty/Funny: Women Comedians and Body Politics* (Austin: University of Texas Press, 2014); Brandy Monk-Payton, "#LaughingWhileBlack: Gender and the Comedy of Social Media Blackness," *Feminist Media Histories* 3, no. 2 (2017): 15–35; Charlene Tung, "Embodying an Image: Gender, Race, and Sexuality in La Femme Nikita," in *Action Chicks: New Images of Tough Women in Popular Culture*, ed. Sherry Inness (Palgrave Mac-Millan, 2004), 95–121; Rebecca Wanzo, "Precarious-Girl Comedy: Issa Rae, Lena Dunham, and Abjection Aesthetics," *Camera Obscura* 31, no. 2 (2016): 27–59.

31 Exceptions include Linda Mizejewski, *Ziegfeld Girl: Image and Icon in Culture and Cinema* (Durham, NC: Duke University Press, 1999); Mizejewski, *Pretty/Funny*; and Jonathan Branfman, "Jewy/Screwy Leading Lady: *Crazy Ex-Girlfriend* and the Critique of Rom-Com Femininity," *Journal of Modern Jewish Studies*, 19, no. 1 (2020): 71–92.

32 Excepting my own article: Branfman, "'Plow Him Like a Queen!'"

33 Roberta Mock, "Female Jewish Comedians: Grotesque Mimesis and Transgressing Stereotypes," *New Theatre Quarterly* 15, no. 2 (1999): 99–108; Hannah Schwadron, *The Case of the Sexy Jewess: Dance, Gender & Jewish Joke-Work in US Pop Culture* (Oxford: Oxford University Press, 2017).

34 Samantha Pickette, *Peak TV's Unapologetic Jewish Woman: Exploring Jewish Women's Representation in Contemporary Television Comedy* (Lanham, MD: Rowman & Littlefield, 2022), 56, 64.

35 Jack Halberstam, *Female Masculinity* (Durham, NC: Duke University Press, 1998).

36 Kortney Ziegler, "Black Sissy Masculinity and the Politics of Dis-Respectability," in *No Tea, No Shade: New Writings in Black Queer Studies*, ed. E. Patrick Johnson (Durham, NC: Duke University Press, 2016), 196–215.

37 Schwadron, *Case of the Sexy Jewess*.

38 Ibid., 14.

39 Ibid., 3, 78.

40 Mizejewski, *Pretty/Funny*, 92, 112.

41 Schwadron, *Case of the Sexy Jewess*, 14, 77–79.

42 Taylor Nygaard and Jorie Lagerwey, *Horrible White People: Gender, Genre, and Television's Precarious Whiteness* (New York: New York University Press, 2020).

43 Ibid., 1–10.

44 Ibid., 5.

45 Ibid., 12, 95–97.

46 Ibid., 134, 147.

47 Ibid., 96–98.

48 Ibid., 152.

49 David Nirenberg, "Deviant Politics and Jewish Love: Alfonso VIII and the Jewess of Toledo," *Jewish History* 21 (2007): 16–17.

50 See Nathan Abrams, *The New Jew in Film: Exploring Jewishness and Judaism in Contemporary Film* (New Brunswick, NJ: Rutgers University Press, 2012); Erdman, *Staging the Jew*, 55; Pellegrini, "Whiteface Performances."

51 Erdman, *Staging the Jew*, 40–60.

52 Matthew Frye Jacobson, *Whiteness of a Different Color: European Immigrants and the Alchemy of Race* (Cambridge, MA: Harvard University Press, 1999), 187–188.

53 "'Jewess' in American English," Google N-Gram, September 10, 2021, https://books.google.com/ngrams.

54 For more on the "JAP" and "Jewish mother" tropes, see Joyce Antler, *You Never Call! You Never Write! A History of the Jewish Mother* (New York: Oxford University Press, 2013); and Riv-Ellen Prell, *Fighting to Become Americans: Jews, Gender, & the Anxiety of Assimilation* (Boston: Beacon Press, 1999).

55 Livia E. Bitton, "Biblical Names of Literary Jewesses," *Names: A Journal of Onomastics* 21, no. 2 (1973): 103–9.

56 See Walter Scott, *Ivanhoe* (Edinburgh: A. Constable, 1820).

57 Charlene A. Lea, *Emancipation, Assimilation & Stereotype: The Image of the Jew in German and Austrian Drama (1800–1850)* (Bonn: Bouvier Verlag Herbert Grundmann, 1978), 61.

58 Daniel Boyarin, Daniel Itzkovitz, and Ann Pellegrini, "Strange Bedfellows: An Introduction," in *Queer Theory and the Jewish Question*, ed. Daniel Boyarin, Daniel Itzkovitz, and Ann Pellegrini (New York: Columbia University Press, 2003), 5.

59 Pellegrini, "Whiteface Performances," 129.

60 Lea, *Emancipation, Assimilation & Stereotype*, 70.

61 On the beautiful Jewess's "Eastern exoticism," see Roberta Mock, *Jewish Women on Stage, Film, and Television* (Basingstoke: Palgrave MacMillan, 2007), 57. On the beautiful Jewess's "stereotypically dark hair and black eyes," see Ann Pellegrini, "Whiteface Performances," 129. On the beautiful Jewess's "serpentine" connotations, see Ann Pellegrini, "Whiteface Performances," 125–126; Keren Rosa Hammerschlag, "'Your Favourite Jewish Girl, Apart From Your Mum': Introducing the Modern Jewess in Image and Text," *Shofar: An Interdisciplinary Journal of Jewish Studies* 39, no. 1 (2021), 4; Roberta Mock, *Jewish Women on Stage, Film, and Television*, 57; Lynn Swarts, "Lilien's Sensual Beauties: Discovering Jewish Orientalism

in Ephraim Moses Lilien's Biblical Women," *Nashim: A Journal of Jewish Women's Studies and Gender Issues* 33 (Fall 2018), 113. On the mixture of "desire and repulsion" that the beautiful Jewess evoked, see Erdman, *Staging the Jew*, 40.

62 Gustav Klimt, *Judith and the Head of Holofernes*, oil on canvas, 1901, Österreichische Galerie Belvedere, Vienna.

63 Carol Ockman, "'Two Large Eyebrows À l'Orientale': Ethnic Stereotyping in Ingres's Baronne de Rothschild," *Art History* 14, no. 4 (1991): 521.

64 See Anthony Trollope, *Phineas Finn*, new edition (Oxford: Oxford University Press, 2011).

65 Bryan Cheyette, *Constructions of "the Jew" in English Literature & Society: Racial Representations, 1875–1945* (Cambridge: Cambridge University Press, 1993), 33.

66 Ibid.

67 Ibid., 34.

68 José Esteban Muñoz, *Disidentifications: Queers of Color and the Performance of Politics* (Minneapolis: University of Minnesota Press, 1999), 11.

69 Henri Regnault, *Salomé*, oil on canvas, 1870, Metropolitan Museum of Art, New York.

70 Metropolitan Museum of Art, "Salomé," 2021, www.metmuseum.org.

71 *Broad City*, "What a Wonderful World."

72 Kate Manne, *Down Girl: The Logic of Misogyny* (Oxford: Oxford University Press, 2017); Kate Manne, *Entitled: How Male Privilege Hurts Women* (New York: Crown, 2020).

73 *Broad City*, season 4, episode 1, "Sliding Doors," directed by Lucia Aniello, aired September 13, 2017, on Comedy Central. Amazon.com.

74 *Broad City*, season 5, episode 8, "Sleep No More," directed by Lucia Aniello, aired March 14, 2019, on Comedy Central. Amazon.com.

75 *Broad City*, "What a Wonderful World."

76 Erdman, *Staging the Jew*, 44.

77 Weaver, *Rhetoric of Racist Humour*, 157.

78 *Broad City*, season 3, episode 6, "Philadelphia," directed by Todd Biermann, aired March 23, 2016, on Comedy Central. Amazon.com.

79 David Burd, "Lil Dicky—White Dude," YouTube video, April 30, 2013, https://www.youtube.com/watch?v=Erg1UXGBowE&sns=em.

80 *Broad City*, "Sliding Doors."

81 *Broad City*, "What a Wonderful World."

82 *Broad City*, season 4, episode 6, "Witches," directed by Abbi Jacobson, aired October 18, 2017, on Comedy Central. Amazon.com.

83 Cheyette, *Constructions of "the Jew" in English Literature & Society*, 34.

84 *Broad City*, season 2, episode 4, "Knockoffs," directed by Lucia Aniello, aired February 4, 2015, on Comedy Central. Amazon.com.

85 See Branfman and Stiritz, "Teaching Men's Anal Pleasure."

86 Nussbaum, "Laverne & Curly."

87 Caitlin Wolper, "How *Broad City* Encouraged Women to Be Their Grossest, Truest Selves," *Vulture*, March 28, 2019, www.vulture.com.

88 Jill Gutowitz, "Abbi Jacobson Just Casually Came Out as Bisexual," *Into*, April 9, 2018, www.intomore.com.

89 Jenavieve Hatch, "How Ilana from *Broad City* Taught Me to Be Unapologetically Bi," *Huffington Post* (blog), August 16, 2016, www.huffpost.com.

90 Mike Albo, "How *Broad City* Became the Greatest Show on Television," *Out Magazine*, February 25, 2016, www.out.com.

91 See James Baldwin, "White Man's Guilt," *Ebony*, August 1965.

92 Cheryl Strayed and Steve Almond, "How Can I Cure My White Guilt?," August 14, 2018, www.nytimes.com.

93 Schwadron, *Case of the Sexy Jewess*, 100–6.

94 *Broad City*, season 4, episode 3, "Just the Tips," directed by Neil Daly, aired September 27, 2017, on Comedy Central. Amazon.com.

95 See Melanie Kaye/Kantrowitz, "To Be a Radical Jew in the 20th Century," in *The Issue is Power: Essays on Women, Jews, Violence & Resistance*, ed. Melanie Kaye/Kantrowitz (San Francisco: Aunt Lute Books, 1992), 108–9; Melanie Kaye/Kantrowitz, *The Colors of the Jews: Racial Politics & Radical Diasporism* (Bloomington: Indiana University Press, 2007), 33.

96 Gretchen Bakke, "Dead White Men: An Essay on the Changing Dynamics of Race in US Action Cinema," *Anthropological Quarterly* 2 (2010): 400–28; Russell Meeuf, *Rebellious Bodies: Stardom, Citizenship, and the New Body Politics* (Austin: University of Texas Press, 2017), 129–33.

97 See Richard Dyer, *White: Essays on Race and Culture* (New York: Routledge, 1997), especially 108–10.

98 Meeuf, *Rebellious Bodies*, 129–33.

99 For more on hyperwhiteness in *Blade*, see Meeuf, *Rebellious Bodies*, 129.

100 For more on hyperwhiteness in *Harry Potter*, see Marcelle Kosman and Hannah McGregor, "The Chamber of Whiteness," *Witch, Please!*, April 6, 2015. Podcast. 59 min. http://ohwitchplease.ca.

101 Meeuf, *Rebellious Bodies*, 133.

102 Ibid.

103 *Broad City*, season 1, episode 6, "Stolen Phone," directed by Lucia Aniello, aired February 26, 2014, on Comedy Central. Amazon.com.

104 *Broad City*, "What a Wonderful World."

105 Katie Couric and Dwayne Michael Carter Jr., "Lil Wayne Interview with Katie Couric [Full 11 Min Interview]," CBS News, YouTube video, 11:19, July 6, 2013, https://www.youtube.com/watch?v=QF5sKeuD2Ck.

106 See Frantz Fanon, *Black Skin, White Masks*, trans. Charles Lam Markmann (New York: Grove Press, 1967), 170.

107 Arielle Bernstein, "Joy Is a Feminist (Comedy) Act," *Salon* (blog), April 2, 2016, www.salon.com.

108 For more on this legacy of appropriating Black "gestural vocabularies," see Jayna Brown, *Babylon Girls: Black Women Performers and the Shaping of the Modern* (Durham, NC: Duke University Press, 2008), 3.

109 See Hadley Freeman, "Miley Cyrus's Twerking Routine Was Cultural Appropria-
tion at Its Worst," *The Guardian*, August 27, 2013, www.theguardian.com; Kyra D.
Gaunt, "YouTube, Twerking & You: Context Collapse and the Handheld Co-
presence of Black Girls and Miley Cyrus," in *Voicing Girlhood in Popular Music:
Performance, Authority, Authenticity*, ed. Jacqueline Warwick and Allison Adrian
(New York: Routledge, 2016), 208–34.

110 Jenna Amatulli, "Here's the Real Origin of the Word 'Yas,'" *Huffington Post*,
September 4, 2017, www.huffingtonpost.com.

111 Albo, "How *Broad City* Became the Greatest Show on Television."

112 See Amatulli, "Here's the Real Origin of the Word 'Yas'"; Ziwe Fumudoh and
Ilana Glazer, "Ilana Glazer Sides with the Sun in the Climate Change Debate,"
excerpted from *ZIWE*, season 2, episode 4, "Hot!," directed by Ziwe Fumudoh, aired May 22, 2022, on Showtime, accessed as a YouTube video, 11:24,
uploaded to YouTube on May 23, 2022, https://www.youtube.com/watch?v
=iqg6BdMc1c4.

113 Priscilla Peña Ovalle, *Dance and the Hollywood Latina: Race, Sex, and Stardom*
(New Brunswick, NJ: Rutgers University Press, 2010), 4; Schwadron, *Case of the
Sexy Jewess*, 1.

114 Ovalle, *Dance and the Hollywood Latina*, 8.

115 Cheyette, *Constructions of "the Jew" in English Literature & Society*, 34.

116 Ovalle, *Dance and the Hollywood Latina*, 8.

117 *Broad City*, season 1, episode 8, "Destination: Wedding," directed by Nicholas
Jasenovec, aired March 12, 2014, on Comedy Central. Amazon.com.

118 Nussbaum, "Laverne & Curly."

119 Schwadron, *Case of the Sexy Jewess*, 77–8.

120 Lauren Michele Jackson, "The Women 'Black-Fishing' on Instagram Aren't Exactly Trying to Be Black," *Slate*, November 29, 2018, https://slate.com.

121 *Broad City*, season 2, episode 8, "Kirk Steele," directed by Lucia Aniello, aired
March 4, 2015, on Comedy Central. Amazon.com.

122 *Broad City*, season 3, episode 2, "Co-Op," directed by Ryan McFaul, aired February 24, 2016, on Comedy Central. Amazon.com.

123 See Lauren Michele Jackson, "The Women 'Black-Fishing' on Instagram Aren't
Exactly Trying to Be Black," *Slate*, November 29, 2018, https://slate.com.

124 Diyora Shadijanova, "Ariana Grande Is a Blackfish and These Are the Receipts,"
The Tab (blog), February 8, 2019, https://thetab.com.

125 See Isabelia Herrera, "The Evolution of Dominican Drake," *Remezcla* (blog),
September 21, 2015, https://remezcla.com.

126 See Laura Limonic, *Kugel and Frijoles: Latino Jews in the United States* (Detroit:
Wayne State University Press, 2019).

127 *Broad City*, season 3, episode 4, "Rat Pack," directed by Ryan McFaul, aired March 9,
2016, on Comedy Central. Amazon.com.

128 Jenni Miller, "11 Things We Learned at the New Yorker Festival's *Broad City*
Panel," *Vulture*, October 3, 2015, www.vulture.com.

129 *Broad City*, season 3, episode 7, "B&B-NYC," directed by Lucia Aniello, aired March 30, 2016, on Comedy Central. Amazon.com.

130 Jackson, "Black-Fishing."

131 *Broad City*, season 5, episode 5, "Artsy Fartsy," directed by Ilana Glazer, aired February 21, 2019, on Comedy Central. Amazon.com.

132 Jackson, "Black-Fishing."

133 Ibid.

134 The BoSHEmian, "The OG JEWESS Hoops!," Etsy, 2020, www.etsy.com.

135 Lily Drazin, "My Intersectional Feminist Queen, Ilana Wexler," *Jewish Women's Archive* (blog), March 11, 2019, https://jwa.org.

136 "About," Jewish Women's Archive, 2022, https://jwa.org.

137 "Lily Drazin," Jewish Women's Archive, 2022, https://jwa.org.

138 See Zeba Blay, "On Watching 'White Feminist' TV When You're a Black Girl," *Huffington Post* (blog), May 23, 2016, www.huffingtonpost.com; Nussbaum, "Laverne & Curly."

139 *Broad City*, season 2, episode 1, "In Heat," directed by Lucia Aniello, aired January 14, 2015, on Comedy Central. Amazon.com.

CHAPTER 4. BOYS JUST WANT TO HAVE FUN?

1 Amazon Bio, "Seth Rogen," 2021, www.amazon.com.

2 IMDb, "Freaks & Geeks," n.d., www.imdb.com.

3 *Knocked Up*, directed by Judd Apatow (Universal Pictures, 2007), Amazon.com.

4 Peter Travers, "Best and Worst Movies of 2007," *Rolling Stone*, December 27, 2007, www.rollingstone.com.

5 Natalie Robehmed, "Seth Rogen, Jonah Hill among Newcomers to Highest-Paid Actors List," *Forbes*, August 4, 2015, www.forbes.com.

6 *Broad City*, season 2, episode 1, "In Heat," directed by Lucia Aniello, aired January 14, 2015, on Comedy Central. Amazon.com.

7 "Seth Rogen's Vancouver High School Misadventures Hit the Big Screen," *CBC News*, August 17, 2007, www.cbc.ca.

8 See *Pam & Tommy*, season 1, episode 1, "Drilling and Pounding," directed by Craig Gillespie, aired February 2, 2022, on Hulu. Hulu.com.

9 "Knocked Up," Rotten Tomatoes, n.d., www.rottentomatoes.com.

10 Decca Aitkenhead, "Seth Rogen on Fame, Smoking Weed and Why His Films Have Not Aged Well," *The Times* (London), May 9, 2021, www.thetimes.co.uk.

11 *Pineapple Express*, directed by David Gordon Green (Columbia Pictures, 2008), Amazon.com.

12 José Esteban Muñoz, *Disidentifications: Queers of Color and the Performance of Politics* (Minneapolis: University of Minnesota Press, 1999), 11.

13 Apatow, *Knocked Up*.

14 Seth Rogen, "Seth Rogen Testifies before Congress," *Daily Conversation*, YouTube video, 7:57, February 26, 2014, https://www.youtube.com/watch?v =hvdbHSGWAgs.

15 *Donnie Darko*, directed by Richard Kelly (Pandora Cinema, 2001), Amazon.com.

16 See Abby Ferber, "The Culture of Privilege: Color-Blindness, Postfeminism, and Christonormativity," *Journal of Social Issues* 68, no. 1 (2012): 63–77.

17 *The 40-Year-Old Virgin*, directed by Judd Apatow (Universal Pictures, 2005), Amazon.com.

18 Ibid.

19 Casey Ryan Kelly, *Abstinence Cinema: Virginity and the Rhetoric of Sexual Purity in Contemporary Film* (New Brunswick, NJ: Rutgers University Press, 2016), 69, 72.

20 *Funny People*, directed by Judd Apatow (Universal Pictures, 2009), Amazon.com.

21 Bob Kronbauer, "Seth Rogen Wants to Do the TransLink Voice Ads in Place of Morgan Freeman," *Vancouver Is Awesome* (blog), May 24, 2018, www.vancouverisawesome.com.

22 Claire Sisco King, "It Cuts Both Ways: Fight Club, Masculinity, and Abject Hegemony," *Communication and Critical/Cultural Studies* 6, no. 4 (2009): 366–85.

23 Ibid.

24 See Debbie Ging, "Alphas, Betas, and Incels: Theorizing the Masculinities of the Manosphere," *Men & Masculinities* 22, no. 4 (2017): 638–57; Bruce Hoffman, Jacob Ware, and Ezra Shapiro, "Assessing the Threat of Incel Violence," *Studies in Conflict & Terrorism* 43, no. 7 (2020): 565–87.

25 Hoffman, Ware, and Shapiro, "Incel Violence," 569.

26 See Claire Cain Miller, "Republican Men Say It's a Better Time to Be a Woman Than a Man," *New York Times*, January 17, 2017, www.nytimes.com.

27 Ging, "Alphas, Betas, and Incels," 639.

28 Ging, "Alphas, Betas, and Incels."

29 Ibid.

30 Alexandra Brodsky, "Rape Adjacent: Imagining Legal Responses to Nonconsensual Condom Removal," *Columbia Journal of Gender and Law* 32, no. 2 (2017): 183–210.

31 Ibid., 189.

32 Ibid., 188.

33 Apatow, *Knocked Up*.

34 Ging, "Alphas, Betas, and Incels," 649.

35 David Burd, "Lil Dicky—Lemme Freak (Official Video)," directed by Tony Yacenda, YouTube video, 5:04, September 17, 2014, https://www.youtube.com/watch?v=ocGiulPm3IU.

36 Apatow, *Knocked Up*.

37 Rotten Tomatoes, "Knocked Up."

38 David Greven, "'I Love You, Brom Bones': Beta Male Comedies and American Culture," *Quarterly Review of Film and Video* 30 (2013): 405–20.

39 Ibid., 410.

40 Ibid., 405.

41 Apatow, *40-Year-Old Virgin*; Apatow, *Knocked Up*; Green, *Pineapple Express*.

42 Kelly, *Abstinence Cinema*, 55.

43 See Viveca Greene, "'Deplorable' Satire: Alt-Right Memes, White Genocide Tweets, and Redpilling Normies," *Studies in American Humor* 5, no. 1 (2019): 31–69.

44 Aitkenhead, "Seth Rogen on Fame."

45 Ellise Shafer, "Seth Rogen and Ted Cruz Clash on Twitter over Paris Climate Agreement and Disney's 'Fantasia,'" *Variety*, January 24, 2021, https://variety.com.

46 Lauren Anderson, "Lil Dicky Speaks Out about George Floyd, Encourages Fans to Take Action against Racism," *Cheat Sheet* (blog), June 2, 2020, www.cheatsheet .com.

47 Zack Sharf, "Seth Rogen: I Do Not Plan to Work with James Franco Right Now after Sexual Misconduct Claims," *IndieWire* (blog), May 10, 2021, www.indiewire .com.

48 Greven, "Beta Male Comedies," 414.

49 Nathan Abrams, *The New Jew in Film: Exploring Jewishness and Judaism in Contemporary Film* (New Brunswick, NJ: Rutgers University Press, 2012), 32.

50 Greven, "Beta Male Comedies," 414.

51 *Funny People*, directed by Judd Apatow (Universal Pictures, 2009), Amazon.com.

52 Meghan O'Rourke, "Katherine Heigl's Knocked Up," *Slate*, December 11, 2007, www.slate.com.

53 William Shakespeare, *The Taming of the Shrew* (New York: Signet Classic, 1998).

54 Phyllis Rackin, *Shakespeare and Women* (Oxford: Oxford University Press, 2005), 54.

55 Greven, "'Beta Male Comedies," 418.

56 Susan Douglas, *Enlightened Sexism: The Seductive Message That Feminism's Work Is Done* (New York: Times Books, 2010); Diane Negra, *What a Girl Wants? Fantasizing the Reclamation of Self in Post-Feminism* (New York: Routledge, 2009).

57 Ging, "Alphas, Betas, and Incels," 639.

58 Ibid.

59 "The Montreal Massacre," CBC Digital Archives, December 6, 1989, https://web .archive.org/web/20110604052652/http://archives.cbc.ca/society/crime_justice /topics/398-2235/.

60 Philip Galanes, "Lena Dunham and Judd Apatow on Girls, Geeks and Trolls," *New York Times*, February 11, 2017, www.nytimes.com.

61 Greven, "Beta Male Comedies," 406.

62 John Alberti, "'I Love You, Man': Bromances, the Construction of Masculinity, and the Continuing Evolution of the Romantic Comedy," *Quarterly Review of Film & Video* 30, no. 2 (2013): 159.

63 Apatow, *Knocked Up*.

64 Eve Sedgwick, *Between Men: English Literature and Male Homosocial Desire* (New York: Columbia University Press, 1985).

65 See Linda Mizejewski, *It Happened One Night* (Hoboken, NJ: Wiley-Blackwell, 2009), 34.

66 Ibid.

67 Alberti, "Bromances," 164.

68 Apatow, *Knocked Up*.

69 Judd Apatow, "Funny People—Trailer," YouTube video, 3:33, June 30, 2009, https://www.youtube.com/watch?v=kzciY15Q3BA.

70 *The Night Before*, directed by Jonathan Levine (Columbia Pictures, 2015), Amazon.com.

71 Apatow, *Knocked Up*.

72 Weaver, *Rhetoric of Racist Humour*, 157.

73 *Neighbors 2: Sorority Rising*, directed by Nicholas Stoller (Universal Pictures, 2016), Amazon.com.

74 See Abby Ferber, "The Construction of Black Masculinity: White Supremacy Now and Then," *Journal of Sport & Social Issues* 31, no. 1 (2007): 18.

75 Labradoodle Home, "Labradoodle Price Guide 2021," 2021, https://labradoodlehome.com.

76 Apatow, *Knocked Up*; Levine, *The Night Before*; Stoller, *Neighbors 2: Sorority Rising*.

77 See Ferber, "Construction of Black Masculinity," 18.

78 O'Rourke, "Katherine Heigl's Knocked Up."

79 See Gretchen Bakke, "Dead White Men: An Essay on the Changing Dynamics of Race in US Action Cinema," *Anthropological Quarterly* 2 (2010): 400–28; Russell Meeuf, *Rebellious Bodies: Stardom, Citizenship, and the New Body Politics* (Austin: University of Texas Press, 2017), 129–33.

80 Meeuf, *Rebellious Bodies*, 133.

81 Ibid.

82 Stoller, *Neighbors 2*.

83 Ironically, this gentile hyperwhite shrew is played by Jewish actress Lisa Kudrow.

84 Dave Itzkoff, "Judd Apatow's Family Business," *New York Times*, November 14, 2012, www.nytimes.com.

85 Apatow, *Knocked Up*.

86 See Ging, "Alphas, Betas, and Incels."

87 Greven, "Beta Male Comedies," 411.

88 Apatow, *Knocked Up*.

89 Green, *Pineapple Express*.

90 *Do the Right Thing*, directed by Spike Lee (Universal Pictures, 1989), DVD.

91 N.W.A., *Straight Outta Compton* (Audio Achievements, 1988).

92 Amanda Nell Edgar, "Commenting Straight from the Underground: N.W.A., Police Brutality, and YouTube as a Space for Neoliberal Resistance," *Southern Communication Journal* 81, no. 4 (2016): 223–36.

93 Apatow, *Knocked Up*.

94 Elizabeth Freeman, *Time Binds: Queer Temporalities, Queer Histories* (Durham, NC: Duke University Press, 2010), 3; Dana Luciano, *Arranging Grief: Sacred Time and the Body in Nineteenth-Century America* (New York: New York University Press, 2007), 9.

95 Elizabeth Freeman, *Time Binds*, 3–4.

96 Ibid., 4.
97 Jack Halberstam, *In a Queer Time & Place: Transgender Bodies, Subcultural Lives* (New York: New York University Press, 2005), 1–2.
98 Greven, "Beta Male Comedies," 405.

CHAPTER 5. FROM BLUE-EYED DEMON TO NICE JEW-ISH GOY

1 Adam DeVine, Blake Anderson, and Anders Holm, "The Workaholics Guys Find a New Cubicle Mate (Feat. Seth Rogen and Zac Efron)—Uncensored," Comedy Central, YouTube video, 6:37, April 16, 2014, https://www.youtube.com/watch?v =qMzt3yQFT-Q.
2 *High School Musical*, directed by Kenny Ortega (Disney-ABC Domestic Television, 2006), Amazon.com.
3 *High School Musical 2*, directed by Kenny Ortega (Disney-ABC Domestic Television, 2007), Amazon.com; *High School Musical 3: Senior Year*, directed by Kenny Ortega (Walt Disney Studios Motion Pictures, 2008), Amazon.com; *Hairspray*, directed by Adam Shankman (New Line Cinema, 2007), Amazon.com.
4 Josh Dean, "Zac Efron Got So Insanely Jacked Even the Rock Thinks He's an 'Animal.' Here's How," *Men's Fitness*, May 16, 2016, www.mensfitness.com.
5 *Charlie St. Cloud*, directed by Burr Steers (Universal Pictures, 2010), DVD; *The Lucky One*, directed by Scott Hicks (Warner Bros. Pictures, 2012), DVD; *At Any Price*, directed by Rahmin Bahrani (Sony Pictures Classics, 2012), DVD. For an example of these films' reviews, see Peter Bradshaw, "The Lucky One—Review," *The Guardian*, May 3, 2012, www.theguardian.com.
6 For past uses of the term "goyface," see Vincent Brook and Marat Grinberg, eds., *Woody on Rye: Jewishness in the Films & Plays of Woody Allen* (Waltham, MA: Brandeis University Press, 2013), xiv; Jeffrey Israel, Living with Hate in American Politics and Religion: How Popular Culture Can Defuse Intractable Differences (New York: Columbia University Press, 2019), 259; Michael O'Malley, "Dark Enough as It Is: Eddie Lang and the Minstrel Cycle," *Journal of Social History* 52, no. 2 (2018): 244.
7 *Neighbors*, directed by Nicholas Stoller (Universal Pictures, 2014), Amazon.com.
8 Devine, Anderson, and Holm, "Workaholics Guys Find a New Cubicle Mate."
9 *Neighbors 2: Sorority Rising*, directed by Nicholas Stoller (Universal Pictures, 2016), Amazon.com.
10 Daniel Montgomery, "2018 Razzie Award Winners," *GoldDerby* (blog), March 3, 2018, www.goldderby.com.
11 *The Greatest Showman*, directed by Michael Gracey (20th Century Fox, 2017), Amazon.com.
12 Jean-Paul Sartre, "Black Orpheus," in *"What Is Literature?" and Other Essays* (Cambridge, MA: Harvard University Press, 1988), 291.
13 Ibid.
14 George Yang and Tracey Ann Ryser, "Whiting Up and Blacking Out: White Privilege, Race, and White Chicks," *African American Review* 42, no. 3–4 (2008): 731–46.
15 Stoller, *Neighbors 2*.

16 Jean Twenge, "Millennials: The Me Me Me Generation," *Time*, May 9, 2013, https://time.com (quote from magazine cover subheadline).

17 Kate Taylor, "The Decade of 'Millennials Killing' Things Has Come to an End," *Business Insider*, January 1, 2020, www.businessinsider.com.

18 Mickey Rapkin, "The Zen of Zac," *Elle*, May 18, 2016, www.elle.com.

19 Stoller, *Neighbors*; Stoller, *Neighbors 2*.

20 Sandra Korn, "When No Means Yes," *The Crimson*, November 12, 2010, www.thecrimson.com.

21 *Mike and Dave Need Wedding Dates*, directed by Jake Szymanski (20th Century Fox, 2016), Amazon.com.

22 Maggie Lange, "Getting Weird with the Real Mike and Dave Who Needed Wedding Dates," *GQ*, July 7, 2016, www.gq.com.

23 Josh Peter, "Charges against US Swimmer Ryan Lochte Over 2016 Olympics Incident in Brazil Are Dismissed," *USA Today*, July 8, 2021, www.usatoday.com; Although Lochte's mother is Cuban, this Latino ancestry has not shaped his public image of white masculinity. On this topic, see Leah Donnella, "Roundup: Smart Thoughts on Ryan Lochte and White Privilege," *Code Switch* (blog), August 19, 2016, www.npr.org/codeswitch.

24 *Baywatch*, directed by Seth Gordon (Paramount Pictures, 2017), Amazon.com.

25 Ibid.

26 Claire Sisco King, "It Cuts Both Ways: Fight Club, Masculinity, and Abject Hegemony," *Communication and Critical/Cultural Studies* 6, no. 4 (2009): 366–85.

27 Julia Kristeva, *Powers of Horror: An Essay on Abjection*, trans. Leon S. Roudiez (New York: Columbia University Press, 1982).

28 *Fight Club*, directed by David Fincher (20th Century Fox, 1999), DVD.

29 See Gretchen Bakke, "Dead White Men: An Essay on the Changing Dynamics of Race in US Action Cinema," *Anthropological Quarterly* 2 (2010): 400–28; Russell Meeuf, *Rebellious Bodies: Stardom, Citizenship, and the New Body Politics* (Austin: University of Texas Press, 2017), 129–33.

30 Meeuf, *Rebellious Bodies*, 133.

31 Ibid.

32 Ibid.

33 *Blade*, directed by Stephen Norrington (New Line Cinema, 1998), DVD.

34 King, "Abject Hegemony," 377.

35 Marjorie Garber, *Symptoms of Culture* (New York: Routledge, 2002), 75, 79.

36 Janet Adelman, "Her Father's Blood: Race, Conversion, and Nation in 'The Merchant of Venice,'" *Representations* 81, no. 1 (2003): 8–10.

37 Chris Holmlund, *Impossible Bodies: Femininity & Masculinity at the Movies* (New York: Routledge, 2002), 5.

38 Holly Millea, "Zac Attack: High School Musical Star Zac Efron Moves to the Head of the Class in Hairspray," *Elle*, 2008, http://photobucket.com.

39 Holly Millea, "All the Right Moves," *Elle*, April 6, 2009, www.elle.com.

40 Dean, "Zac Efron Got So Insanely Jacked."

41 See Ben Freiburger, "20 Movie Stars You Didn't Know Were Jewish," *MTV News* (blog), December 10, 2012, www.mtv.com; Ashley Rocks, "Zac Efron," *Information about My Favorite Celebrities!!!!* (blog), June 23, 2006, http://zac-efron-2813 .blogspot.com.

42 Katie Franks, *Zac Efron* (New York: Rosen Publishing Group, 2008); Freiburger, "20 Movie Stars You Didn't Know Were Jewish."

43 Freiburger, "20 Movie Stars You Didn't Know Were Jewish."

44 Rick Kissell and Michael Schneider, "*High School Musical 2* Aces Test," *Variety*, August 18, 2007, http://variety.com.

45 "Zac Efron," in *Urban Dictionary*, accessed February 13, 2018, www .urbandictionary.com.

46 *Saturday Night Live*, season 39, episode 11, "Drake," directed by Don Roy King, aired January 18, 2014, on NBC. www.nbc.com.

47 José Esteban Muñoz, *Disidentifications: Queers of Color and the Performance of Politics* (Minneapolis: University of Minnesota Press, 1999), 11.

48 Ibid.

49 Devine, Anderson, and Holm, "Workaholics Guys Find a New Cubicle Mate."

50 Ibid.

51 See Harriet Hartman and Moshe Hartman, *Gender and American Jews: Patterns in Work, Education, and Family in Contemporary Life* (Waltham, MA: Brandeis University Press, 2009), 62–63.

52 Devine, Anderson, and Holm, "Workaholics Guys Find a New Cubicle Mate."

53 Daniel Harrison, "Rethinking Circumcision and Sexuality in the United States," *Sexualities* 5, no. 3 (2002): 300.

54 Jonathan Freedman, "Coming Out of the Jewish Closet with Marcel Proust," in *Queer Theory and the Jewish Question*, ed. Daniel Boyarin, Daniel Itzkovitz, and Ann Pellegrini (New York: Columbia University Press, 2003), 335.

55 Devine, Anderson, and Holm, "Workaholics Guys Find a New Cubicle Mate."

56 Dean, "Zac Efron Got So Insanely Jacked."

57 Gordon, *Baywatch*.

58 "How Zac Efron Got His Epic Tan for *Baywatch*," *Access Hollywood*, YouTube video, 1:24, April 24, 2017, https://youtu.be/n19iA_OGpKA.

59 Stoller, *Neighbors*.

60 Ibid.

61 Gordon, *Baywatch*.

62 Ibid.

63 Stoller, *Neighbors*.

64 *White Hot: The Rise & Fall of Abercrombie & Fitch*, directed by Allison Klayman (Netflix, 2022), Netflix.com.

65 Stoller, *Neighbors*.

66 Szymanski, *Mike and Dave Need Wedding Dates*.

67 Gordon, *Baywatch*.

68 See Jack Beresford, "Dwayne Johnson's Little Known Irish Heritage Revealed," *The Irish Post*, May 2, 2021, https://www.theirishopost.com; Dana Rose Falcone, "An Actress Advocating for Refugees," *Time* (blog), September 22, 2017, https://content .time.com.

69 Stoller, *Neighbors*.

70 Gordon, *Baywatch*.

71 Elizabeth Freeman, *Time Binds: Queer Temporalities, Queer Histories* (Durham, NC: Duke University Press, 2010), 3–4.

72 Stoller, *Neighbors*.

73 Stoller, *Neighbors 2*.

74 Lisa Duggan, "The New Homonormativity: The Sexual Politics of Neoliberalism," in *Materializing Democracy: Toward a Revitalized Cultural Politics*, ed. Russ Castronovo and Dana Nelson (Durham, NC: Duke University Press, 2002), 175–94.

75 Stoller, *Neighbors 2*.

76 Gordon, *Baywatch*.

77 Stoller, *Baywatch*; Stoller, *Neighbors*; Stoller, *Neighbors 2*.

78 See Sander Gilman, *The Jew's Body* (New York: Routledge, 1991).

79 See Jeffrey Herf, *The Jewish Enemy: Nazi Propaganda During World War II and the Holocaust* (Cambridge, MA: Harvard University Press, 2008); "Pages from the Antisemitic Children's Book The Poison Mushroom," Holocaust Sources in Context, United States Holocaust Memorial Museum, accessed on December 20, 2023, www.ushmm.org; Schulte-Sasse, Linda, "The Jew as Other Under National Socialism: Veit Harlan's *Jüd Süß*," The German Quarterly 61, no.1 (1988), 22–49.

80 Ibid.

81 See Lori Lefkovitz, "Coats and Tales: Joseph Stories and Myths of Jewish Masculinity," in *A Mensch among Men: Explorations in Jewish Masculinity*, ed. Harry Brod (Freedom, CA: Crossing Press, 1987), 28.

82 Gordon, *Baywatch*.

83 Stoller, *Neighbors*.

84 David C. Atkinson, "Charlottesville and the Alt-Right: A Turning Point?," *Politics, Groups, Identities* 6, no. 2 (2018): 309–15.

85 Stoller, *Neighbors*; Stoller, *Neighbors 2*.

86 Gordon, *Baywatch*.

87 Beyoncé Knowles, "Beyoncé—Single Ladies (Put a Ring on It) (Video Version)," directed by Jake Nava, YouTube video, 3:20, October 2, 2009, https://www .youtube.com/watch?v=4m1EFMoRFvY.

CONCLUSION

1 Brian Scott Lipton, "Whoopi Goldberg Wins Daytime Emmy Award," *Theater Mania* (blog), August 30, 2009, www.theatermania.com.

2 Kenan Malik, "Whoopi Goldberg's Holocaust Remarks Drew on a Misguided Idea of Racism," *The Guardian*, February 6, 2022, www.theguardian.com.

3 James Hibberd, "Whoopi Goldberg Apologizes and Seemingly Doubles Down on Holocaust Comments," *Hollywood Reporter*, February 1, 2022, www .hollywoodreporter.com.

4 Ibid.

5 Ibid.

6 Malik, "Whoopi Goldberg's Holocaust Remarks."

7 See Matthew Frye Jacobson, *Whiteness of a Different Color: European Immigrants and the Alchemy of Race* (Cambridge, MA: Harvard University Press, 1999).

8 Hibberd, "Whoopi Goldberg Apologizes."

9 Ibid.

10 Daniel Solomon, "David Duke Says Jews Aren't White—and Jews Clap Back," *Forward*, December 6, 2016, http://forward.com.

11 Malik, "Whoopi Goldberg's Holocaust Remarks."

12 "Whoopi Goes Square on Us," CBS News, February 9, 2000, www.cbsnews.com.

13 Gabe Friedman, "Are Jews White? Is Whoopi Goldberg Jewish? *The View* Holocaust Controversy, Explained," *Jewish Chronicle*, February 2, 2022, www.jta.org.

14 Robert Viagas, "Whoopi Tells How She Got Her Name," *Playbill* (blog), January 6, 1997, https://playbill.com.

15 Friedman, "Are Jews White? Is Whoopi Goldberg Jewish?"

16 Viagas, "Whoopi Tells How She Got Her Name."

17 Jessica Elgot, "Whoopi Goldberg: I'm Jewish and I Talk to God," *Jewish Chronicle*, May 12, 2011, www.thejc.com.

18 Pew Research Center, "A Portrait of Jewish Americans," Pew Research Center, October 1, 2013, www.pewforum.org.

19 Elgot, "Whoopi Goldberg."

20 Allison Berry, "Top 10 Most Ridiculous Celebrity Name Changes," *Time* (blog), September 16, 2011, https://content.time.com.

21 "5 of Kanye West's Antisemitic Remarks, Explained," *American Jewish Committee* (blog), December 2, 2022, www.ajc.org.

22 Julianne McShane, "Whoopi Goldberg Faces Backlash after Repeating False Holocaust Comments," *NBC News*, December 27, 2022, www.nbcnews.com.

23 See Loubna Qutami, "Censusless: Arab/Muslim Interpolation into Whiteness and the War on Terror," *Journal of Asian American Studies* 23, no. 2 (2020): 161–200; Neda Maghbouleh, *The Limits of Whiteness: Iranian Americans and the Everyday Politics of Race* (Stanford, CA: Stanford University Press, 2017); Nancy Raquel Mirabal, "'Ser De Aquí': Beyond the Cuban Exile Model," *Latino Studies* 1 (2003): 366–82; Sigal Samuel, "For Sephardic and Mizrahi Jews, Whiteness Was a Fragile Identity Long before Trump," *Forward*, December 6, 2016, http: //forward.com.

24 See Marla Brettschneider, *The Jewish Phenomenon in Sub-Saharan Africa: The Politics of Contradictory Discourses* (Lewiston, NY: Edwin Meller Press, 2015); Bryan Roby, "How Race Travels: Navigating Global Blackness in J. Ida Jiggetts's

Study of Afro-Asian Israeli Jewry," *Jewish Social Studies* 27, no. 1 (2022): 1–42; Noah Tamarkin, *Genetic Afterlives: Black Jewish Indigeneity in South Africa* (Durham, NC: Duke University Press, 2020).

25 Samantha Pickette, "The Last Black (Jewish) Unicorn: Tiffany Haddish's *Black Mitzvah* and the Reframing of Jewish Female Identity," *Studies in American Jewish Literature* 41, no. 2 (2022): 165–84.

26 Simon Weaver, *The Rhetoric of Racist Humour: US, UK and Global Race Joking* (Farnham, UK: Ashgate Publishing, 2011), 156.

27 *Aloha*, directed by Cameron Crowe (Sony Pictures Releasing, 2015), Amazon.com.

28 Jens Manuel Krogstad, "Hawaii Is Home to the Nation's Largest Share of Multiracial Americans," Pew Research Center, June 17, 2015, www.pewresearch.org.

29 See Ben Child, "Cameron Crowe Apologises for Casting Emma Stone as 'Part-Asian' in *Aloha*," *The Guardian*, June 3, 2015, www.theguardian.com; "Karl Marx and Yellowface In *Aloha*," *Asian American Popular Culture* (blog), January 30, 2017, https://asianamericanpopularculturew17.wordpress.com.

30 Krin Gabbard, *Black Magic: White Hollywood and African American Culture* (New Brunswick, NJ: Rutgers University Press, 2004), 19.

31 Ibid.

32 Ibid., 21.

33 Hannah Schwadron, *The Case of the Sexy Jewess: Dance, Gender & Jewish Joke-Work in US Pop Culture* (Oxford: Oxford University Press, 2017), 15.

34 Karim Kharbouch, "French Montana—No Shopping Ft. Drake," directed by Carlos Suarez, produced by Epic Records, YouTube video, 5:21, July 29, 2016, https://www.youtube.com/watch?v=mDU-5jwPKmQ.

35 See Brandon Caldwell, "French Montana Opens Up about His Rap Peers Surpassing Him," *Hip Hop DX* (blog), December 5, 2021, https://hiphopdx.com.

36 Viveca Greene, "'Deplorable' Satire: Alt-Right Memes, White Genocide Tweets, and Redpilling Normies," *Studies in American Humor* 5, no. 1 (2019): 31–69.

37 See Matt Sienkiewicz and Nick Marx, *That's Not Funny: How the Right Makes Comedy Work for Them* (Oakland: University of California Press, 2022).

38 See Charles Blow, "Tucker Carlson and White Replacement," *New York Times*, April 11, 2021, https://www.nytimes.com; Sienkiewicz and Marx, *That's Not Funny*.

39 See Paul Elliot Johnson, "Walter White(Ness) Lashes Out: 'Breaking Bad' and Male Victimage," *Critical Studies in Media Communication* 34, no. 1 (2017): 14–28.

40 Kathleen Rowe, *The Unruly Woman: Gender and the Genres of Laughter* (Austin: University of Texas Press, 1995).

41 Gretchen Bakke, "Dead White Men: An Essay on the Changing Dynamics of Race in US Action Cinema," *Anthropological Quarterly* 2 (2010): 400–28; Russell Meeuf, *Rebellious Bodies: Stardom, Citizenship, and the New Body Politics* (Austin: University of Texas Press, 2017), 129.

42 See Aslı Tunç, "Claire Underwood: Feminist Warrior or Shakespearean Villain? Re-Visiting Feminine Evil in 'House of Cards,'" in *Female Agencies and*

Subjectivities in Film and Television, ed. Diğdem Sezen et al. (Cham, Switzerland: Palgrave Macmillan, 2020), 87–105.

43 See *Twilight*, directed by Catherine Hardwicke (Summit Entertainment, 2008).

44 See *Dear White People*, season 2, episode 2, "Chapter II," directed by Kevin Bray, aired May 4, 2018, on Netflix. Netflix.com.

45 See *Abbott Elementary*, season 2, episode 3, "Story Samurai," directed by Jay Karas, aired October 5, 2022, on ABC. Hulu.com.

INDEX

Page numbers in *italics* refer to figures.

ABOUT THE AUTHOR

JONATHAN BRANFMAN is the Eli Reinhard Postdoctoral Fellow in Jewish Studies at Stanford University. His scholarship links Jewish studies, media studies, gender studies, and critical race studies.